Praise for *Memoirs*

"[*Memoirs* is] densely yet nimbly written, and you sense Lowell's judgment and discrimination in every paragraph . . . Lowell freshens the eye . . . This book's editors, Steven Gould Axelrod and Grzegorz Kosc, silently and deftly amend, in their footnotes, Lowell's many small errors of fact, and point out where he seems to have invented characters."

—Dwight Garner, *The New York Times*

"It is the candour of [Lowell's] confession, the satiric self-critique of his earlier work, that continues to draw us to this astonishing body of poetry."

—Marjorie Perloff, *The Times Literary Supplement*

"Reading through *Memoirs*, we pick up on phrases and images that reappear in poems. A single vivid sensibility is at work in both forms . . . Axelrod and Kosc have done Lowell and his readers a service by bringing this material together in a carefully edited and annotated volume."

—William Doreski, *Harvard Review*

"[*Memoirs*] vividly show[s] how a poet's beginnings shape his end."

—Michael Knox Beran, *Air Mail*

"A good summation of the boy, the poet and the man . . . We might say of him what he said of his dearest friend, Randall Jarrell, that he was a 'noble, difficult, and beautiful soul.' And a great poet."

—John Banville, *Irish Independent*

"To anyone addicted to Lowell's spiralling, symphonic prose style, freighted with triple adjectives and hallucinatory details summoned from the depths of memory, this volume is manna from heaven."

—Mark Ford, *The Times Literary Supplement*

ROBERT LOWELL

Memoirs

Edited and with a Preface by
Steven Gould Axelrod and Grzegorz Kosc

ROBERT LOWELL (1917–1977) was the renowned and pathbreaking author of many leading works in American poetry, including *Life Studies* (FSG, 1959), *For the Union Dead* (FSG, 1964), and *Day by Day* (FSG, 1977).

STEVEN GOULD AXELROD is the author of *Robert Lowell: Life and Art* and *Sylvia Plath: The Wound and the Cure of Words*; the coauthor of *Robert Lowell: A Reference Guide*; and the coeditor of the three-volume *New Anthology of American Poetry*. The president of the Robert Lowell Society, he is a Distinguished Professor of English at the University of California, Riverside.

GRZEGORZ KOSC is the author of *Robert Lowell: Uncomfortable Epigone of the Grands Maîtres* and *Robert Frost's Political Body*. His writing has been published in *Partial Answers*, *a/b: Auto/Biography Studies*, and *College Literature*, among other journals. He is also the coeditor of *Robert Lowell in Context*, to be published by Cambridge University Press in 2024. He is an associate professor of English and the director of the American Studies Center at the University of Warsaw.

ALSO BY ROBERT LOWELL

Land of Unlikeness (1944)

Lord Weary's Castle (1946)

The Mills of the Kavanaughs (1951)

Life Studies (1959)

Phaedra (translation) (1961)

Imitations (1961)

For the Union Dead (1964)

The Old Glory (plays) (1965)

Near the Ocean (1967)

Prometheus Bound (translation) (1967)

The Voyage & Other Versions of Poems by Baudelaire (1968)

Notebook 1967–68 (1969)
(*Notebook*, revised and expanded edition, 1970)

History (1973)

For Lizzie and Harriet (1973)

The Dolphin (1973)

Selected Poems (1976) (revised edition, 1977)

Day by Day (1977)

The Oresteia of Aeschylus (translation) (1978)

Collected Prose (1987)

Collected Poems (2003)

The Letters of Robert Lowell (2005)

Selected Poems: Expanded Edition (2007)

*Words in Air: The Complete Correspondence Between
Elizabeth Bishop and Robert Lowell* (2008)

New Selected Poems (2017)

*The Dolphin Letters, 1970–1979: Elizabeth Hardwick,
Robert Lowell, and Their Circle* (2019)

Memoirs

Memoirs

ROBERT LOWELL

Edited and with a Preface by

STEVEN GOULD AXELROD

AND GRZEGORZ KOSC

PICADOR

FARRAR, STRAUS AND GIROUX

NEW YORK

Picador
120 Broadway, New York 10271

Some items in Part III originally appeared in *Partisan Review*, *Sewanee Review*,
The New York Review of Books, *Agenda*, *Hudson Review*, and *Salmagundi*.

Grateful acknowledgment is made to Sarah Payne Stuart for permission
to publish selected photographs from her personal collection.

The Library of Congress has cataloged the Farrar, Straus and Giroux hardcover edition as follows:
Names: Lowell, Robert, 1917–1977, author. | Axelrod, Steven Gould, 1944– editor. |
    Kość, Grzegorz, editor.
Title: Memoirs / Robert Lowell ; edited and with a preface by Steven Gould Axelrod and
    Grzegorz Kosc.
Description: First edition. | New York : Farrar, Straus and Giroux, 2022. | Includes bibliographical
    references and index.
Identifiers: LCCN 2022009258 | ISBN 9780374258924 (hardcover)
Subjects: LCSH: Lowell, Robert, 1917–1977. | Lowell, Robert, 1917–1977—Childhood and youth. |
    Poets, American—20th century—Biography. | Lowell, Robert, 1917–1977—Mental health. |
    Manic-depressive persons—United States—Biography. | Lowell, Robert, 1917–1977—Friends
    and associates. | Authors, American—20th century—Biography. | Lowell, Robert, 1917–1977—
    Prose. | LCGFT: Autobiographies | Biographies
Classification: LCC PS3523.O89 Z46 2022 | DDC 811/.52 [B]—dc23
LC record available at https://lccn.loc.gov/2022009258

Paperback ISBN: 978-1-250-87286-9

Designed by Gretchen Achilles

Our books may be purchased in bulk for promotional, educational, or business use.
Please contact your local bookseller or the Macmillan Corporate and Premium Sales Department at
1-800-221-7945, extension 5442, or by email at MacmillanSpecialMarkets@macmillan.com.

For book club information, please email marketing@picadorusa.com.

picadorusa.com • Follow us on social media at @picador or @picadorusa

1   3   5   7   9   10   8   6   4   2

CONTENTS

APPENDIX: SELECTED FRAGMENTS
FROM THE MANUSCRIPTS

PREFACE

ROBERT LOWELL ONCE WROTE, "In truth I seem to have felt mostly the joys of living; in remembering, in recording, thanks to the gift of the Muse, it is the pain."* But perhaps that was the opposite of what he meant or felt. Certainly he experienced pain in living through the late 1940s and the 1950s, when his severe bipolar disorder struck in full force, landing him in jails and then, recurrently, in psychiatric hospitals. The turning point came in 1954 after his most violent attack of mania yet. He was committed to the Payne Whitney Psychiatric Clinic in New York for a prolonged stay, during which he received for the first time a clear diagnosis and sustained talk therapy.

It was here that the poet began writing autobiographical prose, as part of his therapeutic regimen. It was a writing project that sustained him for three years, and that continued in a different, attenuated form for the rest of his life. From 1954 to 1957 Lowell explored and memorialized his childhood memories as well as his present state of confusion and despair. When that vein of silver ran out in 1957, he returned to poetry, writing the autobiographical poems of *Life Studies*, which was published in 1959 and became a landmark in world poetry. In 1959 he also resumed his memoir project, though in an altered format. From this point forward, his memoirs centered on other writers. Whereas he chose to publish only one of his earlier

* Robert Lowell, *Notebook 1967–68* (New York: Farrar, Straus and Giroux, 1969), 160.

autobiographical memoirs ("91 Revere Street," included in *Life Studies*), he regularly published his memoirs of other writers in literary magazines. He appeared as a character in these memoirs too, but in a healthier condition than before, as the self-assured observer and narrator.

Lowell wrote the introspective memoirs of 1954 to 1957 in a torrent, using them as a method to understand himself, in his past and present guises, and as a potential "way to get well," as he later wrote.* He composed the outer-directed memoirs of 1959 to 1977 in a trickle, as small narratives marking his connection to admired writers and ultimately registering their deaths and foreseeing his own. Taken together, these memoirs begun in crisis and ending with his death were the closest thing to a prose autobiography that Lowell ever wrote.

This present volume gathers Lowell's childhood memoirs in Part I, and his narratives of his adult life in and out of psychiatric hospitals in Part II. Lowell chose, or was encouraged, not to publish these texts, for reasons that will be explored in our introductions. Many of these memoirs lack that last coat of finish he normally applied to his published work. Some are fragmentary, though others are virtually completed. Together they tell a powerful story of a soul in pain and a writer searching, with courage and discipline, for a way forward. In a contrary fashion, many of the memoirs in Part III were indeed finished and published. Whereas the initial examples show a sociable, genial Lowell in conversation with his creative peers, the later examples present a Lowell shaken by the deaths of his friends.

We believe these prose memoirs display another dimension of Lowell's artistry. Although their imagery and fantasy complement his poems, these prose works also stand apart, using their medium's discursiveness to achieve something different from what could be attained through poetic condensation. The memoirs tell a story that is paradoxically extreme and ordinary. In living through the calamitous events evoked in Parts I and II, and through the losses in Part III, Lowell must have felt great pain; in writing about those events with such verve and moral imagination, he must have felt blessed with joy.

---

* Robert Lowell, *Collected Poems*, edited by Frank Bidart and David Gewanter (New York: Farrar, Straus and Giroux, 2003), 834.

PART I

My
Autobiography

INTRODUCTION

I N OCTOBER 1954, Robert Lowell wrote to his friend John Berryman: "I've just started messing around with my autobiographical monster."* In April 1955, he signed a contract for this work with Robert Giroux of Farrar, Straus and Cudahy. At about the same time, he wrote to Peter Taylor: "I want to invent and forget a lot, but at the same time have the historian's wonderful advantage—the reader must always be forced to say, 'This is tops, but even if it weren't it's true.'"[†] Lowell continued to work on the project until early February 1957, when he told Elizabeth Bishop that he was "stalling."[‡] After six months of troubled silence, he began to write autobiographical poems instead. These poems would appear as the "Life Studies" sequence in *Life Studies*, published in 1959. Lowell ultimately published only one chapter of his prose memoir, "91 Revere Street," which saw print first in *Partisan Review* and then in *Life Studies*.[§]

Lowell's initial intention to write a book about his childhood reflected

---

* Robert Lowell, *The Letters of Robert Lowell*, edited by Saskia Hamilton (New York: Farrar, Straus and Giroux, 2005), 240.

† *Letters*, 245.

‡ Elizabeth Bishop and Robert Lowell, *Words in Air: The Complete Correspondence Between Elizabeth Bishop and Robert Lowell*, edited by Thomas Travisano with Saskia Hamilton (New York: Farrar, Straus and Giroux, 2008), 195: "So many relatives don't like it. But that isn't the trouble; rather it's laziness and feeling that I must store up more drive and wisdom."

§ Robert Lowell, "91 Revere Street," *Partisan Review* 23, no. 4 (Fall 1956): 445–77; *Life Studies* (New York: Farrar, Straus and Cudahy, 1959), 11–46.

his experience with psychoanalysis during an extended stay at the Payne Whitney Psychiatric Clinic in the summer of 1954. He hoped he could use that immersion into memory as a way to overcome the writer's block that had been haunting him. The project gained added resonance in late 1955 when he and Elizabeth Hardwick purchased a house on Marlborough Street—"a block from where I grew up," as he wrote to William Carlos Williams.* Although Lowell later implied that his memoir merely prepared the way for *Life Studies*, it is a powerful text in its own right. He kept "bits" of it in his desk for years, and as late as 1972 he dreamed of completing it, "if I can find a new form that will let me write at greater length."† With relatively few overlaps, "My Autobiography" and the "Life Studies" sequence illuminate and challenge each other, and reveal the opportunities and limitations inherent in their different genres.

Lowell originally planned to begin his memoir with his birth and conclude in the summer of 1934, when he was seventeen and attending St. Mark's School. The text would end with "a period of enthusiasm," which occurred a few months before he "*found*" himself, presumably as a writer.‡ "My Autobiography," however, does not follow through with this plan. For one thing, it includes a chapter depicting his parents' courtship ("I Take Thee, Bob"), which occurred before his birth. Presented almost as if Lowell witnessed the events, and written in a style that mimicked his mother's "exaggerating humor,"§ this chapter breaks with memoir convention and prepares us for the extent to which fantasies, imagined voices, and second-hand stories will contribute to the text: that is, the extent to which Lowell's narratives are as much a dream of the past as a recounting. Moreover, "My Autobiography" does not carry us into 1934 but instead stops, or almost stops, in 1930 as the young Lowell, aged thirteen, apprehensively prepares to enter St. Mark's School. Skipping over his boarding-school years entirely,

* *Letters*, 249.

† *Letters*, 317; Lowell to Robert Giroux, July 12, 1972, quoted in Robert Giroux, "Homage to a Poet," in *Robert Lowell: Interviews and Memoirs*, edited by Jeffrey Meyers (Ann Arbor: University of Michigan Press, 1988), 260.

‡ Robert Lowell, "For two years I have been cooling off," reproduced in Part II of this volume.

§ Robert Lowell, "To Mother," in *Day by Day* (New York: Farrar, Straus and Giroux, 1977), 78; reprinted in *Collected Poems*, edited by Frank Bidart and David Gewanter (New York: Farrar, Straus and Giroux, 2003), 789.

the story then jumps to his bittersweet last meeting with his grandfather, Arthur Winslow, in December 1937, when Lowell was twenty.

Despite its deviation from the initial plan, "My Autobiography" seems roughly complete. The first eight chapters articulate the social world of Lowell's early and middle childhood. This initial sequence resolves in the most sustained chapter of the memoir, "91 Revere Street." In this chapter, the young boy, now eight, demonstrates characteristics that are to stay with him a lifetime: intelligence, keen observational powers, rebelliousness, impulsiveness, inner turmoil, and creativity. One might consider the next sequence of nine chapters, from "Pictures of Rock" through "Arthur Winslow V," to be Lowell's pastoral. They focus on his experiences with his grandfather in mostly rural settings, even as Lowell's father is experiencing disastrous career reverses back in the city. Then "My Autobiography" shakes off the leisure of middle childhood in two climactic chapters: "My Crime Wave" and "Entering St. Mark's." These chapters return us to the urbanity of Boston, without the daily protective presence of Grandfather Winslow. Lowell is now entering early adolescence, a time of considerable perturbation. Grandfather Winslow returns in the memoir's coda, a poetic evocation of the last meeting between the old man, now dying, and the grandson, now approaching adulthood. Transitioning from patriarch to angel, Winslow has an effect that is both paralyzing and soothing. "My Autobiography" concludes with a vision of the grandfather as a "white blur," presiding over memories that are themselves fading to a blur.

Lowell never showed this memoir to Giroux. He apparently shared it only with his wife, Elizabeth Hardwick, who read at least one chapter, "Entering St. Mark's," and suggested some word changes. When Lowell moved on to *Life Studies* in August 1957, he left his prose memoir behind. He wrote to Giroux in October: "My autobiography is on the shelf (or rather in my desk-drawer where I have a hundred tousled pages) for the moment."* Despite the implication that he would return to this work, he never did. He explained that "working out transitions and putting in things that didn't seem very important but were necessary to the prose continuity" became

---

* *Letters*, 296. He actually had more than three hundred pages of drafts, though some of these were redundant.

"tedious."* Writing to Richard Tillinghast in August 1969, he mentioned several other issues as well—"a dread of more of the same, impossibility of honestly showing the living, at loss for a plot to pass beyond childhood"— yet he continued to insist that it was the tedium of plugging holes and re-typing pages that ended the project.† In fact, he had nearly completed a first draft of his childhood recollections. He could have asked an editor or Hard-wick to help him with the revisions. Perhaps the strain of scrutinizing his life in such harrowing detail finally overwhelmed him. He later said, "In *Life Studies*, I caught real memories in a fairly gentle style,"‡ and so he did if you compare the poems to the prose memoir.

Although Lowell never published "My Autobiography," he kept the typescript safe for seventeen years before selling it to Harvard in 1973, along with a good portion of his archive. There it sat, in the stacks of the Houghton Library, rarely disturbed for more than forty years. Now it ap-pears to us from out of the past, a moving work by one of our great writers.

A memoir always highlights the passage of time. Lowell's "My Autobi-ography" does so with rare plangency. From its opening citation of *The Education of Henry Adams* (1918) to its stylistic allusions to Henry James's *A Small Boy and Others* (1913), Lowell's memoir acknowledges the self-representational strategies of two early modern masters. In its resemblance to Elizabeth Bishop's autobiographical story "In the Village" (1953), which Lowell thought "wonderful,"§ "My Autobiography" also connects to midcentury discourses of traumatic memory. Whereas Adams and James evoked their own nineteenth-century development from the standpoint of an emergent modernity, Lowell sought to half recover and half create early modernity itself.

Time is embedded in each of Lowell's chapters. The first, "Antebellum Boston," begins with his birth. The sequence of chapters loops back to the courtship of his parents, and then rushes forward to his infancy, his middle

---

* "An Interview with Frederick Seidel" (1961), in Robert Lowell, *Collected Prose*, edited by Robert Giroux (New York: Farrar, Straus and Giroux, 1987), 243.

† *Letters*, 522.

‡ Robert Lowell, "A Conversation with Ian Hamilton" (1971), in *Collected Prose*, 286.

§ *Words in Air*, 173–74.

childhood, his unhappy pubescence, and finally his last meeting with his dying grandfather—a vision in white underwear, part specter, part angel, and part object of desire. Each chapter presents a subtly different view of Lowell, his family members, and their social milieu—each new perspective an ironic commentary on the hopes and disappointments that have come before.

Anxieties about time contributed to the composition of "My Autobiography" in the first place. Following the death of his mother in 1954, Lowell became severely manic and was eventually committed to the Payne Whitney Psychiatric Clinic in New York. He described himself spending the next two years dreaming at night that he was like one of Michelangelo's statues that can be "tumbled downhill without injury," but feeling in the morning as though he "had been flayed, and had each nerve beaten with a rubber hose."* He added: "I am writing my autobiography literally to 'pass the time.' I almost doubt if the time would pass at all otherwise." Thus, he composed "My Autobiography," which narrates the passage of time, because he felt that time had come to a standstill. He needed to restart it discursively in order to feel it again in his mind and body. He intended the story of his birth and growth to foster a rebirth and new growth as he entered middle age: "I also hope the result will supply me with my swaddling clothes, with a sort of immense bandage of gauze and ambergris for my hurt nerves." A movement backward into his painful past might regenerate his barely existent present, like an electroshock, and might regenerate his movement into the future.

In "My Autobiography" Lowell wrote about himself as a small boy in the company of nearly unfathomable others. Most important among these were his self-important yet affectionate grandfather; his gifted, frustrated mother; and his increasingly withdrawn and deflated father. As Lowell wrote, "My grandfather, mother, father, and I were those that mattered, the rest of the world was allegory."† It was the Freudian Oedipal triangle plus one; the family romance spread out across three generations; an Oedipal quartet. "My Autobiography" provides a *Künstlerroman* of a complicated and, in many ways, unlikable young person surrounded by a triad of sim-

---

* "For two years I have been cooling off."

† "My Crime Wave," reproduced below in "My Autobiography."

ilarly difficult elders—controlling giants restraining their inheritor, who
wants to be a controlling giant too. The dynamics among these four main
characters, and the more peripheral family members, friends, and servants
who drift through the pages, dominate the text's vision of the past and its
diagnosis of pain.

Young Lowell's orderly movement from infancy to adolescence and
beyond is impeded by the egotistical and evanescent quality of the love
offered by his elders, and also by his own combination of creativity and
"psychoticism"*—that is, by his extraordinary involvement with language
and fantasy in alliance with his aggressive and hostile impulses. "My Autobiography" is an act of recollection, and to that extent seems to confirm
Lowell's late lament that "sometimes everything I write / with the thread-
bare art of my eye / seems a snapshot."† Yet the narrative frequently portrays times when his fantasies take hold of him and won't let go. It also
shows the memoirist recalling events he couldn't possibly have witnessed,
or telling the same story twice, in different literal circumstances. We see in
this text not the aging poet who feels walled off from "something imagined"
but the reverse: a writer vivified and possessed by things imagined.

At the same time as "My Autobiography" focuses on four unique indi-
viduals, it re-creates a lost time and milieu: the fading grandeur of an Anglo-
American family endowed with wealth and privilege, in rough contact
with a wider society of immigrants, the poor, subalterns, and emancipated
women, all attempting to rise in the world. The story concerns more than
a family; it provides a portrait of social change and resistance, the sense
that one's privilege is never enough. The declining yet still powerful white
aristocrats of this text insistently disrespect people who are not "of the right
sort."‡ They call both Native Americans and citizens of India "Injuns."§
They place Boston's "Irish, Negroes, Latins" on the same discursive plane

* H. J. Eysenck and S. B. G. Eysenck, *Psychoticism as a Dimension of Personality* (London: Hodder and
Stoughton, 1976); Hans J. Eysenck, "Creativity and Personality: Suggestions for a Theory," *Psychological
Inquiry* 4, no. 3 (1993): 147–78.

† Robert Lowell, "Epilogue," in *Collected Poems*, 838.

‡ "91 Revere Street."

§ "I Take Thee, Bob," reproduced below in "My Autobiography."

as "grit, litter."* They pair "Bravas" (mixed-race immigrants from Cape Verde) with "children"; consider Portuguese Americans "exotic"; call Chinese Americans "Chinamen"; and divide Italian Americans into grades A and B.† Even insults aimed at other white men serve to police the margins: "anile," "quee-eers."‡

At the same time, a constant fluidity of identity threatens these hierarchic attitudes. Under the slightest pressure, the structures of white heterosexual selfhood begin to crumble, revealing uncertainties about gender, sexuality, and ethnic otherness. In "91 Revere Street," it is revealed that Lowell's family tree includes at least one "swarthy" Jew. "My Crime Wave" explores not only young Lowell's compulsive need to perform violence on a male Jewish body but also his romantic yearning for a second Jewish boy, whom he thinks of as a "girl." The young Lowell not only wishes he "were an older girl,"§ his phallic mother half-heartedly beseeches his father to be a man, his father fails to be the man his wife demands (but doesn't want), and his bad-boy grandfather joins with his grandson in a sort of homosocial coupling. Seemingly solid identities tremble and break when the memoirist casts his cold eye on them.

"My Autobiography" vibrates between comedy and tragedy, critique and compassion. It reveals the degree to which Lowell himself participated in the flawed behavior depicted, with the consolation that the troubled boy portrayed in these pages grew up to be the brilliant ironist who wrote them. Lowell wanted to both mock and mourn his family, his social world, himself. He wanted, in his famous phrase, to "say what happened,"¶ and he wanted to say what he felt and imagined. Most of all, he aimed to turn his memories into art.

---

* "91 Revere Street."

† Respectively, "Forty-Four West Cedar Street and Barnstable," "Entering St. Mark's," "Arthur Winslow IV," and "91 Revere Street."

‡ "91 Revere Street."

§ "91 Revere Street."

¶ "Epilogue," in *Collected Poems*, 838.

A NOTE ON THE TEXTS

L OWELL'S "MY AUTOBIOGRAPHY" has twenty chapters, seventeen of which appear here for the first time. The texts derive from the typescripts in the Robert Lowell Papers at the Houghton Library, Harvard University.

Of the three chapters that have been previously published, the best known is "91 Revere Street," which appeared for the first time in the fall 1956 issue of *Partisan Review* and then as Part 2 of Lowell's *Life Studies* in 1959 (though not in the Faber and Faber edition). The *Life Studies* version included sixty-seven small changes in the text, most of them improvements. We have used that version here, correcting only obvious errors. Thus, we replaced "cameraderie" with "camaraderie" and "patroling" with "patrolling." Some (though not all) of these corrections also appear in the Vintage Books edition of *Life Studies* (1959) and in Robert Giroux's edition of Lowell's *Collected Prose* (1987)—but not in Lowell's *Collected Poems* (2003) nor in *Selected Poems: Expanded Edition* (2007).

The other previously printed items are "Antebellum Boston" and "Philadelphia." Giroux's edition of Lowell's posthumous *Collected Prose* printed both chapters, combined into one and titled simply "Antebellum Boston." We have returned to Lowell's typescripts, omitting Giroux's editorial interventions and presenting the two chapters individually, as Lowell wrote them.

The purpose of our edition is to provide a version of Lowell's "My

Autobiography" that is as complete, as readable, and as close to Lowell's intentions as possible. We have arranged the chapters in the chronological order of the scenes portrayed, as was Lowell's design. He left some of the chapters—for example, "Antebellum Boston" and "Washington, D.C."—in single, well-edited typescripts, virtually ready to go to press. But he left other chapters in multiple versions, often with further changes inserted in his sometimes illegible script. As a rule, we chose the latest, fullest version of each chapter. In "Forty-Four West Cedar Street and Barnstable," "Arthur Winslow V," and "Entering St. Mark's," however, we inserted one or more paragraphs from another version (or several other versions) into the main one, footnoting the location of the added material.

We have provided titles for seven chapters that Lowell left untitled: "Philadelphia," "Arms-of-the-Law," "The House at Rock," "Arthur Winslow II," "Uncle Cameron," "18 Chestnut Street," and "Arthur Winslow VI." Although Lowell indicated his intention to number the Arthur Winslow chapters, he only numbered the first. We arranged and numbered the rest.

If Lowell omitted, misspelled, or mistyped a word, we made a silent correction. If we felt an irregular spelling served a purpose (for example, "Hindoo" in "I Take Thee, Bob"), we left it alone. We also lightly regularized Lowell's punctuation. We use standard capitalization and hyphenation of family titles, except in "91 Revere Street," where we occasionally adhere to the text published in his lifetime in *Life Studies*. If he crossed out a word or phrase and penciled in a legible substitute above it or in the margin, we chose the substitute. If he proposed an alternative word or phrase, but did not cross out the original, we made our best effort to choose the word that seemed most likely to be the one he would have chosen. In the few instances where we added a word or phrase to improve comprehensibility, the addition appears in square brackets. In several chapters, Lowell began new sections by retyping sentences from an earlier section, seemingly to keep himself focused. We deleted these repetitions, indicating their absence with bracketed ellipses.

Elizabeth Hardwick made a number of corrections in the only surviving typescript of "Entering St. Mark's." The corrections range from commas and disambiguated pronouns to extra phrases and additional sentences. She also crossed out some sentences. We adopted these changes selectively, more often preferring to return to Lowell's original wording.

We have lightly annotated people, events, and contexts when such information would be difficult for readers to find on their own. In general, we have let Lowell tell the stories he wanted to tell, in the words he wanted to use. To facilitate reading, we have provided genealogical charts analogous to the ones Lowell developed to assist him in composition, and we have also supplied a biographical time line.

Antebellum Boston

L IKE HENRY ADAMS, I, too, was born under the shadow of the Boston State House, and under Pisces, the Fish, on the first of March 1917.* America was entering the First World War and was about to play her part in the downfall of five empires: the Austrian, the German, the Russian, the French and the English. At this moment, the sons of most of the old, aristocratic, Republican Boston families were waiting on their doorsteps like spent Airedales or poodles. They were, these children and parents, waiting and hoping for a second wind. James Michael Curley was out of jail and waiting for a mandate from the people to begin the first of his many terms as mayor of Boston. Nothing from now on was to go quite as expected—even downhill.

My grandfather Winslow had chosen to live at 18 Chestnut Street, high on Beacon Hill. In his doorway were two loutish, brownstone pillars copied from the Temple of the Kings at Memphis.† Here, each afternoon, my grandfather would pause for a few minutes at four o'clock and finger his cane, inscribed with the names and altitudes of mountains in Norway which he had climbed. Looking about, he took satisfaction in seeing himself surrounded

---

* A reference to the famous first sentence of *The Education of Henry Adams*.

† The great temple in Memphis, Egypt, was dedicated to the local god Ptah, though several smaller temples were dedicated in part to the deified King Rameses II. Lowell may have meant the Temple of Seti I at Abydos, famous for its colonnades, described in Algernon Thomas St. George Caulfeild's well-known *The Temple of the Kings at Abydos* (1902).

by neighbors whose reputations had made state, if not universal, history. When these people died, their houses, resting on the solid brick of their names, were starred in the guidebooks. Across the street Edwin Booth had lived; across the street Julia Ward Howe still lived; across the street Ralph Adams Cram had lately settled.* Edwin Booth had been so famous one could forget he was an actor; Julia Ward Howe was so old and so distinguished one could forget she was only a woman; Cram, he decided, went rather fatiguingly far afield in his search for old ways of building new churches. Grandfather was not content with Cram, yet he kept Cram drawings scattered over the wormy desk he had brought home from Palermo—thus enjoying the exalted ceremonial of seeing his own just derision continually defeated by his good nature. Twenty houses down Chestnut Street stood the house that had belonged to Francis Parkman, and near was the house in which Oliver Wendell Holmes had lately died, another in which Percival Lowell had also lately died.† My grandfather was a Boston boy who had made good as a mining engineer in Colorado. He was proud of being self-made. He was proud, too, of his descent from New England Winslows who had supported George the Third in the eighteenth century, just as furiously as they had supported Cromwell a century earlier. These Winslows had been ruined and even, temporarily, exiled to Canada during the American Revolution. My grandfather wanted everyone to be pre-revolutionary and self-made. In the mornings he would declare that everyone in Boston was an opportunist and a *parvenu*; in the evenings he would glumly suggest that his neighbors were decadents who lived on their mere names. In 1917, my grandfather was well satisfied. Yet from time to time, something of the poison of his later agony would show; his vitals burned and he looked out with a pale, aching eye.

From my mother's scrapbooks and from her reminiscences, I can imagine scenes that took place in 1915. Perhaps it is fraudulent for me to describe recollections of things I did not see. Nevertheless, the two years before my

---

* Edwin Booth (1833–1893), renowned American actor; Julia Ward Howe (1819–1910), American author, lecturer, and suffragist; Ralph Adams Cram (1863–1942), American architect, the foremost advocate of Gothic revival.

† Francis Parkman (1823–1893), American historian; Oliver Wendell Holmes Sr. (1809–1894), American poet and physician ("lately" is inaccurate, for Holmes had died in 1894, whereas his son, the Supreme Court justice, was still alive); Percival Lowell (1855–1916), Lowell's distant cousin, was a noted astronomer, mathematician, and author.

birth are more real to me than the two years which followed. America entered the war and my mother entered marriage in the two years after 1915. I was often glad I could not be blamed for anything that happened during the months when I was becoming alive.

When I was three or four years old I first began to think about the time before I was born. Until then Mother had been everything; at three or four she began abruptly and gratingly to change into a human being. I wanted to recapture the mother I remembered and so I began to fabricate. In my memory she was a lady preserved in silhouettes, outlines and photographs; she sat on a blue bench; she wore a blue serge dress; she smiled at my father, a naval lieutenant in a collarless blue uniform. Blue meant the sea, the navy, and manhood. Blue was the ideal, defining color Mother had described to Father as his "Wagnerian theme," the absolute he was required to live up to. I was a little doll in a white sailor suit with blue anchors on the pockets, a doll who smiled impartially upon his mother and father and in his approbation thus made them husband and wife. But when I was at last three years old all that began to change. I could no longer see Mother as that rarely present, transfigured, Sunday-best version of my nurse. I saw her as my mother, as a rod, or a scolding, rusty hinge—as a human being. More and more I began to try to imagine Mother when she was happier, when she had been merely her father's favorite daughter, when she was engaged but unmarried. Perhaps I had been happiest then too, because I hadn't existed and lived only as an imagined future.

I found that all I had to do was to hold my breath when Mother talked about her girlhood and then it all came vividly to me. The large houses, the staff of servants, the immense house parties, the future—I was there, living it all. One day I held my breath longer and longer and more perfectly than ever before. I found myself breathing with ponderous, earthy effort. I found I was ill with croup. I could, in reality, hardly breathe. I lay staring at my black fingernails outlined against the white sheet. "You are a design for mourning," Mother said. "If you try to clean your fingernails, you'll have to dig in up to your elbows. You'll come out on the other side of the earth, in China."

For three long breathless nights I lay awake, blowing on the flame of my croup kettle to keep it burning. I breathed the deadening, aromatic benzene and felt it was the myrrh of the Magi. Traditionally, they came at first with

lambs and camels, but later my delirious visitors brought me bizarre, comforting, unorthodox creatures: flying squirrels, jumping mice, a duck-billed platypus. My animal sights danced about the benzene flame all night long in a command performance, and it pleased me to believe that they had chosen me to visit rather than President Coolidge, whose son had just died.*
Mother sat by me on the same blue bench. She remained as long as I could keep my eyes open, which was for three days and nights. I watched the planes, gyres and pyramids of her amazingly abundant brown hair and tried to explain to her that flying squirrels were whirling joyously over her head, going on tirelessly like children on the swings of an all-day recess; and, the jumping mice were burying glittering trinkets in the loops of her hair; the platypus was imitating a clipped-wing duck by flapping his paws like wings and making nutcracker sounds. Then, the scene changing, I would pass away the sick hours looking at Raphael's *Portinari* and the madonnas of Carlo Dolci in Mother's scrapbook.† There was Mother with her brother and sister, arranged in various photographs taken of the family from time to time. There were snapshots from house parties; five colored postcard poses of Sarah Bernhardt as l'Aiglon.‡ I wondered why the picture pasting had left off when the book was only half full. One of the last pictures showed my mother and grandfather together. My grandfather had written their initials in white ink on the black paper: *A. W. and C. W., 1915.*

I can still see Mother as she was in that picture, posed before the brownstone pillars of 18 Chestnut Street. I see her strong, firmly modeled chin, her pulled-in, tiny waist, her flounces, her beaver muff, and her neck, which was like a swan's neck crowned with an armful of pyramidal hair and an ostrich feather. She seemed a lady out of Edith Wharton's *Age of Innocence.* The time covered in the novel would have been at least a decade earlier, but Boston and my grandfather proudly worked at lagging behind the fashions,

---

* President Calvin Coolidge's younger son, Calvin Jr., died suddenly from a blood infection in July 1924 at the age of sixteen, when Lowell was seven.

† Probably *The Portinari Altarpiece* by Hugo van der Goes (ca. 1440–1482) in Florence. Carlo Dolci (1616–1686) painted many madonnas—e.g., *Madonna in Glory*, *The Blue Madonna*, and *Madonna and Child*—all of them in blue.

‡ L'Aiglon, French for "the eaglet," was a posthumous nickname given to Napoleon II (1811–1832), the son of Emperor Napoleon I and his second wife, Empress Marie Louise. Bernhardt created the title role of Edmond Rostand's play about Napoleon II, *L'Aiglon*, in Paris at the Théâtre Sarah Bernhardt in 1900. She played the role again in London at Her Majesty's Theatre in 1901.

a precise and mysterious degree of lagging, just as difficult to comprehend as the latest fashion itself. In the photograph of Mother snapped in front of the Chestnut Street house, my grandfather stood behind her in the doorway. He wore a round fur cap which made him look like a Cossack and he was smiling; to my curious eye he seemed not so much a person as a fascinating, ever-new face with a grin, and a lasso of fur about him.

I imagined Mother waiting to be handed into her touring car, a frail, ailing, indestructible, thirty-foot, carriage-like affair which already had the distinguished and obsolete air of a museum piece or a prop in a silent movie. Mother, her strong chin unprotected and chilled in the helpless autumn, seemed to me the young Alexander, all gleam and panache, Alexander, as in her copy of Plutarch, conferring with his *aide-de-camp* before the Battle of the Granicus. Mother, also, was a sort of commander-in-chief of her virgin battlefield. Steaming up out of my croupy delirium, I saw horses, wondrously tall, stepping up Chestnut Street—horse-chestnut street where the stables were even then being altered into garages. The horses looked down their bald, bleached Norman noses at me, and shook awkward silver bells that turned out to be my christening cups which Mother had sold because she wanted to clear her shelves. My horses reached their noses into the upper foliage of trees and pulled down bushels of green and gold leaves; they nibbled grotesquely and dribbled out of the sides of their mouths a landslide of green slates that were slipping from the stable roofs. A flight of green umbrellas drifted through the air, upside down. On another page of Mother's scrapbook I saw crowds in London, Brussels and Paris; the people grimaced under their shiny, rained-on umbrellas. They had the look of spectators at a gladiatorial show. They were listening to the declaration of World War I.

If you looked quickly at the snapshot I have mentioned, you first noticed only my mother and grandfather. It took a second glance to reveal that my father was also "in the picture"—and this recessiveness, within the family portrait, was not, alas, an accidental aspect of a single photograph but the genuine and enduring placement at all times. Even Father's four disturbingly evident initials (R.T.S.L.) retreated into corners of the album. He was a young man in a collarless blue lieutenant's uniform, always slightly out of place, with even his scrupulous neatness appearing somewhat impersonal, not really his, but as if he and his clothes were each morning hastily cleaned and pressed after a night of neglect. He smiled and smiled in his photographs, just as he smiled and smiled in life. He would look into the faces of others as if he expected to find himself reflected in their eyes. He was a man who treated even himself with the caution and uncertainty of one who has forgotten a name, in this case, his own. Father was not too straightforward, nor too backward, neither too slack nor too hard; the refusal of overstatement was the pillar he leaned on, the inclining Tower of Pisa which was his pose, his definition, his color and his support. In the photograph, Father was self-consciously holding a leash which had on its end a tobacco-colored, senile Sealyham. Old as the creature was, it nevertheless suggested that my father was its slave, rather embarrassingly serving as attendant on walks. In the picture, Mother seemed to be caught on an exciting and fated young day, as if at this moment she had found the courage to say to my grandfather, "Papá, Lieutenant Lowell and I want to be engaged," and then daring to add, or at least to think, "And Bob hasn't a mean or an extraordinary bone in his body."

Mother's conception of her father was very different from her notion of her Lieutenant Lowell. Even her military notions were reserved for her father, who was a great conquering emperor in her mind. Six years before, she had read the Duchess D'Abrantès's *Memoirs of Napoleon*. "In short, when I recollect Napoleon entering the courtyard of the Hotel de la Tranquillité in 1793, with a shabby round hat drawn over his forehead, and his ill-powdered hair hanging over the collar of his grey great-coat, which afterwards became as celebrated as the white plume of Henry IV, without gloves, because he used to say they were a useless luxury, with boots ill-made and ill-blackened, with his thinness and his sallow complexion . . ." Yes, he was "a sloven," but Mother, with her intense and extraordinary neatness, could love this personage she wished to tidy, could imagine herself as a tidying, organizing hand to greatness. She began to bolt her food, and for a time slept on an army cot and took cold dips in the morning. In all this she could be Napoleon made over in my grandfather's Prussian image. It was always my grandfather she admired, even if she called him Napoleon. She might run into her father's library and say, "I wish you were puny and green in the face with genius, and not six feet tall with a red and brown face." She had learned how to lead her father: she had only to let him dominate.

My grandfather's behavior inclined strongly toward exaggeration. When Mother's suitors came, he acted with a bossy, tense attentiveness that was absurd even in that era of protective patriarchs. Mother and the young man would sit down in the "Louis Seize Room" at Chestnut Street. My grandmother and grandfather sat in the next room only a few feet away. They were partially visible and utterly audible. But, with the plea that they were thinking of Mother's privacy, they would stubbornly refuse to be introduced and said that no indication need be made that the young people were mindful of their presence, a forgetfulness no one was ever visited by, however.

In the war years there was much talk about the Prussians and the Austrians. My grandmother Winslow came from Raleigh, North Carolina.* She was too joyful, quick and amused to blame my grandfather for the Civil War, although in her heart she may have decided that "his kind" was at fault. She couldn't imagine ranting about family, or pretending to be discontent with the wealth my grandfather had won for her. Still, she could never quite swallow New England. It was a place peculiarly designed to irritate. She did not feel that New England had formed my grandfather so much as that his strictness had somehow chosen New England for its proper setting. When Austria came up in conversation, my grandmother would grow excited with critical feeling; she would say, "If only those humorless, crop-haired Prussians would stay in their own country." She would grunt and condemn and mix up Von Moltke, General Sherman, Rutherford B. Hayes, and Prince Hohenlohe. My grandfather would immediately and violently take offense. He would repeat that he had spent two years studying in Stuttgart, and to good effect; he would insist that northern climes were the nurses of character. As he talked, his bulletins from the English-Speaking Union† would slide from the table, and he would brush aside the cuttings from the *National Geographic* which he had fastened together with paper clips and which he meant to mail to some country relative. In argument he grew heated and sometimes even stamped the floor. Whenever one of my mother's utterly subdued young men said something Grandfather disapproved of, he would cough. No one ever coughed back. Before he could propose to Mother, my father had to break through all these coughs, disapprovals, impediments.

---

* Mary Livingston Devereux (1862–1944) of Raleigh, North Carolina, whom Arthur Winslow married on May 19, 1887. Lowell's grandfather met his wife in Raleigh while he ran a private practice there as a geologist and mining engineer.

† Charitable educational organization, founded in Britain in 1918, seeking to promote the English language and to provide educational opportunities for English-speaking people around the world.

———

The wedding took place. Photographs of the bride and her bridesmaids remained, yellowing on the mantels; there also remained the tale of a gold and platinum watch chain given to Father by his shipmates. Never before had there been a chain fashioned with such an abundance of precious material. It was interestingly costly and pronounced scandalous in the tastelessness of its design. Mother somehow managed to dispose of this chain—she was not one whose hand was stayed from destruction by sentiment. Because it had been so outlawed, and yet strangely unkillable at least as a topic of conversation, I used even years later to wish that I might see the heavy, hopeless chain for myself. Mother never liked the presents she received; she either exchanged the gift or had it in some vaguely accusing fashion remodeled. If you gave her a silver belt buckle, she would have one half made into a pin for her coat; if you gave her a traveling case, she would say with a sigh that she never hoped to see another train or boat as long as she lived.

For their honeymoon my parents took a two-week journey to the Grand Canyon. The choice was so heroic and unoriginal that it left them forever after with a feeling of gaping vacuity: the whole thing was also inexplicable because my parents, in great moments at least, fell in with what was fashionable and accepted: coming-out parties, grand tours, good hotels, photographs by Bachrach, dresses by Worth. Striking the common, humble, young-honeymooners note in the Grand Canyon was for them a peculiar dissonance, always a bit jarring. I have never thought our lives determined by the stars and yet at idle moments I could imagine myself stamped with the mark of the Grand Canyon, as if it were a sticker on an automobile. The Canyon's hollow hugeness was a sort of bad start for us all. I have never seen it; it is, indeed, too familiar to be seen.

Immediately after their marriage, Mother went to Jamestown, or rather she was taken there or *sent* there.* My father was stationed at this inexpensive little haven near Newport. Father had often to be away for weeks at sea, but Jamestown had the grandeur of its nearness to Newport, some society and a great deal of solitude to offer my mother. She made a great point of liking it all. As a very green and reckless housekeeper, for a whole week she

---

* Jamestown in Newport County, Rhode Island.

ordered three quarts of cream a day under the impression it was only grade A milk. Her new husband had no complaints to offer; he did not presume to advise and direct. Mother sighed for her father, whose urgent domination she had long been accustomed to and been sustained by.

Winter came and my father went off to Guantanamo. Mother was then sent to Staten Island, across the bay from New York City, to stay with my grandmother Lowell and great-grandmother Myers, Father's mother and grandmother.* To Mother's unhappy eyes, Grandmother Lowell appeared to be sapless, resigned, depressed, dependent and contented. She had lovely, soft white hair which she wore in braid; her husband, my father's father, had died in the fifth month of their marriage, five months before my father was born.†

This terrible, early bereavement bewildered my grandmother Lowell. She remained a young girl, chaste, tender, sentimental and sad. She adored her son and looked forward with girlish delight to the hope that my mother would bring something fresh and gay into her life. But Mother felt mislaid and lost in a household without brothers and sisters, men, arguments, explosions. She didn't enjoy Grandmother Lowell and Great-Grandmother Myers at all; she was miserable with them. The only thing she enjoyed was taking brisk walks and grieving over the fact that she was pregnant. She took pride in looking into the great Atlantic Ocean and saying, without a trace of fear or illusion, "I wish I could die."‡ On her insistence, and certainly contrary to my father's wishes, we made our first of those many intense moves back to Boston from where my father's life and work had sent us. My mother's true lover was Boston, or living in Boston, or perhaps *not* living away from Boston; she died during the separations. I was born at my grandfather Winslow's, on the first of March 1917.

---

* Kate Bailey Myers Lowell (1859–unknown) and her mother, Caroline Chappell Myers (1835–1930).

† Robert T. S. Lowell II, born 1860, died on March 17, 1887, four months before Lowell's father was born (July 15, 1887).

‡ Compare to "Unwanted," in Robert Lowell, *Day by Day* (New York: Farrar, Straus and Giroux, 1977), reprinted in *Collected Poems*, edited by Frank Bidart and David Gewanter (New York: Farrar, Straus and Giroux, 2003), 833: "I wish I were dead, I wish I were dead."

I Take Thee, Bob

IN THE WINTER OF 1915, my mother, Charlotte Lowell [née Winslow], first met my father, Robert Traill Spence Lowell, at a dinner given by Beatrice Lowell* for her son, Alfred Putnam Lowell, who was announcing his engagement to Mother's best friend, Kitty Bowles.† Of course, Mother had been in on the secret for two months, and for two months she had been in a tizzy asking Kitty half-envious, half-flattering questions about the Lowells. One afternoon Mother even acted out a slightly hysterical one-man charade, entitled, *The Lowells: Have they tails or have they wings?* A few of Mother's skits have been remembered. There was her A. Lawrence Lowell,‡ the genial President of Harvard, awarding Alfred his A.B. and saying lugubriously, "Go west, young man, avoid Miss Bowles." There was Percival Lowell, the brilliant but unsociable astronomer, who looked through the wrong end of my grandfather Winslow's telescope, and said, "I have discovered *Percival*, the minutest living planet." Then there was Mother all padded out with pillows and laundry bags, and with a clothespin

---

* Born in Middlesex, England, Beatrice Kate Lowell, née Hardcastle (1848–1930), was the widow of Charles Lowell (1855–1906), Robert Lowell's great-uncle (and the son of his namesake, Robert Traill Spence Lowell).

† Catherine Hay Bowles (1890–1969), the daughter of Rear Admiral Francis Tiffany Bowles and Adelaide Hay Bowles, née Savage.

‡ Abbott Lawrence Lowell (1856–1943), the brother of Amy Lowell and Percival Lowell, and Robert Lowell's distant cousin.

in her mouth; pretending to be Amy Lowell,* and exclaiming, "Hold me, John Keats, I am as light as the *Lusitania*." There was Judge James Lowell,† himself a charader, for Mother made him talk with a Jewish accent and play the role of King Solomon giving judgment. "Oi yoi, scut do kiddo in bieces." There was the imaginary Augustus "Awful" Lowell, the cotton plutocrat, who earned more money yearly than the government adding machines could add, and was therefore decorated with the blue ribbon that had hitherto belonged to Mother's Scottie, Mac. There was Cornelius Lowell, the historian of the French Revolution, writing an article for the *Atlantic Monthly* entitled, "Notes on the Monetary Background of Charlotte Corday."‡ There was Guy Lowell,§ the architect, being consulted on a building for the Boston Fine Arts Museum. He was holding up photographs of St. Peter's, the Pitti Palace, the Taj Mahal, the Parthenon and the Eiffel Tower, and saying, "Take your pick." There was Mrs. John Lowell, the President of the Colonial Dames, who was blackballing an application for membership made by the wife of President Wilson. There was Mrs. Gus Lowell . . . but why go on? At the end, all but two of the Lowells were awarded wings. Tails went to the unspeakable Amy and to Cornelius, whom my grandfather Winslow impulsively described as a "cad, a smart Alec and a Pink."

Mother's Reading Club—Rosy Bigelow, Franny Kittredge, Connie Codman and Kitty Bowles—were out in force for the one-man charade. Politely, they had almost died laughing, but on the way home, Connie had said, "Well, I must admit that Charlotte is an uproarious sport." And Kitty had said, "Yes, Charlotte is emphatic, but that's why we love her." And Franny had said, "Sometimes I worry."

Kitty Bowles was taut, timid, freckled and a believing Unitarian. For two years, she had actually run her mother's hen yard at Barnstable, and insisted on helping her maid make and unmake the beds. She spoke perhaps too stridently about the need for people to be plainspoken, considerate and sincere. I can see her shaking her honest, puzzled red head at the world's

---

* Amy Lowell (1874–1925), an avant-garde poet and a biographer of John Keats. The clothespin in Charlotte's mouth stands for a cigar, which Amy Lowell habitually smoked.

† James Arnold Lowell (1869–1933), a federal judge in Massachusetts and Robert Lowell's distant cousin.

‡ Presumably Lowell did not mean "Cornelius" but Edward J. Lowell (1845–1894), a Suffolk County lawyer, the author of *The Eve of the French Revolution* (1892).

§ Guy Lowell (1870–1927), architect, landscape designer, and Robert Lowell's distant cousin.

profusion and horror. "But the Kaiser had all the advantages," she would say. "Can you honestly understand why he *refused* to look into his own heart?"* Kitty, as Mother insisted, was an "honest to goodness *person*"; that's why it was amusing to try and figure out just what she saw in Alfred Lowell. Alfred looked as though he had been born in his black bowler hat, his black mustache, his black coat, his black waistcoat, his black striped trousers, and his cold, chewed black cigar. He was a first-rate yachtsman and a first-rate squash player; his skill in carving a fowl was already beginning to be talked about. He had a sinister eye for women, which may have been Platonic. He belonged to two or three good clubs. By his stiffness and slang, he kept the world at arm's length. He was high church, had a horror of stereotyped velleities, and there was no subject on earth which he was unable to analyze in terms of firsthand Boston anecdotes. All in all, the Reading Club was upset, and couldn't believe that Alfred was at all Kitty's dish of tea. Mother took a more down-to-earth and Machiavellian view. She thought that a Lowell with a perfectly good Harvard Law School degree was nothing to be sneezed at in Boston. "Alfred may be a stick," she would say, "but he does have style."

Mother asked Kitty hundreds of humorous questions about Alfred's first cousin, Robert. Mother would say, "A Lowell *and* a naval officer! He must be a genius and a buccaneer. I love him sight unseen!" Then Kitty would answer, "Bob is the most gentle, the most cheerful, the most modest, the most Euclidean man I have ever met." This last was Kitty's affectionate translation of the one sentence that was used by everyone to characterize Lieutenant Lowell. "Can't say much about Robert. I hear he got straight A's at Columbia for his work in radio." Then Kitty would wrinkle up her frail freckled nose. She was determined to be sincere as well as considerate, but Bob was a puzzler to sum up. She remembered a lecture on Psychology given by Professor James.† Franny's father, Professor Kittredge,‡ "Kitty," had insisted on taking the entire Reading Club. Kitty Bowles said, "Bob's mind-stuff is recessive, because Bob's father died before Bob was born."

---

* Kaiser Wilhelm II (1859–1941), the emperor of Germany, was Queen Victoria's grandson and once a British Army officer, but by 1915 many English speakers viewed him as a betrayer.

† William James (1842–1910), a professor of psychology and philosophy at Harvard, the author of *The Principles of Psychology* (1890).

‡ George Lyman Kittredge (1860–1941), a Harvard professor and celebrated scholar of Shakespeare, Chaucer, and Malory.

When my father had been a mere midshipman, he had spent his summer vacations with his Aunt Beatrice and Alfred. Beatrice once amused my
grandmother Winslow by waving her arms in the air and crying, "Little
Boy Blue is here. My nephew dogs Alfred all day as though he were Alfred's
navy-blue shadow." And even now, almost fifteen years later, my father had
the reputation in Boston of being something of a spook, who didn't know
his way about. Aunt Beatrice was British, barking, squat and tyrannous. She
had a tongue in her head, and she believed that *noblesse oblige* "obliged" her
to use her tongue on Boston. People said that this was because she was a
widow, a foreigner and arthritic.

What had really spoiled Aunt Beatrice was that the first two years of her
marriage to Uncle Charles had been spent in India, where she had queened
it over a staff of thirty Hindoo servants. She only wore ugly earth-brown
dresses ornamented with dim sand-brown spots. If some ignorant guest flattered Aunt Beatrice on her colors, she would shriek, "Brown favors me! Isn't
it a scream! I dress like a gilded toad so as not to be mistaken for a hollow-
hipped, flyblown Boston bluestocking." She was dying to be taken for an
enfant terrible. "Would you believe it?" she would giggle. "Boston wants to
behead me because I have never learned Bridge!" After dinner, she would
force her guests to listen to her sing old French songs which she had translated. She accompanied herself on a harpsichord which she had imported
from Budapest. She sang off-key; the harpsichord was never in tune. For
years she had kept two pacifist clergymen in tow. "Aren't they darling?" she
would say. "They have walked straight out of the Vedanta."*

Once she had disgusted my grandfather Winslow by saying, "Stop beating around the bush, Arthur. Of course, it's a racket! You may be Mr. Up-
right Citizen, but I know I am just what Karl Marx says I am. I am a corrupt
old crow, with more money than is good for her, and who wouldn't lift a finger to help my fellow man, especially if it meant work. Do you know what
I am writing on my gravestone? 'Riches were my greatest responsibility.' I
would rather be damned than give a nickel to the Reds or the Red Cross."
Aunt Beatrice's comments on Amy Lowell's free-verse poem *Patterns* went
something like this: "No tumpty-tump-tump. No jamble-jam. The woman
in *Patterns* is an honest-to-God eighteenth-century rococo striptease. I hear

---

* One of the six orthodox schools of thought in Hindu philosophy.

the Old Howard Burlesque House* is after her. But she says, 'Down with the stage! I am descended from Governor Winthrop on both sides, and swear to abide by the blue laws.'" The person who maddened Aunt Beatrice more than all others was my father. She would say, "Bob hasn't a mean bone, an original bone, a funny bone in his body! That's why I can't get a word he says. If he were mine, I'd lobotomize him and stuff his brain with red peppers."

Thirty Hindoo servants with thirty mops would have had a hard time of it trying to clean 10 Clarendon St. in time for the engagement party.[†] Though set in the middle of Boston, 10 Clarendon stood on a corner and was as big and as wayward as a Newport mansion. On the grounds, an acre of sickly yews gathered dust and survived; indoors, an acre of possessions bred and multiplied. The ceilings were twenty feet high. The walls' four-inch-thick oak panels were said to have been taken from the frigate *Constitution* when it was being remodeled twenty years earlier. The floors were red, black-speckled tiles stamped with sixteenth-century Spanish coats-of-arms. They had been imported from Bruges by Mrs. Jack Gardner,[‡] rejected, and sold to Aunt Beatrice for a song. Suits of armor stood on duty in nooks and held up unlit tapers as big as the paschal candle. Banners and frocks of chain mail hung on prongs of maces, and looked like dust cloths lost in the gloom. In the drawing room, there was a huge Dresden china chandelier, in which colored Madame de Pompadours and gamboling goats alternated as candleholders. The light flickered rudely on two bad oil portraits of full-length Bengalee bankers, who wore tuxedoes, turbans, and cordons of the Legion of Honour.

Here, Aunt Beatrice sat and received. Mother came near. Mother waved her fan at the swarthy, swathed, painted faces and said in a little girl's voice, "Mrs. Lowell, I admire your beaux, your white knights."

Aunt Beatrice said, "When you really get to know them, no one is more bourgeois than a Brahmin."

---

* The Old Howard (1845–1953), located in Scollay Square, was the best-known burlesque theater in Boston.

† By all indications, the address of Beatrice Hardcastle Lowell and Alfred Putnam Lowell was different at the time—namely, 277 Beacon Street. See "277 Beacon," Back Bay Houses, Genealogies of Back Bay Houses, https://backbayhouses.org/277-beacon/.

‡ Isabella Stewart ("Mrs. Jack") Gardner (1840–1924) was an art collector, philanthropist, and founder of the Isabella Stewart Gardner Museum in Boston.

Mother said, "Oh, then Papá needn't make us memorize Emerson's essay on 'Friendship.'"

Aunt Beatrice looked blank. Alfred Lowell said, "Charlotte, Ma isn't talking about old Ralph Waldo and Frankie Parkman's uncle.* Her Brahmins is Injuns."†

Aunt Beatrice beckoned to my father. "Miss Winslow," she said to Mother, "I implore you to bestow your 'Friendship' on the Lieutenant. Robbie is as close and romantic as the Orient."

[...] In such a setting, Mother fell in love with Father's shyness, his name, and his deep collarless blue ensign's uniform. Up till a little more than a year before this, Mother had still been sleeping on a hard army cot, and pinning up prints of Napoleon at Arcola, Austerlitz and St. Helena. She prized the fall above the grandeur and felt that Napoleon in exile was a man you could talk to. Two men she despised above all others. One was Sir Hudson Lowe, the roast-beef-faced St. Helena jailer.‡ The other was the puny, green-cheeked eaglet, l'Aiglon, Napoleon's legitimate son, who hadn't the strength to live.§ Mother had a picture of her father, the patriarchal Arthur Winslow, which was hard to explain. He was a Napoleon disguised as Sir Hudson Lowe.

Mother thought about her father day and night, but this evening she looked at Robert Lowell. "Will he do?" she said to herself. She was impressed by Father's short, mumbled, strictly factual comments on the European War. Further down the table, another officer, Ensign MacRae, was talking on this same subject with the patronizing verbosity of an insider. Father whispered in Mother's ear, "Poor Mac, he sounds like Admiral Sims, but he is going to be retired next spring, because he has no bean for math." Mother felt that

---

* Ralph Waldo Emerson (1803–1882), an essayist and poet, and George Parkman (1790–1849), a physician, philanthropist, and murder victim. Francis Parkman (1823–1893), George Parkman's nephew, was an American historian.

† Alfred uses the derogatory term for American Indians to refer to citizens of India. Charlotte had thought Alfred and Beatrice were referring to so-called Boston Brahmins, members of the city's elite, like Ralph Waldo Emerson and Francis Parkman.

‡ Lowe (1769–1844), an Anglo-Irish soldier who served as governor of St. Helena, was in effect the "jailer" of Napoleon Bonaparte.

§ Napoleon II, always sickly, died of tuberculosis at twenty-one.

this was hardly the cry of the Eagle, but she remembered that Napoleon himself had been an artillery officer. Was it the surly, low-browed General Augereau, or Shakespeare's Iago, who had spoken of his better as a mere mathematician?*

Mother began to venture a few impersonal but somewhat emphatic opinions. She said that Southerners had execrable taste in clothes, but the only presentable manners in America. She said that Theodore Roosevelt made her think of Rudyard Kipling dressed up as Mowgli in a charade. Then Father would apologetically chime in and support Mother with long, pliant platitudes. One thing was disconcerting. Every now and then Father's mind would wander; he would show an unexpected and unwarranted warmth for nonsensical whimsy. He called the suits of armor *Don Carmen*. Mother had to laugh out loud. She was a little frightened.

[. . .] On the night when Mother was to meet Father, Aunt Beatrice was seated at her harpsichord and playing an old French song that she had translated. [. . .] She began to sing in a hoary, coughing cracked contralto:

> *Le tems a laissie son manteau*
> *de vent, de froydure, et de pluye,*
> *et s'est vestu de Broderye,*
> *de soleil raiant, cler et beau.*

She sang the words again in her English translation:

> The year has sloughed her winter coat
> of wind and wet and night;
> and now she walks in tapestry
> of bird and bud and light.

---

* Pierre-Francois-Charles Augereau (1757–1816), the son of a servant, rose to the positions of general and commander in Napoleon's army but ultimately clashed with both Napoleon and Louis XVIII. Resentful of Bonaparte's brilliant career, Augereau reportedly once said of him, "An insignificant figure! He is said to be a mathematician and a dreamer!" See Hippolyte Adolphe Taine, *The Origins of Contemporary France: The Modern Regime*, vol. 1, translated by John Durand (New York: Henry Holt, 1890), 15. In *Othello*, Iago derides Cassio, reputedly a "great mathematician," as merely a "counter-caster" (1.1.33).

My father compared the music to a platinum filament, and found that he was beginning a lecture on filaments.

"Tinkle and toffee," Aunt Beatrice said. "It's pre-Adamite, I mean a pre-Bach fugue. A child could do better today."

My father said, "Say, what a translation. My aunt is a poet and a scholar."

Aunt Beatrice said, "If the Navy had taught my nephew Robbie two words of French, he would realize that my translation is, to use a naval expression, bilge. Well, as I told Amy Lowell, I may not say anything, but at least I chime."

Mother looked shyly at my father, then she said to Aunt Beatrice, "Mrs. Lowell, when I hear you singing, I believe that I too am 'sloughing my winter coat of *froydure*.'"*

Mother blushed. Her accent was a strange mixture of Kansas City, Raleigh, North Carolina, and Beacon Hill Boston.† Aunt Beatrice listened for a moment with amusement, then she said with gentle derision, "Why Charlotte dear, you mustn't strain to speak English, when it isn't your native language. Robbie will understand you, he's a globe-trotting sailor. He's an honest Abe from Staten Island." She stopped a minute, and then said very slowly and seriously, "Since Robbie was fourteen, the Navy has been his father, a mother and wife."

---

* Intense cold (medieval French).

† Charlotte spent childhood years in Missouri (first in Jefferson City, then in Kansas City). Her father was the state geologist in Jefferson City from 1889 to 1894. Her Southern inflection came from her mother, Mary Livingston Devereux.

Philadelphia

W HAT I KNOW of my parents' engagement, marriage and honeymoon comes from what I have been told later and from what I can imagine out of my knowledge of my parents' lives and characters. Of the first years of my own life I remember quite a bit, and of course much was told to me, and I have imagined much. In my mind white sunlight on white sand stays with a brute, unlocked, dumb insistence.

On the top floor of our house, in a room that was dark but always germ-free because the windows were open, I used to lie on my back, hold my knees and vibrate. *Stop rocking*, my nurse or Mother would say. I remember this trembling fury but I do not know its reason. Remembering, I seem to see water dripping from the ceiling, down on the wallpaper, but that happened later, when we rented our house to people who were "irresponsible vandals." I can see sunlight striking our gray carpet, the rays falling on the sideboard and the marmalade jar in our Brimmer Street house. The house was the first my parents owned in Boston as newlyweds. It was a financial miracle; Mother hadn't paid a penny for it. My grandfather Winslow had first taken a mortgage and then a second mortgage to pay the first; then he took out a loan of some kind in order to pay the second mortgage, then he gave Mother a Christmas present to pay the interest on the loan.* Perhaps there were other

---

* Lowell's grandfather took the mortgages in his daughter's name. He presumably arranged for several mortgages and a loan on her property, each to pay off the previous indebtedness, and then he gave her the

steps in these exciting negotiations, maybe even third and fourth mortgages, all taken by my grandfather, who was reputed to be a wizard in such affairs and who had plenty of time on his hands in order to execute his amazing financial schemes.

When Mother finally sold the house on Brimmer Street she paid off all the debts on it and cleared a thousand dollars. The room where I had held my knees and trembled with stubbornness has faded; more alive, more vivid long after is the sensation of the resentment occasioned by the fact that my father's naval duties forced to us to move from Boston. Mother, despising the demands the navy made upon her, would say mysteriously that she needed character and courage to prevent my father from allowing things simply to take their quiet course and, thereby, ruin us.

From the period of the Brimmer Street house a scene remains, a childish drama embarrassingly heavy with religious symbolism and black magic. When real events are so starkly allegorical, the accidental nature of such happenings is blackly underscored. When I was two years old I had a young nurse who was, herself, only eighteen or so years old and had come to Boston from Ireland. She was always spoken of as a beautiful girl, firmly conforming to her national pattern: she had raven hair which was soft and wavy, sky blue eyes, fair skin, and an exquisite brogue. She was pious, irreverent and loose-limbed—the pretty possessor of what Grandfather Winslow described as a "loosely-laced mind." Her name was Katherine. Katherine's rosary was a memorable work of religious mass production. It was designed with a Celtic exaggeration and the beads were made of some material which had the appearance and texture of rock candy. These beads were so hard, cold and precious and of such fascination that immediately the fat, warm, wooden beads which decorated my crib lost all their appeal to me. But what I loved more than the beads of Katherine's rosary was the silver crucifix. It was heavy, intricate and important, as I could see from Katherine's awed and loving glance upon it. Katherine told me about Jesus and I regret to recall that my feelings were highly egocentric: I saw, with despair, that I was second fiddle even in my nurse's affections. And then suddenly the rosary disappeared and the house was disturbed by the mystery. I was questioned,

money to pay the interest on the loan. When she sold the property, she paid off the principal from the sale and kept the profit.

but I merely gaped sweetly and presented myself as a figure of innocence, all sunlight and brown curls. I smiled and smiled and smiled, very much in the perplexing way my father smiled and smiled and smiled. A day or so later the rosary was found, hidden under the corner of the rug, where it had slipped by mistake according to the decision taken by the household. However, it was noted that the Christus was missing and also, with embarrassment, that the chain of the rosary had been chewed. I returned to my denying smile, but later Mother saw me pushing a strip of paper down the register. "You will burn up the house," she said. But two days later she again saw me pushing a whole handful of paper strips down the register, "You are setting the furnace on fire," she said. I smiled and smiled, to her intense displeasure. "Yes, I know," I said. "That's where Jesus is."

My father was sent to Philadelphia and so we were to be packed up and sent there, too, for my third and fourth winters. These years were unhappy, or so they were always described by my mother, who did not want to go to Philadelphia or any place else. The theme of her early married life was clear and constant and alarming: *I want to live in Boston.* I can still feel the bite of those two Philadelphia winters and the dismal chill of the scene, a clammy, snowless, sooty, sunless prospect of an insupportably long street bordered by indistinguishable residences. Now, looking back, I can wonder why Mother pronounced Philadelphia "absolutely unbearable." Wasn't it, after all, just a bigger, warmer, Boston?

Philadelphia—our winters there leave an unpleasant trace in my history, like a metallic taste in the mouth. This, I suppose, came from Mother's utter detestation of this period, because I could not have cared one way or another. I remember our train journey, very snug and very serious. I felt I was setting sail for Europe or another age and that it was only my steady courage and enduring patience which made the arrival possible. Mother undertook the trip with all the bravado of unpleasant duty, which seemed to say that if she was wrong in not wishing to go she was at least triumphantly admirable in going anyway. Her dress, her proud walk, her dramatic tension which made her assume in moments of stress an abnormally casual and indifferent air! I discovered at this time that adults enjoyed drama, even painful drama, for only then when they were boiling and raging inside could they act calmly, with a sense of importance and control.

We did, at last, solemnly and importantly and dutifully arrive in Philadelphia. We had taken an apartment which had a certain number of distinct
rooms but was, nevertheless, quite small. The windows ran from floor to
ceiling and admitted little sunlight, but much electric glare, dust and drafty
air; the window panes were blue-gray and framed in iron—all of our glassy
view of the outside and inside world was a little shadowed and askew, like
the decor for a German expressionist film. The apartment's bedrooms, servant's room, dining room, nursery and parlor were a Lilliputian annex to a
kitchen which was covered with a peeling black and white linoleum. When
we had finally arrived, my parents spent hours screwing in light bulbs, while
I sat serenely crackling the paper in a box of Fig Newtons. The confusion
of the move, the disappointment of the apartment threw everything out of
balance and accounted for the unprecedented availability of the Fig Newton
box and even for the cookie itself, a rich, exotic mixture disapproved of,
unlike the salutary New England Graham Cracker.

Philadelphia: one afternoon at about four o'clock, when winter and coal
smoke had already made the sky impenetrably black, I wandered out of
our long kitchen and to my horror saw Father lying in his brown, monkish
wrapper on a sofa that had been moved into the hall. He was ill with flu;
his temperature was 103, and he lay back, sack-like, and smiling still. Father
looked cold and waxen and I thought his cheap Chinese slippers very
much like little snowshoes. On the hard chair at his elbow, lay his shirt and
underwear—he seemed somehow on the alert. Father, in his illness, had
removed himself from the bedroom he shared with Mother so that the room
might remain healthy and germ-free and spared the disorder of his convalescing presence. In his quiet, smiling, feverish banishment, he meant to be
an ideal husband whose demands were infinitesimal. But, nevertheless, every time we moved we stumbled gracelessly upon the unselfish invalid. The
strain brought about by his effort to make himself heroically nonexistent
was extreme; all was hushed, vexed and ajar. Still after a day of such exposure and boldness, Father was cured. It did not pay to be sick in this way and
it seemed to me that the cure had come from some glorious modesty and
self-sacrifice on Father's part. His object, however, was defeated because
Mother caught flu and was sick for a week. She lay in warmth and splendor
in her bedroom, supported by hot water bottles, gardenias, doctors, and

trays with pink napkins on them. In her self-indulgent illness nothing was set at odds in the household; instead everything was more smooth than ever, as if music were playing and we were all living in a floating palace.

This Philadelphia illness was my first experience with the strange contraries of hardiness and sickness which were always a great part of our family life. At this time I, too, came down with flu which mysteriously lasted for three weeks. I felt very close to Mother because she took joy in giving me every comfort and care and I was even allowed to feel that the very act of being sick for three long weeks was an extraordinary accomplishment. This feat gave much trouble and expense and yet it was the kind of trouble that one need not be ashamed of. Here was a difficulty Mother could rise to. She made sickness something of a pleasure and a privilege and surrounded it with good sense, humor and ease. Yet, mentally or verbally, it was hardiness which was always praised and when, later, I simply would not be sick, hardiness was fine and yet somehow associated in my mind with perverse stubbornness, with an assertion of my will against my mother's. Hardiness could be hardness of heart, self-love, whereas a few convenient light illnesses were an announcement of one's tenderness, tolerance, and family spirit.

On the matter of illness, Mother was perplexed, and theory and practice were not always united. She believed desperately in hardiness and always said firmly, "I am never ill," but meanwhile she spent several days every month in bed for one reason or another. When the men of her household were sick, her duties were definite, domesticity soared in importance and the stubborn wills around her were pleasantly resting and recuperating. Sickness was at once the supreme proof of masculine recklessness and absurdity and a penalty which strangely eased domestic tensions. If one was sick, he was culpable and unworthy, but on the other hand his behavior was better, more considerate: an ill man won't be late to dinner. A passive, emergency object could be dealt with in prescribed terms and the emergency, itself, gave a pleasant drama to the routine days.

When I was convalescing from flu, Christmas holidays arrived and I associated in my mind the lazy, indulgent recovering days with actual calendar holidays. My father was away at sea and Grandfather Winslow made us a surprise visit from Boston. My father sent me a big bundle of toys and in my self-concentration I thought I had the toys only because Father was

away and so his absence seemed delighted.* When he returned, I ran up to
him with tears in my eyes and said, "Daddy, I love you, but please go away
again so that Santa can mail us a wagonload of toys." Father seemed rather
queasy in the face of this demonstration from his son.†

The toys had been chosen with the notion of impressing upon me the
glamor of Father's naval career by comparison with mere civilian life and
parenthood. Someone in the Philadelphia Yard had ordered naval toys
wholesale from Japan and was selling them at a discount to men in the service. Among my gifts was a grim, gray wooden model of a German U-boat.
By pressing a button, I could snap a trap-like spring inside the U-boat which
made its gear collapse on the carpet, as though the thing had been hit by a
depth bomb. This device was meant to teach children that wars meant business and, further, it was the very magic of the toy itself and so I was dismayed when Mother snatched my prize from me, disemboweled it of its
spring, and then returned it, a miserable, weightless, warped wreck of its
former warlike self. The intricate and banned U-boat gave a fascination to
the German character which had produced it. I thought they must be amazing people with their model boats, and guns and torpedoes; I imagined they
were the sort to hide stones in snowballs and put barbs back on fishhooks.
When my father came home he told me my toy submarine was skippered
by a six-foot blond boy from Stuttgart, a creature named Fritz Shoemaker,
who was drowned whenever the spring was snapped. For a few nights I had
nightmares in which I saw poor Fritz's cold, stiff, lifeless German body.

I was partially consoled for the loss of my U-boat by another gift, a set
of six hand-painted French sailors, with red tufts on the top of their sailor
hats. All through Christmas morning I kept wretchedly fumbling about in
the heavy sheets of brown paper in which the sailors had been wrapped.
Concealed in the heavy paper, I had been told, was a seventh sailor. I

* Lowell left us here with a mixed construction. Was he trying to say that the father's absence was *delightful* or that the son was *delighted* that the father was away? Perhaps he wanted to keep both shades of
meaning—or to suggest the father's delight in being absent.

† In the manuscript, Lowell wrote an alternative to the first two letters of "Father" before he typed "F-a"
over them. The typed-over letters look like "M-o" (though they could conceivably be "F-6"). Did Lowell
originally write, "Mother seemed rather queasy"? In that possible variant, the mother serves as witness to
even this most intimate instance of the son's ambivalence toward his father—or at least she did until Lowell
saw what he had written and corrected it.

wanted the other sailor and when I couldn't find him I had the desperate feeling that my method for looking for him was wrong, that somewhere in the paper he lay and that it was only my clumsiness and headlong, impatient ways which prevented him from being instantly revealed. My grandfather Winslow walked up and down in front of the fireplace, snapping his gold matchbox open and shut. Mother jokingly said the sailor was in the matchbox, but I looked and saw only a green-black musty darkness. This looking for the sailor was filled with anguish, self-hatred for my ineptness, genuine despair. I felt shaken and believed I had not only known how, but had actually experienced the finding of the sailor, that I had mastered the mystery of the folded paper, but had somehow mysteriously lost my knowledge. The joy of hunting, my tireless and awkward persistence which had in it a certain measure of satisfaction, went along with my grief and anxiety. Now, I cannot decide whether there had ever truly been a seventh sailor in a seventh hat with a red tassel on it.

Philadelphia was a watery dinginess, like the black cement floor of its own principal railroad station. The ice floes of white enamel in our long kitchen shivered and shimmered; soot floated calmly in the air and the windows glared steel blue. In the newness of our life, the unfamiliarity, the fact that we wouldn't stay long enough ever to be really of the city, all of this meant that about us, people existed, lived, gossiped and accepted their lives, but we did not exist. We seemed to be treading water all day, getting nowhere. Mother felt Philadelphia society was a bit limp and peripheral, an oversized and ersatz Boston. Some natives of the city called upon us. The visits passed with tenderness and mutual respect, but my mother thought these lone ladies and dignified couples peculiarly lacking in gaiety and eccentricity. They were, in character at least, Quakerish, serenely accustomed to the bromidic flow of life.

One day a person named Martha Bent came to call. She had a nose like an acorn and her penitential purple hat threw a friendly shadow over her eyes. Around her neck she wore a plain black cord upon which she had attached a cracked ivory elephant, the color of jaundice and no bigger than a man's molar. Mother could not prevent Martha from "theeing and thouing" Father and calling him "Cousin Bob." She also had an unfortunate, showy way of giggling every time he spoke to her or talked naval shop in an urgent voice. As the weeks passed, Martha Bent became what is called "a fixture about the house." She was, indeed, a piece of machinery, always making its own characteristic noise as it worked away. She adored children and liked to drop in on me once a day; the time she chose was nearly always around teatime when Father would be getting back from the yard. Martha was what my father liked to call "a regular fella," and he didn't waver from this sturdy opinion even when my mother said she was dreary and a flirt. On the subject of Martha Bent I was torn in two, accepting painfully the attitudes of my parents as correct and finding myself left with a person who was both to be wooed and to be rejected, an object as mixed and bewildering as Philadelphia itself. I already felt the stirrings of revolt against my mother's judgment; I already felt an attraction to what she rebuked or condemned; in her enemies, or at least in her castoffs, I always saw a possible ally of my own. In my grim self-adoration I devised a way to try Martha Bent's patience, to prove her goodness, test her loyalty. She must give me her ivory elephant! I wanted the elephant not only as proof of devotion, but greedily for itself, because it was small, heavy, precious, useless—the heart that Martha wore on her sleeve as well as the absurd animal around her neck. Then somehow I had been "given" the elephant: I lay back in my bed, looking at the dusty, gray sunlight which filtered through the window shade I had drawn in order to enjoy my treasure unseen, in near darkness. I tapped the ivory and tested it with my teeth and then it went down. Doctors were told with a shrug, "Bobby has swallowed an elephant!" And that was the sly, stupid end of a little trinket cherished by a foolish woman and by me.

Arthur Winslow I

O<small>N THE FIRST</small> of March 1920, only about seven months after our arrival in Philadelphia, and early in the morning of my third birthday, Arthur Winslow, my mother's father, paid us a surprise visit. He entered with the faraway freshness of his night's sleep on the Pullman, the jaunty calm of the rolling wheels. When I kissed his pink cheek, I tasted bay rum; his coat held the tobacco flavor of his quick after-breakfast loll in the smoker. "Hie on," he shouted to me, as though he were training a young retriever, "hie on." He tapped me gently with his cane, winked, and kept nodding with a deadpan severity toward his neat leather handbag. He was trying to make me see my present, a badly hidden silver-papered box. The handbag looked like my doctor's. It was stuffed with my grandfather's typical train reading: an old red-and-gold-lettered volume from his set of Winston Churchill's novels,* a *Boston Transcript* folded to the real estate pages, a ploddingly penciled copy of his *Quarterly of the English-Speaking Union*,† which stuck up untidily like a stethoscope.

When I had rummaged through the handbag and failed to realize that the silver box was mine, my grandfather leant with both elbows on the immaculate white mantelpiece. With playful courtesy, he began to flatter and

---

* This was the American Winston Churchill (1871–1947), a best-selling novelist who lived most of his adult life in Cornish, New Hampshire, and whose books included *Richard Carvel* (1899) and *The Crossing* (1904).

† The English-Speaking Union published a monthly, not quarterly, magazine, *The Landmark*, from 1919 to 1938.

josh, treating me as though I were at least five. I grew more and more excited. Everyone in the room, my mother, my nurse, and even my grandfather, grew giddy. In those days my grandfather wore simple but formal
English suits, which, a moderate rebuke to the times, were always slightly
out of date. He himself, a six-footer, had, even without the help of his good
clothes, the stamp of being imported, well made, and tried. Yet his tiepin,
a biggish pearl set in a tiny gold nugget, and his starched collar, described
by my grandmother as "fit for an old-fashioned country Sunday in New
Hampshire," now gave his round head and small period mustache an air of
fussy unease.

For all his manliness, he seemed intimidated and headstrong. At fifty-
eight, he was puppyish. Though ruddy and enjoying the indulgence of a
semiretirement, he had slowly grown less in key with himself than he had
been in 1880 as a poor, pasty and whiskered MIT senior. There he had tasted
his first whiskey and enjoyed his first ceremonial and forbidden cigars.
Though propped up by the stiff regalia of the era, he had suffered nightmares. He feared his mother had been too complex, humorous, and impoverished for his understanding. As he surveyed metallurgical fieldwork,*
his studies were interrupted by dreams of his pre-Revolutionary merchant
ancestors. He commissioned a copy of an ancient red-coated portrait of
Edward Winslow, the Boston silversmith and King's high sheriff.† He somehow imagined that there was a congenial sternness and something of the
underdog about pomp and place in old New England. All his life, he had
tried to live with clashing passions; his intemperate reverence for propriety
was confused by a still more overbearing drive toward solitude.

* Winslow was the president of several companies that mined precious metals at the time.

† Edward Winslow Jr. (1669–1753), a grandson of Mary Chilton and a grandnephew of the Plymouth
Colony governor Edward Winslow (1595–1655), was an ancestor of Arthur Winslow. A famous American
silversmith, he served as sheriff in Suffolk County, Massachusetts Colony. The copy Arthur ordered was
presumably that of the 1730 portrait of Edward Winslow by the Scottish painter John Smibert, today held
at Yale University Art Gallery.

Forty-Four West Cedar Street
and Barnstable

T HE WINTERS OF 1921–22 and 1922–23 flash with brightness for
me.* Philadelphia was at last safely behind us; Boston was again
all about us.† Mother had complained of the enervating dirtiness
of Philadelphia, but she now found no fault with the equally dirty air of
Boston—it had been purified by hill, river, cold, and familiarity. In Philadelphia I felt like one of the dull larvae which looked like little dill pickles
to me when, on a nature outing, I used to rake with my net in the mirthless,
green underwater of a cow pond. In Boston, no longer a worm, I emerged
as a dragonfly and spread my mica wings. I lived in a world of undisciplined
grandparents bearing gifts. Our lives by becoming cozy had suddenly become romantic.

The knocker on the front door of our 44 West Cedar Street house was
a simple and distinguished brass eagle. The door was dark green; its frame,
a luxurious cream color, was of a quaint and spare design. Age had given
the freshly restored brick front many disarming irregularities. The back of

---

* The first, third, and fourth paragraphs come from a typescript with the title above; the second paragraph
derives from a variant typescript describing the same house; and the final nine paragraphs come from two
untitled typescripts, one focusing on Grandmother and Mrs. Bowles and the other on Mr. Bowles.

† In 1921 the Lowells moved to 44 West Cedar Street on Boston's Beacon Hill, near the home of Charlotte
Lowell's parents. Summers were spent at Rock Village (see footnote on p. 91), with frequent visits to Barnstable, on Cape Cod.

the house exploited an abrupt slope in the ground to drop ten or twelve feet and thrillingly add an extra story and emphasize the precarious immensity of a full-grown elm in our backyard. When one climbed to the top rear bedrooms, there was suddenly a view of the defiant, mobile, unmetropolitan blue of the Charles River Basin. This outlook, so refreshing in itself, was also a romantic symbol for my father's naval profession.

I seemed to be sunning myself all day under the skylight of my attic nursery. I leaned with both my elbows on the wooden tool chest designed by that clever carpenter, my Uncle Devereux. It was as cumbersome and complicated as a man's loom, and yet as mysterious as some piece of furniture belonging to medieval guildsmen. Because the only tool I was allowed was a broken folding ruler, I grew tired of the chest. I covered my bright hardwood floor with great jigsaw puzzles and nearly went blind piecing together spotted cows and clouds against a blue sky.

Forever I sat listening to my mother read aloud from boys' books dominated by colored illustrations, which caught the light like pictures on glass windows. There, peering sailors from Salem Massachusetts and Bristol England climbed crow's nests or Caribbean crags. They all stared at clouds on blue sky. These were my heroes—law-abiding, steady men, who wore the bloody sashes and nicked cutlasses of pirates. Forgetfulness and the histrionics of memory have certainly simplified and overdrawn the bright gaiety of these two years. Yes, I saw life then with the simple animal eye of a child.* The agile fullness of consecutive memory was beginning in me, but I was still too young for the drudging drill of school. I was still illiterate, and wanted my mother to read aloud to me by the hour.

Once a week my grandmother and Mrs. Bowles† were partners at bridge, once a week they were opponents. They had been having it out for forty years. Defeat had never dulled their wits or buoyancy; winning no longer turned their heads. More and more, a miraculous finesse was shown in their

---

* Perhaps an allusion to Wordsworth's recollection in "Tintern Abbey" of "The coarser pleasures of my boyish days, / And their glad animal movements."

† Adelaide Hay Bowles, née Savage (1861–1949), called by her family "Dada," was a friend of the Winslows and the mother of Kitty Bowles, Charlotte's close friend. Adelaide had a house at 148 Marlborough Street, in Boston, and a summer house in Barnstable. Mary Winslow frequently visited Adelaide's Barnstable home in the summer, Barnstable being fifty minutes by car from the Winslow farm at Rock.

choice of second prizes. For, if starting a rubber was a lark on the outrageous roulette wheel at Monte Carlo, its completion was the giving and receiving of comfort.

Something more heartfelt and personal was perhaps at issue in their war of the teacakes. Cooks were advertised for, cooks were fired. The criterion was cakes. Some, scoops from display windows, were bought ready-made, some were executed from recipes invented by their grandmothers, some were impromptus and made with their own hands on barn-like and abandoned kitchen ranges. This was on Thursdays when the servants had an afternoon off to visit relatives in ghastly environs. Mrs. Bowles pretended to my less outspoken grandmother that she was learning cooking in order to ship Mamie, Eileen and Kathleen back to Cork and elect an Anglo-Saxon Mayor of Boston.

Verbally, they both regretted the incorruptible Peters, who had been landslided into office by the election of William Howard Taft. Peters, our last Republican mayor, had been a flash in the pan, expired after two years, and had had less side and conversation than a totem pole or Calvin Coolidge.* Mayor Curley came to Boston.† He came, he went, he came. His demagogic speeches were larded with barrel-loads of quotations from the Bard of Avon. Graft snowballed. For the first time in history, our streets and alleys were properly cleaned and snowplowed. Cardinal O'Connell came.‡ He banned books. He was as big as A. Lawrence Lowell, the president of Harvard, when he sauntered with his henchmen down the sunny side of Commonwealth Avenue as if he owned it. He shoveled out Boston money to unearth a Mithraic temple under a crummy, venerable Catholic church in Rome. My grandmother and Mrs. Bowles continued to play auction bridge. One could

---

* Andrew J. Peters (1872–1938), a Democrat and a former assistant secretary of the Treasury in the Woodrow Wilson administration, was the mayor of Boston from 1918 to 1922. His election was part of the Democratic swing that commenced with the defeat of Taft by Wilson in 1914. Peters was one of the last Protestant mayors of the city. The last Republican mayor of Boston was Malcolm Nichols (1926–1930).

† James Michael Curley (1874–1958), the son of Irish immigrants, was a popular and effective mayor of Boston, serving four nonconsecutive terms in 1914–1918, 1922–1926, 1930–1934, and 1946–1950. During his career in public office, he was convicted twice of fraud. His political rise coincided with a demographic rise of Irish Americans in Boston and the flight of white Protestants to the suburbs.

‡ William Henry O'Connell (1859–1944), the archbishop of Boston from 1907 and a cardinal of the Roman Catholic Church from 1911. A powerful force in Boston, he actively supported the Vatican's campaign in the 1920s against books deemed immoral.

see that it was a school of manners. As with the teacakes, disturbing inno-vations here were taboo; repetition turned out to be variation. In time, the two ladies became so advanced that connoisseurs among their friends were unable to recognize, let alone judge, each new challenge. They knew life from womb to tomb. When they took up a subject, they named their cards. Their conversation was yea, yea and nay, nay.

They called each other simply by their first names, Mary and Adelaide. Formality fatigued them, they blushed at the inconsequence of nicknames. But after their grandchildren were born one took to calling them Gaga and Dada. Dada was big, outright in her carriage, and acted the part of her coeval Queen Mary, not merely in some fly-by-night and speechless charade, but to the life or a little better. Gaga was rococo and smaller than Napoleon. During the full tide of the teacakes, old Miss Susan Stackpole, who had a "knack" for puffing up commonplaces, named Dada "the Bayreuth Festival."* Gaga was the Raleigh, North Carolina violet by a mossy stone. Gaga smoothed and teased. Dada was high-handed, emotional, and sincere. Dada got servants, Gaga kept them. When Gaga read Zola's "Siege of Paris"† in the original, Dada reacted by buying a flock of twenty geese. Each died in her eighties. They really loved talking and never sounded like poultry.

It was what he had done and done, of course, and not at all a play for the grandstand, or the whirl of a man standing upside down and pushing pin-wheels with both his bare feet for the benefit of Bravas‡ and children; but all through my first summer at Barnstable, former rear admiral Bowles seemed to live in his black town clothes.§ When he turned down his mouth at the corners for us, it hurt the wart on his chin. His cuffs were starched, his collar

* The Bayreuth Festival is an annual music festival held in Bayreuth, Germany, which features perfor-mances of Richard Wagner's operas.

† Presumably Émile Zola's novel *La Débacle* (1892), describing the Franco-Prussian War of 1871, but possi-bly his 1873 novel *Le Ventre de Paris* (The Belly of Paris), contrasting the excesses of food displayed in Les Halles with the privations of the workers who staffed the market.

‡ Bravas are immigrants to Massachusetts from Cape Verde, off the coast of Africa. Of mixed West African and Portuguese ancestry, they often settled on Cape Cod and around New Bedford.

§ Rear Admiral Francis Tiffany Bowles (1858–1927), Dada's husband and Kitty's father. Between 1888 and 1903 he worked as a naval constructor, first in Norfolk, Virginia, then in the New York Navy Yard, where he eventually became the chief of the Bureau of Construction and Repair with the rank of rear admiral.

was limp, his vest was an outrage, for it matched his half-bald head and belonged in the mid-August Episcopal bazaar. His hullo meant goodbye. Children were a hallucination to him.

His favorite exercise was riding on the commuters' train to Boston. He loved crooked country walking, and always made a beeline on foot for the station. Coming home, he would dawdle and bargain with the small Portuguese truck farmers for berries. Ironically, he would call this "casting my bread on the waters." If he realized no such tenfold profits as the Bible promises, it is probable that he got as good as he gave, and those parodies of the mercantile triumphs of his forebears amused his pride by tickling his funny bone. No one ever bothered him for attentions and spoil at such times, but it was stupid of us to want to meet him halfway on the road. "Excuse me, excuse me, excuse me my dears. I have one foot in the grave, and I am taking it with me." His geese were a sideshow. They were forever taking the stage. I can see them vaunting and bowing and hissing and honking about him. They had blocked him off from his driveway. "Dada, dada, dada." He was shaking his railroad ticket and trying to put his cane in his pocket.

Once in town, he would shut himself up in his fourth-floor sitting room. Chairs in their white slipcovers stood like dunes about him. He wolfs through packets of gilt-edged securities. He stares across the Charles River at the Massachusetts Institute of Technology. He sees concrete buildings, concrete domes, his son—a Tech student who died of a blood blister in one of the German Baden in Edwardian days.* Albums, albums, albums! Life's in those picture books. "I am a squid in the boiling armor of a lobster."†

In one of his boathouses there was a secondhand telescope on a tripod. It had the floor all to itself, and it always pointed at a forty-five degree angle to the World War I artillery range on the midriff of Sandy Hook.‡ Old skin on black cloth, brass on black leather, water on sand—man, instrument, and outlook might have made a marriage of it. But you couldn't really call him admiral, because he had resigned from the navy and joined the staff of

---

* On August 14, 1910, at the age of twenty-two, Thomas Savage Bowles, Adelaide and Francis's son and a member of the Class of 1912 at Harvard, died of pneumonia in Nuremberg, Germany, while on vacation, only a week after he had done some mountain hiking in the Alps.

† A variant elucidates this passage: "Albums, albums, albums! That would have been living for him. Instead he was crawling through life like a squid in the boiling armor of a lobster."

‡ Presumably, Lowell has in mind Sandy Neck, a barrier beach protecting Barnstable.

the shipyard at Fore River.* You couldn't really call him mister, because he had been an admiral. You couldn't really call him Father or Grandfather, because his wife was Dada.

Dada, Dada, Dada. That's what all children, even her grandchildren Frances, Biddie and Chrissie, said to the geese all day.† They snored Dada in their dreams. Dada's poultry kicked up arrowheads in her hen yards, her cranberries attracted red-winged blackbirds and cedar waxwings, red-shouldered hawks dozed on her telephone poles. Servants, services, bridge, wardrobes of grandchildren. Neckers pursued their mysteries on the fringe of Barnstable and gave her estate a wide berth. Summer long, her sky was a daylight bulb. Dada was immense. Viva Dada. She was Barnstable. Poor Bowles was in the boathouse.

* Having resigned from the navy, Admiral Bowles served between 1903 and 1914 as the president of the Fore River Shipyard, in Quincy near Boston.

† Dada and Admiral Bowles's grandchildren—that is to say, the children of Kitty Bowles and Alfred Putnam Lowell (Robert Lowell's first cousin once removed)—were Frances, Beatrice, and Christina; later their full names were Frances Bowles Hunsaker (1916–2011), Beatrice Hardcastle Magruder (1918–2013), and Christina Brazelton (1921–2015).

Washington, D.C.

"WEEL-A-WAW, WEE-EE-EEL-A-WAW, WEELAWAW," went the high voice. "Anh, anh, anh, anh," went the low. They had closed the door to the upstairs sitting room, and except for an occasional shrill *Bobby*, I couldn't hear a word.

But an hour before, and for about an hour (I had gone to bed early for this purpose), I had been waiting for Mother and thinking out what I was going to tell her. I was going to let her know that the first grade was very tedious and frightening for me, and not something I enjoyed every minute of like kindergarten of the year before. If Mother asked me *how* or *how come*, I had, I felt certain, logical, almost mathematical proofs. They went like this: either kindergarten was meant to teach, or it was not meant to teach; but it *was* meant to teach, otherwise I couldn't have learned those stories, illustrated and edifying, of Samuel and King David, also how to play soccer, and the game of the good deed, making someone smile once a day. But the first grade was *only* meant to teach, therefore, etc., etc. I was afraid, though, lest Mother ask me *how* in quite a different sense, that I would have to tell her *everything that had happened*. And how could I tell her all about David Scull being, not bigger than I was, but stronger; about David Scull, not not talking to me, but talking and looking in such and such a way that was, well, what I called scary and tiresome? And then there was long division, but the dry, frightening part was just the part I didn't understand, and anyway the one joy of long division was that I was expected to be so much better at it than Mother, but the only part that would have impressed Mother was the part, as I had said, that I couldn't understand, and therefore couldn't describe. *Therefore, therefore, therefore,* I kept saying: my newly learned, unemotional, day-school, daylight, man's word. At the end of almost an hour's thought I knew that I couldn't make Mother understand. I couldn't describe day school minute by minute, and therefore didn't know just how in words and images I wanted it remade into kindergarten. Yet I knew already there was one way I could have made sense and made my point with Mother. I could have said, "Washington sure isn't Boston!" Then Mother could have calmly explained to herself, my father, and above all me, why all my tortures came from living in Washington.* Then perhaps Mother's reasons, if believed, would have really been so, the skies would have lightened and I would have spared myself years and years of kicking against the goad. Anyway, I couldn't say Boston, and I couldn't say what had really happened.

Mother sat on the foot of my bed, and showed me a photograph of the model Dolley Madison† at the Smithsonian Museum. Mother and two other Colonial Dames were in the photograph because they were working on a new dress. But the dress seemed so far from my *therefore, therefore,* my release from first grade. If only Mother could read thoughts! Rage, shyness. "Mother," I said, "I know something." I squeezed my pillow as roughly as I dared. "I know how to give this pillow an hourglass waist."

Talking with Daddy before bed was different. Father respected a man and didn't ask what had happened. Maybe he didn't care. And there was no magic phrase, like "Let's go back to Boston," that would have made my father happy. Of course he smiled when I said I wanted to be a naval officer, but it was a distant smile for the time was distant, and not real like my *D* in long division. What I was always wanting to tell Mother was: "Everything you want to know about my day will be tabulated on my monthly report

---

* In the summer of 1923 the navy transferred Bob Lowell to Washington, D.C., where he and his family stayed until moving back to Boston in the summer of 1925.

† Dolley Madison (1768–1849), the wife of James Madison, an influential Washington figure in the early Republic and First Lady of the United States between 1809 and 1817.

card much more precisely than I can say it." What I wanted to say to my father was: "The real Bobby Lowell is not just numbers and letters on a card."

"Wheel-a-waw, wee-ee-eehl-a-waw, wheel-a-waw," went the high voice. "Anh, anh, anh, anh," went the low. As I pressed my nose between the bars of the bannister, and sighted with one eye down the dark stairway broken by blotches of orange light, I pretended that I was "The Legree,"* a Rebel iron-clad sniping at the giant green statue of Admiral "Damn-the-Torpedoes" Farragut.† The Admiral stood in the hallway by the front door, and was fitting on his bronze gloves, like a professional throttler. "The only good Reb is a dead Reb," he said. I took these words at their face value and was getting ready to perish at my post and so win the Admiral's approval. "Wheel-a-waw," "Anh, anh." Argument, resolution, crescendo, diminuendo: ever the same and ever new—truth! Part of my pleasure was that I couldn't make out a word, except for an occasional shrill "Bobby." The door to the up-stairs sitting room was closed. I had never felt so near my parents, so inside them. The conversation was universal, nothing; but more and more I could almost taste the personalities of the talkers. Sometimes, I pictured my father bent back in a swivel chair, and grunting and grunting, as he played a tar-pon that skittered and broke water all over the ocean; sometimes my mother was jumping up and down a red mudbank, frolicking into shallow water and skipping back, as she worked to land a sullen, tugging catfish—sheer weight and burden. The door opened; Father said, "I'll take care of the little fellow."

But it was fun playing hooky from Sunday School with Father on that March Sunday in 1923, shortly after President Harding's death.‡ Father had a way of making his favorite Liggett's Drugstore seem like a Mark Twain saloon on a Mississippi paddle wheeler. When he ordered us two cups of Maxwell House Coffee, he pointed to the can. "It says: Good to the last drop. That means, Good *except* for the last drop." The waitress smiled

---

* Named after Simon Legree, a villainous slaveholder in Harriet Beecher Stowe's *Uncle Tom's Cabin*.

† David G. Farragut (1801–1870), a Union admiral in the Civil War.

‡ President Warren G. Harding died on August 2, 1923. Later in this paragraph, Lowell, who was born on March 1, 1917, calls himself "seven years old and five days." Given that the Lowells did not live in Washington in March 1923, we might surmise that the date was March 6, 1924, rather than the indicated "March Sunday in 1923," except that March 6, 1924, was a Thursday. In another draft, Lowell writes that this was "the Sunday afternoon after President Harding's death," which would make it August 6, 1923.

strenuously at Father, as though she had passed a secondary incident in a test for promotion. Her starch stiffened before our eyes, and she touched the signature, *Liggett's*, on her cap. Our Chevy outmaneuvered taxis. Perfectly, impersonally, it ran as if by remote control. I was seven years old and five days, but I had never been alone in a car with Father, or seen such driving. "No Maggie," I said, "No backseat skipper." I was too shy to explain that Maggie meant both Mother and the horror who stunned Jiggs with a rolling pin in the comics.* We came to the Smithsonian. "Last one in," I said, "is a big fat female." We passed by Cousin Cassie James's 1840s slippers; we passed by Dolley Madison's inaugural dress that Mother, a newly elected Colonial Dame, was collaborating on. We stopped by the tableau of Lieutenant-Commander Carpenter's destroyer torpedoed by a German U-boat in World War I.† "This is the one major American naval loss in modern times." Father's inside version of the disaster emphasized Carpenter's English accent and low grades at Annapolis. Something in Father's voice made me think of a robot criticizing strawberry shortcake. I remembered the iconoclastic joviality of his reading an exposé of Custer. "If General Custer had been in the Navy," I said, "would he have stayed ashore on radio like you during the war, or would he have commanded a destroyer and become a vice-admiral like Uncle Cameron?"‡ Once again, Father gave me a feeling of remote control and ebullience. "Custer would have been ploughed his Plebe year!" he said. "Daddy," I said, "Grampa says that our New England stock makes me good officer material." Father was always taken aback by the personal assertion that decorated my references to his father-in-law. When he answered, however, his tone was oddly lackadaisical and had lost its usual overeager levelheaded stubbornness. "Officers have to be regular fellows. I guess your grandfather had to be pretty fair at math when he was at Tech."

Nursing a single small martini, served in a demitasse to confuse the servants and teetotalers, my father spoke sentences of admiration for his classmate Kent Hewett. The eulogy, one that harped on Kent's up-to-date

---

* Reference to George McManus's *Bringing Up Father*, an influential comic strip by 1913 and featuring a quarreling married couple named Maggie and Jiggs.

† Apparently a fictional or composite figure.

‡ Lowell's great-uncle on his mother's side.

training and lack of side, seemed double-edged and to timidly disparage both Carpenter and my great-uncle Cameron, the Admiral. At dinner, Father was abstracted and rather too boyish in his compliments for the Yorkshire pudding, mint jelly, and chocolate ice cream with chocolate sauce. Mother said, "I don't see how that stupid Dr. Brague or *Brag* can help Bobby when he let President Harding die!"* A few days before, I had been initiated into a club called "The Filibusters." The big neighborhood boys had posed me like a scarecrow under F's statue† and lambasted me with mud balls for fifteen minutes. Then I was told that "The Filibusters" had voted to support Calvin Coolidge and had dissolved. I came home looking like an unwashed clam. My new and first suit, a blue plum–colored tweed chosen after a two-hour debate at a Woodward and Lothrop's department store, was ruined. I showed what Mother believed were symptoms of asthma. "Papá ran into Dr. Fritz Talbot at the Somerset Club. Dr. Talbot says if it weren't for cod liver oil," her voice broke mockingly, "no children would survive this Washington climate. What Bobby needs are bracing winters and a daily walk around the Basin in Boston." For all her pride and stamina, Mother had lately been having dizzy spells. New naval people, a new city, and new child problems made her hysterical. She was fond of saying, "I am *never* sick. When I motor with your poor deaf Cousin Fanny in her car with shock-absorbers, I feel I could hop out and walk to Boston." Mother waved away the chocolate sauce. "Bob," she said, "please stop saying *Bully*. Please stop repeating, *Beat him when he sneezes, he only does it because he knows it teases.*"‡

For Mother, Boston meant her mother, her sister, her reading club, and Papá.§ There was iron in the air for her will, taste in the drawing rooms; wherever she turned in Boston, she met herself. But Father was only two-thirds through the first year in his two-year term at the Washington Naval Yard. An immediate winter move was out of the question. The real battle

---

* President Harding's personal physician was Dr. Charles E. Sawyer. "Dr. Brague" seems to be an invention.

† Presumably the David G. Farragut Memorial at Farragut Square, though it is a thirty-minute walk from where young Lowell lived.

‡ From a lullaby sung by the Duchess in chapter 6 of Lewis Carroll's *Alice's Adventures in Wonderland*.

§ Charlotte's sister is Sarah H. Winslow, later Cotting (1893–1992). Lowell usually refers to her as "Young Aunt Sarah."

was over where we should go for the summer. "Papá has that mortgage on the Sarah Barnard Cottage at Matt.* Last summer when you were at sea, and I was already installed in the Handy House at Barnstable, he was always pressing me to take it off his hands for the upkeep." Father was glad that the conversation was no longer impossible. He said vaguely, "No one has better intentions than your father."

We sat in the downstairs den. Mother was shuffling the calling cards of the loud naval wives and their husbands, as though she were playing double Canfield† with her father. A dress sword with black crape on its hilt for President Harding hung over our radio, on a wire from the antenna as big and ornamental as a clothesline. The sun was uncomplimentary to the prints of Japanese prostitutes, and to the long photograph of my father with his engineering staff aboard the Battleship "Pennsy."‡ An unfinished mah-jongg game occupied a cheap card table. Mother's swinging slipper and ankle cast a repelling shadow out into the hallway and on the lace curtains that covered the glass panes of the inner front door. Whenever Ito Mancuso, our temporary Filipino, announced another visitor, Mother would say, "Ito, Mrs. Lowell is not at home." Through a wide-open window and a wildly blowing organdy, Washington steamed like a herd of tepid elephants sinking in seedy mud. Mother said, "Daddy was teasing when he asked you how you would like to board for the summer with Grandmother Lowell and Great-Grandmother Myers on Staten Island."

My father and Commander Brook were kneeling on the society section of the Sunday paper. They were adding four new tubes to the radio, a mass of unshelled apparatus that filled all three shelves of our bookcase. Both men were wearing earphones and couldn't hear a word that was being said. The radio's specialty was getting Australia. Commander Brook wasn't a real commander, an Annapolis man. He was a paymaster. He had married

---

* "Matt" is short for Mattapoisett, a coastal village on Buzzards Bay in Plymouth County, Massachusetts. Rock Village, the site of Arthur Winslow's farm, was twenty minutes by car. Winslow kept two yachts, *Water Witch* and *Narcissus*, in Mattapoisett boatyard. Apparently, he also bought a cottage in Mattapoisett on a mortgage loan, probably 6 Shipyard Lane, where they'd often stay in the 1920s. The name of the cottage comes from the Barnard family, whose members built dozens of cottages along the beaches to rent out to summer residents.

† A solitaire game played independently by two people.

‡ The *Pennsylvania*, one of two super-dreadnought battleships built by the U.S. Navy before the American entry into the Great War.

someone my father described as "the cook." I preferred Commander Brook to Commander Hewett, because he had given me an expensive mariner's compass. He was so docile and attentive to my father that Mother forgave him his lack of parts. Still, it was boring when Commander Brook looked up and said, "Bob, I hear the Union Station is advertising a five o'clock forty-minute commuter's train from Washington to Boston."

The doorbell kept ringing, Ito kept repeating "not at home," pollen blew from the window to the mah-jongg pieces. Father was terrified by Mother's rudeness to the visitors. He grew more and more fascinated by the tubes. Instead of answering "bully," he now said merely "fine." Mother made no effort to be impressed when the radio got Schenectady where Great-Grandmother Myers was born. Mother snatched up the telephone. "Boston, long distance," she said. "No, no! I am Mrs. R.T.S. . . . L, L, L, for Lowell, 2229 Q St., N.W.—D.C.—U.S.A.—U.S.N."* She pronounced these single letters with drama and worried the operator. Mother meant for her humorous exaggerations to hide her suspense and to imply that she was impractical, but a character. "Oh Papá," Mother said, "Bob insists that Bobby is dying for a breath of fresh air." When the telephone conversation was over, Mother turned to Father with a laugh. "Papá is so funny. He is so afraid you will think he is bossy. He is dying for us to take the Barnard Cottage and won't say a word in its favor. He says Matt is half summer colony, half Irish, half Portuguese, and half Yankee—a Biarritz in Sleepy Hollow." This was how I learned that my mother and grandfather had decided that we would be staying that summer at Matt.

---

* In "The Balanced Aquarium," Lowell identifies their Washington address as 2129 Bancroft Place. This seems confirmed by photograph 8, included in this volume, showing Charlotte in front of the entryway to 2129 Bancroft Place. Bancroft Place is also mentioned among penciled notes on the reverse of a draft page of "Rock."

Arms-of-the-Law

T HE "CONTRACT" with Mother and Father had been that I could stay home from the Trinity Church Sunday School if I would work at improving my penmanship for Miss Bundy at the Brimmer Boys and Girls' School on Brimmer St.* One shoe was untied. One stocking was wrinkling down to my ankle. I was wearing a "Byronic" as Mother called it, a soft collar which had been specially fitted to my ordinary shirt to ease my breathing because I was still thought to be suffering from asthma. I sat in my father's favorite chair, spread out his mechanical drawing board, and began my composition. Miss Bundy had said that the script I had learned at my school in Washington, D.C., was a snake dance. I was learning to print. I wrote in ugly legible letters:

ARMS-OF-THE-LAW, A HORRID SPOOF†

Arms-of-the-Law was a horrid spoof most of the time, but an all-right guy on the 29th of February. He was also a Bostonian, an Irish

---

* In Boston, to which the Lowells returned from Washington, D.C., in 1925.

† In Ian Hamilton, *Robert Lowell: A Biography* (New York: Random House, 1982), John Thompson is quoted as having explained that Lowell's standard tease was to talk about "bear-characters," which he sometimes also called "berts." He would invent parables and dramas involving these bears, each of them named individually and impersonating one of his relatives or friends. Lowell would usually be the chief bear, Arms-of-the-Law, a police officer who scolded and arrested others for misbehavior.

policeman and a bear. Miss Bundy, I wish you could hear Arms talking big about his make-believe mansion with a mansard roof on Commonwealth Avenue. The house Arms was really and truly brought up in was a calcified tooth, which the neighbors mistook for a sugarloaf. The room he like better than all other rooms in the whole world was a mushroomy brown abscess called "my cave." Arms like sleep better than liquor or living. He like hoofing and whooping after cave men. He also like to take Sunday afternoon tours with Father on the Fenway in the old Hudson. Arms thought bellyaching at Father's driving was more fun than a barrel of monkeys. The blood that Arms' heart beat up was the tobacco-colored juice of a squashed grasshopper in a lawn mower . . .

91 Revere Street

THE ACCOUNT OF HIM is platitudinous, worldly and fond, but he has no Christian name and is entitled merely Major *M.* Myers in my Cousin Cassie Mason Myers Julian-James's privately printed *Biographical Sketches: A Key to a Cabinet of Heirlooms in the Smithsonian Museum.** The nameplate under his portrait used to spell out his name bravely enough: he was Mordecai Myers. The artist painted Major Myers in his sanguine War of 1812 uniform with epaulets, white breeches, and a scarlet frogged waistcoat. His right hand played with the sword "now to be seen in the Smithsonian cabinet of heirlooms."† The pose was routine and gallant. The full-lipped smile was good-humoredly pompous and embarrassed.

Mordecai's father, given neither name nor initial, is described with an air

---

* Major Mordecai Myers was Robert Lowell's great-great-grandfather on the side of his father's mother, Kate Bailey Myers Lowell. Cassie Mason Myers, later Julian-James (1851–1922), was the cousin of Kate Bailey Myers Lowell. All the details Lowell is discussing here—including the Mason-Myers bookplate auguring his father's timidity—can be found online at the HathiTrust Digital Library website, in a scanned copy of the book Lowell is using: Cassie Mason Myers Julian-James, *Biographical Sketches of the Bailey-Myers-Mason Families, 1776–1905: Key to a Cabinet of Heirlooms in the National Museum, Washington* (1908).

† Lowell has in mind the circa 1810 oil-on-wood-panel portrait by John Wesley Jarvis (1781–1840) of Mordecai Myers in uniform, today part of the collection of the Toledo Museum of Art in Toledo, Ohio; Julian-James, in *Biographical Sketches*, prints only a sepia-colored "sketch" of the painting (on page 7). In Lowell's original publication of this essay in *Partisan Review* (Fall 1956), Major Myers's hand "clenched" rather than "played with" the sword. "Played with" seems less accurate, unless Myers "played" with it in the sense of pretending to clench it for an imaginary fight.

of hurried self-congratulation by Cousin Cassie as "a friend of the Reverend Ezra Styles, afterward President of Yale College." As a very young man the son, Mordecai, studied military tactics under a French émigré, "the Bourbons' celebrated Colonel De la Croix." Later he was "matured" by six years' practical experience in a New York militia regiment organized by Colonel Martin Van Buren. After "the successful engagement against the British at Chrysler's Field, thirty shrapnel splinters were extracted from his shoulder." During convalescence, he wooed and won Miss Charlotte Bailey, "thus proving himself a better man than his rivals, the united forces of Plattsburg." He fathered ten children, sponsored an enlightened law exempting Quakers from military service in New York State, and died in 1870 at the age of ninety-four, "a Grand Old Man, who impressed strangers with the poise of his old-time manners."

Undoubtedly Major Mordecai had lived in a more ritualistic, gaudy, and animal world than twentieth-century Boston. There was something undecided, Mediterranean, versatile, almost double-faced about his bearing which suggested that, even to his contemporaries, he must have seemed gratuitously both *ci-devant* and *parvenu*.* He was a dark man, a German Jew—no downright Yankee, but maybe such a fellow as Napoleon's mad, pomaded son-of-an-innkeeper-general, Junot, Duc D'Abrantès;† a man like mad George III's pomaded, disreputable son, "Prinny," the Prince Regent. Or he was one of those Moorish-looking dons painted by his contemporary, Goya— some leader of Spanish guerrillas against Bonaparte's occupation, who fled to South America. Our Major's suffering almond eye rested on his luxurious dawn-colored fingers ruffling an off-white glove.

Bailey-Mason-Myers! Easy-going, Empire State patricians, these relatives of my Grandmother Lowell seemed to have given my father his character. For he likewise lacked that granite *back-countriness* which Grandfather Arthur Winslow attributed to his own ancestors, the iconoclastic, mulish Dunbarton New Hampshire Starks. On the joint Mason-Myers bookplate, there are two merry and naked mermaids—lovely marshmallowy, boneless,

---

* *Ci-devant* is a French expression meaning "from before" or "former," originally used as an adjective designating a person's status as a French aristocrat overthrown by the French Revolution; a *parvenu* is a person of low origins suddenly risen to high position.

† Andoche Junot, duke d'Abrantès (1771–1813), the son of a farmer and one of Napoleon's generals.

Rubensesque butterballs, all burlesque-show bosoms and Flemish smiles. Their motto, *malo frangere quam flectere*, reads: "I prefer to bend than to break."*

Mordecai Myers was my Grandmother Lowell's grandfather.† His life was tame and honorable. He was a leisured squire and merchant, a member of the state legislature, a mayor of Schenectady, a "president" of Kinderhook village. Disappointingly, his famous "blazing brown eye" seems in all things to have shunned the outrageous. After his death he was remembered soberly as a New York State gentleman, the friend and host of worldly men and politicians with Dutch names: De Witt Clinton, Vanderpoel, Hoes, and Schuyler. My mother was roused to warmth by the Major's scarlet vest and exotic eye. She always insisted that he was the one properly dressed and dieted ancestor in the lot we had inherited from my father's Cousin Cassie. Great-great-Grandfather Mordecai! Poor sheepdog in wolf's clothing! In the anarchy of my adolescent war on my parents, I tried to make him a true wolf, the wandering Jew!‡ *Homo lupus homini!*§

Major Mordecai Myers's portrait has been mislaid past finding, but out of my memories I often come on it in the setting of our Revere Street house, a setting now fixed in the mind, where it survives all the distortions of fantasy, all the blank befogging of forgetfulness. There, the vast number of remembered *things* remains rocklike. Each is in its place, each has its function, its history, its drama. There, all is preserved by that motherly care that one either ignored or resented in his youth. The things and their owners come back urgent with life and meaning—because finished, they are endurable and perfect.

---

* Actually, the Latin motto says the opposite: "I prefer to break than to bend."

† There was another Mordecai in Lowell's lineage on his mother's side. The grandfather of his grandmother Gaga (Mary Livingston Devereux) on *her* mother's side was Judge Moses Mordecai (1785–1824). See Lowell's sonnet "Hudson River Dream," in *History* (New York: Farrar, Straus and Giroux, 1973), in which Charlotte is described as "one-eighth Jewish, and *her* mother two-eighths." Compare in Sarah Payne Stuart, *My First Cousin Once Removed: Money, Madness, and the Family of Robert Lowell* (New York: HarperCollins, 1998), 36.

‡ According to medieval legend, the Wandering Jew was cursed to roam the earth until the Second Coming of Christ in punishment for having taunted Jesus when Jesus was on the way to his crucifixion. Some romantic and postromantic texts transformed him into a heroic outsider.

§ Traditionally with a different word order, *Homo homini lupus*, the Latin expression means "Man is wolf to man."

———

Cousin Cassie only became a close relation in 1922. In that year she died. After some unpleasantness between Mother and a co-heiress, Helen Bailey, the estate was divided. Mother used to return frozen and thrilled from her property disputes, and I, knowing nothing of the rights and wrongs, would half-perversely confuse Helen Bailey with Helen of Troy and harden my mind against the monotonous *parti pris* of Mother's voice. Shortly after our move to Boston in 1924,* a score of unwanted Myers portraits was delivered to our new house on Revere Street. These were later followed by "their dowry"—four moving vans groaning with heavy Edwardian furniture. My father began to receive his first quarterly payments from the Mason-Myers Julian-James Trust Fund, sums "not grand enough to corrupt us," Mother explained, "but sufficient to prevent Daddy from being entirely at the mercy of his salary." The Trust sufficed: our lives became tantalized with possibilities, and my father felt encouraged to take the risk—a small one in those boom years—of resigning from the Navy on the gamble of doubling his income in business.

I was in the third grade and for the first time becoming a little more popular at school. I was afraid Father's leaving the Navy would destroy my standing. I was a churlish, disloyal, romantic boy, and quite without hero worship for my father, whose actuality seemed so inferior to the photographs in uniform he once mailed to us from the Golden Gate. My real *love*, as Mother used to insist to all new visitors, was toy soldiers. For a few months at the flood tide of this infatuation, people were ciphers to me—valueless except as chances for increasing my armies of soldiers. Roger Crosby, a child in the second grade of my Brimmer Street School, had thousands—not mass-produced American stereotypes, but hand-painted solid lead soldiers made to order in Dijon, France. Roger's father had a still more artistic and adult collection; its ranks—each man at least six inches tall—marched in glass cases under the eyes of recognizable replicas of mounted Napoleonic captains: Kléber, Marshal Ney, Murat, King of Naples. One delirious afternoon Mr. Crosby showed me his toys and was perhaps the first grownup to talk to me not as a child but as an equal when he discovered how feverishly I

* The Lowells did not move back to Boston from Washington, D.C., until the summer of 1925.

followed his anecdotes on uniforms and the evolution of tactical surprise. Afterwards, full of high thoughts, I ran up to Roger's play room and hoodwinked him into believing that his own soldiers were "ballast turned out by central European sweatshops." He agreed I was being sweetly generous when I traded twenty-four worthless Jordan Marsh* papier-mâché doughboys for whole companies of his gorgeous, imported Old Guards, Second Empire "redlegs," and modern *chasseurs d'Alpine* with sky-blue berets. The haul was so huge that I had to take a child's wheelbarrow to Roger's house at the top of Pinckney Street. When I reached home with my last load, Mr. Crosby was talking with my father on our front steps. Roger's soldiers were all returned; I had only the presence of mind to hide a single soldier, a peely-nosed black sepoy† wearing a Shriner's fez.

Nothing consoled me for my loss, but I enjoyed being allowed to draw Father's blunt dress sword, and I was proud of our Major Mordecai. I used to stand dangerously out in the middle of Revere Street in order to see through our windows and gloat on this portrait's scarlet waistcoat blazing in the bare, Spartan whiteness of our den-parlor. Mordecai Myers lost his glory when I learned from my father that he was only a "major *pro tem.*" On a civilian, even a civilian soldier, the flamboyant waistcoat was stuffy and no more martial than officers' costumes in our elementary school musicals.

In 1924 people still lived in cities. Late that summer, we bought the 91 Revere Street house, looking out on an unbuttoned part of Beacon Hill bounded by the North End slums, though reassuringly only four blocks away from my Grandfather Winslow's brown pillared house at 18 Chestnut Street. In the decades preceding and following the First World War, old Yankee families had upset expectation by regaining this section of the Hill from the vanguards of the lace-curtain Irish. This was bracing news for my parents in that topsy-turvy era when the Republican Party and what were called "people of the right sort" were no longer dominant in city elections. Still, even in the palmy, laissez-faire '20s, Revere Street refused to be a straightforward, immutable residential fact. From one end to the other,

---

* Jordan Marsh was a New England department store chain headquartered in Boston.

† An Indian soldier serving under the orders of the British colonial army.

houses kept being sanded down, repainted, or abandoned to the flaking of decay. Houses, changing hands, changed their language and nationality. A few doors to our south the householders spoke "Beacon Hill British" or the flat *nay nay* of the Boston Brahmin. The parents of the children a few doors north spoke mostly in Italian.

My mother felt a horrified giddiness about the adventure of our address. She once said, "We are barely perched on the outer rim of the hub of decency." We were less than fifty yards from Louisburg Square, the cynosure of old historic Boston's plain-spoken, cold roast elite—the Hub of the Hub of the Universe.* Fifty yards!

As a naval ensign, Father had done postgraduate work at Harvard. He had also done postgraduate work at M.I.T., preferred the purely scientific college, and condescended to both. In 1924, however, his tone began to change; he now began to speak warmly of Harvard as his second alma mater. We went to football games at the Harvard Stadium, and one had the feeling that our lives were now being lived in the brutal, fashionable expectancy of the stadium: we had so many downs, so many minutes, and so many yards to go for a winning touchdown. It was just such a winning financial and social advance that my parents promised themselves would follow Father's resignation from the Navy and his acceptance of a sensible job offered him at the Cambridge branch of Lever Brothers' Soap.

The advance was never to come. Father resigned from the service in 1927, but he never had a civilian *career*; he instead had merely twenty-two years of the civilian *life*. Almost immediately he bought a larger and more stylish house; he sold his ascetic, stove-black Hudson and bought a plump brown Buick; later the Buick was exchanged for a high-toned, as-good-as-new Packard with a custom-designed royal blue and mahogany body. Without drama, his earnings more or less decreased from year to year.

But so long as we were on Revere Street, Father tried to come to terms with it and must have often wondered whether he on the whole liked or disliked the neighborhood's lack of side. He was still at this time rather truculently democratic in what might be described as an upper middle-class, naval, and Masonic fashion. He was a mumbler. His opinions were almost

---

* "Hub of the Universe" was one of Boston's popular nicknames; it originated in Oliver Wendell Holmes once calling the Boston State House "the hub of the solar system."

morbidly hesitant, but he considered himself a matter-of-fact man of science and had an unspoiled faith in the superior efficiency of northern nations. He modeled his allegiances and humor on the cockney imperialism of Rudyard Kipling's swearing Tommies, who did their job. Autochthonous Boston snobs, such as the Winslows or members of Mother's reading club, were alarmed by the brassy callousness of our naval visitors, who labeled the Italians they met on Revere Street as "grade-A" and "grade-B wops." The Revere Street "grade-B's" were Sicilian Catholics and peddled crummy second-hand furniture on Cambridge Street, not far from the site of Great-great-Grandfather Charles Lowell's disused West Church, praised in an old family folder as "a haven from the Sodom and Gomorrah of Trinitarian orthodoxy and the tyranny of the letter." Revere Street "grade-A's," good North Italians, sold fancy groceries and Colonial heirlooms in their shops near the Public Garden. Still other Italians were Father's familiars; they sold him bootleg Scotch and *vino rosso* in teacups.

The outside of our Revere Street house was a flat red brick surface unvaried by the slightest suggestion of purple panes, delicate bay, or triangular window-cornice—a sheer wall formed by the seamless conjunction of four inseparable façades, all of the same commercial and purgatorial design. Though placed in the heart of Old Boston, it was ageless and artless, an epitome of those "leveler" qualities Mother found most grueling about the naval service. 91 Revere Street was mass-produced, *regulation-issue*, and yet struck Boston society as stupidly out of the ordinary, like those white elephants—a mother-of-pearl scout knife or a tea-kettle barometer—which my father used to pick up on sale at an Army-Navy store.

The walls of Father's minute Revere Street den-parlor were bare and white. His bookshelves were bare and white. The den's one adornment was a ten-tube home-assembled battery radio set, whose loudspeaker had the shape and color of a Mexican sombrero. The radio's specialty was getting programs from Australia and New Zealand in the early hours of the morning.

My father's favorite piece of den furniture was his oak and "rhinoceros hide" armchair. It was ostentatiously a masculine, or rather a bachelor's, chair. It had a notched, adjustable back; it was black, cracked, hacked, scratched, splintered, gouged, initialed, gunpowder-charred and tumbler-ringed. It looked like pale tobacco leaves laid on dark tobacco leaves. I doubt

if Father, a considerate man, was responsible for any of the marring. The
chair dated from his plebe days at the Naval Academy, and had been bought
from a shady, shadowy, roaring character, midshipman "Beauty" Burford.
Father loved each disfigured inch.

My father had been born two months after his own father's death.* At
each stage of his life, he was to be forlornly fatherless. He was a deep boy
brought up entirely by a mild widowed mother and an intense widowed
grandmother. When he was fourteen and a half, he became a deep young
midshipman. By the time he graduated from Annapolis, he had a high sense
of abstract form, which he beclouded with his humor. He had reached, perhaps, his final mental possibilities. He was deep—not with profundity, but
with the dumb depth of one who trusted in statistics and was dubious of personal experience. In his forties, Father's soul went underground: as a civilian
he kept his high sense of form, his humor, his accuracy, but this accuracy was
henceforth unimportant, recreational, *hors de combat*. His debunking grew
myopic; his shyness grew evasive; he argued with a fumbling languor. In
the twenty-two years Father lived after he resigned from the Navy, he never
again deserted Boston and never became Bostonian. He survived to drift
from job to job, to be displaced, to be grimly and literally that old cliché, a
fish out of water. He gasped and wheezed with impotent optimism, took on
new ideals with each new job, never ingeniously enjoyed his leisure, never
even hid his head in the sand.

Mother hated the Navy, hated naval society, naval pay, and the trip-
hammer rote of settling and unsettling a house every other year when Father was transferred to a new station or ship. She had been married nine or
ten years and still suspected that her husband was savorless, unmasterful,
merely considerate. Unmasterful—Father's specialized efficiency lacked utterly the flattering bossiness she so counted on from her father, my Grandfather Winslow. It was not Father's absence on sea-duty that mattered; it
was the eroding necessity of moving *with* him, of keeping in step. When
he was far away on the Pacific, she had her friends, her parents, a house

---

* Robert T. S. Lowell III was born on July 15, 1887, nearly four months after Robert T. S. Lowell II died
on March 17, 1887.

to herself—Boston! Fully conscious of her uniqueness and normality she basked in the refreshing stimulation of dreams in which she imagined Father as suitably sublimed. She used to describe such a sublime man to me over tea and English muffins. He was Siegfried carried lifeless through the shining air by Brünnhilde to Valhalla,* and accompanied by the throb of my Great Aunt Sarah playing his leitmotif in the released manner taught her by the Abbé Liszt.† Or Mother's hero dove through the grottoes of the Rhine and slaughtered the homicidal and vulgar dragon coiled about the golden hoard.‡ Mother seemed almost light-headed when she retold the romance of Sarah Bernhardt in *L'Aiglon*, the Eaglet, the weakling! She would speak the word *weakling* with such amused vehemence that I formed a grandiose and false image of l'Aiglon's Father, the *big* Napoleon: he was a strong man who scratched under his paunchy little white vest a torso all hair, muscle, and manliness. Instead of the dreams, Mother now had the insipid fatigue of keeping house. Instead of the *Eagle*, she had a twentieth-century naval commander interested in steam, radio, and "the fellows." To avoid naval yards, steam, and "the fellows," Mother had impulsively bought the squalid, impractical Revere Street house. Her marriage daily forced her to squander her subconsciously hoarded energies.

"*Weelawaugh, we-ee-eeelawaugh, weelawaugh,*" shrilled Mother's high voice. "*But-and, but-and, but-and!*" Father's low mumble would drone in answer. Though I couldn't be sure that I had caught the meaning of the words, I followed the sounds as though they were a movie. I felt drenched in my parents' passions.

---

* An allusion to the final opera, *Götterdämmerung*, of Richard Wagner's cycle *Der Ring des Nibelungen* (1876). In Wagner's rendition of the Nibelung myth, however, Brünnhilde burns the German warrior Siegfried on a funeral pyre and she herself rides into the flames that flare up and destroy Valhalla, the Hall of the Gods.

† Sarah Stark Winslow (1858–1938), Lowell's great-aunt and Arthur Winslow's sister. Lowell usually refers to her as "Old Aunt Sarah." Franz Liszt (1811–1886), a Hungarian pianist and composer. Never ordained a priest, Liszt became an abbot in 1865 and took to wearing the habit of the Franciscan order (hence "Abbé"). Sarah Stark Winslow attended the Conservatory of Music in Stuttgart, Germany, from 1871 to 1876. It seems implausible that she actually took master classes with Liszt, who was not affiliated with the Stuttgart conservatory and lived in Budapest at the time. Sarah is not listed in a comprehensive catalog of Liszt pupils and disciples compiled by Alan Walker in *Franz Liszt: The Final Years, 1861–1886*, vol. 3 (Ithaca, NY: Cornell University Press, 1997), 249–52.

‡ Siegfried, the same whose body burns in Wagner's opera, was originally the hero of the great German epic poem *Nibelungenlied*, in which, among several complications, one finds the motif of him killing a dragon and coming into possession of a hoard.

91 Revere Street was the setting for those arthritic spiritual pains that troubled us for the two years my mother spent in trying to argue my father into resigning from the Navy. When the majestic, hollow boredom of the second year's autumn dwindled to the mean boredom of a second winter, I grew less willing to open my mouth. I bored my parents, they bored me.

"Weelawaugh, we-ee-eelawaugh, weelawaugh!" "But-and, but-and, but-and!"

During the weekends I was at home much of the time. All day I used to look forward to the nights when my bedroom walls would once again vibrate, when I would awake with rapture to the rhythm of my parents arguing, arguing one another to exhaustion. Sometimes, without bathrobe or slippers, I would wriggle out into the cold hall on my belly and ambuscade myself behind the banister. I could often hear actual words. "Yes, yes, yes," Father would mumble. He was "backsliding" and "living in the fool's paradise of habitual retarding and retarded do-nothing inertia." Mother had violently set her heart on the resignation. She was hysterical even in her calm, but like a patient and forbearing strategist, she tried to pretend her neutrality. One night she said with murderous coolness, "Bobby and I are leaving for Papá's." This was an ultimatum to force Father to sign a deed placing the Revere Street house in Mother's name.

I writhed with disappointment on the nights when Mother and Father only lowed harmoniously together like cows, as they criticized Helen Bailey or Admiral De Stahl. Once I heard my mother say, "A *man* must make up his *own* mind. Oh Bob, if you are going to resign, do it *now* so I can at least plan for your son's *survival* and education on a single continent."

About this time I was being sent for my *survival* to Dr. Dane, a Quaker chiropractor with an office on Marlborough Street. Dr. Dane wore an old-fashioned light tan druggist's smock; he smelled like a healthy old-fashioned drugstore. His laboratory was free of intimidating technical equipment, and had only the conservative lay roughness and toughness that was so familiar and disarming to us in my Grandfather Winslow's country study or bedroom. Dr. Dane's rosy hands wrenched my shoulders with tremendous éclat and made me feel a hero; I felt unspeakable joy whenever an awry muscle fell back into serenity. My mother, who had no curiosity or imagination for cranky occultism, trusted Dr. Dane's clean, undrugged manliness—so like home. She believed that chiropractic had cured me of my undiagnosed asthma, which had defeated the expensive specialists.

"A penny for your thoughts, Schopenhauer," my mother would say.

"I am thinking about pennies," I'd answer.

"When *I* was a child I used to love telling Mamá everything I had done," Mother would say.

"But you're not a child," I would answer.

I used to enjoy dawdling and humming "Anchors Aweigh" up Revere Street after a day at school. "Anchors Aweigh," the official Navy song, had originally been the song composed for my father's class.* And yet my mind always blanked and seemed to fill with a clammy hollowness when Mother asked prying questions. Like other tongue-tied, difficult children, I dreamed I was a master of cool, stoical repartee. "What have you been doing, Bobby?" Mother would ask. "I haven't," I'd answer. At home I thus saved myself from emotional exhaustion.

At school, however, I was extreme only in my conventional mediocrity, my colorless, distracted manner, which came from restless dreams of being admired. My closest friend was Eric Burckhard, the son of a professor of architecture at Harvard. The Burckhards came from Zurich and were very German, not like Ludendorff,† but in the kindly, comical, nineteenth-century manner of Jo's German husband in *Little Men*, or in the manner of the crusading *sturm und drang* liberal scholars in second year German novels.‡ "Eric's mother and father are *both* called Dr. Burckhard," my mother once said, and indeed there was something endearingly repellent about Mrs. Burckhard with her doctor's degree, her long, unstylish skirts, and her dramatic, dulling blond braids. Strangely the Burckhards' sober continental bourgeois house was without golden mean—everything was

---

* Indeed, the official song of the U.S. Navy, "Anchors Aweigh," composed by Lieutenant Charles A. Zimmerman, was dedicated to the Academy Class of 1907, of which Robert T. S. Lowell III was a member. Lowell's classmate Alfred Hart Miles wrote the song's title and the original lyrics.

† Erich Ludendorff (1865–1937), a Prussian general who planned Germany's strategy in the latter phase of World War I.

‡ *Sturm und Drang*, which in English means "storm and stress," was a German romantic literary movement of the late eighteenth century.

either hilariously old Swiss or madly modern. The Frau Doctor Burckhard used to serve mid-morning hot chocolate with rosettes of whipped cream, and receive her friends in a long, uncarpeted hall–drawing room with lethal ferns and a yellow beeswaxed hardwood floor shining under a central skylight. On the wall there were large expert photographs of what at a distance appeared to be Mont Blanc—they were in reality views of Frank Lloyd Wright's Japanese hotel.*

I admired the Burckhards and felt at home in their house, and these feelings were only intensified when I discovered that my mother was always ill at ease with them. The heartiness, the enlightenment, and the bright, ferny greenhouse atmosphere were too much for her.

Eric and I were too young to care for books or athletics. Neither of our houses had absorbing toys or an elevator to go up and down in. We were inseparable, but I cannot imagine what we talked about. I loved Eric because he was more popular than I and yet absolutely *sui generis* at the Brimmer School. He had a chalk-white face and limp, fine, white-blond hair. He was frail, elbowy, started talking with an enthusiastic Mont Blanc chirp and would flush with bewilderment if interrupted. All the other boys at Brimmer wore little tweed golf suits with knickerbockers, but Eric always arrived in a black suit coat, a Byronic collar, and cuffless gray flannel trousers that almost hid his shoes. The long trousers were replaced on warm days by gray flannel shorts, such as were worn by children still in kindergarten. Eric's unenviable and freakish costumes were too old or too young. He accepted the whims of his parents with a buoyant tranquility that I found unnatural.

My first and terminating quarrel with Eric was my fault. Eventually almost our whole class at Brimmer had whooping cough, but Eric's seizure was like his long trousers—untimely: he was sick a month too early. For a whole month he was in quarantine and forced to play by himself in a removed corner of the Public Garden. He was certainly conspicuous as he skip-roped with his Swiss nurse under the out-of-the-way Ether Memorial Fountain far from the pond and the swan boats.† His parents had decided that this was an

---

* Frank Lloyd Wright (1867–1959), drawing on the architectural aesthetics of the Maya, designed the Imperial Hotel built in Tokyo in 1923. The hotel was demolished in 1968.

† Lowell has in mind the Ether Monument commemorating the first use of ether as an anesthetic at Massachusetts General Hospital in 1846. The monument, which is also a fountain, is located in the northwest corner of the Boston Public Garden, a three-minute walk from the dock where the swan boats are moored.

excellent opportunity for Eric to brush up on his German, and so the absoluteness of his quarantine was monstrously exaggerated by the fact that child and nurse spoke no English but only a guttural, British-sounding, Swiss German. Round and round and round the Fountain, he played intensely, fraily, obediently, until I began to tease him. Though motioned away by him, I came close. I had attracted some of the most popular Brimmer School boys. For the first time I had gotten favorable attention from several little girls. I came close. I shouted. Was Eric afraid of girls? I imitated his German. *Ein, swei, drei, BEER.** I imitated Eric's coughing. "He is afraid he will give you whooping cough if he talks or lets you come nearer," the nurse said in her musical Swiss-English voice. I came nearer. Eric flushed, grew white, bent double with coughing. He began to cry, and had to be led away from the Public Garden. For a whole week I routed Eric from the Garden daily, and for two or three days I was a center of interest. "Come see the Lake Geneva spider monkey!" I would shout. I don't know why I couldn't stop. Eric never told his father, I think, but when he recovered we no longer spoke. The breach was so unspoken and intense that our classmates were actually horrified. They even devised a solemn ritual for our reconciliation. We crossed our hearts, mixed spit, mixed blood. The reconciliation was hollow.

My parents' confidences and quarrels stopped each night at ten or eleven o'clock, when my father would hang up his tuxedo, put on his commander's uniform, and take a trolley back to the naval yard at Charlestown. He had just broken in a new car. Like a chauffeur, he watched this car, a Hudson, with an informed vigilance, always giving its engine hair-trigger little tinkerings of adjustment or friendship, always fearful lest the black body, unbeautiful as his boiled shirts, should lose its outline and gloss. He drove with flawless, almost instrumental, monotony. Mother, nevertheless, was forever encouraging him to walk or take taxis. She would tell him that his legs were growing vestigial from disuse and remind him of the time a jack had slipped and he had broken

---

The swan boats are traditional pleasure boats on the garden's pond, so named because adorned, at the stern, with oversized white swans covering the pedaling of the boats' operators.

* Two of the German numerals, meaning "one, two, three," are misspelled. Correctly, they should read "*Eins, zwei, drei.*" The errors probably suggest Bobby's ignorance of or disdain for German. "*BEER*" puns on "*vier,*" meaning "four."

his leg while shifting a tire. "Alone and at night," she would say, "an amateur driver is unsafe in a car." Father sighed and obeyed—only, putting on a
martyred and penny-saving face, he would keep his self-respect by taking the
trolley rather than a taxi. Each night he shifted back into his uniform, but his
departures from Revere Street were so furtive that several months passed before I realized what was happening—we had *two* houses! Our second house
was the residence in the Naval Yard assigned to the third in command. It was
large, had its own flagpole, and screen porches on three levels—yet it was
something to be ashamed of. Whatever pomp or distinction its possession
might have had for us was destroyed by an eccentric humiliation inflicted
on Father by his superior, Admiral De Stahl, the commandant at Charlestown. De Stahl had not been consulted about our buying the 91 Revere Street
house. He was outraged, stormed about "flaunting private fortunes in the
face of naval tradition," and ordered my father to sleep on bounds at the
Yard in the house provided for that purpose.

On our first Revere Street Christmas Eve, the telephone rang in the
middle of dinner; it was Admiral De Stahl demanding Father's instant return to the Navy Yard. Soon Father was back in his uniform. In taking leave
of my mother and grandparents he was, as was usual with him under pressure, a little evasive and magniloquent. "A woman works from sun to sun,"
he said, "but a sailor's watch is never done." He compared a naval officer's
hours with a doctor's, hinted at surprise maneuvers, and explained away the
uncommunicative arrogance of Admiral De Stahl: "The Old Man has to be
hush-hush." Later that night, I lay in bed and tried to imagine that my father
was leading his engineering force on a surprise maneuver through arctic
wastes. A forlorn hope! "Hush-hush, hush-hush," whispered the snowflakes
as big as street lamps as they broke on Father—broke and buried. Outside, I
heard real people singing carols, shuffling snow off their shoes, opening and
shutting doors. I worried at the meaning of a sentence I had heard quoted
from the *Boston Evening Transcript*: "On this Christmas Eve, as usual, the
whole of Beacon Hill can be expected to become a single old-fashioned
open house—the names of mine host the Hill, and her guests will read like
the contents of the Social Register." I imagined Beacon Hill changed to the
snow queen's palace, as vast as the north pole. My father pressed a cold finger to his lip: "hush-hush," and led his surprise squad of sailors around an
altar, but the altar was a tremendous cash register, whose roughened nickel

surface was cheaply decorated with trowels, pyramids, and Arabic swirls. A great drawer helplessly chopped back and forth, unable to shut because choked with greenbacks. "Hush-hush!" My father's engineers wound about me with their eye-patches, orange sashes, and curtain-ring earrings, like the Gilbert and Sullivan pirates' chorus* . . . Outside on the streets of Beacon Hill, it was night, it was dismal, it was raining. Something disturbing had befallen the familiar and honorable Salvation Army band; its big drum and accordion were now accompanied by drunken voices howling: *The Old Gray Mare, she ain't what she used to be, when Mary went to milk the cow.* A sound of a bosun's whistle. Women laughing. Someone repeatedly rang our doorbell. I heard my mother talking on the telephone. "Your inebriated sailors have littered my doorstep with the dregs of Scollay Square."† There was a gloating panic in her voice that showed she enjoyed the drama of talking to Admiral De Stahl. "Sir," she shrilled, "you have compelled my husband to leave me alone and defenseless on Christmas Eve!" She ran into my bedroom. She hugged me. She said, "Oh Bobby, it's such a comfort to have a man in the house." "I am not a man," I said. "I am a boy."

Boy—at that time this word had private associations for me; it meant weakness, outlawry, and yet was a status to be held onto. Boys were a sideline at my Brimmer School. The eight superior grades were limited to girls. In these grades, moreover, scholarship was made subservient to discipline, as if in contempt of the male's two idols: career and earning power. The school's tone, its *ton*, was a blend of the feminine and the military, a bulky reality governed in turn by stridency, smartness, and steadiness. The girls wore white jumpers, black skirts, stockings, and rectangular low-heeled shoes. An ex–West Pointer had been appointed to teach drill; and, at the moment of my enrollment in Brimmer, our principal, the hitherto staid Miss Manice, was rumored to be showing signs of age and of undermining her position with the school trustees by girlish, quite out of character, rhapsodies on the varsity basketball team, winner of two consecutive championships. The lower four grades, peaceful and lackadaisical, were, on the other hand, almost a separate establishment. Miss Manice regarded these "coeducated" classes with amused

---

* Comic opera of 1879, *The Pirates of Penzance*, composed by Arthur Sullivan (1842–1900) and with a libretto by W. S. Gilbert (1836–1911).

† Scollay Square was Boston's traditional red-light neighborhood, sailor-frequented and disreputable, known for its saloons, striptease clubs, tattoo parlors, slapstick vaudeville, and movie theaters.

carelessness, allowed them to wear their ordinary clothes, and . . . carelessness, however, is incorrect—Miss Manice, in her administration of the lower
school, showed the inconsistency and euphoria of a dual personality. Here she
mysteriously shed all her Prussianism. She quoted Emerson and Mencken,*
disparaged the English, threatened to break with the past, and boldly coquet-
ted with the non-military American genius by displaying movies illustrating
the careers of Edison and Ford. Favored lower school teachers were permitted
to use us as guinea pigs for mildly radical experiments. At Brimmer I *un-
learned* writing. The script that I had mastered with much agony at my first
school† was denounced as illegible: I was taught to print according to the
Dalton Plan—to this day, as a result, I have to print even my two middle
names and can only really *write* two words: "Robert" and "Lowell." Our
instruction was subject to bewildering leaps. The usual fall performance by
the Venetian glass blowers was followed by a tour of the Riverside Press.‡
We heard Rudy Vallee, then heard spirituals sung by the Hampton Institute
choir. We studied grammar from a formidable, unreconstructed textbook
written by Miss Manice's father. There, I battled with figures of speech and
Greek terminology: *Chiásmus*, the arrangement of corresponding words in
opposite order; *Brachylogy*, the failure to repeat an element that is supplied
in more or less modified form. Then all this pedantry was nullified by the
introduction of a new textbook which proposed to lift the face of syntax by
using game techniques and drawings.

Physical instruction in the lower school was irregular, spontaneous, and
had nothing of that swept and garnished barrack-room camaraderie of the
older girls' gymnasium exercises. On the roof of our school building, there
was an ugly concrete area that looked as if it had been intended for the top
floor of a garage. Here we played tag, drew lines with chalk, and chose
up sides for a kind of kids' soccer. On bright spring days, Mr. Newell, a
submerged young man from Boston University, took us on botanical hikes
through the Arboretum. He had an eye for inessentials—read us Martha
Washington's poems at the Old State House, pointed out the roof of Brimmer School from the top of the Customs House, made us count the steps

* In the *Partisan Review* version, it was William James rather than H. L. Mencken. The revision makes Miss
Manice seem more iconoclastic, if less Bostonian.

† The Potomac School at 2144 California Street, Washington, D.C., which Lowell attended from 1923 to 1925.

‡ Riverside Press, established in 1852, was a printing house in Cambridge, Massachusetts.

of the Bunker Hill Monument, and one rainy afternoon broke all rules by
herding us into the South Boston Aquarium in order to give an unhealthy,
eager little lecture on the sewage-consumption of the conger eel. At last
Miss Manice seemed to have gotten wind of Mr. Newell's moods. For an afternoon or two she herself served as his substitute. We were walked briskly
past the houses of Parkman and Dana, and assigned themes on the spunk of
great persons who had overcome physical handicaps and risen to the top of
the ladder. She talked about Elizabeth Barrett, Helen Keller; her pet theory, however, was that "women simply are not the equals of men." I can
hear Miss Manice browbeating my white and sheepish father, "How can we
stand up to you? Where are our Archimedeses, our Wagners, our Admiral
Simses?"* Miss Manice adored "Sir Walter Scott's *big bow-wow*," wished
"Boston had banned the tubercular novels of the Brontës," and found nothing in the world "so simpatico" as the "strenuous life" lived by President
Roosevelt. Yet the extravagant hysteria of Miss Manice's philanthropy meant
nothing; Brimmer was entirely a woman's world—*dumkopf*,† perhaps, but
not in the least Quixotic, Brimmer was ruled by a woman's obvious aims
and by her naive pragmatism. The quality of this regime, an extension of
my mother's, shone out in full glory at general assemblies or when I sat with
a handful of other boys on the bleachers of Brimmer's new Manice Hall. In
unison our big girls sang "America"; back and forth our amazons tramped—
their brows were wooden, their dress was black and white, and their columns
followed standard-bearers holding up an American flag, the white flag of the
Commonwealth of Massachusetts, and the green flag of Brimmer. At basketball games against Miss Lee's or Miss Winsor's, it was our upper-school
champions who rushed onto the floor, as feline and fateful in their pace as
lions. This was our own immediate and daily spectacle; in comparison such
masculine displays as trips to battle cruisers commanded by comrades of my
father seemed eyewash—the Navy moved in a realm as ghostlike and removed from my life as the elfin acrobatics of Douglas Fairbanks or Peter
Pan. I wished I were an older girl. I wrote Santa Claus for a field hockey
stick. To be a boy at Brimmer was to be small, denied, and weak.

---

* William S. Sims (1858–1936), one of the greatest admirals in American military history, was the commander of the U.S. fleet in European waters during World War I.

† Misspelled in Lowell's text, *Dummkopf* means "fool" or "blockhead" in German.

I was promised an improved future and taken on Sunday afternoon
drives through the suburbs to inspect the boys' schools: Rivers, Dexter,
Country Day. These expeditions were stratagems designed to give me a
chance to know my father; Mother noisily stayed behind and amazed me
by pretending that I had forbidden her to embark on "men's work." Father,
however, seldom insisted, as he should have, on seeing the headmasters
in person, yet he made an astonishing number of friends; his trust begat
trust, and something about his silences encouraged junior masters and even
school janitors to pour out small talk that was detrimental to rival insti-
tutions. At each new school, however, all this gossip was easily refuted;
worse still Mother was always ready to cross-examine Father in a manner
that showed that she was asking questions for the purpose of giving, not
of receiving, instruction; she expressed astonishment that a wishy-washy
desire to be everything to everybody had robbed a naval man of any reliable concern for his son's welfare. Mother regarded the suburban schools as
"gerrymandered" and middle-class; after Father had completed his round
of inspections, she made her own follow-up visits and told Mr. Dexter and
Mr. Rivers to their faces that she was looking for a "respectable stop-gap"
for her son's "three years between Brimmer and Saint Mark's." Saint Mark's
was the boarding school for which I had been enrolled at birth, and was due
to enter in 1930. I distrusted change, knew each school since kindergarten
had been more constraining and punitive than its predecessor, and believed
the suburban country day schools were flimsily disguised fronts for refor-
matories. With the egotistic, slightly paranoid apprehensions of an only
child, I wondered what became of boys graduating from Brimmer's fourth
grade, feared the worst—we were darkly imperiled, like some annual bevy
of Athenian youths destined for the Minotaur. And to judge from my father,
men between the ages of six and sixty did nothing but meet new challenges,
take on heavier responsibilities, and lose all freedom to explode. A ray of
hope in the far future was my white-haired Grandfather Winslow, whose
unchecked commands and demands were always upsetting people for their
own good—he was all I could ever want to be: the bad boy, the problem
child, the commodore of his household.

When I entered Brimmer I was eight and a half. I was distracted in my
studies, assented to whatever I was told, picked my nose whenever no one
was watching, and worried our third-grade teacher by organizing creepy

little gangs of boys at recess. I was girl-shy. Thick-witted, narcissistic, thug-
gish, I had the conventional prepuberty character of my age; whenever a
girl came near me, my whole person cringed like a sponge wrung dry by a
clenching fist. I was less rather than more bookish than most children, but
the girl I dreamed about continually had wheel-spoke black and gold eye-
lashes, double-length pageboy blond hair, a little apron, a bold, blunt face,
a saucy, shivery way of talking, and . . . a paper body—she was the girl in
John Tenniel's illustrations to *Alice in Wonderland*. The invigorating and
symmetrical aplomb of my ideal Alice was soon enriched and nullified by a
second face, when my father took me to the movies on the afternoon of one
of Mother's headaches. An innocuous child's movie, the bloody, all-male
Beau Geste had been chosen, but instead my father preferred a nostalgic tour
of places he had enjoyed on shore leave. We went to the Majestic Theater,
where he had first seen Pola Negri—where we too saw Pola Negri, sloppy-
haired, slack, yawning, ravaged, unwashed . . . an Anti-Alice.

Our class belles, the Norton twins, Elie and Lindy, fell far short of the
Nordic Alice and the foreign Pola. Their prettiness, rather fluffy, freckled,
bashful, might have escaped notice if they had been one instead of two, and
if their manners had been less good-humored, entertaining, and reliable.
What mattered more than sex, athletics, or studies to us at Brimmer was
our popularity; each child had an unwritten class-popularity poll inside his
head. Everyone was ranked, and all day each of us mooned profoundly on
his place, as it quivered like our blood or a compass needle with a thousand
revisions. At nine, character is, perhaps, too much *in ovo* for a child to be
strongly disliked, but sitting next to Elie Norton, I glanced at her and gulped
prestige from her popularity. We were not close at first; then nearness made
us closer friends, for Elie had a gracious gift, the gift of gifts, I suppose, in
a child: she forgot all about the popularity-rank of the classmate she was
talking to. No moron could have seemed so uncritical as this airy, chatty,
intelligent child, the belle of our grade. She noticed my habit of cocking my
head on one side, shutting my eyes, and driving like a bull through opposition at soccer—wishing to amuse without wounding, she called me Buffalo
Bull. At general assembly she would giggle with contented admiration at
the upper-school girls in their penal black and white. "What bruisers, what
beef-eaters! Dear girls," she would sigh, parroting her sophisticated mother,
"we shall all become fodder for the governess classes before graduating from

Brimmer." I felt that Elie Norton understood me better than anyone except my playful little Grandmother Winslow.

One morning there was a disaster. The boy behind me, no friend, had been tapping at my elbow for over a minute to catch my attention before I consented to look up and see a great golden puddle spreading toward me from under Elie's chair. I dared not speak, smile, or flicker an eyelash in her direction. She ran bawling from the classroom. Trying to catch every eye, yet avoid commitment, I gave sidelong and involuntary smirks at space. I began to feel manic with superiority to Elie Norton and struggled to swallow down a feeling of goaded hollowness—was I deserting her? Our teacher left us on our honor and ran down the hall. The class milled about in a hesitant hush. The girls blushed. The boys smirked. Miss Manice, the principal, appeared. She wore her whitish-brown dress with darker brown spots. Shimmering in the sunlight and chilling us, she stood mothlike in the middle of the classroom. We rushed to our seats. Miss Manice talked about how there was "nothing laughable about a malaise." She broke off. Her face took on an expression of invidious disgust. She was staring at me . . . In the absentmindedness of my guilt and excitement, I had taken the nearest chair, the chair that Elie Norton had just left. "Lowell," Miss Manice shrieked, "are you going to soak there all morning like a bump on a log?"

When Elie Norton came back, there was really no break in her friendliness toward me, but there was something caved in, something crippled in the way I stood up to her and tried to answer her disengaged chatter. I thought about her all the time; seldom meeting her eyes now, I felt rich and raw in her nearness. I wanted passionately to stay on at Brimmer, and told my mother a fib one afternoon late in May of my last year. "Miss Manice has begged me to stay on," I said, "and enter the fifth grade." Mother pointed out that there had never been a boy in the fifth grade. Contradicted, I grew excited. "If Miss Manice has begged me to stay," I said, "why can't I stay?" My voice rose, I beat on the floor with my open hands. Bored and bewildered, my mother went upstairs with a headache. "If you won't believe me," I shouted after her, "why don't you telephone Miss Manice or Mrs. Norton?"

Brimmer School was thrown open on sunny March and April afternoons and our teachers took us for strolls on the polite, landscaped walks of the Public

Garden. There I'd loiter by the old iron fence and gape longingly across Charles Street at the historic Boston Common, a now largely wrong-side-of-the-tracks park.* On the Common there were mossy bronze reliefs of Union soldiers, and a captured German tank filled with smelly wads of newspapers. Everywhere there were grit, litter, gangs of Irish, Negroes, Latins. On Sunday afternoons orators harangued about Sacco and Vanzetti,† while others stood about heckling and blocking the sidewalks. Keen young policemen, looking for trouble, lolled on the benches. At nightfall a police lieutenant on horseback inspected the Common. In the Garden, however, there was only Officer Lever, a single white-haired and mustached dignitary, who had once been the doorman at the Union Club. He now looked more like a member of the club. "Lever's a man about town," my Grandfather Winslow would say. "Give him Harris tweeds and a glass of Scotch, and I'd take him for Cousin Herbert." Officer Lever was without thoughts or deeds, but Back Bay and Beacon Hill parents loved him just for being. No one asked this hollow and leonine King Log‡ to be clairvoyant about children.

One day when the saucer magnolias were in bloom, I bloodied Bulldog Binney's nose against the pedestal of George Washington's statue in full view of Commonwealth Avenue; then I bloodied Dopey Dan Parker's nose; then I stood in the center of a sundial tulip bed and pelted a little enemy ring of third-graders with wet fertilizer. Officer Lever was telephoned. Officer Lever telephoned my mother. In the presence of my mother and some thirty nurses and children, I was expelled from the Public Garden. I was such a bad boy, I was told, "that *even* Officer Lever had been forced to put his foot down."

---

* Tram tracks used to run on Charles Street, which divides the Boston Public Garden from the Boston Common. The two green public spaces, positioned side by side, are historically quite different. While the former is a manicured botanical garden closely monitored and subject to strict park regulations, the latter, meant to embody the ideals of civic and political freedom, is less strictly policed and maintained. The Common, therefore, is less genteel and more likely to witness "vandalism, drug dealing, and sidewalk gambling"; see Stephen Carr et al., *Public Space* (New York: Cambridge University Press, 1992), 182–85.

† Nicola Sacco (1891–1927) and Bartolomeo Vanzetti (1888–1927) were two Italian American political radicals convicted of murder in a trial that progressives viewed as unfair and politically motivated. Abbott Lawrence Lowell, the president of Harvard, headed a review committee that upheld the verdict. As a result, the two men were executed.

‡ In one of Aesop's fables, "King Log," frogs ask Zeus to give them a king. When he sends them a log, the frogs begin to grumble about its passivity. Their complaints eventually provoke the god to send them a stork. The bird, with the usual energy of a predator, devours them.

New England winters are long. Sunday mornings are long. Ours were often made tedious by preparations for dinner guests. Mother would start airing at nine. Whenever the air grew so cold that it hurt, she closed the den windows; then we were attacked by sour kitchen odors winding up a clumsily rebuilt dumb-waiter shaft. The windows were again thrown open. We sat in an atmosphere of glacial purity and sacrifice. Our breath puffed whitely. Father and I wore sleeveless cashmere jerseys Mother had bought at Filene's Basement.* A do-it-yourself book containing diagrams for the correct carving of roasts lay on the arm of Father's chair. At hand were Big Bill Tilden on tennis, Capablanca on chess, newspaper clippings from Sidney Lenz's bridge column, and a magnificent tome with photographs and some American's nationalist sketch of Sir Thomas Lipton's errors in the Cup Defender races.† Father made little progress in these diversions, and yet one of the authors assured him that mastery demanded only willing readers who understood the meaning of English words. Throughout the winter a graywhiteness glared through the single den window. In the apoplectic brick alley, a fire escape stood out against our sooty plank fence. Father believed that churchgoing was undignified for a naval man; his Sunday mornings were given to useful acts such as lettering his three new galvanized garbage cans: R.T.S. LOWELL—U.S.N.

Our Sunday dinner guests were often naval officers. Naval officers were not Mother's sort; very few people *were* her sort in those days, and that was her trouble—a very authentic, human, and plausible difficulty, which made Mother's life one of much suffering. She did not have the self-assurance for wide human experience; she needed to feel liked, admired, surrounded by the approved and familiar. Her haughtiness and chilliness came from apprehension. She would start talking like a *grande dame* and then stand back rigid and faltering, as if she feared being crushed by her own massively intimidating offensive.

Father's old Annapolis roommate, Commander Billy "Battleship Bilge"

---

* Filene's Basement was a discount section of Filene's department store at the Downtown Crossing in Boston.

† Sir Thomas Lipton (1848–1931), the famous Scottish tea merchant, sailed as many as five times in the America's Cup, never winning it.

Harkness,* was a frequent guest at Revere Street and one that always threw Mother off balance. Billy was a rough diamond. He made jokes about his "all-American family tree," and insisted that his name, pronounced H*a*rkness, should be spelled H*e*rkness. He came from Louisville, Kentucky, drank whiskey to "renew his Bourbon blood," and still spoke with an accent that sounded—so his colleagues said—"like a bran-fed stallion." Like my father, however, Commander Billy had entered the Naval Academy when he was a boy of fourteen; his Southernisms had been thoroughly rubbed away. He was teased for knowing nothing about racehorses, mountaineers, folk ballads, hams, sour mash, tobacco . . . Kentucky Colonels. Though hardly an officer and a gentleman in the old Virginian style, he was an unusual combination of clashing virtues: he had led his class in the sciences and yet was what his superiors called "a *mathmaddition* with the habit of command." He and my father, the youngest men in their class, had often been shipmates. Bilge's executive genius had given color and direction to Father's submissive tenacity. He drank like a fish at parties, but was a total abstainer on duty. With reason Commander Harkness had been voted the man most likely to make four-star admiral in the class of '07.

Billy called his wife *Jimmy* or *Jeems*, and had a rough friendly way of saying, "Oh, Jimmy's bright as a penny." Mrs. Harkness was an unpleasant rarity: she was the only naval officer's wife we knew who was also a college graduate. She had a flat flapper's figure, and hid her intelligence behind a nervous twitter of vulgarity and toadyism. "Charlotte," she would almost scream at Mother, "is this mirAGE, this MIRacle your *own* dining room!"

Then Mother might smile and answer in a distant, though cozy and amused, voice, "I usually manage to make myself pretty comfortable."

Mother's comfort was chic, romantic, impulsive. If her silver service shone, it shone with hectic perfection to rebuke the functional domesticity of naval wives. She had determined to make her *ambiance* beautiful and luxurious, but wanted neither her beauty nor her luxury unaccompanied. Beauty pursued too exclusively meant artistic fatuity of a kind made farcical

---

* There was no William Harkness in the Class of 1907. Lowell once made a comment on the fictitiousness of many of his characters in his poetry, one that is pertinent to his autobiographical prose as well: "My characters are purely imaginary, except when I've used myself or occasionally named actual people in poems. I've tried to buttress them by putting images I've seen and in indirect ways getting things I've experienced into the poem." See "Applause for a Prize Poet," *Life*, February 19, 1965, 55.

by her Aunt Sarah Stark Winslow, a beauty too lofty and original ever to marry, a prima donna on the piano, too high-strung ever to give a public recital. Beauty alone meant the maudlin ignominy of having one's investments managed by interfering relatives. Luxury alone, on the other hand, meant for Mother the "paste and fool's-gold polish" that one met with in the foyer of the new Statler Hotel.* She loathed the "undernourishment" of Professor Burckhard's Bauhaus modernism, yet in moments of pique she denounced our pompous Myers mahoganies as "suitable for politicians at the Bellevue Hotel." She kept a middle-of-the-road position, and much admired Italian pottery with its fresh peasant colors and puritanical, clean-cut lines. She was fond of saying, "The French *do* have taste," but spoke with a double-edged irony which implied the French, with no moral standards to support their finish, were really no better than naval yahoos. Mother's beautiful house was dignified by a rich veneer of the useful.

"I have always believed carving to be *the* gentlemanly talent," Mother used to proclaim. Father, faced with this opinion, pored over his book of instructions or read the section on table carving in the *Encyclopædia Britannica*. Eventually he discovered among the innumerable small, specialized Boston "colleges" an establishment known as a carving school. Each Sunday from then on he would sit silent and erudite before his roast. He blinked, grew white, looked winded, and wiped beads of perspiration from his eyebrows. His purpose was to reproduce stroke by stroke his last carving lesson, and he worked with all the formal rightness and particular error of some shaky experiment in remote control. He enjoyed quiet witticisms at the expense of his carving master—"a philosopher who gave himself all the airs of a Mahan!"† He liked to pretend that the carving master had stated that "No two cuts are identical," *ergo*: "each offers original problems for the *executioner*." Guests were appeased by Father's saying, "I am just a plebe at this guillotine. Have a hunk of my roast beef hash."

What angered Father was Mrs. Harkness's voice grown merciless with

* The Statler Hotel opened in March 1927.

† Alfred Thayer Mahan (1840–1914), a U.S. Navy officer, a maritime historian, and an influential exponent of the role of America's sea power in its newly defined security and new global responsibilities.

excitement, as she studied his hewing and hacking. She was sure to say something tactless about how Commander Billy was "a stingy artist at carving who could shave General Washington off the dollar bill."

Nothing could stop Commander Billy, that born carver, from reciting verses:

"By carving my way
I lived on my pay;
This reeward, *though small,*
Beats none at all . . .

My carving paper-thin
Can make a guinea hin,
All giblets, bones, and skin,
Canteen a party of tin."

And I, furious for no immediate reason, blurted out, "Mother, how much does Grandfather Winslow have to fork up to pay for Daddy's carving school?"

These Sunday dinners with the Harknesses were always woundingly boisterous affairs. Father, unnaturally outgoing, would lead me forward and say, "Bilge, I want you to meet my first coupon from the bond of matrimony."

Commander Billy would answer, "So this is the range-finder you are raising for future wars!" They would make me salute, stand at attention, stand at ease. "Angel-face," Billy would say to me, "you'll skipper a flivver."*

"Jimmy" Harkness, of course, knew that Father was anxiously negotiating with Lever Brothers' Soap, and arranging for his resignation from the service, but nothing could prevent her from proposing time and again her "hens' toast to the drakes." Dragging Mother to her feet, Jimmy would scream, "To Bob and Bilgy's next battleship together!"

What Father and Commander Billy enjoyed talking about most was their class of '07. After dinner, the ladies would retire to the upstairs sitting room. As a special privilege I was allowed to remain at the table with the men. Over and over, they would talk about their ensigns' cruise around the world, escaping the "reeport," gunboating on the upper Yangtze during the Chinese

* To "skipper a flivver," means to be a captain of a cheap car.

Civil War, keeping sane and sanitary at Guantanamo, patrolling the Golfo del Papayo during the two-bit Nicaraguan Revolution, when water to wash in cost a dollar a barrel and was mostly "alkali and wrigglers."* There were the class casualties: Holden and Holcomb drowned in a foundered launch off Hampton Roads; "Count" Bowditch, killed by the Moros and famous for his dying words to Commander Harkness: "I'm all right. Get on the job, Bilge."†

They would speak about the terrible 1918 influenza epidemic, which had killed more of their classmates than all the skirmishes or even the World War. It was an honor, however, to belong to a class which included "Chips" Carpender, whose destroyer, the *Fanning*, was the only British or American warship to force a German submarine to break water and surrender.‡ It was a feather in their caps that three of their classmates, Bellinger, Reade, and another, should have made the first transatlantic seaplane flight.§ They put their faith in teamwork, and Lindbergh's solo hop to Paris struck them as unprofessional, a newspaper trick. What made Father and Commander Billy mad as hornets was the mare's-nest made of naval administration by "deserving Democrats." Hadn't Secretary of State Bryan ordered their old battlewagon the *Idaho* to sail on a goodwill mission to Switzerland?¶ "Bryan, Bryan, Bryan,"** Commander Billy would boom, "the pious swab had been told that Lake Geneva had annexed the Adriatic." Another "guy with false gills," Josephus Daniels, "ordained by Divine Providence Sec-

---

* Refers to the presence of the U.S. Pacific fleet off the western shores of Nicaragua, including the Gulf of Papagayo at the border between Nicaragua and Costa Rica, in the years 1909 through 1912, when the United States repeatedly intervened in Nicaragua to protect perceived U.S. interests.

† Moros: Muslim peoples on several islands of the Philippines whom the United States tried to assimilate into the Philippine nation after 1898 when the archipelago became an American possession. "Bowditch" was killed in the Moro Rebellion (1901–1913), the second and lesser-known front of the Philippine war against U.S. domination, on the island of Mindanao.

‡ Arthur S. Carpender (1884–1960)—the commander of the celebrated USS *Fanning*, which in 1917 forced a German U-boat to surrender—was a member of the Class of 1908, not 1907. "Chips" was a traditional nickname used for a ship's carpenter.

§ Patrick N. L. Bellinger, Albert C. Read, and John Towers commanded three seaplanes, Curtiss NC "flying boats," which made the first air crossing of the Atlantic in May 1919. Achieved eight years before Charles Lindbergh's crossing, the feat had to include several stops on the way. Of the three men, only Towers was not Bob Lowell's classmate, having graduated from Annapolis a year earlier.

¶ In fact, William Jennings Bryan, the secretary of state from 1913 to 1915, made a related diplomatic blunder. In 1914 he invited the Swiss government to send its navy to the gala opening of the Panama Canal.

** An ironic echo of Vachel Lindsay's poem in favor of William Jennings Bryan called "Bryan, Bryan, Bryan, Bryan" (1919).

retary of the Navy," had refused to send Father and Billy to the war zone. "You are looking," Billy would declaim, "at martyrs in the famous victory of red tape. Our names are rubric." A man they had to take their hats off to was Theodore Roosevelt; Billy had been one of the lucky ensigns who had helped "escort the redoubtable Teddy to Panama." Perhaps because of his viciously inappropriate nickname, "Bilge," Commander Harkness always spoke with brutal facetiousness against the class *bilgers*, officers whose "services were no longer required by the service." In more Epicurean moods, Bilge would announce that he "meant to accumulate a lot of dough from complacent, well-meaning, although misguided West Point officers gullible enough to bet their shirts on the Army football team."

"Let's have a squint at your *figger* and waterline, Bob," Billy would say. He'd admire Father's trim girth and smile familiarly at his bald spot. "Bob," he'd say, "you've maintained your displacement and silhouette unmodified, except for somewhat thinner top chafing gear."

Commander Billy's drinking was a "pain in the neck." He would take possession of Father's sacred "rhino" armchair, sprawl legs astraddle, make the tried and true framework groan, and crucify Mother by roaring out verbose toasts in what he called "me boozy cockney-h'Irish." He would drink to our cocktail shaker. "'Ere's to the 'older of the Lowelldom nectar," he would bellow. "Hip, hip, hooray for senor Martino, h'our h'old hipmate, 'elpmate, and hhonorary member of '07—h'always h'able to navigate and never says dry." We never got through a visit without one of Billy's "Bottoms up to the 'ead of the Nation. 'Ere's to herb-garden 'Erb." This was a swaggering dig at Herbert Hoover's notoriously correct, but insular, refusal to "imbibe anything more potent than Bromo-Seltzer" at a war-relief banquet in Brussels. Commander Billy's bulbous, water-on-the-brain forehead would glow and trickle with fury. Thinking on Herbert Hoover and Prohibition, he was unable to contain himself. "What a hick! We haven't been steered by a gentleman of parts since the redoubtable Teddy." He recited *wet* verses, such as the following inserted in Father's class book:

"I tread the bridge with measured pace;
Proud, yet anguish marks my face—
What worries me like crushing sin
Is where on the sea can I buy dry gin?"

In his cups, Commander Bilge acted as though he owned us. He looked like a human ash heap. Cigar ashes buried the heraldic hedgehog on the ashtray beside him; cigar ashes spilled over and tarnished the golden stork embroidered on the table-cover; cigar ashes littered his own shiny blue-black uniform. Greedily Mother's eyes would brighten, drop and brighten. She would say darkly, "I was brought up by Papá to be like a naval officer, to be ruthlessly neat."

Once Commander Billy sprawled back so recklessly that the armchair began to come apart. "You see, Charlotte," he said to Mother, "at the height of my *climacteric* I am breaking Bob's chair."

Harkness went in for tiresome, tasteless harangues against Amy Lowell, which he seemed to believe necessary for the enjoyment of his after-dinner cigar. He would point a stinking baby stogie at Mother. "'Ave a peteeto cigareeto, Charlotte," he would crow. "Puff on this whacking black cheroot, and you'll be a match for any reeking senorita *femme fatale* in the spiggotty republics, where blindness from Bob's bathtub hooch is still unknown. When you go up in smoke, Charlotte, remember the *Maine*.* Remember Amy Lowell, that cigar-chawing, guffawing, senseless and meterless, multimillionheiress, heavyweight mascot on a floating fortress. Damn the *Patterns*!† Full speed ahead on a cigareeto!"

Amy Lowell was never a welcome subject in our household. Of course, no one spoke disrespectfully of Miss Lowell. She had been so plucky, so *formidable, so beautifully and unblushingly immense*, as Henry James might have said. And yet, though irreproachably decent herself apparently, like Mae West she seemed to provoke indecorum in others. There was an anecdote which I was too young to understand: it was about Amy's getting her migraine headaches from being kept awake by the exercises of honeymooners in an adjacent New York hotel room. Amy's relatives would have liked to have honored her as a *personage*, a personage a little *outrée* perhaps, but perfectly within the natural order, like Amy's girlhood idol, the Duse.‡ Or at

---

* USS *Maine* was an American battleship blown up and sunk in the Havana harbor in 1898, when Cuba was a Spanish colony. "Remember the *Maine*" became the rallying cry of many Americans for war against the Spanish, who were blamed for the catastrophe and whose colonial presence in the Caribbean was resented.

† "Patterns" is the title of one of Amy Lowell's poems.

‡ Eleonora Duse (1858–1924), an Italian actress, famous for her roles in plays by D'Annunzio and Ibsen.

least she might have been unambiguously tragic, short-lived, and a classic, like her last idol, John Keats. My parents piously made out a case for Miss Lowell's *Life of Keats*, which had killed its author and was so much more manly and intelligible than her poetry. Her poetry! But was *poetry* what one could call Amy's loud, bossy, unladylike *chinoiserie*—her free verse! For those that could understand it, her matter was, no doubt, blameless, but the effrontery of her manner made my parents relish Robert Frost's remark that "writing free verse was like playing tennis without a net."

Whenever Amy Lowell was mentioned Mother bridled. Not distinguishing, not caring whether her relative was praised or criticized, she would say, "Amy had the courage of her convictions. She worked like a horse." Mother would conclude characteristically, "Amy did insist on doing everything the *hard* way. I think, perhaps, that her brother, the President of Harvard, did more for *other* people."

Often Father seemed to pay little attention to the conversation of his guests. He would smack his lips, and beam absentmindedly and sensuously, as if he were anticipating the comforts of civilian life—a perpetual shore leave in Hawaii. The Harknesses, however, cowed him. He would begin to feel out the subject of his resignation and observe in a wheedle obscurely loaded with significance that "certain *cits*, no brighter than you or I, pay income taxes as large as a captain's yearly salary."

Commander Harkness, unfortunately, was inclined to draw improper conclusions from such remarks. Disregarding the "romance of commerce," he would break out into ungentlemanly tirades against capital. "Yiss, old Bob," he would splutter, "when I consider the ungodly hoards garnered in by the insurance and broking gangs, it breaks my heart. Riches, reaches, overreaches! If Bob and I had half the swag that Harkness of Yale has just given Lowell of Harvard to build Georgian houses for Boston quee-eers with British accents!"* He rumbled on morosely about retired naval officers "forced to live like coolies on their half-pay. Hurrah for the Bull Moose Party!" he'd shout. "Hurrah for Boss Curley! Hurrah for the Bolshies!"

Nothing prevented Commander Billy from telling about his diplomatic

---

* The multimillionaire and philanthropist Edward S. Harkness (1874–1940) of Yale made a major donation to Harvard in 1929 for the establishment of an undergraduate house system. Abbott Lawrence Lowell was the president of Harvard at the time.

mission in 1918, when "his eyes had seen the Bolshie on his native heath." He had been in Budapest "during the brief sway of Béla Kun.* Béla was giving those Hunkyland money-bags and educators the boot into the arms of American philanthropy!"

Then Mother would say, hopefully, "Mamá always said that the *old* Hungarians *did* have taste. Billy, your reference to Budapest makes me heartsick for Europe. I am dying for Bob and Bobby's permission to spend next summer at Étretat."†

Commander Billy Harkness specialized in verses like "The Croix de Guerre":

> "*I toast the guy, who, crossing over,*
> *Abode in London for a year,*
> *The guy who to his wife and lover*
> *Returned with conscience clean and clear,*
> *Who nightly prowling Piccadilly*
> *Gave icy stares to floozies wild,*
> *And when approached said, 'Bilgy Billy*
> *Is mama's darling angel child—'*
> *Now he's the guy who rates the croy dee geer!*"

Mother, however, smiled mildly. "Billy," she would say, "my cousin, Admiral Ledyard Atkinson,‡ always has a twinkle in his eye when he asks after your *vers de société*."

"'Tommy' Atkins!" snorted Commander Billy. "I know Tommy better than my own mother. He's the first chapter in a book I'm secretly writing and leaving to the archives called *Wild Admirals I Have Known*. And now my bodily presence may no longer grace the inner sanctum of the Somerset

---

* Béla Kun (1886–1938?), a Hungarian Communist leader, was the prime minister in a Communist–Social Democratic coalition government that came to power in March 1919 and ruled Hungary until August. The *Life Studies* version of this memoir adds "Whon" to Kun's surname, making it "Kun-Whon." It is unclear why the "Whon" was added to the Hungarian leader's name. Later in the chapter, the name appears correctly as "Béla Kun," and it appears that way in both occurrences in the earlier *Partisan Review* version. Because the "Whon" seems to be a copyediting mistake, we have omitted it.

† A coastal town in Upper Normandy, known for its beautiful chalk cliffs.

‡ Apparently one of Lowell's fictional or composite characters.

Club, for fear Admiral Tommy'll assault me with five new chapters of his *Who Won the Battle of Jutland?*"

After the heat and push of Commander Billy, it was pleasant to sit in the shade of the Atkinsons. Cousin Ledyard wasn't exactly an admiral: he had been promoted to this rank during the World War and had soon reverted back to his old rank of captain. In 1926 he was approaching the retiring age and was still a captain. He was in charge of a big, stately, comfortable, but anomalous warship, which seldom sailed further than hailing distance from its Charlestown drydock. He was himself stately and anomalous. Serene, silver-maned, and Spanish-looking, Cousin Ledyard liked full-dress receptions and crowed like a rooster in his cabin crowded with liveried Filipinos, Cuban trophies, and racks of experimental firearms, such as pepper-box pistols and a machine gun worked by electric batteries. He rattled off Spanish phrases, told first-hand adventure stories about service with Admiral Schley,* and reminded one of some landsman and diplomat commanding a galleon in Philip II's Armada. With his wife's money he had bought a motor launch which had a teak deck and a newfangled diesel engine. While his warship perpetually rode at anchor, Cousin Ledyard was forever hurrying about the harbor in his launch. "Oh, Led Atkinson has dash and his own speedboat!" This was about the best my father could bring himself to say for his relative. Commander Billy, himself a man of action, was more sympathetic: "Tommy's about a hundred horse and buggy power." Such a dinosaur, however, had little to offer an '07 Annapolis graduate. Billy's final judgment was that Cousin Ledyard knew less *trig* than a schoolgirl, had been promoted through mistaken identity or merely as "window-dressing," and "was really plotting to put airplane carriers in square sails to stem the tide of our declining Yankee seamanship." Mother lost her enthusiasm for Captain Atkinson's stately chatter—he was "unable to tell one woman from another."

Cousin Ledyard's wife, a Schenectady Hoes distantly related to my still living Great-Grandmother Myers, was twenty years younger than her husband. This made her a trying companion; with the energy of youth she demanded the homage due to age. Once while playing in the Mattapoisett tennis tournament, she had said to her opponent, a woman her own age

---

* Winfield Scott Schley (1839–1911), a rear admiral in the U.S. Navy who made his name as the hero of the Battle of Santiago de Cuba during the Spanish-American War.

but married to a young husband, "I believe I'll call you Ruth; you can call me Mrs. Atkinson." She was a radiant Christian Scientist, darted about in smart serge suits and blouses frothing with lace. She filled her purse with Science literature and boasted without irony of "Boston's greatest grand organ" in the Christian Science mother temple on Huntington Avenue. As a girl, she had grown up with our Myers furniture. We dreaded Mrs. Atkinson's descents on Revere Street. She pooh-poohed Mother's taste, snorted at our ignorance of Myers family history, treated us as mere custodians of the Myers furniture, resented alterations, and had the memory of a mastodon for Cousin Cassie's associations with each piece. She wouldn't hear of my mother's distress from neuralgia, dismissed my asthma as "growing-pains," and sought to rally us by gossiping about healers. She talked a prim, sprightly babble. Like many Christian Scientists, she had a bloodless, euphoric, inexhaustible interest in her own body. In a discourse which lasted from her first helping of roast beef through her second demitasse, Mrs. Atkinson held us spellbound by telling how her healer had "surprised and evaporated a cyst inside a sac" inside her "major intestine."

I can hear my father trying to explain his resignation from the Navy to Cousin Ledyard or Commander Billy. Talking with an unnatural and importunate jocularity, he would say, "Billy Boy, it's a darned shame, but this State of Massachusetts doesn't approve of the service using its franchise and voting by mail. I haven't had a chance to establish residence since our graduation in '07. I think I'll put my blues in mothballs and become a *cit* just to prove I still belong to the country. The directors of Lever Brothers' Soap in Cambridge . . . I guess for *cits*, Billy, they've really got something on the ball, because they tell me they want me on their team."

Or Father, Cousin Ledyard, Commander Billy, and I would be sitting on after dinner at the dining-room table and talking man to man. Father would say, "I'm afraid I'll grow dull and drab with all this goldbricking ashore. I am too old for tennis singles, but too young for that confirmed state of senility known as golf."

Cousin Ledyard and Commander Billy would puff silently on their cigars. Then Father would try again and say pitifully, "I don't think a naval man can ever on the *outside* replace the friends he made during his years of wearing the blue."

Then Cousin Ledyard would give Father a polite, funereal look and say, "Speaking of golf, Bob, you've hit me below the belt. I've been flubbing away at the game for thirty years without breaking ninety."

Commander Billy was blunter. He would chaff Father about becoming a "beachcomber" or "purser for the Republican junior chamber of commerce." He would pretend that Father was in danger of being jailed for evading taxes to support "Uncle Sam's circus." *Circus* was Commander Billy's slang for the Navy. The word reminded him of a comparison, and once he stood up from the table and bellowed solemnly: "Oyez, oyez! Bob Lowell, our bright boy, our class baby, is now on a par with 'Rattle-Ass Rats' Richardson, who resigned from us to become press agent for Sells-Floto Circus, and who writes me: 'Bilgy Dear—Beating the drum ahead of the elephants and the spangled folk, I often wonder why I run into so few of my classmates.'"

Those dinners, those apologies! Perhaps I exaggerate their embarrassment because they hover so grayly in recollection and seem to anticipate ominously my father's downhill progress as a civilian and Bostonian. It was to be expected, I suppose, that Father should be in irons for a year or two, while becoming detached from his old comrades and interests, while waiting for the new life.

I used to sit through the Sunday dinners absorbing cold and anxiety from the table. I imagined myself hemmed in by our new, inherited Victorian Myers furniture. In the bleak Revere Street dining room, none of these pieces had at all that air of unhurried condescension that had been theirs behind the summery veils of tissue paper in Cousin Cassie Julian-James's memorial volume. Here, table, highboy, chairs, and screen—mahogany, cherry, teak— looked nervous and disproportioned. They seemed to wince, touch elbows, shift from foot to foot. High above the highboy, our gold National Eagle stooped forward, plastery and doddering. The Sheffield silver-plate urns, more precious than solid sterling, peeled; the bodies of the heraldic mermaids on the Mason-Myers crest blushed a metallic copper tan. In the harsh New England light, the bronze sphinxes supporting our sideboard looked as though manufactured in Grand Rapids. All too clearly no one had worried about synchronizing the grandfather clock's minutes, days, and months with its mellow old Dutch seascape-painted discs for showing the phases of the moon. The stricken, but still striking gong made sounds like steam banging through pipes. Colonel Myers' monumental Tibetan screen had been impiously shortened to fit it for a low Yankee ceiling. And now, rough and gawky, like some Hindu water buffalo killed in mid-rush but still alive with mad momentum, the screen hulked over us . . . and hid the pantry sink.

Our real blue-ribbon-winning *bête noire* was of course the portrait of Cousin Cassie's father, Mordecai Myers' fourth and most illustrious son: Colonel Theodorus Bailey Myers.* The Colonel, like half of our new portraits, was merely a collateral relation; though really as close to us as James Russell Lowell, no one called the Colonel "Great Grand Uncle," and Mother playfully pretended that her mind was overstrained by having to remember his full name, rank, and connection. In the portrait, Colonel Theodorus wore a black coat and gray trousers, an obsequiously conservative costume which one associated with undertakers and the musicians at Symphony Hall. His spats were pearl gray plush with pearl buttons. His mustache might have been modeled on the mustache of a bartender in a Western. The majestic Tibetan screen enclosed him as though he were an ancestor-god from Lhasa, a blasphemous yet bogus attitude. Mr. Myers' colonel's tabs were crudely stitched to a civilian coat; his New York Yacht Club button glowed like a carnation; his vainglorious picture frame was a foot and a half wide. Forever, his right hand hovered over a glass dome that covered a model locomotive. He was vaguely Middle-Eastern and waiting. A lady in Mother's sewing circle had pertly interpreted this portrait as, "King Solomon about to receive the Queen of Sheba's shares in the Boston and Albany Railroad." Gone now was the Colonel's place of honor at Cousin Cassie's Washington mansion; gone was his charming satire on the belles of 1850, entitled, *Nothing to Wear*, which had once been quoted "throughout the length and breadth of the land as generally as was Bret Harte's *Heathen Chinee*";† gone was his priceless collection of autographed letters of *all* the

---

* Colonel Theodorus Bailey Myers (1821–1888) was Lowell's great-grand-uncle, that is, his grandmother Kate Bailey Myers Lowell's uncle.

† Lowell is again quoting Julian-James's *Biographical Sketches of the Bailey-Myers-Mason Families, 1776–1905*, 28–29.

Signers of the Declaration of Independence—he had said once, "my letters will be my tombstone." Colonel Theodorus Bailey Myers had never been a New Englander. His family tree reached to no obscure Somersetshire yeoman named Winslowe or Lowle. He had never even, like his father, Mordecai, gloried in a scarlet War of 1812 waistcoat. His portrait was an indifferent example from a dull, bad period. The Colonel's only son had sheepishly changed his name from Mason-Myers to Myers-Mason.

Waiting for dinner to end and for the guests to leave, I used to lean forward on my elbows, support each cheekbone with a thumb, and make my fingers meet in a clumsy Gothic arch across my forehead. I would stare through this arch and try to make life stop. Out in the alley the sun shone irreverently on our three garbage cans lettered: R.T.S. LOWELL—U.S.N. When I shut my eyes to stop the sun, I saw first an orange disc, then a red disc, then the portrait of Major Myers apotheosized, as it were, by the sunlight lighting the blood smear of his scarlet waistcoat. Still, there was no *coup de théâtre* about the Major as he looked down on us with his portly young man's face of a comfortable upper New York State patroon and the friend of Robert Livingston and Martin Van Buren. Great-great-Grandfather Myers had never frowned down in judgment on a Salem witch. There was no allegory in his eyes, no *Mayflower*. Instead, he looked peacefully at his sideboard, his cut-glass decanters, his cellaret—the worldly bosom of the Mason-Myers mermaid engraved on a silver-plated urn. If he could have spoken, Mordecai would have said, "My children, my blood, accept graciously the loot of your inheritance. We are all dealers in used furniture."

The man who seems in my memory to sit under old Mordecai's portrait is not my father, but Commander Billy—*the* Commander after Father had thrown in his commission. There Billy would sit glowing, perspiring, bragging. Despite his rowdiness, he even then breathed the power that would make him a vice-admiral and hero in World War II. I can hear him boasting in lofty language of how he had stood up for democracy in the day of Lenin and Béla Kun; of how he "practiced the sport of kings" (i.e., commanded a destroyer) and combed the Mediterranean, Adriatic, and Black Seas like gypsies—seldom knowing what admiral he served under or where his next meal or load of fuel oil was coming from.

It always vexed the Commander, however, to think of the strings that had been pulled to have Father transferred from Washington to Boston. He would ask Mother, "Why in God's name should a man with Bob's brilliant cerebellum go and mess up his record by actually *begging* for that impotent field nigger's job of second in command at the defunct Boston Yard!"

I would squirm. I dared not look up because I knew that the Commander abhorred Mother's dominion over my father, thought my asthma, supposedly brought on by the miasmal damp of Washington, a myth, and considered our final flight to Boston a scandal.

My mother, on the other hand, would talk back sharply and explain to Billy that there was nothing second-string about the Boston Yard except its commandant, Admiral De Stahl, who had gone into a frenzy when he learned that my parents, supposed to live at the naval yard, had set themselves up without his permission at 91 Revere Street. The Admiral had *commanded* Father to reside at the yard, but Mother had bravely and stubbornly held on at Revere Street.

"A really great person," she would say, "knows how to be courteous to his superiors."

Then Commander Harkness would throw up his hands in despair and make a long buffoonish speech. "Would you believe it?" he'd say. "De Stahl, the anile slob, would make Bob Lowell sleep seven nights a week and twice on Sundays in that venerable twenty-room pile provided for his third in command at the yard. 'Bobby me boy,' the Man says, 'henceforth I will that you sleep wifeless. You're to push your beauteous mug into me boudoir each night at ten-thirty and each morn at six. And don't mind me laying to alongside the Missus De Stahl,' the old boy squeaks; 'we're just two oldsters as weak as babies. But Robbie boy,' he says, 'don't let me hear of you hanging on your telephone wire and bending off the ear of that forsaken frau of yours sojourning on Revere Street. I might have to phone you in a hurry, if I should happen to have me stroke.'"

Taking hold of the table with both hands, the Commander tilted his chair backwards and gaped down at me with sorrowing Gargantuan wonder: "I know why Young Bob is an only child."

Pictures of Rock

N AKED EXCEPT FOR thirty-two patches of adhesive tape, I lay
on a fluffy, lettuce-green Turkish towel.* My towel, a few inches
off-center, was enframed by the red diamond of a Navajo blanket.
I was the hub of the wheel. Wheel on wheel of red tiles, octagonal or hex-
agonal, rayed out from me. Some were mossy and sweating, others were
covered with the powdery punk of anthills. Whenever I looked up, I saw a
pale, pastel-colored china statuette of Huckleberry Finn perched on the rim
of an unpolished cement basin. The basin looked like a sand dollar the size
of a mill wheel. The statuette held a sand-colored wisp of bamboo, and was
supposed to be fishing. The dry, brilliant, brutal, ubiquitous July afternoon
penetrated everywhere. A feeble sprinkle of water fell with the sound of fine
sand. My grandfather fussed ineffectually in the fountain with a brass-shod
stick. His smart sport khaki shirt was hot as a washrag with sweat. He was
drained, paralyzed, bleached by the heat. I saw him as a warped bamboo
fishing pole propped over a pool.

The statuette was one that my grandmother Winslow had discovered
at the general store in Middleborough, and brought home because she
thought it Sicilian. And now, as it perched in its Chinese coolie's hat, its

* This chapter is set in Rock, a village in the town of Middleborough, Plymouth County, Massachusetts.
Rock is forty miles south of Boston, forty-five miles northeast of Barnstable, and twenty-four miles northeast of the seaside resort of Mattapoisett. Arthur Winslow's big vacation house was located on Marion Road
just to the northeast of the Narrows linking Assawompset and Pocksha Ponds.

dim, boudoir, Boucher hues,* and its wisp of dry bamboo, my grandfather had just hung a green ribbon with a card around its neck. The card said: "I am a callow youth. My name is Verdant Green."† Grandfather had done this when he had seen me stretched out on the green towel and smarting from the stings of thirty-two hornets. I felt humored by his whimsical, didactic attention.

And all about me soared the works of my grandfather's hands:‡ a row of blistered wooden ducks, chairs with the bark still on their frames, screens, invisible from one angle, but blacker than railroad sidings from another, and artificially decayed beams as cracked and tobacco-brown as Grandfather's stogies. The porch was ranch style, and like everything my grandfather did or built, it was stern, overgrown, unfashionable, and an inextricable tangle of rigor and languor. But what were those pumpkins, sunflowers, balloons? They were my grandparents' pitchers of afternoon ice tea, and floating with oases of mint.

All afternoon I had been moving up the back lawn on my hands and knees, and keeping an eye on the sunset cabin. The sunset cabin was made of logs and the bark had been left on, so as to have it in keeping with the chairs and tables on the screen porch. But I knew the bark would strip off and explode to powder. *Pop, pop, pop*: went the logs when I peeled them— firecrackers. But the shy, pale wood under the bark made me think of Grandfather's legs in his purple wool stockings. The knots in the wood were the knots of his varicose veins. Each piece of bark was a scab itching unbearably to pull loose. Then I saw them: the drops, the yellow drops, the sticky ooze of honey, the yellow flies bigger than a man's thumb. Little Black Sambo's tigers, miners with lamps pasted on their backs: the yellow jackets came on. Bowmen in zebra jerkins, they bent shoulder and torso. One needled me.

---

* François Boucher (1703–1770), a French rococo painter known for his pinks and blues.

† Besides simply the naïveté connoted by "green," Grandfather has in mind *The Adventures of Mr. Verdant Green* by Cuthbert M. Bede (Edward Bradley), a well-known book of 1853–1857 about the experiences and travels of a first-year Oxford undergraduate. This novel is associated with Mark Twain's *The Adventures of Huckleberry Finn* (1884–1885) below.

‡ Compare Isaiah 45:11: "This is what the Lord says—the Holy One of Israel, and its Maker: Concerning things to come, do you question me about my children, or give me orders about the work of my hands?" This allusion, along with many of the images in this paragraph, reappears in the first part of "My Last Afternoon with Uncle Devereux Winslow" in *Life Studies* (New York: Farrar, Straus and Cudahy, 1959), 59–60, reprinted in *Collected Poems*, edited by Frank Bidart and David Gewanter (New York: Farrar, Straus and Giroux, 2003), 163–64.

Then another needled me. Then another needled me. Thirty-two hornets stung me. Then the whole household stood around. I was the hub of the wheel. I saw Mr. Pittman, the farmer, run from the stable. I held up two fistfuls of grease that looked like Vaseline. I knew I was alive.

The china Huckleberry Finn from the general store in Middleborough has pale Fragonard colors. He fishes with a broom straw in a cement basin, about the size of Uncle Devereux's archery target. Out in the garden, my cousin Arthur* is winging arrows at an empty wasp's nest he has placed on the wine cup of a plaster Hebe. Pine trees peal audibly, a wooden decoy blisters and fades on a ledge; there has been no rain for twenty days. I squat on my hands and knees and pretend I am Huck Finn's dog or a camel. [. . .] My cousin Arthur's loosened bowstring barks like a revolver and just misses the china fisherman and snaps the broom-straw. "Woof, woof," I bark. "For God's sake stop acting your age!" [. . .]

I wear the calling card tied to a green ribbon. Here my grandfather has written in green ink, "I am a callow youth. My name is Verdant Green." I am a camel. A bottle of homemade beer chugs and explodes into a stein of flat homemade root beer. What are these sunflowers? They are pitchers of ice tea, floating green oases of mint. Here everything cold and drinkable tastes better than anywhere else in the world. But neither ice tea nor beer can really hold a candle to Old Aunt Sarah. Beautiful Sarah, blue eyes on a straw chaise longue . . . she is a colored target. All I can see reflected in the basin is a clothes hanger hung with pink and gray muslin. She says, "As you see, there's the world. But you mustn't worry, Bobby. There's always another on top of it, and another on top of that, and another. Do you know what's laughing all over the face of everything? *Made and given away for keeps by your fond grandfather, Arthur Winslow.*" My grandfather wears Prussian riding breeches, woolen stockings an inch thick, and he holds a handkerchief knotted in four corners. Old Aunt Sarah says, "Poor Huck, he's deaf as a post, and athirst for game." My grandfather unknots his handkerchief; he puts a paper clip in his copy of the *National Geographic Magazine* to mark

---

* Arthur Winslow (1913–1987), Lowell's first cousin once removed (his mother's first cousin), the son of Theodora Havemeyer and Admiral Cameron McRae Winslow.

pictures of the mountains near his mine in Telluride, Colorado. He prods at the water with a little stick that no one else is allowed to handle. A spout hits the beams; then the basin sprinkles. "Mercy Arthur!" Old Aunt Sarah says as she makes a dumb show of clapping her hands. "Bravo Arthur, it's the fountains of Versailles fed by the Ganges."

"I can't wait, I can't wait, I can't wait." That's what we are both thinking as Old Aunt Sarah shuffles my cards for a last game of muggins. We hear the Pierce Arrow blasting its way out of the stable. The Ford follows. My grandfather, my grandmother, Young Aunt Sarah* and all the servants are off to the Brockton Fair. "Goodbye, Verdant!" It's Cousin Arthur, the courier, perched on the running board, holding a spare tire with one hand and waving a stock catalogue with the other. We are alone.

Old Aunt Sarah is still the loveliest person in the world and a perfect brick, but there are times when small boys . . . She looks at me, pencils a Chinese mustache on the knave of hearts. "You make me tired." Then she says out loud. "Bobby, I think you can be yourself today. I am going to be myself. I am going to be *by* myself. Knock on my door at five and tell me how you do it." She floats off to her bedroom. She draws the outer green shade. She draws the inner white shade. She sleeps. She dresses and undresses. She unfolds hairpins from many-times-used tissue paper, she memorizes another chapter of *The Count of Monte Cristo*, she plays Liszt fantasias on her dummy piano. I stalk and roister through the house as though I owned it. I am Captain Hook the Crook laying a powder chain. I place a billiard ball on each step to the attic. By five I have collected all the keys and torn off the labels. Twenty-seven, almost identical. I jumble them past recognition. I shake them up like a cocktail in Young Aunt Sarah's conical straw garden hat. "Ice-tea man," I shout outside Old Aunt Sarah's door, "ice-tea man." She is telling me about Little Black Sambo and his red jacket. "First you take a cross stitch, then you take a corkscrew stitch . . ." "But what about the tigers?" "Oh they are all lapping up each other's tails and running like a merry-go-round about Little Black Sambo. They are so hot and bored, they turn into a beautiful yellow puddle. They're just like you: butter won't melt in their mouths. Now if you were Sir Walter Raleigh, you would fling Sambo's coat on the puddle, and good Queen Bess—her true

* Charlotte's sister and Lowell's aunt.

name is Goldilocks—would step across and hug you.* But first you must put all the keys back, and by that time you will have a goatee, as white as your teeth, only you won't have any teeth then, and you will be bent like a tire (each step you take, your goatee will polish your shoes), and you won't be able to take me to the Paris opera, where Mary Garden is playing Goldilocks and Queen Bess and Melisande.† Her hair is as long as a tiger . . ."

But when my grandfather returns, I am sent off to bed for supper and the next day, and I hug myself and know that no one will ever reassort the keys.

---

* Sir Walter Raleigh (1554?–1618), English explorer and writer. According to a legend, he laid his cloak over a mud puddle for Queen Elizabeth I to pass dry-footed.

† Mary Garden (1874–1967), Scottish soprano. In 1902 she sang the female lead in Claude Debussy's opera *Palléas et Mélisande*.

The House at Rock

T HE HOUSE AT ROCK was so much better than life; so much dew, so much elbow room, so much solitude. Mother was keeping house for my grandfather—five maids and no neighbors! Domina, the mistress of the house. Strange things stand out for me: the archaic telephone box—Middleborough 3 ring 13—which began the working day each morning with creaky, tense, unhurried conversations with the nearest grocery store, five miles distant; then the fierce midday drowsiness, with its new word "siesta" suggesting Corsican feuds and Southern slaveholding; then the hard old window seat, ten feet long, embroidered, and where the sunset blazed both on the mile-away lake and the empty piano, where Great-Aunt Sarah's Wagnerian themes still silently smoldered.

My life, however, raced into pure actuality each morning. The white front of the house was still mobile with dew, the green shutters were almost black with the early morning shadows, the ant tracks on the great S of inset and spaced out red tiles on the lawn path had not yet turned to dust, the elms were dewily alive, even the intermingled telephone poles seemed kindred to the trees, growing and casual. I would run and run. Past the pansy beds, under the little rose arbor, through the field path leading under dry, pollarded poplars, and into the pine grove.

First I passed the quarter of a mile stretch of tall, spaced, Germanically clean and cleared pine trees. Not a twig was allowed to lie ungathered, and on my left I could see clearly the play cabin with its log window blinds and divided log door, and on my right was the unsightly, ten-foot wire fence that separated Mr. Leland's land from my grandfather's. Then I was passing the statue of Hebe, her cup dewy, one breast showing and the base of her plaster chiton a little green at the edges. And on either side of the built-up path there was still water, four to six feet wide and four to six feet deep. And here, time after time, I could catch the yellow-spotted black turtles, as they flopped off a fallen sapling or moved encumbered through the concealing but stubbornly retarding underbrush.

Then I would run home and drop each new turtle into the garden well— not a real well, but a sort of plaster barrel about as big around as a mill wheel and ornamented with Greeks in procession.* It was an urn: after the number of turtles reached the thirties, they began to die. Despite my putting bits of old meat, green crab apples and buckets of fresh water in the urn, the turtles died and stank. Then did the joy of catching more turtles grow tedious, meaningless, and at last the sickly survivors—ten or so—were released. And the hunt, the single track of my appetite, led nowhere, and I could not understand.

---

* The story here corresponds to the one in "The Neo-Classical Urn," in *For the Union Dead* (New York: Farrar, Straus and Giroux, 1964), 47; reprinted in *Collected Poems*, edited by Frank Bidart and David Gewanter (New York: Farrar, Straus and Giroux, 2003), 358–59.

Rock

B
UT I DON'T WANT to go anywhere; I want to go to Rock."*
     This was how I used to talk in my teens† to Mother and Fa-
ther, when they planned those so highly overcolored hypothetical
summer sea trips to Gibraltar, Puget Sound, Mont-Saint-Michel or Bar Harbor. Then, if we were *en famille*, Father would sink deeper into his chair
which was leather and wood and dark and shabby, because he was a man,
and open one of his many books on self-instruction: How to Play Tennis,
How to Sail, How to Invest. Mother would pout, till her mouth looked like
a hose that had lost its nozzle. "Rock this, and Rock that," she would say.
"Boy, Rock's the word to stop a clock." But if there were guests in the room,
Mother would say, "Rock is Papá's farm *at* Rock. Bobby adores his grandfather." Was the look she gave me one of horrified love, or of loving horror?

I was never in much doubt about my father's feelings. He was most bitterly bored by my obsession. When Mother's voice rose on the words *adores
his grandfather*, Father would give what we called his "presidential" smile,

---

* This sentence prefigures the opening sentence of Robert Lowell. "My Last Afternoon with Uncle
Devereux Winslow," in *Life Studies* (New York: Farrar, Straus and Cudahy, 1959), reprinted in *Collected
Poems*, edited by Frank Bidart and David Gewanter (New York: Farrar, Straus and Giroux, 2003), 163: "I
won't go with you. I want to stay with Grandpa!"

† By "teens," Lowell may mean from the age of nine or ten on. Later in the chapter, he dates one event
as occurring in 1926: a dinner party at which his father wants to tell his friend Billy Harkness that he has
resigned from the Navy and taken a position with Lever Brothers Soap. Robert Lowell was nine in 1926, and
he turned ten in 1927, shortly before his father actually did leave the navy to join Lever Brothers.

a sheepish, terrific, wrinkled, ear-to-ear affair. Father had a peculiar way of acting, whenever he met or heard about his father-in-law, my grandfather, Arthur Winslow. Father was like some unfairly fined motorist appearing before a police captain, who was about to tear up his ticket. My grandfather had a passion for doing favors, and there was often something a little childish, nonsensical and grandiose about his generosity. Father, the recipient, was a little too grateful, a little too frisky. But from time to time, pained puzzled glances or an overly commonsensical comment would indicate that Father felt ashamed and patronized. As I was saying, Father would smile at the mention of Rock and how I adored my grandfather. Then his whole face would drain and grow as blank as if he had been blowing into a brown paper bag and had become that bag.

"Bobby," Mother would sometimes say, "we know you are dying to go to Rock. How many times must I tell you not to address your father with that inane, accusing whine!" Then Father would smile, and make a joke. Always, he seemed to treat me as though I were some relation of Mother's who was visiting and he was waiting to be introduced. He had been told my Christian name and even my nicknames, but somehow or other my surname had escaped. He would rather have had his fingernails pulled one by one than have said anything to me that was impolite, called for, or fatherly. Once though, I heard him apologizing for my manners. Mother was away, and he thought I was out of earshot. His voice was soft, amused and disgusted. "Rock, Rock, Rock," he said, "my boy is a rock-bottom Puritan. I wonder when his grandfather will learn that he dislikes anything anyone else likes."

At this time I was very keen on what I called "living for my finest self." My grandfather had dropped this phrase, in a speech delivered at the Boy Scouts Jamboree held at the old Mechanics Building on Huntington Avenue in Boston. My grandfather's ideals, my grandfather's whimsies, his gestures, his humors, his eccentricities, everything about him, expressed "finest selves." Day and night, I thought about Rock. As I walked down some hall in Boston, I imagined that my cheeks were brushed by dewy cobwebs and that I was clearing a forest path behind my grandfather. Each bath I took was a dip into Rock's Pocsha Pond. Sometimes my concentration and distraction got me into trouble. Twice, despite Grandfather's coaching, I failed my tenderfoot scout knot test. Often I was the butt of Mother's acid, exaggerating teasing. I remember wandering in once on one of her Reading Club teas. I was looking for my Iver Johnson hunting and fishing catalogue. Mother's friends tried to interest me in the book *Scott's Last Expedition to the South Pole*.* The pictures were all that a boy could ask for. There were snow deserts, ice floes, icehouses, icy huskies drawing sleds on ice. There were the heroes—above all Scott: Scott on the first pages clean-shaven, Scott on the later pages bearded; Scott on the first pages sound of limb, Scott on the later pages frost-bitten; Scott at the beginning alive, Scott at the end buried under a pitiful crooked pile of rocks. I seemed to follow the drama languidly. I pointed to some men fishing through the ice. I said, "I bet they wish they had the new South Bend level-winding, anti-backlash reel." "Oh dear," Mother said, "Bobby is thinking, thinking, thinking. His finest self wishes we would drop dead."

I feel a need to splash some whitewash on this picture. Things weren't, of course, all this bad. I have always liked that unimaginable Hieronymus Bosch expression about the "pot painting the kettle black." No less monstrous and grotesque is the picture of a writer in extremis, the writer inspired to give himself black eyes because there is no one else in range, no other way to fill the page. Yet there once really was a day, when I just about wished that everyone would drop dead.

It was a long, dim, thin, grim, gray winter Sunday in 1926. We were at our house at 91 Revere St. in Boston. Mother and Father had invited Father's old classmate Commander Bilge Harkness and his wife, Floride, to dinner. Father sat carving lamb under the gleam and gloom of Cousin Cornelius Mason-Myers' portrait. The lamb had previously been carved by Father at his carving school in Cambridge. The slices, though skillfully put back in their original positions, were overdone and chunky. Mother was looking on with an embarrassed bantering expression. She was struggling not to betray Father. What she wanted to say for the diversion of the table was, "When I first met Bob, he was taking courses in pipe-smoking and proposing to a lady."

---

* Lowell seems to have made a portmanteau of two publications on the subject: *Scott's Last Expedition*, arranged by Leonard Huxley (London: Smith, Elder, 1913), comprising the journals of Captain R. F. Scott himself as well as the reports by surviving members of his team, and the two-volume *The Worst Journey in the World: The Story of Scott's Last Expedition to the South Pole*, by Apsley G. B. Cherry-Garrard, originally published in 1922.

I addressed Commander Harkness with a frank, dishonest stutter. "S-sir?" I said, "does your w-wife let you carve at table?" Now I knew perfectly well that Commander Harkness and my cousin, Alfred Lowell, were the two best carvers in Boston. Once Bilge had served a small chicken to twelve people. He had given third helpings and had heaps of meat left over. My question had been asked during a moment of silence, it was followed by a dead silence. Everybody tried not to notice Father or his leg of lamb. Mrs. Harkness looked over my head, and said to Mother, "Charlotte, did I ever tell you how we lived for the first two years of our marriage on what Bilge saved by his carving?" Then Bilge said for apparently no reason at all that a naval man's pay was small but honorable. "Ha ha," I said, "my grandfather is *the* best carver in the world. He is paying for Daddy's lessons."

Father turned pale. He lifted his martini glass. "I propose a toast to Bilge Harkness. Bilge is an economist and artist. His slices of lamb are thinner than dollar bills." Then he looked to Mother. "Charlotte," he said, "please tell Bobby *for the umpty-umpth* time, that your father is only adequate. My father-in-law is not the best. Bilge is the best. Please tell Bobby that I am not a dog that you are leading on a leash." Mother turned to me. "Bobby," she said dryly. "Your father can carve whenever and wherever he wants to. When he was your age, he was studying algebra, so that he could enter the Naval Academy and support his mother and grandmother." Then Father said to Floride Harkness, but he seemed to be talking almost to himself. "You see I had no one to watch. My father died seven months before I was born."* He went on a little incoherently, "All my life, I have had to make my left hand learn what most men's right hands know by instinct." This was about the only self-pitying or at all personal remark that I ever heard Father make.

Now all this time something unparalleled was going on. The silver cocktail shaker was still going around the table. The reason Father was emotional and annoyed was because he was a little drunk. The reason why he was a little drunk was because he wanted to be openhearted with Commander Harkness. He wanted to be openhearted with Commander Harkness because he wanted to announce his resignation from the Navy, and

---

* A question mark in the draft shows that Lowell wasn't sure about dates here. As a footnote in "91 Revere Street" points out, Robert T. S. Lowell II died *four* months before Robert T. S. Lowell III was born.

even persuade Commander Harkness to join him at his new job with Lever Brothers Soap.

Now I knew there was something special about being the son of a naval officer. I knew that all our relatives and all my father's colleagues felt that Mother was forcing his hand. Desertion, robbery and confusion were looking me in the eyes. Rock was my answer to Lever Brothers. Rock was the iron wedge and abstraction that my fears lest Father resign were driving into my brain. Such a reaching, generalized connection will, I am sure, sound simpleminded and melodramatic. And that was the whole trouble. We were all born with hardening arteries. Our drives ran in grooves. Mother wanted to live in Boston, and be a daughter. Father wanted to live on his battleship, and be a bachelor just about to announce his engagement. I wanted to live at Rock twelve months of the year. I wanted be the Napoleon of my daydreams, an orphan who lived on a trust fund, a fisherman who lived on fish that cooked themselves. "I don't want to go anywhere; I want to go to Rock." This was my confession of faith; I saw no nonsense in it; I meant it word for word.

Father's mind was made up, but somehow he never got up the courage to make his announcement about the resignation. Instead, he began to kid me. "Bilge," Father said, "my son's a second Increasingly Cottonheaded Mather.* He's so straightlaced, he can't give an inch, he can't give a second thought. Boy," my father pointed a finger that trembled on purpose at me, and his voice was an imitation of the passionate croaking bass of my uncle Cameron, the Admiral, "the only thing you will retain or save in life is your face." Then it seemed as though the wind had quickly gone out of the martinis. Father was again levelheaded and sober. "The boy's grandfather, Mr. Winslow, has great plans for him. He has good plans for all of us. Nobody in the world has better intentions than Mr. Winslow. Our trouble has always been in getting down to brass tacks."

I had long known that Father wasn't going to stick in the navy. But I now felt that he would never speak out about anything. I began to dig in my mind through the floor. I was digging to China, and I was just about ready

* A play on the names of two notable Puritan ministers in the Massachusetts Bay Colony: Increase Mather (1639–1723) and his son, Cotton Mather (1663–1728).

to drop us all in it one by one. I was just about ready to wish that we would all drop dead.*

The dining room was as was usual with us on a winter morning, glacial. This was because Mother had been airing since breakfast. She was death on dirt and stuffiness, and believed that a healthy house should be so cold it hurt. When Mrs. Harkness suggested that our pipes were in danger of freezing and bursting, Mother smiled. It was as though she had been told she had the best desserts in Boston.

The dining room was as was usual with us, spotless. This was because Mother was death on dirt. Two hours earlier, she had put on a white chamois glove that covered her forearm. She had then run a finger over and under the windowsills, mantelpiece and table. No groove or corner in chair or table was overlooked. Our upstairs maid, Katherin Gannon, was given hell for each smudge or mote of dust that turned up on the glove. No modern bathroom, no battleship, no country moon in midsummer was as clean as Mother's dining room. I can see her eye following Commander Harkness's hand as he waved a cigarette through the air. How greedily her eyes would brighten and drop. Each ash that fell was a treasure she could dispose of.

---

* Perhaps an expansion on Huckleberry Finn's recurrent invocations of a death wish: for example, "I got to feeling so mean and so miserable I most wished I was dead."

Arthur Winslow II

GRANDFATHER WINSLOW SHREDDED a clot of brown sugar on his huckleberries. He poured on chilled, blue, nonfattening, skimmed milk, then thin cream, then solid cream that had to be coaxed with a spoon. Brown sugar, skimmed milk, thin and solid cream went on his baked apple and on his dish of Dutch clabber. His Colonial salt grinder cackled and squeaked, as he grated out cinnamon. The Lazy Susan in front of him was loaded with honey, Dundee marmalade, five or six flavors of jam, and a dozen varieties of spices. The long copper warming plate behind him was heated by five alcohol lamps and was heaped with fried eggs, bacon, sausages, blueberry muffins, corn muffins, and English muffins.

My grandfather pulled out a notebook and a stubby indelible carpenter's pencil. He gave me a foxy, make-believe stern look. "Lumberjack," he said to me, "shall we show your father how we drink water?" He turned to Mother and began teasing her with a courtly rowdiness. "Charlotte," he said, "I hear Bob is getting rich faster than the Democratic mayor of Boston. I'm going to ask him for a loan. This lumberjack is ruining me by sawing up twenty-five logs a day at a penny a log." For a second, Father looked as though he were being sued by his insurance company. He said, "I'm glad the fellow is earning our breakfast." The eyes of the whole table were on me. I pushed my chair back, and handed Father my napkin, as though I were Gus Sonnenberg,* the wrestler, tossing his gorgeous dressing gown to an attendant. In unison, my grandfather and I gulped down three glasses of cold water straight. "Purge and gorge," he said.

"They certainly are stout fellows," Father mumbled to my grandmother. "Arthur," she called down the table, "I want you to remove those boring placards you tacked up in the bathroom, saying, *Please kindly do not use the water wastefully; the tank is small and the pump old and feeble.* You and Bobby drink the ocean dry, and then expect Bob and Charlotte to use the water in their basins twice." "Papá," Young Aunt Sarah put in, "do you know why Billy Ashton, the lieutenant governor,† is the best preserved man of sixty? Every morning before breakfast and three hundred and sixty-five days of the year, he makes a perfect jackknife dive from his Ipswich pier into the Atlantic." I felt empty and slighted, and thought of how Mother made fun of what she called Sarah's beau monde. "Grampa," I said, "isn't the lieutenant governor pretty small potatoes to a lumberjack?" My grandfather handed me the notebook and pencil. Under the date August 2, 1927, I made three little purple lines for my glasses of water.

Silence. "Papá," Mother said, "don't you think Bob looks peakèd? They call him the undertaker at Lever Brothers. I think he is in love with his soap vat." "Charlotte," my grandmother said, "you talk about Bob as if he were deaf and dumb and two and a doll." Young Aunt Sarah said, "Bob must be tired of a new promotion every month." Father said, "Summer is the season for our all-out Lifebuoy drive."‡ Mother said, "Bob hasn't been promoted *this* summer." Young Aunt Sarah said, "Billy Ashton sponsored President Carpenter§ for the Somerset Club. Shall I ask Billy to put in a word for Bob?"

Mother said, "At the Lever Brothers' reception, Sir Ralph Leverhulme, the son of Lord Leverhulme, the English president, had to rescue me from

---

* Gus Sonnenberg (1898–1944), a German American football player and world heavyweight wrestling champion.

† No Billy Ashton was ever a lieutenant governor of Massachusetts. In 1927, Frank G. Allen (1874–1950) held that office.

‡ Lifebuoy was a brand of notably acidic soap, originally marketed by Bob Lowell's employer, Lever Brothers of Cambridge, Massachusetts.

§ The president of the American branch of Lever Brothers in 1927 was actually Francis A. Countway.

those boring Carpenters.* 'Sir Ralph,' I said, 'I have been telling Mr. Carpenter why your father should make my husband a knight of the Garter.
Bob is the one man in America who really believes it is criminal to buy Ivory
Soap instead of Lux.† I haven't seen my husband for a year. He drags home
at eight in the evening and pretends he is being promoted to Lord Lux.
You and Mr. Carpenter are treating Bob like Egyptian Pharaohs.' 'The Le-
vers are Norman Irish,' he said, 'but the Near Eastern family we are usually
confused with is the Rothschilds, not the Cleopatra.' Well, Sir Ralph was so
witty. I think he had heard the stories about Mr. Carpenter's mother being
the daughter of a Tennessee tenant farmer. Anyway, he burlesqued Mr. Carpenter's accent and said, 'Some Gol-durn mules you can't tote away from
the corncrib, eh Carpenter?' Sir Ralph was most interested in Bob's work in
radio at Washington. 'Are there radios even in *soap*?' 'Gracious Lady, good
heavens! No,' Sir Ralph said. He then told such amusing anecdotes about his
own war service under Lord Jellicoe at Jutland.‡ It seems that Lord Jellicoe
had memorized every order ever given by Nelson and was as out of date
as a commander of our Civil War ironclads. Sir Ralph seemed to be under
the misapprehension that Bob was only on loan to Lever Brothers from the
Navy. He kept saying, 'Ours is a purifying vocation. I am sure that Uncle
Sam won't find your husband corrupted by his stay with us. I said, 'Bob has
resigned forever. Your company made him such brilliant offers.' 'Oh, I see,'
Sir Ralph said, 'your husband is like Eurydice or Lot's wife; one look back
and he will turn into a bar of soap.'"

"Charlotte," my grandfather said, "your uncle Cameron is editing Lord
Jellicoe's papers. Your young man was most misinformed." He looked at
Father: "Bob, does Sir Ralph have any authority over the American branch
of Lever Brothers?" "None," my father said, "I don't see how Carp puts
up with those visiting firemen."§ Young Aunt Sarah leaned toward Father

* At the time, the chair of Lever Brothers was William Hulme Lever (1888–1949), the son of William
Hesketh Lever, 1st Viscount Leverhulme (1851–1925), who founded the company. It was under William
Hesketh Lever that the company purchased a soap manufacturer in Cambridge, Massachusetts, in 1898 and
thus effectively entered the U.S. market. Lowell invented the name of the scion, "Sir Ralph."

† Lux was another Lever Brothers brand. Ivory was a competing soap produced by Procter & Gamble.

‡ John Jellicoe, First Earl Jellicoe (1859–1935), was an Admiral of the Fleet in the British Royal Navy. He
commanded the Grand Fleet at the Battle of Jutland in May 1916 during the Great War. Although the battle
was a British success, Jellicoe's command was controversial, and he was removed from service in 1917.

§ "Fireman" here means a person serving in the U.S. Navy who operates and maintains a ship's engines and
other machinery.

and said in a low voice, "Bob, I think they are so lucky to have you. Billy says that Carpenter is racking his brains for masterful young executives." My father wasn't attending. "The English had the Germans outnumbered two to one," he said to no one in particular, "but ballistics show they were outgunned." "But if the German fleet was bottled up for the duration . . ." Young Aunt Sarah said.

My father seemed deeply absorbed in my grandfather. Without shifting in his chair or bending his back, Grandfather slowly raised a pitcher until it was two feet above his tall cylindrical glass. Unpasteurized milk foamed like beer; pinpoints of milk stippled the Lazy Susan. As Father stretched forward, his clapboard-stiff white flannels and his sleeveless sweater knitted by Mother jerked apart and showed the imitation leather attachments of his Army and Navy Store suspenders. "Oh Bob," Mother said fondly, reproachfully, "you mustn't economize on clothes. You're not like Papá who can wear anything." He could. This morning he presided like Lear at the head of the table in his soft khaki shirt, his stiff khaki riding britches, his old Stuttgart tweed coat, and brown-green hose an inch thick that matched his eyes. Like Lear, he flung his head back and snuffed the steam of unsweetened black chicory-flavored coffee shipped to him from North Carolina by Cousin Nell. His eye passed over the five jam jars and then rested angrily on a streamlined silver cigarette lighter. "Mary," he said, "I never could understand why you adulterate your coffee with sugar."

The day was clearly off on the wrong foot. Just the night before, Grandfather had portentously passed by his usual after-dinner game of cowboy pool, and had brought out the first twenty manuscript pages of his biography of his father: *Francis Winslow, His Forebears and Life*.* The whole gang—Grandmother, Old Aunt Sarah, Young Aunt Sarah, Teddy Brooks, Mother, Father, and I—sat about Grandfather in a circle on the glass porch. Bats hawked across the lavender sky and made the windows look like a Klee painting. Above us, we could hear the pitiful panting of the feeble pump as it labored to refill its small tank. Grandfather started to read. "My father's life, in a modest way, was an epic of a relatively unimportant career, marked by no great events or accomplishments, but characterized by patient persever-

---

* Arthur Winslow, *Francis Winslow: His Forebears and Life* (Norwood, MA: Plimpton Press, private printing, 1935).

ance, coupled with a high sense of honor in his public and private relations. Though my father left his widow and children in very straitened circumstances, he left them an heritage of character and fine conduct which makes a recital of his life well worth while for future generations . . ." The response was less than he might have hoped for. After a sharp debate on the exact location of Tangier and Algiers, stopping points on one of Great-Grandfather Winslow's voyages, my grandmother said, "Arthur, are you certain this small epic should be published? Family memorials are not of interest outside the family." "Why Mary," Old Aunt Sarah said, "your mother's *Plantation Sketches* are charming."* Young Aunt Sarah said, "*All* Southerners are charming talkers and writers." "Sir," my father said, "what was your father's rank when he passed away?" "Mr. Winslow," Teddy Brooks said, "why do you write *he was ten years of age*, instead of *he was ten*?" "Grampa, your father was like Daddy, a naval officer who never was in a war," I said. Mother said, "Papá has spent six months on these thirty pages."

Yes, the day was off on the wrong foot. Young Aunt Sarah, though dutifully down on time, was again insisting on fasting. "Just a thimbleful of orange juice, Ovaltine, and a sliver of burnt toast," she said. "It's so tonic and easy on the servants." "Most unfortunate and inconvenient," my grandfather said. Young Aunt Sarah was lighting up. If there was anything that Grandfather detested, it was a woman smoking at meals. Aunt Sarah's never-inhaled, expensive, and pretentiously innocent denicotinized Parliaments were particularly wounding to him. "Taisy," he said, "the gratuitous vulgarity of your behavior . . ." But Teddy Brooks had been thinking night and day about his school dramatics. "Mr. Winslow," he interrupted, "from the way you swing your arms when you pour milk, I'll bet anything you played Ariel at Boston Latin, and were perfectly stunning." This was hitting below the belt; there were only five diversions Grandfather approved of: farm work, walking, tennis on a homemade court, pool and chess. "In my day," he said, "a boy would rather have been found dead than seen in petticoats." To change the subject, Young Aunt Sarah said, "Isn't Wordly Wallace coming in a few minutes to play with Bobby and Teddy? Papá, I have

---

* Lowell's great-grandmother Margaret Mordecai Devereux (1805–1910) wrote her memoirs of her slave-holding days in *Plantation Sketches* (Cambridge, MA: Riverside Press, private printing, 1906).

just been reading Wordly's father's new printed sermons. Papá, you probably call them light reading, but I find them quite over my head." "New?" Grandfather snapped. "There's nothing new on the New Testament under the sun!" At this point and to keep Grandfather in a good temper, we would all have gladly conceded that even Bible reading was faddish and frivolous.

Arthur Winslow III:
Dunbarton

MY GRANDFATHER WINSLOW was at his best with children in the country. He didn't like his country plain, however, and Grandpa's big moments, his purple passages, were our trips to the Stark Cemetery in Dunbarton, New Hampshire.* One raked leaves or dragged away fallen branches there. A still better way to spend one's time was to collect newts from the disused millpond, whose water, heavily wood-stained, was almost as red as the jackets of silver-wigged Colonial officials, whose portraits hung in the State Capitol in nearby Concord. The newts—that is, the mature ones—were dark yellow and looked like scrolls of old dried-up lemon peel. The young newts were frail and scarlet like a sliver from the setting sun or a candle shining through the rosy, translucent fingers of a little girl.

Before beginning work on the graveyard, my grandfather would drive, if the weather were fair and mild, to East Weare for Mr. Burroughs.† Mr.

---

* When Lowell visited the Stark Cemetery in the 1920s with his grandfather, it was on the west end of Winslow Road by General John Stark's old dam at the tip of Stark Pond (the "disused millpond" below). In 1962 the whole site was moved, along with Lowell's parents' remains, one mile south to higher ground on Mansion Road, away from the area that was in danger of flooding. It was in this new location that Lowell was buried fifteen years later.

† East Weare was a village in the eastern part of Weare, New Hampshire, a town only fifteen minutes from Dunbarton.

Burroughs was ninety or so and a survivor of the last days of the Civil War. He called my grandfather "Arthur" without a "Mister" and made him feel rooted in the soil of New Hampshire. He was tall, quavery-voiced, and had a full head of silver, black and hay-colored hair. He was mild and beautiful and always brought his own lunch. His wife prepared a thermos bottle for him of lukewarm, shockless coffee that was all milk and grounds. If we visited her house in East Weare, she brought out purple glasses that had once belonged to the local Church of England and served us glasses of bad homemade red wine that was so sugary it looked like crab-apple jelly topped with a cake of paraffin. She was dumpy, ugly, shrewish and dying of cancer. Something in the way she used to say my grandfather's name, Mr. Win-slow, has always made me suspect that she had little patience for his role of country squire and patron.

My grandfather Winslow preferred the solitary companionship of his grand-children to human society. In cities, even among the starred historic sites of his revered Boston, he had the bearing of a man monotonously dressed in his Sunday best. His only truly imposing and gay moments indoors were Christmas and Thanksgiving dinners. Then, bountiful Abraham, he stood carving. Our best times together were our long weekend outings to the Stark Cemetery in Dunbarton, New Hampshire. My grandfather's style of driving a car was willful: in order to save gasoline and feel close to nature, he used to coast with his engine switched off. Our drives from Boston into ever colder, rockier and more hilly country, the motor now coughing, now eerily silent, were like going on crusade.

Everything in Dunbarton was an oxymoron, a struggle of good and evil: the sun rose on frozen leaves; all physical and moral color was touched with Caravaggio-like emphasis. We never came indoors until we had seen the sun set. There, somewhat misanthropically, somewhat too hurrahingly, I used to play about the graves of my ancestors. I daydreamed with healthy, burning red cheeks and a mind mossy with the dates on the gravestones. The dates often indicated tragedy: death in childhood, at childbirth, at sea. They were authentic nineteenth-century deaths that each year aged and grew dearer to us. Our Stark forebears, both men and women, seem to have been shy, mannish people, plainspoken to a fault, yet uncouthly poetic in choosing

Dunbarton to be buried in. There, no new house had been built in a hundred years; there, Mount Washington was visible on the clearest days; and there, their quiet, quarrelsome lives still edified without overawing. Nothing came easier to my grandfather than his praise of their hard-won virtues.

I was first taken by my grandfather to enjoy the Stark Cemetery late in the 1920s. The last-laid gravestone was then my grandfather's mother, Mary Nelson Winslow, dead in 1903. Next to her was my grandfather's father, Lieutenant-Commander Francis Winslow, dead in 1862,* next *his* grandmother, Elizabeth née Stark Winslow dead in 1823, at childbirth! The cynosure of the whole family group was the eight-foot obelisk of my grandfather's great-grandfather, Major Caleb Stark.† The obelisk, a dated and now unrecapturable pomposity, used to remind me of the Bunker Hill Monument, the Washington Monument, the gray, flauntingly occult pyramid on dollar bills. The Major's obelisk dwarfed the stones of his descendants, for unlike them he was at least by association historic: he served as a boy of sixteen under the indisputably historic father, General John Stark, the conqueror of the British at Bennington. The General was somehow inevitably *not* buried at Dunbarton. He lay thirty miles away at Manchester. Above him rode his equestrian statue, below him rolled the mill-harnessed Merrimack, all about him lay the gardens of the Stark State Park.‡ This was fame, yet my grandfather curiously took only a lukewarm interest in the General John Stark remains and only once made, half by accident at that, a trip to the Manchester monument.§ Yet the General was the one and true sun by which the graves at Dunbarton shone on us with glory. For the rest my grandfather rejoiced that our people in the Stark Cemetery, no commoners, had possessed the modest grandeur of country gentry in their lives, and were now in their death restfully unknown.

---

* Francis Winslow's body as such is not interred in Dunbarton. A commander of USS *R. R. Cuyler*, he died of yellow fever on August 26, 1862, while at sea. Hence Lowell's allusion in the poem "Dunbarton" to his great-grandfather's "stone but not the bones" at the cemetery.

† Arthur Winslow's grandmother Sarah Stark Winslow (1794–1819) was a daughter of Major Caleb Stark (1759–1838), who served in the Continental Army.

‡ The Stark Park in Manchester is located at River Road.

§ Arthur Winslow could not have visited the equestrian statue of John Stark, for it was not erected until 1948. More likely, Winslow visited Stark Cemetery, with a small obelisk marking General John Stark's grave, located in the same park as the statue, a little over three hundred feet west of it toward the Merrimack River.

My grandmother, Mary née Devereux Winslow, came from Raleigh, North Carolina. Small, witty, untortured, she played bridge twice a week with two different groups and hated two Presidents of the United States: Lincoln, because of the pious tone taken by northerners; and Herbert Hoover, because once, as my grandfather's superior, he had come to dinner with black fingernails. Nothing bored her more than American history, yet she read whatever French novels the Boston Athenaeum supplied and could name and date the kings of France. She found much to be glum about in my grandfather. He liked his relatives, she thought, better than people. He liked his poor and tedious relatives better than the rich and amusing ones. He liked relatives who were unable to manage their affairs better than the ones who could. He liked dead relatives better than the living relatives, and of these preferred those who were mere names to those who had left some mark and needed no help.

All this was true. My grandfather's favorite ancestor was Mary Chilton Winslow, of whom one knew nothing except that she was the first woman to touch Plymouth Rock and had the Chilton Club named in her honor. A great day in my grandfather's life was when he brought his three-year-old granddaughter Mary Chilton Winslow* to assist in the dedication of a statue to the original Mary Chilton. Unfortunately, there was nearby a statue to another of our ancestresses, one only too well known, Anne Hutchinson, in my grandfather's words the notorious troublemaker. Anne Hutchinson had disputed the authority of men, the ministers and Governor Winthrop and had then been luridly massacred by the Indians.

On winter evenings, my grandfather would leave my grandmother as soon as he had finished dinner and shut himself up in his library. This room was an extraordinary one, designed and partially built by my grandfather. It was assertively long, almost as long, it seemed, as one could hit a golf ball. The furniture was oak and leather. The walls were oak panels. In the book cases, leagues of them, there was only an expensive set of Dickens, a dozen copies of *Who's Who*, the *Britannica*, and three autographed copies of

---

* Robert Lowell's cousin Mary ("Polly") Chilton Winslow was the third daughter of the early-deceased John Devereux Winslow and Alice C. Thorndike.

novels by Owen Wister, which had been given to his great-aunt, Charlotte Stark.* There was a glassed-in model of my grandfather's schooner, the *Water Witch*, and two second prizes won by the *Water Witch* in New York Yacht Club races in which there had been only one other boat, the Ayers' *Queen Mab*, in the *Water Witch*'s class.† Lord knows what else filled up space in the library. I remember a shelf with pictures of Norway and walking sticks marked with names of mountain peaks in Norway, which my grandfather had climbed. There were bear rugs, and no one could deny that the library was wonderfully and utterly massive. Yet there were drawbacks. The heating system wouldn't work in the library unless the furnace was turned up to a degree that made the rest of the house like a hothouse. So, shiveringly, one would immediately set to work and light the big oak-paneled fireplace. Unfortunately, the fireplace never drew except when there was a strong south wind. Instead, it reeked and gave out a chill, like the radiator of a car before it has warmed. Then the library windows were thrown open to get rid of the smoke. Then coffee was served and one sat shivering, shuddering and red-eyed and talked to my grandfather.

* Charlotte Stark (1799–1889), sister of Arthur's grandmother Sarah Stark Winslow. Both women are buried in Dunbarton. Lowell misremembered the detail about the autographed copies of Owen Wister's three novels. Given that Wister (1860–1938) published his first book in 1891, Charlotte Stark could not have been given any of them: she died before the first one was published.

† Nathaniel F. Ayer (?–1948) had a seventy-seven-foot Herreshoff yacht called the *Queen Mab*.

Uncle Cameron

O H BOBBY, not the tongs to *poke* with!" The big twin goblets of grade A milk on the fumed oak stool between us had the bubbly watered azure of glass balls used to float lobster nets and local color in the New Bedford glass factory that Mother and I had once rummaged on alternate summer Thursdays for flawed markdowns. Each goblet was half emptied. The untoasted Triscuits on the salver beside them were untouched, and their flesh was half-revealed by a twist of wax paper. I was bending to the fire and tamping about on the hearth with my gross, novel, squeaky shoes like a bear that has just had its claws cut and is learning to walk on two feet. The shoes were unsuitable, had brass toe guards, quasi-octagonal quarter-inch staghorn cleats, and had been bought by my great-uncle Cameron* on a lark for Indian summer golf and maybe to tease my grandfather. After Cameron's death they had lain smothered by mothballs in a wardrobe of castoffs. Grandiose, nouveau riche and obsolete, they looked and smelled like a mah-jongg box. "Great-Uncle Cameron was a dreamboat." Neither Mother nor I could have used this expression, but that's what the shoes said to us each time they marred her hearth.

My uncle liked to live in mint and clover. He had siphons on every table,

---

* Rear Admiral Cameron McRae Winslow (1854–1932), the son of Commander Francis Winslow and older brother of Lowell's grandfather Arthur Winslow, served with distinction in the U.S. Navy during the Spanish-American War and World War I. In 1915 and 1916, he was the commander in chief of the U.S. Pacific Fleet.

six children after he was forty, ten servants, fires that roared like Christmas on all five floors of his house on the sunny side of Commonwealth Avenue.* He was a notorious Anglophile, and if Theodore Roosevelt had still been President, he would have commanded the Atlantic Fleet and held it in readiness on the day when, as he used to say, the Archduke Franz Ferdinand was bushwhacked by Bohemian thugs. He did everything more expensively, smartly and expertly than my grandfather, whose golf, fly casting and puritanical granite gave him the willies. At the time of Cameron's late marriage to Aunt Dora, a Viennese and Manhattan Havemeyer,† there had been much backstage kidding in the family. His two brothers and sister had called the bride the ice, icing, powdered sugar queen. All of them had fallen out with him twice a week and fallen in thrice. But my uncle's hand-me-downs had allowed at least ten nephews to dress on occasion like the London stage, and I can still remember his son Arthur's rawhidy coonskin coat that hung three years in my closet waiting for the Harvard-Yale game.

At the age of seventy-five, and seven months before dying of a brain hemorrhage, my uncle Cameron had gone on an inspection tour to our family graveyard in Dunbarton. His cheeks were pinker than raw salmon and his Edinburgh plaids were stone gray, when, jovial and tough, he went poking and fuming over the grounds, and had run into old Charlie Stark.‡ Charlie, once a fiendish skeet shot and New Hampshire's gold medalist, was a dirty, courteous old squire with his fly unbuttoned. The Winslows, after interminable litigation, had done him out of his wardenship of the graveyard; then, in the twinkling of an eye and helped by the county court which he knew like one of his shotguns, he did Great-Aunt Sarah out of Aunt Lottie's will.§ Meeting my uncle after a quarter-century silence, he pretended to mistake Cam for a lumberjack.

Corporal Bonaparte in his great coat . . . what more Napoleonic could have been said of a gentleman and officer with seven months to live? The

---

* Uncle Cameron's address was 205 Commonwealth Avenue in 1931 and 1932.

† Theodora Havemeyer (1878–1945), a granddaughter of Frederick Christian Havemeyer and co-inheritor of his sugar-refinery fortune.

‡ Charles Frederick Morris Stark (1847–1934), a second cousin of Cameron Winslow—that is, they shared great-grandparents Major Caleb Stark and Sarah Stark. The couple had three daughters: Sarah Stark (Cameron's grandmother), Elizabeth Stark (Charlie F. M. Stark's grandmother), and Charlotte Stark.

§ "Aunt Lottie" is Charlotte Stark (1799–1889). See note * above, on page 114. She was Charles F. M. Stark's great-aunt.

vice admiral's snazzy diesel cutter had been built to order for his flagship in La Spezia.* Neither gunboat *Farragut*† nor the Scotch privateer Jones‡ could have taught him anything about weighing anchor in Newport at the head of a detachment of battle cruisers. But it was only when I went on a fishing trip to Nova Scotia that I learned to value the prestige of his title. My grandfather had the same determined shaving-brush mustaches, the same English outing clothes, a more sarcastic wit, and was three inches taller. But while it was "the admiral this" and "the admiral that," the guides hardly knew what to call Grandpa. One of them even said to me, "You and the admiral's brother hack with your fly rods. Mother of God, what meatballs!" Daddy, whose specialty in the service had been engineering and wireless, had different standards. He was post-Edwardian, post–Teddy Roosevelt, post-horsemanship, post-panache, post-personality and post–World War I. When questioned about his uncle-in-law, he would answer in an affectionate, disappointed undertone, "Winslow had dash and his own speedboat."

---

* A port in northwestern Italy.

† A U.S. Navy destroyer built in 1934, the first of a new class of destroyers.

‡ John Paul Jones (1747–1792), a naval commander of Scottish origins, served in the Continental Navy and was famous for his exploits during the American Revolution.

Arthur Winslow IV

WHEN I WAS eleven or twelve, I was expected to make sense when spoken to and to work at my lessons as if I were being paid. My best times were the weekends when my grandfather Winslow carried me off to *Chardesa*, his farm at Rock.* Rock, some forty miles south of Boston, was a little one-street and one-filling-station village near a group of lakes with Indian names—Snippatuit, Assawamsett, Big and Little Pocshaw!† The Rock I knew in the 1920s was without variety or history. Ignored once by King Philip's braves,‡ Colonial architects and New England men of letters, it now attracted neither society nor factories.§ Its landscape was flat; its houses, very much the real thing, were white

---

* The name Arthur Winslow chose for his estate was not unlike other names wealthy Bostonians coined for their summer homes in Rock, lined along Marion Road and stretching east to Pocksha and Assawompset Ponds. The summer residents expanded existing houses into mansions and gave them posh names. William S. Leland built his "Edgewood" in about 1901, Henry A. Wyman completed his "Chippoponquet" in 1901, and Clifford R. Weld finished his Colonial Revival "Moreland Acres" in 1904. Two of those homes have survived: William Storer Eaton's (on Long Point Road in neighboring Lakeville) and Weld's (at 332 Marion Road).

† Today the names are Snipatuit Pond, Assawompset Pond, and Pocksha Pond. Pocksha Pond designates two connected reservoirs of different sizes. Snipatuit and Assawompset are also mentioned (though spelled differently) in Lowell's poem "My Last Afternoon with Uncle Devereux Winslow," along with Great and Little Quittacas Ponds, which are located immediately south of Pocksha Pond and share waters with it.

‡ Metacomet or Metacom, also known by his English name, King Philip, was the Wampanoag chief who led Native Americans in negotiations with English colonists and then in battle against them in Metacom's (King Philip's) War (1675–1678).

§ Michael Maddigan, who has written a history of South Middleborough, describes the village in the following way: "Rock was not well known and certainly was much less well considered than areas like Mattapoi-

frame, made livable and elbowy, pulled out of shape by verandas, and all built within ten years of 1900; its one boom industry was a cranberry bog, owned by L. O. Atwood, an Englishman from Brockton, Mass.* Our farm's name, *Chardesa*, was derived from the first syllables of my grandfather's three children, Charlotte, Devereux, and Sarah. *Chardesa* had existence in print—on its letterhead stationery, in my grandparents' Social Register listing,† over their letterbox, barn and stable—but was otherwise a dead letter and so seldom spoken that its pronunciation, always chilling, was unfixed. Haphazardly cultivated, spruce, not at all *au courant*, it was too shaggy for a country estate and too baggy for a farm. Here each summer my grandfather tried to moor his family in overblown rustication; here on winter weekends he sometimes escaped from family and city and blew off steam.

Our winter trips to Rock were ostensibly for sawing up trees. We began shortly after Thanksgiving when the marshy scrub woodlands were safely frozen and continued once or twice a month until the first steady black rain in March. Our new house in Back Bay Boston, my parents' main enthusiasm, still got on my nerves. On the morning of a going-to-Rock day, I was unendurably sleepless and nervous. My head so swam with pine boughs, snow, and images of my grandfather that I could hardly handle my silver. I leaned a messy elbow on the dining room table and assumed supercilious, feline poses. I shied whenever my father spoke. Again and again I baited him buffoonishly by pretending anxiety over my mother's health because on this morning, as on all weekdays, she was having her ridiculous orange juice, dry toast and black coffee—more a fast I felt than a breakfast—in bed.

I bolted down my egg and rushed eggy-mouthed to the front door. There, changed utterly and now hysterically a good fellow, I would wave

---

sett or Marion that attracted a larger number of Bostonian social elites. [. . .] The Marion Road set may have wished to perhaps get away from Boston society (which typically packed up and relocated to Buzzards Bay, Cape Cod, the Berkshires, Bar Harbor, etc., for the summer). Rock would have afforded a more secluded location and much less formal atmosphere than the other resorts." Michael J. Maddigan, email message to the editors, February 28, 2016.

* In fact, many of the houses Lowell knew were constructed earlier, in the 1800s. Levi O. Atwood and his father, Charles N. Atwood, were probably American—they were born at Middleborough. L. O. Atwood Company, a lumber and box-making mill, produced cranberry, apple, and fish boxes rather than cranberries themselves. They were the main supplier of boxes to New England Cranberry Sales Company, the first cooperative of cranberry growers in Massachusetts, with its headquarters in the town of Middleborough, where Rock Village is located.

† The name "Chardesa" is indeed mentioned in the *Summer Social Register* of July 1913, in the supplement *Dilatory Domiciles*, on page 576.

at Nelson, who was already hoofing back and forth on the snowy sidewalk. Nelson, my grandfather's chauffeur, was a gross Dane. He had a yielding cinnamon-colored handlebar mustache. In his uniform he was so unnaturally good-humored and conspicuous that he appeared as some young and black-suited Santa Claus nourished on inhuman vegetable fats. He never rang our doorbell. Instead, putting his feet down stealthily and with the chuckle-headed smile of a practical joker, he would parade unnoticed in the cold. Behind him lay the Pierce Arrow limousine. Its accusing bottle-green glossiness, too aloof and severe for the tired city's traffic, seemed already a brook in the woods, a part of the country. I was handed in state to the suede-glove-colored cushions and buried under coarse, costly, wolverine-like lap robes. Then one saw that the barbarous early start was unnecessary and was only to stir up our household, get us on tiptoe, and express my grandfather's puppyish and high-spirited authoritarianism. Nelson would leave the Pierce in second gear and dawdle on detours through downtown Boston. We passed the State House, its Bulfinch* brick still whitewashed a fraudulent white to match its modern marble wings, the jewelers Treffery & Polly,† the cottage of the Anti-Vivisection League,‡ Goodspeed's rare books and prints,§ the Athenaeum, King's Chapel, then Chinamen,¶ an Italian fiesta, the Italian market, Italians playing Italian games under a statue of Paul Revere,** rotten warehouses smelling like a freshly opened tin of Maxwell House Coffee in our pantry, cobblestones the color of dirt in a carpet sweeper. Finally, we would stop at the office on Federal Street.††

---

* Charles Bulfinch (1763–1844), an American architect who designed the Boston State House.

† Probably the well-known Trefry & Partridge silver store at 22 Beacon Street, across from the State House. Lowell could not have passed it in the 1920s, however, for it was not established until 1940.

‡ Presumably, Lowell has in mind the 1920s quarters of the New England Anti-Vivisection Society at Tremont Temple. Neither this office nor its successor at 6 Park Street, where the society moved in 1933, could be called a "cottage."

§ One of several Goodspeed's Book Shops on Beacon Hill, most likely the one at 18 Beacon Street.

¶ Lowell lightly penciled in barely legible words "there were creeping" over the phrase "then Chinamen." He may have been contemplating a change to "then there were creeping Chinamen," though it is unclear whether he wanted to include the addition. He left no caret or line to indicate where it should go, which may suggest indecision.

** In fact, Chinatown and the traditionally Italian North End district are far out of the way if Arthur Winslow's office was the destination. The Paul Revere statue is in the middle of the North End, near the Old North Church. It is best seen from Hanover Street, across from St. Stephen's Catholic Church. As with Trefry & Partridge, the statue was not unveiled until 1940. Lowell combines his memories of the 1920s with later ones.

†† Lowell almost certainly mistakes State Street for Federal Street. In the 1920s Boston Petroleum Com-

Inside the office, my grandfather was busily "putting," as he would say, his "shoulder to the wheel." He would pull out the strong boxes filled with Cousin Belle's and Old Aunt Sarah's sealed and engraved bonds, he would dictate memoranda, he would roll and unroll his obsolete roll-top desk. Above the desk was a fading brown photograph of my grandfather seated at the same desk in an office of unfinished wood. Its inscription said: "Headquarters of the Liberty Bell Mine, Telluride, Colorado." Alongside this was the signed photograph of a very young Herbert Hoover dressed in a belted coat and high collar like someone in a Harvard class picture, but with a curiously Prussian or rather hill-billy haircut. Hoover and my grandfather had worked together on some engineering enterprise. I always winced when it was explained that Hoover, so much younger, plumper and more middle-class looking, was of course, so superior in position that he had scarcely met my grandfather.

Like the sights I had seen on my drives through downtown Boston, the Federal Street office had a strictly-for-adults, males-only atmosphere that was quite proper yet gave a [hint] of the forbidden. Whenever I wanted to go fishing and escape the rolling, sagging, anthill-run tennis court at Rock, my grandfather would tell me that my play should be work. Much of the work at his own office was play. When I arrived there, he would usually be getting into his roughing-it-at-Rock clothes, an extravagant outfit in which London tweeds and whipcords were mixed with all-wear shirts and stockings bought at Raymond's, the worker's department store. My father, with a naval officer's inverted snobbery and indifference, dressed in a manner that defied distinction. A cheap white shirt instantly made his best tailor-made or Brooks Brothers suit look sleazy. My grandfather, however, could wear the worst trash because he had a noble build and had covered it, like his layers of tan, in ages of fine clothes.*

---

pany, under the presidency of Arthur Winslow, had its headquarters at 131 State Street; see *Directory of Directors in the City of Boston and Vicinity*, 1921/22, National Shawmut Bank of Boston, 564. One thirty-one State Street was formerly the address of Winslow's Liberty Bell Gold Mining Company, and it's the address he used on his stationery as late as 1936.

* In a variant of the text, this last sentence is clearer, if still paradoxical: "He had such a fine build and covered it with so many fine clothes that he could get away with wearing almost any sort of trash in moderation."

18 Chestnut Street

I N 1929 MY WINSLOW GRANDPARENTS had many possessions; their house on Chestnut Street had many rooms, and their rooms groaned with many heterogeneous luxuries and curios picked up mostly on trips to Europe. At Chestnut Street I was far from my parents, numbed by the newness and uncertainty of middle age, far from the locker-room acidity of my open-air school. Here, a compact torpedo-like little creature, vague with submerged, half-criminal preadolescent seethings, I drank in all my grandparents' welcome and meandering ostentation. I hoped my mind, like theirs, would grow nimble on deference, years and means.

The Chestnut Street house was prodigiously conventional. Yet even a child was disturbed by the crankiness of its heating. The furnace, now seeming to go backwards, now forwards, was always going dead or jarring into action with sounds like stripping gears. The shiny floor registers always blew too hot or too cold. One room would be as cold as my unheated schoolrooms, the next room would be tropical. Grandfather was continually turning the furnace down so as to reach that state of conscience-clear noble discomfort where he might dream about his ancestors' *Mayflower* misery, their killing first winter in Plymouth, or his own hardening disciplines as a boy in Stuttgart, and his jagged, self-made ascent as a mining engineer in Colorado. My grandmother wanted the house kept at 80. Warm, small, charming, she came from North Carolina. Ruined by Sherman and brought up on plantation stories, she looked on New Englanders as Vandals and witch-burners.*

* Sarah Payne Stuart, in *My First Cousin Once Removed: Money, Madness, and the Family of Robert Lowell* (New York: HarperCollins, 1998), 37, describes the marriage of Arthur and Gaga as an utter failure: "My mother never saw more than a cold good-morning kiss pass between her grandparents. Arthur and Gaga had separate bedrooms and met only at mealtimes. Gaga refused to step into her husband's den—the long, cold, narrow room where Arthur spent his time in the house on Chestnut Street [. . .] Arthur was athletic, disciplined, and exact. Gaga was soft, relaxed, and pointedly uninterested in Arthur's diatribes about the efficiency of the Germans. She loved everything French."

Arthur Winslow V

THE FARM WASN'T really a farm, but my grandfather's shaggy summer place, his "conditioner" in winter.* When the big house was closed, we used to stay at the farmer's.† There at daybreak our loft bedroom was always arctic. I huddled under dull mustard-colored army blankets. Whenever my grandfather looked at me, I held my breath, pretending to be asleep. I whitened. The antiquated brass balls and rods of my bedstead stood out shivering. *If I lie low, I'll outlast him.*

Like a yellowish polar bear, my grandfather humped and fussed in his new Raymond's workingman's winter underwear. Now looking like a dude, now like a tramp, now like a dandy, he worked interminably over our cold, bare heating stove. He stood, legs apart, on a blood-red Navajo rug and fed the stove green brush kindling from a fraying handwoven Navajo basket. The diamond design on the rug matched the diamond design on the basket and was conventional. The green brush, however, was my grandfather's pet inspiration. In a mood of hardiness, waywardness and economy, he would gather it while returning from a day's sawing in the woods. The brush was sopping, and naturally snapped, smoked and refused to catch flame.

* The first four paragraphs appear in the fullest typescript of this chapter, and the last derives from a variant typescript that belongs to the same material and in which the paragraph immediately follows the stove scene.

† If not in the big house, which was presumably unheated in the winter, they would stay in a house on Perry Street, in which Arthur Winslow's caretaker, James MacDonald, resided. The lot on Perry Street was also Winslow's property, which he bought in 1910. Lowell mentions MacDonald in the *Life Studies* poem "Dunbarton" and devotes the *History* sonnet "Two Farmers" to him.

Even in his underwear, his mufti as he called it, my grandfather was a gorgeous fellow, moose-shouldered, black-and-white-mustached, blustery red-brown in the face, and with a gallant waist for a man of almost seventy. His legs spoiled the picture; they were underfed, and even from my bed I could see the varicose veins bulging through his thick, close-fitting underwear legs. The bulges were big, vulnerable, and like white paint blisters on the rowboat we had painted together.

These moments in bed were moments of idleness and high mystery. I had sworn to myself that my grandfather should light the stove without my stirring. I dreamed, then I fumed. Waiting, I could hardly hold myself in. I wanted to make my bed's brass rods wince and throb against my kicking heels. The stove continued to smoke, fail and eat up time. I felt that I was being robbed of my grandfather's strength and energy to amuse me. I ached for him to climb back that instant under the covers. There I could cling to his arms like a fungus. He told lonely, Horatio Alger stories about his silver mine at Telluride, or about his austere boyhood, romantically, economically divided between Stuttgart, Germany and the old Boston Latin School. The stories were men's stories, rather off-bounds, yet morbidly edifying.

A "conservative" believes that happiness comes from duty done. This observation holds, I suppose, for some conservatives; it suited the Cato-the-Younger mind of my grandfather. And yet his sense of duty was partly ornamental. It stemmed from that lonely world, part real and luxurious, part historical and mental, which he built up around himself in his loneliness. When my grandfather retired from business in his early forties in order to do light office work and gamble on heavily mortgaged Boston real estate, the luxury he intended to treat himself to was that of remodeling his leisurely life along the lines of some imaginary rugged old forebear, a martyr to duty. Though largely idle, my grandfather pictured himself as following a stern against-the-spirit-of-the-times course. Though childishly, rather delightfully imperious and bossing everyone in sight, he thought of himself as always wrestling to keep his errant plowshares in the harsh furrow of duty. Though no Platonist, he pictured his worldly though eccentric pleasures as the calling of some higher and spiritual cause. And so it was. Grandfather's duty was to give a rough surfacing to his life of pleasure.

My Crime Wave

1929 WAS A palmy dangerous year for all four of us. I have used the words *all four* inadvertently—a quarter century ago my grandfather, mother, father, and I were those that mattered, the rest of the world was allegory. For about three months, though, my favorite classmate at Rivers Country Day School* was Werner Ash. During those three months he mattered. Later for various reasons he didn't. In 1929 Rivers was an open-air—i.e., unheated—school that was being changed into what we called a *hot-air* school. Scholarship was low, health was high, manners were hearty. Each class met in a separate, small, smoky house; our goings and comings naturally involved a lot of putting on and taking off [of] sheepskins and galoshes, and stamping. At these times even Mr. Rivers, the principal and owner of Rivers, couldn't enforce perfect order. I think I was leaving Miss Brock's English grammar class—feeling baffled and outraged (just as now) by the complex sentence—when I heard Werner making sounds like a toy cat. Taking my heart into my mouth, I meowed. After that, toy cat sounds were as thick as flies. You could make them without moving your lips; and you were practically undetectable. The whole class made toy cat sounds for about two weeks; then the stunt grew insipid and lost its vogue. Werner and I went on meowing. We were bound—*closer than life, closer than breath*, we used to say. I don't know to this day how we did it; but it sure beat work—it beat just about

* Rivers School was at 290 Dean Road in Brookline, a suburb of Boston.

anything. During March Werner and I formed a complicated alliance for playing "potsies," a game of marbles. We never quite cheated; we never quite played fair. Somehow we just "wished" each other's shots into the hole. We left one another rather good lies, and between us won some eight hundred marbles before Easter. Most of these I kept, for I had persuaded Werner that I was willing to relieve him of the sacrificial toil of making the winning shot. The way I did this was . . . well, to tell the truth, Werner was a little less everything than I was: less strong, less unpopular, less stubborn, less a C-minus student, less a child of fortune—less his mother's son.

Our cooperative stealing began with high hopes and a noble intention. We wanted to do something together that would make us better friends. At school they had told us that the value of a present is measured by the thought that has been spent on it, not by its price. We felt just the opposite: the price was all—"It's the risk, not the effort, that counts," I never tired of telling Werner. "Yes," he would answer, "safe risks." "Every day, in every way, I am becoming a better and better friend to Werner Ash": this is how I ended my prayers each night. The way I did it was by a series of furtive, spectacular, safe risks. During the first half of our Easter vacation we rampaged through the Boston Public Garden, and won marbles by the handful from the smaller boys. There were two in particular, the Gerson twins. They had tweed coats, tweed shorts and tweed caps; their woolen stockings were of the same gray color as their tweeds. They had been to a Swiss boarding school and spoke (when they weren't talking French or German to their governess) with a Scotch accent. They were pushovers at marbles. But after they had lost a sky-blue Swiss agate as big as a golf ball, the Gerson twins seemed to lose interest in us. "We can only talk to children who speak French," they said. "*Voulez-vous accepter nos absences, garçons coquins?*"* But later we heard them talking like parrots with their Scotch accents to Phil Lowe and his two sisters who lived at the Ritz Carlton. "Absurd r-r-rogues," they said, and pointed in our direction. Fortunately, the ground froze next morning, marbles were impossible, and we were spared the insult of seeing games stop as we approached.

I don't know why we wanted to steal Thornton Prescott's marbles. Or is it that once I start out thinking out this subject the reasons seem infinite?

---

* "Shall we ask permission to take our leave, naughty boys?"

Day after day the marbles lay in their kid leather bag on the top shelf of Thornton's unlocked locker while he took his shower—exposed, unguarded: thirty of those deluxe marbles we called *moonies*. After ten days of desiring, I thought I would stifle if I didn't steal. Werner and I had many conferences. "It's awful," I would say, "for Thornton to have all these moonies and never play them." "Hoarding," Werner would answer, "goes against laissez-faire." "They are too valuable to pass by," I would say. "Yes, all of a dollar and a quarter," Werner would answer. Werner was always submitting to me and at the same time unintentionally (or so I thought) pulling my leg; that's what made our friendship so seductive and exasperating. "It's not as though they are *really* worth anything, like Phil Lowe's agates; no one will bother to catch us."

This is how we pulled off the job: I stood on guard at the entrance to the shower to give warning if Thornton should start back to his locker. Meanwhile Werner waited till no one was looking in his direction; then he threw his bath towel over the marbles, and quickly removed it with the marbles. Our plan worked like magic—I mean by this that it was something memorable, yet cost us less thought than a one-page composition. My crowning stroke was to walk back with Thornton from the shower, and become the co-discoverer of the theft.

We had gotten away with our deed; but soon the whole business turned out to be a waste and a trap. Mr. Rivers referred to the stolen marbles in his five-minute daily assembly speech. He made a pointed point about its being not the value but the principle. He made the marbles seem of even less value than they actually were. I wished I'd never stolen; I wished we'd taken Phil Lowe's agates. On the third day after the theft, I started to play a game with moonies—some of my own actually. One of our classmates made a wild intuitive joke about stealing. "Prove it!" I screamed angrily, and then tried to laugh. On the fifth day Thornton stopped speaking to me. Werner and I had conference after conference—the air began to feel like prickly heat, but we were awfully relieved to feel so inescapably loyal to one another. We were in it, and nothing could be proved. But somehow the other students didn't talk to us quite as they used to. There was a joke about our playing stinky foot. For two days I played with a fantasy about Thornton Prescott. Prescott suggested William Prescott the historian, whose *Conquest of Mexico* had been read to me by my father. Mexico meant Montezuma, the Aztec king—weak, treacherous, evil, plundered. It was one's duty to rob such people. That's what Thornton was like. But I couldn't quite explain this version of our exploit to Werner—proving the analogy made me tired. So I said, "Thornton's a swarthy Montezuma." On the seventh day we, or rather I, broke; for Werner had never seen where we were going from the first, and had only wanted to go into action with me. "I have an idea," I said. My idea was to put a third of the moonies back in their bag, and then hide the bag under a blanket near Thornton's locker. Again we did the job as planned; that is, Werner returned the marbles.

Everything went wrong. "It will look," I had said, "as though Thornton had just left them there by mistake." It didn't! The blankets had been looked under a hundred times. Everyone knew that the marbles were too few; they were even the wrong color. But worst of all, Pop Foster, the athletics director, seemed to know all about the return. He called in Werner the next afternoon. "You must like playing Santa Claus," he had said. Werner hadn't answered. "You'll like it still better," Pop Foster had said, "if you can be a whole-hog Santa Claus and give back the rest of the marbles." Again Werner hadn't answered. "Who did you do it with and for?" Pop Foster had said. Then Werner grew red and shouted "No one!" Then Pop had said, "There won't be any punishment if you'll be a whole-hog Santa—that means every marble." When Werner told me about his interview, I said, "There'll be no punishment; you'd better give the marbles to Pop. I'd go with you, but it would mix things up; I mean Pop has only promised to let you off, you couldn't tell what he'd do if he learned we were two." That's how we talked. Again Werner acted. Again it was no go.

The next day our section was at rest hour. Mr. Sheehan was reading Cooper's *Deerslayer* aloud to us. Pop stood for five or six minutes in the doorway. "What are you waiting for," Mr. Sheehan (old skinny) had said. "I guess I'm just tired of this tame suburban life, and teaching boys to play the game. I was just imagining I was Natty Bumppo stalking the deer . . . I tell you what," he said a minute later, "I want to talk to Robert Lowell. I think he can tell me . . . how shall I put it, Mr. Sheehan? I haven't done the reading to know how to express myself; but I think Robert Lowell is going to tell me how to influence a friend so as to win him." So at last I was caught. Pop and I talked for an hour. The game was up, and I saw no harm in saying that it was my idea, not Werner's, to steal the marbles. "Well," Pop had said, "if you'll keep your chin up, play square and smile, I won't tell Mr. Rivers, your father or school. Only you'll have to apologize to Thornton Prescott. I don't think he'll tell." And so it happened. I was awfully happy, went on two hikes with Pop and was even one of the five boys asked to Thornton's birthday party. I couldn't help lording it a little over Werner though, who hadn't been asked. After all, I *had* taken the rap; Pop had said, "You are the real bum, the cat behind the cat's paw." For a while I was rather good in some ways; but later I learned that the hundredth sheep that has strayed and been brought back is, well there's no getting around it—he is still a sheep, and a little more sheepish, a little worse, all in all, than his nine and ninety fellows.

Our next campaign was trading soldiers with Roger Crosby.* Roger had also lived abroad too long to know what was what. His soldiers came from Paris, where their manufacture was a national art and honor. They were all hand-painted, solid lead, had removable saddles and historic uniforms. His marshals weren't just anonymous ciphers in gorgeous dress; instead you could really tell Marshal Foch from Marshal Joffre, and Marshal Ney from King Murat. Some of Roger's best pieces were discards from his Father's collection—a hundred or so six-inch replicas of Napoleon's *Grande Armée* on the eve of Austerlitz. Crosby *Père*—that's what Mother called him— used to say, and I don't think he was kidding: "You can tell it is 1805 or '06 by Napoleon's hair and figure, also by the uniforms." Well, Roger had never seen khaki soldiers, he had never seen papier-mâché. We managed to swap twenty Jordan Marsh doughboys for enough French masterpieces to fill a wheelbarrow. We even had to persuade Roger that a ten-for-one ratio was more than we could accept. So we stumbled home with our huge burdens and felt like ascetics, glorious in our denials. Unfortunately, Crosby *Père* arrived just as we were unloading and quarreling over the right division. "I only asked eight for one," I said. The soldiers—that is, most of them— went back.

But the stealing, the real stealing, began with the Thread and Needle Shoppe on Newbury St. between Dartmouth and Exeter.† Miss Frothing-

---

* The Roger Crosby story told here repeats, but changes some details of, the story as it is related in "91 Revere Street."

† Dartmouth and Exeter are two parallel streets crossing Newbury Street, all of them in the Back Bay, quite near Lowell's childhood homes on Revere and Marlborough Streets. In 1929, a store traditionally known as Woodbury Thread and Needle Shop (but by then called Woodbury Shop and Lending Library) was located at the Woodbury Building, 229 Berkeley Street, several blocks from the location indicated in the text and a

ham, who managed the Thread and Needle, wasn't a commercial woman. That's what Young Aunt Sarah had told us—in fact she only worked where she did to raise the standards of Boston taste and (believe it or not) decency. She just loved mothers, little girls, and even little boys, if, as Aunt Sarah put it, they were washed behind the ears and made sense. Werner and I didn't, I guess. We rambled into the Thread and Needle, our pockets full of unreturned Crosby soldiers. But Miss Frothingham, who looked and acted like a well-paid and well-dressed headmistress at a girls' school, wasn't interested in making us an offer. No, she couldn't evaluate them; her own favorites were the wretched papier-mâché doughboys. We pointed to a troop of these under the glass counter. Miss Frothingham, all smiles, got them out, mounted them, arranged them (incorrectly, as we insinuated) for a charge. This took almost ten minutes. Then I said, "I guess I already have this kind." "I guess I have too," Werner said. "Do you have any good shrapnel?" I asked. "Of course not, this isn't an arsenal," Miss Frothingham said. "Have you ever tried to get a job in an Army Navy Store?" Then, to soothe the sting of what I was saying, I added, "They take all sorts of people." At this point it was clear that Werner and I were never going to become favorites with Miss Frothingham. It was maddening though when she turned from us and started a long, fluent, and purely social conversation with the Gerson twins in French and English. We stood watching for five minutes. Then I said, as though I were in a bookstore, "Do you mind if I browse?" "It's best to know what you want before you come"; then, as she turned back winking to the Gersons and taking them into her confidence, she added "Ain't that a fact?"

We felt riled, misunderstanding, and misunderstood. We browsed, we lifted. The store was big. The staff was small, talkative, and genteel-offish but trusting. First we took small game: a pencil sharpener in a red morocco case, then a pincushion, shaped like a Scottie and colored like a zebra. It had been made for Miss Frothingham's Concord "Country Store." Then we saw what we wanted, a $16.50 toy microscope, the most expensive toy

---

nine-minute walk from 170 Marlborough Street, where the Lowells had moved in the spring of 1927. There were no similar stores at the Newbury location the text identifies—only dentists' offices. However, Lowell may have had in mind a retail store carrying "novelties," gifts, and antiques at the corner of Newbury and Dartmouth, just before the block he mentions (147 Newbury). The store was called Black Bear Shop, and Lowell would have needed only four minutes to walk there.

on the top of any counter. Having marked our victim, we departed. Stealing wasn't enough. We wanted to have necessary reasons. "We are going to be scientists," I said. "You've got to do it at home. You've got to have your own microscope, and a good one. A magnifying glass won't do." The actual stealing wasn't hard. I walked in ahead and alone to draw off attention. "Do you still have those old doughboys?" I said to Miss Frothingham. "You're not much of a buyer," she answered. "Or talker either," giggled Miss Frothingham's assistant. I just stared and looked simple. When Werner and I got back to my bedroom, the microscope wouldn't focus. We twisted this, and twisted that. We unscrewed the whole business, and put it together minus one lens that was apparently an extra. It wouldn't focus. We bought a catalogue. But nothing we could do made it possible to see anything at all through the microscope. Then I had a brainstorm. "Why not return it to the Thread and Needle," I said to Werner, "and get our money back?" "We'll settle for a new microscope—one that's not a defective," Werner said.

The return was a failure. "But did you buy it from us? We have no record of the sale," said Miss Frothingham. In no case could we have the money. If we left it there for examination by the factory representative, maybe there could be an exchange. Miss Frothingham and her assistants began to whisper. Yes, decidedly they wanted us to leave the microscope behind. Just when *did* we buy it? What were our names anyway? "Black and Brown," we said and fled. The other day I came on the old microscope. It had not been looked at from then till now—really it was a cheap old thing, not a tool, a precision tool but just a tawdry toy. How tinny and badly put together it looked. Yes, and decidedly it wouldn't work.

One matter—it was what was really closest to heart—but I never said a word about it to anyone, no, not even to Werner. This matter was Buddy Strauss. What made Buddy so attractive was that he was small for his age, and old for his class. He was actually smaller than I was, though two classes ahead of me and three years older—so though in the same weight group, he was five football teams ahead of me. There wasn't a moment of the day in which I didn't dream up scenes in which we were together. Buddy reminded me of the three most exciting objects in the world—(1) Napoleon, as he looked during his Italian campaign, say at Arcola, long-nosed, transparent, mask-like; (2) a girl; and (3) an orangutan. However, I just watched; I could never think of anything to say. Yet in a house, two or three doors up from ours on Marlborough St. there was someone—small, compact, who used to stand by an upstairs bay window in a scarlet jersey. Was it a boy or a girl? It was Buddy Strauss. Or so I thought, for I never dared or cared to find out where Buddy actually lived—yet after a while it was forced on my attention that he lived miles away in a suburban apartment house called Pelham Court. But still I invented a fiction that Buddy was visiting across the street. So we were really awfully close, though we never spoke.

One thing I'm really ashamed of—ashamed pure and simple with no mixed feeling. A touch of horror. Arthur Knowland and I and William Friedman used to come home together in a taxi. The taxi itself was intoxicating—for no one was with us, it was as though we were hiring it with our own money. The first year I had gone to school in the school bus. There were thirty of us—all small, and a teacher to keep order. Then came the trolleys—all by one's self with change to pay. But the taxi was the best of all—fast, comfortable, adult. Arthur Knowland was much more popular and a better athlete than any of my previous friends. He had a braided leather belt, a braided leather watch fob, and a set of long knives. What made the knives so interesting was that there wasn't the slightest suggestion that they were in any way weapons, and indeed they weren't. Arthur used his knives to carve with. During the odd moments of a single day he could make a dory, with removable seats, a rope buffer, and its name, or he could make a coffin that really opened and shut, or it could be a totem pole. Given time, he could make—in fact he was making—a little square-rigged bark. I had no right to be friends with Arthur. This is how I did it. Bill Friedman was a Jew; so was Buddy Strauss. I don't know if I was anti-Semitic. I loved one, and—well, you'll see how I treated the other. Bill Friedman was pale, freckled, he had a nose that bent in a new direction in the middle. He wasn't very pretty, very strong, or very popular. Somehow one day, Arthur pushed Bill Friedman against me in the taxi. I pushed back a little harder. "Bill," I said, "help me *ram* Arthur." I gave Arthur a wink.

There wasn't any really rough stuff at first, only Bill got pushed one way then the other. He never seemed to be doing the pushing, and he wasn't. "Fried Egg Man," we kept shouting, "stop swaying!" But after a week or so it got worse. We used to make Bill sit in the folding seat. Then we pushed it forward. Bill would make breathy sounds, turn white and red, but didn't seem hurt much. One day he said, "I throw up when I get home." Then the next day he said, "My mother wants to know why I throw up. I say I get carsick. She won't believe." At that point Arthur began to feel kindly and scared. We stopped. All well and good, but there had been a time when all through the school day I would look forward to those taxi rides and the squashing and being friends with Arthur. It was like water to a wandering traveler in a desert—like news from a far country.

Entering St. Mark's

MATTAPOISETT LIES ON Buzzards Bay, perhaps the calmest and least spectacular of New England's summer regions.* There are no buzzards, but "Matt," undoubtedly an outpost, seems built to stand against nothing more active than those somnolent and mortuary marauders. Its strength has always been in its tameness, its modest propriety, and its Horatian removal from gross or gallant extravagance. In the '30s its flower-and-vegetable-growing Portuguese population was only moderately exotic and prolific. Their ghetto filled the heart of the village, exerted little pressure, and lay like some tropical fringe or bouquet offered to nineteenth-century colonials. Yankees, three-fourths Portuguese but with *Mayflower* names, ran the post office, fish market and a half dozen summer shops. Once a year the New York Yacht Club entered Mattapoisett's large, smooth, reef-less harbor, and rode at anchor for an evening, night and morning, magnificently vegetating. Our only live wires were the summer perennials, a score or so of wives between the ages of forty-five and fifty-five. They wore white felt hats, white button-up jerseys, and white flannel skirts. In cars and with newly won licenses, they drove like horseshoe crabs, black, stalled, unwieldy, murderously erratic. On foot, the shore trembled beneath their firm white leather shoes. Their solid and prudent gossip seldom missed

---

* The first paragraph appears on one sheet of a variant typescript of this chapter; the next four paragraphs come from another sheet of the variant; and the rest of the chapter reproduces the fullest typescript.

the target. Their children were all under seven; their husbands, agile fig-
ureheads, commuted on weekends, and spent the five remaining days two
and a half hours away in Boston, three or four often sharing a house in the
suburbs.

In 1930 all the Barnard Estate cottages were still rented, all the Herreshoff
yachts were still in the water, the tennis club had even increased its waiting
list. On weekends we still motored from unpretentious Mattapoisett to the
more *à la mode* Marion,* paid high fees to play on its famous landscaped golf
course, and brought home our Sunday quart of fresh crushed strawberry
sherbet. Nevertheless, this was the summer of 1930; everywhere the Great
Depression was moving across the world of the moderately rich with a
steady, chafing, out-at-the-elbows motion. Each new patch of flaking paint,
each splinter was a signal. Fathers, released by their cocktails, talked up the
advantages of the democratic public schools. The stock market no longer
worked while we slept.

Our class's old friends, the future, the workaday, the real became nations
at war with us. Minds, once practical, grew speculative, moved in an air of
vaguely nauseated musing.

About this time I got into the habit of waking up early. No light, no
sounds. Soon, however, the night betrayed its pitiable lack of staying power.
Again and again came the anxious duplicity of drawing out my dreams, and
waiting for the furtive, methodical, swishing thud of Father's Chinese sandals in our shared bathroom. At last I was sure I had gained precisely twenty
minutes of compulsory idleness. Then the warship-gray softwood floor of
my bedroom would reflect like a mirror, and here and there catch the shine
of my scalloped white curtains, perfect as those of a doll's house and thin
as handkerchiefs. On the leaving day, nothing except my pillow, a little salt
marsh, showed the sweat and strain of the moment. Five hours and hundred
miles or so away was St. Mark's School waiting for my entrance.†

What I kept trying to see was a green double-sterned rowboat, a short
rapier baitcasting rod, and three long rods, one telescopic steel, one jointed

---

* Another coastal town about five miles northeast of Mattapoisett.

† It was about seventy-five miles away, a two-hour trip in 1930.

cane, one an expensive and inappropriate four-ounce fly rod. All had colored bobbers and held live yellow perch hooked through their backs. Huge, kindly, profitless, Harold Thomas, a retired grocer, reigned over the boat. He cut tobacco, poured a can of urine overboard for luck. He wore a gray bathing suit top. And now in bed, on this, my departure day, I too wore a gray bathing suit top. It was my skull and bones, my banner of classless defiance.

By six-thirty on the morning of Friday, the seventeenth of September, 1930,* I had already massaged away the crick in my neck that had come from falling asleep with my chin in my fingers. In the colorless dawn-dusk, my whole bedroom had the whittled-down transparency of an X-ray photograph. "What next!" Mother had said during my last Easter vacation. "Dr. Dane opines that Bobby has had prenatal rickets." Dr. Dane's diagnosis turned out to be doubtful, but for several months I imagined that rickets and my bones were conferring mutual honors on one another. "When I am dead," I had said, "my skeleton is going to hang with the skeleton of the spare chimpanzee in the cellar of the Natural History Museum on Berkeley Street. 'Bobby (R.T.S.L. Jr.), rickets.'" That was when I had my crush on Chimp Austin, the Rivers' goal guard, and used to daydream of *Swiss Family Robinson* island heavens, where Chimp and I, impervious, stopped a thousand hockey pucks, and then swaggered about in our lettered blazers, giving ground to no one, and eating red bananas.

Wanting a prop to break the suddenness of getting up, I let my arm dangle and felt for Bowser's forehead. Bowser was not there. Then I clenched my eyes lest the nothing I touched should develop into desertion and terror. Then I remembered that the little hound hadn't limped away to my father's room, but had been driven off to Rock for the winter. All summer, Bowser's running out on me had made my nights a formless underworld. Bowser was *my* dog; I and no one else fed her; I and no one else took her daily on two-mile walks to Ned's Point.† Each night for an hour we were friends; our noses had the same temperature. Then she was off. I couldn't face it, and after a month I took to closing my bedroom door. "The draft gives me

---

* September 17, 1930, was a Wednesday not a Friday.

† Ned's Point Lighthouse, Mattapoisett, one mile southeast of the village.

earaches," I said. We stifled together. Bowser grew puffy and bored. Each morning I had to wring the sweat from my pillow. One night my father cracked my door, and gently closed it after Bowser had escaped. Later that night, I strode like a hiker into my father's room, picked Bowser up by the scruff of her neck and bolted my door. Nothing was ever said. I reveled in unloved righteousness and plumed myself on acquiring the granite New England character, so esteemed by my grandfather.

This morning, as always, I could hear the furtive swishing thud of my father's feet moving into his Chinese sandals. He was half everyman, half Huck Finn back from the Orient; there was no naval officer or ex-naval officer in the world who rattled his sword less. I was for once more or less sincerely determined to beat him to the bathroom. [But first] there was an important dream to be decoded and reassembled. Darks, lights, pouring sand, knots of sword grass, a tennis court, a roller, an up-and-down feel in my stomach, barked knees. I was pushing the roller and trailing my grandfather across the tennis court. Each time I touched his tough riding britches, the roller grew too heavy for the sand and plowed up a bunker. I gulped from an empty canteen, and felt charged with kindly, contemplative consideration. I had all morning. Suddenly the roller was bounding ahead like a corkscrew, it flattened grass at the side of the court, and bumped my knees together like dice. What was my grandfather saying? Was it Headless Heedlong, or Lazy Susan? His mustache was misshapen from biting. Deep in my pocket, I found his ivory knife of all purposes with its sixteen blades. There was no purpose now in catching up . . . I had the dream's clue.

That's why it was so awfully thin and unfair, this waking up and finding nothing except memories of St. Mark's School between me and the bathroom.* I saw the pale slate roofs of St. Mark's, as green as the edges of plate glass, and stretching as far as two of our Marlborough Street blocks in Boston; the school corridors as angular and stained-woody as the old country desk I had taken the knife from in my dream; a steel engraving of General Israel Putnam in a wolf's cave; the bleached Indian profile of Mrs. Thayer, the ex-headmistress serving tea.† Mrs. Thayer treated the small boys like

---

* Lowell's "memories" of the boarding school that he is only about to attend were, presumably, of being interviewed for a spot there the year before.

† Violet Otis Thayer (1871–1962) was the wife of William Greenough Thayer, the headmaster of St. Mark's from 1894 until October 1930. "Ex-headmistress" probably means the wife of the ex-headmaster, Thayer

grads, and the grads like schoolboys. Her parlor was fit for a stern, brisk, happy family. "Not like mine," I thought . . .

I rowed backward and forward in my bed, and the huge main building of St. Mark's seemed to rouse [before me,] our meeting place in the later afternoon.* I pushed a hand under my pajamas and roughened my fingers like a cat on my red and gray bathing-suit top, a replica of the one worn by Uncle Harold† when we went fishing for freshwater bass. I got out of bed. "Anchors aweigh, old fellow," I shouted to my father as I wiped his razor marked Friday. I brushed my teeth twice for good luck, but a single semi-circular gouging sweep with the damp bath towel did for my cheeks.

Mother, down for breakfast to give verve to the occasion of my leaving for prep school, was like the youngish Napoleon writing dispatches on a drumhead before the Battle of Marengo. Her hand moved with decisive, dramatic thrusts, as she checked off items of clothing on a two-foot list. "What is l'Aiglon, I mean your royal highness, thinking of?" she said. "Uncle Harold and Number One," my father answered. I knew I must say something. Torn between making trouble and opening my heart, I thought about the faded blue and gold binding of *Antony Brade*, Great-Grandfather Lowell's novel about St. Mark's.‡ How dim and proper this work seemed after my hockey hero Chimp Austin and Kipling's *Stalky and Co.*§ Still, the "hunting chapters" were really snug and nifty. It was ominous, though, that Mrs. Thayer had misunderstood me a year ago, when I had asked how

---

retiring precisely when RL entered the school in the fall of 1930. The new headmaster was Francis Parkman (1898–1990), a historian from Harvard.

* If he dreaded going to St. Mark's, the experience indeed turned out to be traumatic. He describes his misery there in "St. Mark's, 1933," in Robert Lowell, *Day by Day* (New York: Farrar, Straus and Giroux, 1977), reprinted in Robert Lowell, *Collected Poems*, edited by Frank Bidart and David Gewanter (New York: Farrar, Straus and Giroux, 2003), 800–801. In a letter of August 7, 1963, to Mary McCarthy, he describes "the world of St. Mark's" as "curious clubby monosexual, but seething with tentacles [. . .]. How close the eye was for changes and vicissitudes of character! I think the whole form's popularity chart could have been made from one to thirty-seven, and each week two or three digits would have to be changed"; see Robert Lowell, *The Letters of Robert Lowell*, edited by Saskia Hamilton (New York: Farrar, Straus and Giroux, 2005), 431.

† The manuscripts make clear that this "Uncle Harold" is the same as "Harold Thomas," mentioned earlier in the chapter. The term "Uncle" is an honorific indicating affection. Young Lowell is worried that in entering St. Mark's he will be leaving Uncle Harold and childhood behind.

‡ Robert Traill Spence Lowell, *Antony Brade* (Boston: Roberts Brothers, 1874). Great-Grandfather Lowell (1816–1891) had a notable career as clergyman, author of uplifting books of fiction and poetry, and, for four years, headmaster of St. Mark's School.

§ Rudyard Kipling's *Stalky & Co.* (1899) is a collection of rowdy short stories about three adolescent boys, Stalky and his two best friends, at a British boarding school.

the fisher martins* were doing. "Marden?" she said. "But I think the boy's name is Cyrus; his father was a Brotherhood man and set our record for the shot put."

I saw that Mother was bolting her coffee and off in the clouds. I looked at my father: "Let's shove, old fellow, I want to have time for buying those steel traps at Iver Johnson's."† "But Bobby, I know you want to wait and see what styles of traps your classmates are using." I saw that I had lost the first round. My outburst about the traps, though circuitous to the point of dishonesty, had been obvious. The only traps I had ever handled were illustrations. I had been trying to goad Mother into saying that I knew perfectly well that there was no longer any trapping at St. Mark's. Then I could say that I was entering this silly, sissyish school as a martyr to my parents. They would agree. I would either stay on at my present Rivers, or gracefully accept the role of family champion, and even, impossibly, its breadwinner. "We are so proud of Bobby. He has left his wonderful open-air school, Uncle Harold, Earnest Manahan, and Earnest Seaton Thompson behind him. He's not confiding and talkative, because . . ." Here I found that even the praise I was imagining was an intrusion. *Because*: I pondered hundreds of preverbal completions. *Because he is a goal guard.* I wasn't. "I meant . . ." I held my breath, and grew tight and swollen with meaning like an inner tube. Mother gave me one of her bewildered, jaw-thrust-out looks. "I don't think your father can afford traps until Christmas." That's what she had said last year and then bought me five neckties, twenty handkerchiefs, a mackinaw (a dreary brown one) and some dancing pumps.

I realized with stiffening excitement that we were approaching the old fished-out argument about the expense of my tuition at St. Mark's. My defense, brief, practiced, deadly, was almost as fine a thing as Chimp's goal guarding. "Ten traps cost $17.50; St. Mark's costs $2000. If you can't pay, why make me go? It wasn't my idea." Mother talked on with a hard, hopeless bravado. It was maddening to be talking to a stone and stuck with a theme that ruled out humor and all her wonderfully good-natured and de-

---

* Fishers and martens are two closely related varieties of weasel native to New England and Canada. Bobby's question apparently stemmed from his previous reading of *Antony Brade*, which portrays St. Mark's students of the nineteenth century setting traps for small game.

† Iver Johnson's Arms and Cycle Works was a Massachusetts manufacturer and purveyor of bicycles, firearms, and other outdoor equipment.

tailed exaggerations. Still, she had lived all summer on just this. Now, [what] if the hot bath she had so lovingly drawn should turn out to be a rock pile?

She wasn't so common and nouveau riche as to name or even quite remember the exact figures; still, anyone could see that this gross tuition was something in black and white, a cold demonstrable proof of giving. *Money talks.* She might have said this if she had had more of it, and a less Puritan, less genteel conscience. What she so deeply felt was that only spiritual pain is deserving, and that if, despite her feelings, she had had oceans of just this, oh nauseating oceans, and all nearly impossible to exhibit to others . . . well, she deserved a vacation she could pay for. Ever since her marriage she had been modeling a statue called *I am a mother.* If sending me off to boarding school was buying the pedestal ready-made, surely she had shown genius in her choice.

In all this vibrating torment, it was as though Mother and I were battling down a list of statements and answers.

Statement: your father and I are paying a great deal to give you the advantage of St. Mark's.
Answer: I only thank for what I ask for.
Statement: $2000.
Answer: my allowance is twenty-five cents a week.
Statement: the return we expect is improved conduct.
Answer: love and admire what I already am!
Statement: most boys are unable to go to St. Mark's.
Answer: that means I can't play with Earnest Manahan.
Statement: your great-grandfather was headmaster of St. Mark's.
Answer: I am afraid to mention him.
Statement: he was a great man.
Answer: probably he was mean and couldn't keep order.
Statement: we are giving you the best education.
Answer: you mean blue serge suits seven days a week and music lessons.

And so on; at the end of the list Mother wrote: "we are breathless, someone else must take over." I said, "Eskimos fish every day of the year, except when they are hibernating." Mother and I loved knocking our heads together until they bled. Worn, jumpy, exhilarated from such bloodletting, we could not live a day without it. My father drained his great cereal bowl of a coffee cup. "Maxwell House," he said, "good *except* for the last drop."*

The closest I had ever come to understanding that money was something that changed numbers into things and things into numbers was when I had won fifty agates, and started a savings account and a miser's hoard for myself by refusing to sell them. Mother knew the price of food and the price of clothes; the cost of a house was incomprehensible to her, but she knew what it was to sell one for twice what she had paid. For my father, money was the oxygen he survived on. Since he had resigned from the Navy, he learned that the money a man makes is his rank in society. He was doing badly in business; his rank was falling. Spending and even using money made him tired. This morning he looked at his wife with a gentle, exhausted admiration. He looked at his son with a gentle, exhausted exhaustion. Old naval habits, an old meekness, an old faith in little duties, an automatic optimism that was mostly a tone of voice—these, and a new almost imperceptible itch for luxury and affection, kept him going.

At the table, he buried himself in roadmaps and sketched out the Taunton detour. He made us feel that this was a man's work, like drinking a pint of coffee. "Charlotte is too heady to hear me," he was thinking. "If Bobby ever deviated into sense, I would send him to a public school, and turn in the old Hudson for a new Packard."†

The last I can remember of Mattapoisett on that day is that I was pressing down on the lid of a garbage can and studying the mole on my whitened, angry right hand. The mole was stimulating me with its familiar, powerful, and imbecile message: "You are Bobby. You are awfully right-handed. No one from the time of Adam and Methuselah till kingdom come and the end of people in storybooks can ever have had a mole in just this position." A dwarf and twisted pear tree stood a few feet to one side, and seemed to ape my stance and thoughts. "This mole in just this spot on my right hand," I thought. "Ergo: I am. Mother can't ever take this away. I have won the game." What the game was, I had no idea. But this I knew: do what I might,

---

* Maxwell House Coffee began to use its signature advertising slogan "Good to the last drop!" in 1917.

† In "91 Revere Street" Lowell indicates that his father sold his Hudson and bought a Buick in 1927, and then later traded up to "a high-toned, as-good-as-new Packard." In the scene depicted here, taking place in 1930, Lowell seems to elide the Buick.

lose what I might, I held one immeasurable trump card. It was like discovering the nonexistence of God. Perhaps that was why I motioned Mother away so energetically with my other hand and didn't even deign to look at the half-unstitched moccasins of mine that she was holding up two feet in front of her like a dirty mud turtle, beginning to throw them in the rubbish. "Why don't you throw away my new city shoes? Those moccasins took all summer to break in so that they were finally *mine*."

The garbage can lid was still dented and bent from the flying pears it had stopped, when I had used it as my buckler in a gang battle one afternoon five years before. I had gone into that battle with a broken arm, and the splint with its gauze and adhesive tape had hidden my mole from everyone except myself. "Why don't you make friends with Tommy Whitney?" Mother had said. But I had stood off multitudes with only my garbage can shield, a little girl a head shorter than I was, and a boy hardly tall enough to walk on two feet. As I now stood by the garbage can, I suddenly understood why I always fell asleep with my chin in my fingers. I wanted to handle and draw strength from my scar. David Howe did it in a duel with sawed-off broomsticks. When the blood came, it made me friends with David, a hero to his sister, and later, when the scar formed, Mother called me "old soldier."

Arthur Winslow VI

SUMMER, AUTUMN, WINTER—these three seasons, and particularly their fierce transitory extremes, had always suited Grandfather Winslow. My last visit to him was on a cloudless, snowless, unencumbered December afternoon.* For some reason he was sitting in his dining room, the sunniest and sparest room in the apartment. The brief hard sunlight blazed suavely on the red-blue of the Turkish carpet, then almost sightlessly on the silver, on the tops of waves out on the Esplanade.† There Grandfather had walked for thirty-five years—three and a half miles a day, at first alone, and then with dogs, always decreasing in size.

For the first time since I had known him, Grandfather was physically changed. He was shrunken and irritable. His neck couldn't fill his high starched collar; his watch chain seemed crudely bloated. The ranging cancer scars on his cheeks and throat were like ivy turning scarlet. I looked at him with captivated embarrassment, found nothing to say, and began to boast irrelevantly about the Virgil I had been translating. My face was somewhat broken out, and Grandpa asked disgustedly why I had so many *bruises* on my face.

I suppose hardly a day has passed since his death without my turning

* Presumably December 1937, before Arthur Winslow's death in March 1938.

† The Charles River Esplanade, especially its traditional section between today's Hatch Shell and the Longfellow Bridge. In the apartment building at 10 Otis Place, where the Winslows moved after they had been forced to sell 18 Chestnut Street, many windows look out on the Esplanade and the river.

back to him. Often I try to catch the old man off guard, and all my visual, auditory and nervous impressions gasp away into a white blur. Soothed and a little paralyzed, I dwell on this whiteness and hoard it to me. I see a knotted pillow, two woolen sheets, a ridge of virgin snow on the sill of an open window, the gray-white vacuity of the window blanking into winter sky. My grandfather stands by me in his white winter underwear.

PART II

Crisis and Aftermath

INTRODUCTION

FROM LATE 1954 to early or mid-1956, at roughly the same time as Lowell was "messing around" with his "autobiographical monster,"* his memoir of childhood, he also worked on another memoir titled "Near the Balanced Aquarium" in one early draft but otherwise simply "The Balanced Aquarium." (Lowell never called it "Near the Unbalanced Aquarium," the title Robert Giroux affixed to it in 1987 when he published a heavily pruned version in Lowell's posthumous *Collected Prose*.) Both "My Autobiography" and "The Balanced Aquarium" grew out of a series of life-altering events in the early 1950s. Lowell had been suffering from an undiagnosed mood disorder at least since the summer of 1934, when at the age of seventeen he experienced "a period of enthusiasm."† Signs of Lowell's mood shifts were probably present even earlier, in his difficult childhood and especially in his tumultuous relations with his parents—disturbances made evident in both "My Autobiography" and "The Balanced Aquarium."

Lowell experienced recurrent cycles of what he called "enthusiasm" and "depression."‡ These bipolar episodes accelerated in his thirties, and lasted

---

* Robert Lowell, *The Letters of Robert Lowell*, edited by Saskia Hamilton (New York: Farrar, Straus and Giroux, 2005), 240.

† Phrase stricken from manuscript of "For two years I have been cooling off" (Robert Lowell Papers at the Houghton Library, Harvard University).

‡ For discussions of Lowell's mood disorder, see Lowell, "Seven years ago I had an attack of pathological enthusiasm"; Paul Mariani, *Lost Puritan: A Life of Robert Lowell* (New York: W. W. Norton, 1994); and

throughout his life (except, as Kay Redfield Jamison has pointed out, in some of the later years when his doctors and his second wife, Elizabeth Hardwick, prevailed on him to take prescribed doses of lithium). In a typical cycle, he would start out feeling fine; then he would sense, ominously, that his mind was racing. In full-blown mania, he might commence passionate affairs with newly met women or threaten violence against friends or strangers, fall under the grip of fantasies or hallucinations,* inveigh against Communists or, conversely, insist on Alger Hiss's innocence, barricade himself in his room or wander the streets all night, foam at the mouth, talk nonstop, and wind up in police custody and then in a hospital room or a padded cell. Following the death of his mother in February 1954, Lowell suffered his worst manic attack yet, resulting in electroshock treatment at a Cincinnati hospital and then transference to a locked cell in the Payne Whitney Psychiatric Clinic in New York. From then on, all of his major manic attacks culminated in a stay at a psychiatric institution—generally McLean Hospital just outside of Boston. Initially he was involuntarily committed, but then, as he gained an understanding of his condition, he voluntarily admitted himself. In the hospital, he would descend into quietude, remorse, and intense self-criticism. And then, often quickly, he would be fine again, for a while.

Although Lowell composed "My Autobiography" and "The Balanced Aquarium" at roughly the same time, and seemed at the outset to regard them as part of the same autobiographical project, he eventually saw them as divergent texts in terms of their form and subject matter. "My Autobiography" begins with his birth in 1917 and, after looping backward for one chapter, proceeds in a linear fashion to his departure for St. Mark's School in 1930, with a coda evoking his last meeting with his grandfather in 1937. In contrast, "The Balanced Aquarium" focuses on his hospitalization at Payne Whitney from May to September 1954, and it interleaves those scenes from the institution with elegiac memories of his mother, father, and uncle. Whereas "My Autobiography" generally moves forward in fragments of time, "The Balanced Aquarium" oscillates between his recent experi-

---

especially Kay Redfield Jamison, *Robert Lowell, Setting the River on Fire: A Study of Genius, Mania, and Character* (New York: Alfred A. Knopf, 2017).

* Mariani relates Peter Taylor's account of Lowell's manic behavior in March 1949 in Bloomington, Indiana. "Do you smell that?" he asked Taylor. When Taylor said he couldn't smell anything, Lowell told him he smelled brimstone. Then, as Mariani writes, Lowell "began looking around the room, trying to locate the devil"; see Mariani, *Lost Puritan*, 182–83.

ences at Payne Whitney and more distant, burdensome memories of family events. The three main autobiographical texts that Lowell wrote in the 1950s ("My Autobiography," "The Balanced Aquarium," and *Life Studies*) compose an extended conversation he had with himself about himself—and a three-pronged experiment in turning memories into art.

Lowell's intentions for "The Balanced Aquarium" are uncertain. In March 1956, Hardwick (writing for Lowell) suggested to *Partisan Review* editors that they publish "The Balanced Aquarium" instead of "91 Revere Street," but that substitution never happened.* During 1957 and 1958, Lowell rewrote some of its flashback scenes for five poems in Part IV of *Life Studies* (see "A Note on the Texts"), and from that point forward its publication as a separate item dropped from his agenda. Perhaps the repurposing of a handful of pages led him to think of "The Balanced Aquarium" as merely a rough draft for his poems. But given the high regard in which he once held the memoir, and the time and care he devoted to it, it is clearly much more than that.

In any case, Lowell never published "The Balanced Aquarium." A decade after Lowell's death, his longtime editor Giroux published an edited and retitled version of the text in *The New York Review of Books* (March 12, 1987) and in his edition of Lowell's *Collected Prose* (1987). In so doing, he deleted or shortened many of the flashback scenes. The present volume presents "The Balanced Aquarium" in the form Lowell left it. This version highlights Lowell's nonlinear arrangement, presents the remembered scenes in full, and restores the text's stylistic quirks and intended conclusion. By restoring Lowell's childhood memory of his mother "coming into the upstairs den 'undressed,'" this version adds detail to Lowell's representation of the fraught mother-son bond. By reinstating his account of his father's last days, as well as a portrait of a fellow patient (Prince Scharnhorst) who reminded Lowell of his father, this version also returns the father-son relationship to its intended prominence. Finally, this version recovers Lowell's

* Hardwick to Catharine Carver, March 7, 1956, *Partisan Review* Collection #1028, box 4, folder 2, Howard Gotlieb Archival Research Center, Boston University. It's likely that Lowell never actually sent "The Balanced Aquarium" to Philip Rahv and Catharine Carver at *Partisan Review*. Probably he revised the initially "rougher" "91 Revere Street" and sent that revision instead, sometime in mid-April. In May, in unpublished letters now at the Houghton Library, Rahv called the childhood memoir "an excellent job of writing, something quite new and original, full of buoyancy and humor" and Carver called it "a triumph." In the excitement, "The Balanced Aquarium" was forgotten. See Rahv to Lowell, May 5, 1956, box 4 (986), and Carver to Lowell, May 27, 1956 (355), Robert Lowell Papers, MS Am 1905, Houghton Library, Harvard University.

own title, which refers to the "balanced" aquarium described toward the end of the memoir. A self-sustaining ecosystem of fish, plants, and mollusks of a kind popular in the nineteenth century, the aquarium helps to calm the patients. Lowell jokes about "the aquarium being a sanitarium within a sanitarium." The joke depends on a contrast between the aquarium's balanced ecosystem and the presumptively unbalanced psychology of the patients. But it also implies that the clinic itself is "the balanced aquarium," that the clinic's patients and doctors compose an orderly world in contrast to the chaos beyond its borders.

"The Balanced Aquarium" vibrates between the off-kilter sociality of the hospital as a final safe space and Lowell's tragicomic memories of the childhood events that brought him to that place. If "My Autobiography" is Lowell's prose epic of childhood, and *Life Studies* is his effort to write memoir as a poetic sequence, then "The Balanced Aquarium" is a postmodern psychomachy, an evocation of his internal turmoil.

The nine items that follow "The Balanced Aquarium" are peripheral to it and to "My Autobiography." They fill in gaps and provide a metacommentary on both major prose memoirs. Lowell composed seven of these items at about the same time as he wrote the two major memoirs. "I suffer from periodic wild manic explosions" and "Seven years ago I had an attack of pathological enthusiasm" focus on the psychological disability that landed Lowell in Payne Whitney. "For two years I have been cooling off" begins by meditating on the purpose of "My Autobiography," veers into a fantasy about a father-hating dog, and concludes with a wish for peace between Lowell and his father's memory. Taking the form of a therapeutic self-analysis, it ends by sounding like a canned response to such questions as "How do you think therapy can help you?" The memoiristic fragments "Our dining room at 239 Marlborough St." and "I might have been fifteen, or I might have been thirty-five" are perhaps additional adjuncts to "My Autobiography," whereas "On Black Israelites" and especially "Dreams" feel like further responses to psychiatric assignments, but this time with more complex resolutions.

Lowell wrote "Death, the Rich City" later, in 1962, after a vacation with Hardwick in Puerto Rico. Rather than being a factual account of the visit, it evokes an imagined encounter with a charismatic populist named "El Butano." Using his powers of fantasy, as he was encouraged to do in psychotherapy, Lowell stages the encounter as a confrontation between contrastive self-images: the peaceful lapsed Catholic still yearning for faith and the violent, atheistic revolutionary who challenges his interlocutor's assumptions.

"The Raspberry Sherbet Heart," Lowell's only real short story, was also composed in the 1960s. The mother and father in the story seem to be fictionalized portraits of Hardwick and Lowell in their domestic roles of spouses and parents. Despite the resemblances of the parents in the story to Hardwick and Lowell, they also resemble Lowell's own parents, especially in their propensity to argue.* The son Charles, the story's protagonist, may be based both on Lowell as a child and on his daughter, Harriet, who was between four and eight years old when the story was composed. Initially a literalist who doesn't comprehend his father's metaphorical speech, Charles soon grows to be even more figurative in his thinking than his father. In the latter sections of the story, the boy seems to stand allegorically for his father's, or Lowell's own, imaginative capacity—a figure, perhaps, of Lowell's fear of being swept away by his fantasies into madness.

Beyond the story's focus on the imagination, "The Raspberry Sherbet Heart" seems to be addressing another of Lowell's recurrent concerns: a son's troubled relations with his emotionally inaccessible father. Lowell's failure to find an authoritative ending to the story—he tried out new alternatives even on the last extant typescript—indicates that his confusions about the father-son relationship did not resolve, and therefore the story could not reach a definitive conclusion. Nor did he ever return to the story to try to work out its meanings anew—as he did with the late poem "To Daddy."† He left the story sitting in a library archive as an enduring, insoluble conundrum.

* For more details on the origins of the story, see Terri Witek, "The Boy with the Raspberry Sherbet Heart," *Shenandoah* 43, no. 2 (1993): 107–19. Witek quotes Hardwick as observing: "Perhaps the interesting thing is that Cal [Lowell] is both the child and the father!"

† The first published version of "To Daddy," in Robert Lowell, *History* (New York: Farrar, Straus and Giroux, 1973), posits the father as an "airhole" for his son, whereas the second published version, in Robert Lowell, *Selected Poems* (New York: Farrar, Straus and Giroux, 1976), rejects that generous interpretation.

A NOTE ON THE TEXTS

THE TEXT FOR "The Balanced Aquarium," the memoir that opens this section, has been culled from the typescripts in the Robert Lowell Papers at the Houghton Library, Harvard University. Although some of its pages are misfiled, after we re-sorted them, we found the text to be in good shape, indeed quite as Elizabeth Hardwick describes it in a March 1956 letter to *Partisan Review* editors—that is to say, as "already written in a good draft," "already nearly done," and needing only "to be revised for the last time."* It was so well developed by then that Hardwick offered it to the magazine for the planned publication of a sample of Lowell's new prose in lieu of "91 Revere Street," which had seemed rougher in comparison (though eventually it was the latter that was printed).

Nevertheless, "The Balanced Aquarium" is notably different from "Near the Unbalanced Aquarium," a version of the memoir that Robert Giroux quarried for his edition of Lowell's *Collected Prose* (1987). "The Balanced Aquarium" as published here offers the fullest version of the original text, one that includes as many as eleven pages missing from Giroux's version. It incorporates seven pages from the middle, which the previous editor seems to have deliberately omitted, as well as four other pages that are clearly part of the original draft but that Giroux probably overlooked; one

---

* Elizabeth Hardwick, letter to Catharine Carver, assistant editor of *Partisan Review*, March 7, 1956 (*Partisan Review* Collection #1028, box 4, folder 2, Howard Gotlieb Archival Research Center, Boston University).

of them was misfiled when the collection was catalogued, and three must have been placed in the wrong file later on, after the collection had been made available to researchers.

In addition, Giroux, as Lowell's lifetime editor, did not hesitate to make major revisions in his text. He cut single words, sentences, and in one case an entire paragraph. In particular, he rid the text of several poignantly symbolic, condensed passages and haunting but sudden flashbacks—fragments he must have thought were more appropriate to poetry than to prose. In the version of "The Balanced Aquarium" included in this volume, we have restored all of the passages and words Giroux deleted. Of several divergent drafts of the memoir's opening paragraphs, we selected the fullest version, which happens to be the same one Giroux chose. (Two alternatives appear in the Appendix.) At the end of "The Balanced Aquarium," the reader will not find the paragraphs Giroux tacked on to his version, for these are from other miscellaneous manuscripts and were not intended for this memoir. The pagination and the formal features of typescript pages show that the last paragraphs we provide are the real ending. We restored Lowell's preferred final title, "The Balanced Aquarium" (though in one early version of the opening paragraphs, the title is "Near the Balanced Aquarium," which is almost Giroux's title, one that the editor modified only slightly by adding to the adjective the prefix "Un-," making its meaning opaque). We retained Lowell's characteristic asterisk lines marking the transitions between his near-present-time narrative at the Payne Whitney Psychiatric Clinic and his flashbacks to the past.

The language and stories in "The Balanced Aquarium" occasionally remind one of the poems in *Life Studies*. The memoir first foreshadows "Sailing Home from Rapallo," and then, in order of appearance, "Terminal Days at Beverly Farms," "For Sale," "During Fever," and "My Last Afternoon with Uncle Devereux Winslow." Despite what Lowell implied after the fact,* the prose is too strong to be treated merely as source material for poetry.

"Seven years ago I had an attack of pathological enthusiasm," "For two

---

* Lowell explained: "There's a long first section in *Life Studies* called 'Last Afternoon with Uncle Devereux Winslow' which was originally written in prose. I put it aside and later cut things out and re-arranged it and made different transitions and put it into verse, so there is that connection and perhaps the style comes out of writing prose"; see Robert Lowell, "Robert Lowell in Conversation with A. Alvarez," *Review*, August 1963, 36–40.

years I have been cooling off," and "On Black Israelites" all originate in the Houghton Library collection, from sketches Lowell made as he was working on "The Balanced Aquarium." Giroux, incidentally, used "For two years I have been cooling off" for the ending of "Near the Unbalanced Aquarium," though Lowell nowhere indicated that it actually belonged there. "Our dining room at 239 Marlborough St." and "I might have been fifteen, or I might have been thirty-five" are transcribed from loose miscellaneous worksheets, also part of the Houghton Library collection. "I suffer from periodic wild manic explosions" and "Dreams" collect materials donated by Hardwick in 1990 to the Harry Ransom Center at the University of Texas, Austin. They come from the files of Dr. Vernon Williams, a psychiatrist treating Lowell in Boston in the late 1950s. "Dreams," however, additionally incorporates a page from a different folder in the Harry Ransom Center collection, with similar accounts of two other dreams. We decided that all the dreams belonged together in terms of their subject matter and style; they clearly are part of Lowell's project at the time of recording his dreams. The last section of "Dreams" derives from an isolated page on dreams in the Houghton Library. We left Lowell's accounts of his dreams underpunctuated in order to keep the note- and dream-like elements intact and to preserve the hazy effect of adjectives merging with each other.

"Death, the Rich City" is transcribed from one of several typescript drafts in the Harry Ransom Center collection. Some alternative drafts bear such titles as "Death, the Rich Port" and "Puerto Rico." They also show Lowell's efforts to turn the prose fantasy into a poem. The version we quote, though the best-developed of the prose versions, comes from a typescript with many corrections and variant words written between the lines or on the margins.

"The Raspberry Sherbet Heart" derives from a typescript at the Houghton Library. Little is known about the text. In 1989 and 1990, Terri Witek corresponded with Hardwick, who helped establish that "The Raspberry Sherbet Heart" was written in the 1960s, and was inspired by his family life with Hardwick and their daughter, Harriet, in New York City. The only significant change we introduced in our edition of the text is to make the protagonist's name consistently "Charles." The alternative name "David" appears on one page of the typescript, which seems to have come from a different draft than all of the other pages.

Except in "Dreams," we applied the same editorial principles we used in "My Autobiography." We preserved the anachronistic lowercase "oriental" for the same reason we kept the quaintly spelled "Hindoo" previously, as markers of the culture Lowell is evoking. Occasionally we had to correct or provide pronouns, prepositions, and other links of standard grammar. We entered Lowell's handwritten corrections if the typed words they were to replace were struck; if they weren't, we considered the corrections one by one and chose the best ones, which in our estimation were most likely to have found their way to the final text. We had to give up some corrections when we could not read them or determine where exactly they were intended, there being no carets or arrows signaling their placement.

The Balanced Aquarium

ONE MORNING IN July of 1954 I sat brooding by the open door of my bedroom on the third floor of the Payne Whitney Clinic.* For a few minutes I had been trying to get my picture of myself straight, and what I saw whenever I looked up were the blind, white bricks of the New York Hospital rising in my window.† Down the corridor, almost a city block away, I heard the elevator jar shut and steam like a kettle as it soared with its second and last allotment of my fellow patients to Occupational Therapy. My mind, somewhat overliterary and muscle-bound, hunted for the clue to the right picture of itself, and seemed to be chasing its own shuffle down the empty ward. In my distraction, the outer and inner walls of the hospital seemed to change shape like baggy, white clouds. I imagined that I saw a hard, enameled wedding cake, and beside it, holding the blunt silver knife of ritual, stood the tall, white stone bride . . . my mother in the brief, sacrificed frost of her wedding dress on a day in 1916 now forever less

---

* This was the second time Lowell received treatment at Payne Whitney Psychiatric Clinic. He had been admitted there in the late summer of 1949 to treat depression following a major manic episode. After his mother's death in February 1954, Lowell had another severe bipolar episode, was treated for six weeks at Jewish Hospital in Cincinnati (where he underwent electroshock therapy), and then was admitted again to Payne Whitney, staying from mid-May until mid-September 1954.

† New York–Presbyterian Hospital / Weill Cornell Medical Center, called in the 1950s New York Hospital and housing Payne Whitney Psychiatric Clinic, is located at East Sixty-Eighth Street and York Avenue in Manhattan. Architecturally inspired by the fourteenth-century Palace of the Popes in Avignon, France, the campus consists of a white skyscraper with a cascade of smaller buildings in the same style. With intricate brickwork and Gothic-influenced arches, the complex looks like a medieval fortress.

a lived day than the surface of its photograph on my father's bureau. There was something wonderful, overweening and dated about the architecture of the hospital, a fine and standard skyscraper surfaced with once avant-garde fifteenth-century Gothic . . . groin, coign and stainless steel! I thought of an island on the Seine, that little Manhattan with river water on both sides, the island of King Louis's Sainte-Chapelle, all heraldry and color, thoughtless as a chessman and innocent . . . built to house a thorn!* Under its lacquer of white brick, how merely geometrical this New York Hospital was, how safely skeletonized with indestructible stainless steel, how purely and puritanically confined to its office of cures! I counted the tiers of metal-framed windows, and in their place I imagined such a wall as the Assyrian, ruthless in his love of spick-and-span materials, might have reared, a wall bedizened with sparkling new tessellation, thousands of molasses-golden lions rampant on blue tiles.† In my mind the tiles were as blue as sky, yet I was unable to prevent their glowing from time to time with the lurid, self-advertising, chlorinated blue-green of an indoor swimming pool. Brick by brick, and white block by block, I was myself as if building this hospital like a child.

Below, occupying less space than five or six large living room carpets, was a formal, flowerless French garden. There the depressed patients were taking their morning airing, for they were too melancholy for athletics or occupational therapy. There segregation of the sexes was discouraged; in twos the patients circled the bright, gray, octagonal paving stones. Mixed couples, *Mann und Weib*,‡ and often not unwilling, the patients worked off their

---

* Built by King Louis IX of France, Sainte-Chapelle is located on the Île de la Cité, an island in the Seine as it flows through the heart of Paris. Until the French Revolution, the chapel housed the Crown of Thorns, one of Europe's most important Christian relics, believed to have been placed on Jesus's head for the Crucifixion.

† Life-sized enameled golden lions in bas-relief lined the walls of the Processional Way, which led from Ishtar Gate to the inner city of Babylon. Built under King Nebuchadnezzar II between 615 and 575 BCE, the passageway was considered to be one of the Seven Wonders of the World. The walls and the gate were covered with the background of deep-blue lapis lazuli tiles. Lowell echoes the book of Judith, which in a famous error identifies Nebuchadnezzar as an Assyrian, whereas the king was a Babylonian.

‡ German for "man and wife." In act one of Mozart's 1791 opera *The Magic Flute*, Papageno and Pamina praise the virtues of traditional marriage. They repeat in a duet, "*Nichts Edlers sei, als Weib und Mann. / Mann und Weib, und Weib und Mann, / Reichen an die Gottheit an*" (There is nothing nobler than wife and man. / Man and wife, and wife and man, / reaching toward the Deity). Lowell later used "Man and Wife" as the title for a rather dissonant marriage poem in *Life Studies*. One of his working titles for the poem was "Mann und Weib."

morning rounds. Student nurses with pageboy bobs and blue denim blouses
sat at picturesque and strategic angles. Crisp white medieval caps and stiff
*Herald Tribune*s caught the sun and glared like headlights. The unflowering,
jade-green garden shrubbery was fresh though formal, and apparently the
patients were also cool, contented, ingenuous and patterned. A black iron
gate, twenty feet high, divided the patients from the dust, heat and humanity of New York. Pains had been taken to make this gate appear unimpris-
oning and simply florid. Looking beyond the patients and over the caps and
newspapers of the nurses, I saw the blinding sparkle of the East River, the
filthy East River. An orange tugboat was lifting and lifting the monstrous
fleece-and-rawhide buffer that protected its prow. It nudged the sides of the
concrete embankment, as if arguing for admission to our asylum.

****

Mother had had no business coming into the upstairs den "undressed." She
wore pale pink slippers, a pale pink nightgown, a pale pink woolen throw-
over and a pale pink lace nightcap. Her wrapper, coral pink, was decorated
with blanched, massed pink thread work which repeated an overornate ori-
ental† arrangement of clustered cranes, crags and samurai dirks. All was
hushed, effete, tubercular and sacred. Mother was one of those lavishly
designed and colored pieces in our mah-jongg set called Seasons; or the
reeking, steaming, shrieking birdhouse at Franklin Park Zoo. I knew that
pink was a sissy color, and probably invented by a sissy, whom my grandmother Winslow, Gaga, called Louis Quinze. I felt like pushing in all directions with my arms, and making pink stay put in Mother's bedroom. And
here was Mother cruising throughout the house, and spilling all out over
everything, like some Chinese dragon jack-in-the-box with too powerful a
spring. I felt meshed and menaced.

One way to get around Mother was to think of the man's colors, blue
and tan. Father's chair was leather and oak. The water in his two photographs of the battleships *New York* and "Pennsy" was a gray that stood for

---

* This is the first of nine instances of an unusual punctuation feature Lowell uses in "The Balanced Aquarium" and nowhere else: an extended line of asterisks marking a suture between remembered times.

† We have left Lowell's adjective as he typed it, without an initial capital, though it is possible he or an editor
might have changed it in copyediting.

blue. I was a tower of muscle rushing into air and water. Then I did my best to look straight ahead and into Mother without seeing her.

****

My mind moved through the pictures of conscience, and remained in its recollections, weightless, floating, in medias res! I remembered the red storm lights and the brown tobacco spaces of night and the city's sky. On a sallow sheet of onionskin paper, whose semitransparency half revealed and half concealed the pink pads of my fingers and the royal blue abracadabra of the blotter, I wrote:

> In Boston the Hancock Life Insurance Building's beacon flared
> Foul weather, Father, as far as to the Charlestown Naval Yard,
> And almost warmed . . .

In February, on the nights when Mother was dying all alone at that little private hospital in Rapallo, the needle of the Hancock Life Insurance Building was flashing storm warnings.* On the road to the airport, I watched the angry discouraging red lights go on and off,† and far to my left, men were working with blowtorches on the blistered gray of old battleships that had been scrapped at the Charlestown naval yard, Father's old hunting ground, and the last place he had found employment worthy of his optimistic esprit de corps and his solid grounding in higher mathematics. In New Hampshire, the White Mountains would have been freezing to stone. And at our family cemetery in Dunbarton, the black brook, the pruned fir trunks, the iron spear fence, and the memorial slates would have been turning blacker. The motto on Father's family crest would still say *Occasionem Cognosce*,‡ as

---

* Charlotte had been spending her winter in Europe, where she went on October 17, 1953. After Lowell received a cable about his mother's critical situation following a major stroke in early February, he delayed his journey to Rapallo by taking a long circuitous route from Cincinnati "to Boston to New York to London to Paris," where he dillydallied for another night to spend the evening with Blair Clark. Clark noticed Lowell's dilatory manner and signs of mania. See Ian Hamilton, *Robert Lowell: A Biography* (New York: Random House, 1982), 201–2.

† The Old John Hancock Tower at 200 Berkeley Street, in the Back Bay, the second of three John Hancock buildings built in Boston, is known for its flashing weather beacon at the top. The building was completed in 1947, and its beacon has been in service since 1950. When flashing red, the beacon forecasts heavy snowfalls.

‡ Latin for "Recognize [your] opportunity." There is no family crest—to say nothing of the Lowell motto—on the father's tombstone, but rather the U.S. Navy officer badge.

he lay buried under his ostentatiously recent, unacclimatized tombstone, a wifeless, childless man, the single Lowell among some twenty-five Starks and Winslows. And as the moonlight and the burning cold illuminated the carved names of Father's in-laws, one might have thought they were in pain and were protesting Father's right to hold a single precious inch of the over-crowded soil there . . . unless he produced a dead wife, a Winslow.

I arrived at Rapallo half an hour after Mother's death.* On the next morning, the hospital where she died[†] was a firm and tropical scene from Cézanne: sunlight rustled through watery, plucked pines, and streaked the verticals of a Riviera villa above the Mare Ligure. Mother lay dappled by the brilliant blacks and greens and tans and flashings from her window. Her face was too formed and fresh to seem asleep. There was a bruise the size of an earlobe over her right eye.[‡] The nurse who had tended Mother during her ten days' dying stood at the bed's head. She was a great gray woman and wore glasses whose diaphanous blue frames were held together with a hairpin. With a flourish, she had just pulled aside the sheet that covered Mother's face, and now she looked daggers at the body as if death were some sulky animal or child that only needed to be frightened. We stood with tears running down our faces, and the nurse talked to me for an hour and a half in a patois that even Italians would have had difficulty under-standing. She was telling me everything she could remember about Mother. For ten minutes she might just as well have been imitating water breaking on the beach, but Mother was alive in the Italian words. I heard how Mother thought she was still at her hotel and wanted to go walking, and said she was only suffering from a little indigestion, and wanted to open both French windows and thoroughly air her bedroom each morning while the bed was still unmade; and how she kept trying to heal the hemorrhage in her brain by calling for her twenty little jars and bottles with pink plastic covers, and kept dabbing her temples with creams and washes, and always felt guilty because she wasn't allowed to take her quick cold bath in the morning and her hot aromatic bath before dinner. She kept asking about Bob and Bobby.

---

* Charlotte died of several strokes on February 13, 1954, shortly before midnight.

† Villa Chiara, where Ezra Pound was hospitalized in 1962 and 1963.

‡ After the first stroke, she was presumably prescribed blood-thinning medicines, which often result in bruising.

"*I have never been sick in my life.*" Nulla malattia mai! Nulla malattia mai!* And the nurse went out. Qua insieme per sempre.† She closed the door, and left me in the room.

That afternoon I sat drinking a Cinzano with Mother's doctor.‡ He showed me a copy of Ezra Pound's *Jefferson and/or Mussolini*, which the author had personally signed with an ideogram and the quotation, "Non . . . come bruti . . ."§

And at the Italian funeral, I did everything that my father could have desired. I met the Rapallo English colony, Mother's brief acquaintances. I made arrangements at the simple redbrick English Chapel;¶ I engaged a sober Church of England clergyman. Then I went to Genoa and bought Mother a black-and-gold baroque casket that would have been suitable for burying her here, Napoleon at *Les Invalides*. It wasn't disrespect or even impatience that allowed me to permit the undertakers to take advantage of my faulty knowledge of Italian and Italian values and to overcharge me and to make an ugly and tasteless error. They misspelled Mother's name on her coffin as *Lowel*.** While alive, Mother had made a point of spelling out her name letter by letter for identification. I could almost hear her voice correcting the workmen. "I am Mrs. Robert Lowell of One Seventy Marlborough St., Boston. L, O, W, E, *double* L."

On Sunday morning when we sailed, the whole shoreline of the Golfo di

---

* Not standard Italian. Charlotte had taken Italian lessons in the summer of 1953. Literally, the sentence means "No illness ever."

† Italian for "Here together forever."

‡ Dr. Giuseppe Bacigalupo (1912–1988), who himself describes the circumstances of Charlotte's death in his book *Ieri a Rapallo* (Udine: Companotto Editore, 1993).

§ On the margin of the manuscript Lowell penciled in the word "Cantos" which indicates he contemplated replacing *Jefferson and/or Mussolini* with *Cantos*. "*Non . . . come bruti . . .*" seems to be an allusion to well-known words uttered by Ulysses in Dante's Canto xxvi, words for which the hero was damned in the Florentine's Hell as "evil counselor." Ulysses is quoted as having said, in an address to his companions, that they "were not made to live like brutes or beasts," and therefore they have a natural craving for knowledge, however dangerous the pursuit may be: "*fatti non foste a viver come bruti.*" If Pound thought it a fitting inscription in a book, he seems to have disregarded the sinful dimension of Ulysses's speech and appreciated instead its emphasis on the human thirst for experience and novelty.

¶ Presumably, Rapallo's one and only Anglican chapel, the Church of St. George at the crossing of Via Aurelia Ponente and Via Costaguta. Built in 1902 to serve the growing English community and often used for funeral services, it is neither redbrick nor simple. Sold in 1975, the building is no longer a place of worship.

** In the analogous scene in the *Life Studies* poem "Sailing Home from Rapallo," written several years later, the mother's name is misspelled "Lovel." In a March 11, 1954, letter to Blair Clark, Lowell describes the misspelling on the casket still differently: "*Charlotte Winslon*"; see Robert Lowell, *The Letters of Robert Lowell*, edited by Saskia Hamilton (New York: Farrar, Straus and Giroux, 2005), 214.

Genova was breaking into fiery flower. A crazy Piedmontese raced about us in a parti-colored sea sled, whose outboard motor was, of course, unmuffled. Our little liner was already doing nearly twenty knots an hour, but the sea sled cut figure eights across our bows. Mother, permanently sealed in her coffin, lay in the hold. She was solitary, just as formerly, when she took her long walks to the Ned's Point Lighthouse by the Atlantic at Mattapoisett in September, which she called "the best season of the year" after the summer people had gone. She shone in her bridal tinfoil and hurried homeward with open arms to her husband lying under the White Mountains.*

****

When Mother died, I began to feel tireless, madly sanguine, menaced and menacing. I entered the Payne Whitney Clinic for "all those afflicted in mind." One night I sat in the mixed lounge, and enjoyed the new calm which I had been acquiring with much cunning during the few days since my entrance. I remember coining and pondering for several minutes such phrases as "the Art of Detachment," "Offhanded Involvement," and "Urbanity: A Key to the Tactics of Self-Control." But the old menacing hilarity was growing in me. I saw Anna and her nurse walk into our lounge. Anna, a patient from a floor for more extreme cases, was visiting our floor for the evening. I knew that the evening would soon be over, that the visitor would probably not return to us, and that I had but a short time to make my impression on her. Anna towered over the piano, and thundered snatches of Mozart sonatas, which she half remembered and murdered. Her figure, a Russian ballerina's or Anna Karenina's, was emphasized, and *illuminated*, as it were, by an embroidered, middle-European blouse that fitted her with the creaseless, burnished, curved tightness of a medieval breastplate. I throbbed to the music and the musician. I began to talk aimlessly and loudly to the room at large. I discussed the solution to a problem that had been bothering me about the unmanly smallness of the suits of armor that I had seen "tilting" at the Metropolitan Museum. "Don't you see?" I said, and pointed to Anna, "the armor was made for *Amazons*!" But no one took up my lead. I

---

* The mountain range in New Hampshire where Bob Lowell was buried and where the poet was taking his mother's body. The graveyard was subsequently relocated less than a mile from its original site.

began to extol my tone-deafness; it was, I insisted, a providential flaw, an auditory fish weir that screened out irrelevant sonority. I made defiant adulatory remarks on Anna's touch. Nobody paid any attention to me.

Roger, an Oberlin undergraduate and fellow patient, sat beside Anna on the piano bench. He was small. His dark hair matched his black flannel Brooks Brothers suit; his blue-black eyes matched his blue-black necktie. He wore a light cashmere sweater that had been knitted for him by his mother, and his yellow woolen socks had been imported from the Shetlands. Roger talked to Anna with a persuasive shyness. Occasionally, he would stand up and play little beginners' pieces for her. He explained that these pieces were taken from an exercise book composed by Béla Bartók in protest against the usual, unintelligibly tasteless examples used by teachers. Anna giggled with incredulous admiration as Roger insisted that the clinic's music instructor could easily teach her to read more skillfully. Suddenly, I felt compelled to make a derisive joke, and I announced cryptically and untruly that Rubinstein had declared the eye was of course the source of all evil for a virtuoso. "If the eye offends thee, pluck it out." No one understood my humor. I grew red and confused. The air in the room began to tighten around me. I felt as if I were squatting on the bottom of a huge laboratory bottle and trying to push out the black rubber stopper before I stifled. Roger sat like a rubber stopper in his black suit. Suddenly, I knew I could clear the air by taking hold of Roger's ankles and pulling him off his chair. By some crisscross of logic, I reasoned that my cruel boorishness would be an act of self-sacrifice. I would be bowing out of the picture, and throwing Roger into the arms of Anna. Without warning, but without lowering my eyes from Anna's splendid breastplate blouse, I seized Roger's yellow ankles. I pulled; Roger sat on the floor with tears in his eyes. A sigh of surprised repulsion went round the room. I assumed a hurt, fatherly expression, but all at once I felt eased and sympathetic with everyone.

When the head nurse came gliding into the lounge, I pretended that I was a white-gloved policeman who was directing traffic. I held up my open hands, and said, "No roughage, Madam; just innocent merriment!" Roger was getting on his feet; I made a stop signal in his direction. In a purring, pompous James Michael Curley voice, I said, "Later, he will thank me." The head nurse, looking bored and tolerant, led me away to watch the Liberace program in the men's television parlor. I was left unpunished. But next morning, while I was weighing in and "purifying" myself in the cold shower, I sang

Rex tremendae majestatis
qui salvandos salvas gratis*

at the top of my lungs and to a melody of my own devising. Like the catbird, who will sometimes "interrupt its sweetest song by a perfect imitation of some harsh cry such as that of the Great Crested Flycatcher, the squawk of a hen, the cry of a lost chicken, or the spitting of a cat,"[†] I blended the lonely tenor of some fourteenth-century Flemish monk with bars of "Yankee Doodle," and the *Mmm Mmm* of the padlocked Papageno.[‡]

I was then transferred to a new floor where the patients were deprived of their belts, pajama cords and shoestrings. We were not allowed to carry matches, and had to request the attendants to light our cigarettes. For holding up my trousers I invented an inefficient, stringless method which I considered picturesque and called Malayan. Each morning before breakfast, I lay naked to the waist in my knotted Malayan pajamas and received the first of my round-the-clock injections of chlorpromazine: left shoulder, right shoulder, right buttock, left buttock. My blood became like melted lead. I could hardly swallow my breakfast, because I so dreaded the weighted bending down that would be necessary for making my bed. And the rational exigencies of bed making were more upsetting than the physical. I wallowed through badminton doubles, as though I were a diver in the full billowings of his equipment on the bottom of the sea. I sat gaping through Scrabble games unable to form the simplest word; I had to be prompted by a nurse, and even then couldn't make any sense of the words the nurse had formed for me. I watched the Giants play the Brooklyn Dodgers on television.

Prince Scharnhorst, the only other patient watching the game, was a pundit and could have written an article for the Encyclopedia on each bat-

---

* A couplet from the thirteenth-century Latin hymn Dies Irae. Translated in 1849 by William Josiah Irons, it reads: "King of Majesty tremendous, / Who dost free salvation send us."

† The quotation, almost verbatim, comes from Edward Howe Forbush, *Birds of Massachusetts and Other New England States* (Boston: Massachusetts Department of Agriculture, 1929), 324.

‡ Papageno is a character in Mozart's *Magic Flute*. A bird catcher, the boy gets a padlock on his mouth as punishment for lying and for a time can sing only "Hm! hm! hm!"

ter's technique and the type of pitching that had some chance of outwitting him. The Prince understood the catcher Roy Campanella's signals to the Dodgers' pitchers, and criticized Campanella's strategy sympathetically, but with the authority of an equal. My head ached, and I couldn't keep count of the balls and strikes for longer than a single flash on the screen. I went back to my bedroom and wound the window open to its maximum six inches. Below me, patients circled in twos over the bright gray octagonal paving stones of the courtyard. I let my glasses drop. How freely they glittered through the air for almost a minute! They shattered on the stones. Then everyone in the courtyard came crowding and thrusting their heads forward over my glasses, as though I had been scattering corn for pigeons. I felt my languor lift and then descend again. I already seemed to weigh a thousand pounds because of my drug, and now I blundered about nearly blind from myopia. But my nervous system vibrated joyfully, when I felt the cool air brushing directly on my eyeballs. And I was reborn each time I saw my blurred, now unspectacled, now unprofessorial face in the mirror. Yet all this time I would catch myself asking whining questions. Why don't I die, die? I quizzed my face of suicide in the mirror; but the body's warm, un-awed breath befogged the face with a dilatory inertia.

I said, "My dreams at night are so intoxicating to me that I am willing to put on the nothingness of sleep. My dreams in the morning are so intoxicating to me that I am willing to go on living."* Even now I can sometimes hear those two sentences repeating themselves over and over and over. I say them with a chant-like yawn, and feel vague, shining, girlish, like Perdita,† or one of the many willowy allegoric voices in Blake's prophetic books.‡ "For my dreams, I will endure the day; I will suffer the refreshment of sleep." In one's teens these words, perhaps, would have sealed a Faustian compact. Waking, I suspected that my whole soul and its thousand of spiritual fibers, immaterial ganglia, apprehensive antennae, psychic radar, etc., had been bruised by a rubber hose. In the presence of persons, I was ajar.

---

* Here Lowell echoes the passage that appears as the conclusion to "Dreams."

† In Shakespeare's *The Winter's Tale*.

‡ The poet William Blake (1757–1827), whose prophetic books include *America: A Prophecy*, *The Book of Urizen*, *The Book of Los*, *Milton*, and *Jerusalem*.

But in my dreams, I was like one of Michelangelo's burly ideal statues that can be rolled downhill without injury.

****

My last images of Father were of something anxious, wordless and repetitive. But how blindingly he stood out to me, when he would hover on the porch of the Beverly Farms house, two, three, five, ten, or maybe twenty days before his third coronary thrombosis and abrupt, unprotesting death!* I have never known the night when Father failed to appear in some brusquely emphatic change of dress for dinner; these evenings he wore an imported English cream-colored dinner jacket and an indigo silk cummerbund. And this dashing and deftly careless costume was the final triumphant and surprising flower of his evolution; or rather it was a reversion to the glory of those blue-and-gold, white-and-gold naval uniforms, which he had abandoned when he had resigned from the service in 1927. I do not know whether it was ignorance (Father had been a naval man since the age of fourteen and a half) or whether it was some self-distrusting wish to jar others that made him choose dress clothes that were "small-town" or peasant *endimanché*.† There was something hopelessly dull and lumpish about his twin penguin tuxedoes, bought somewhere at a twelve percent serviceman's discount, worn with their boiled shirts stiff as bathtubs, summer and winter—one tux alternating with the other night after night after night! And his many pairs of white flannels looked as though they had been starched by mistake, and were always an inch or so too long because Father, penny-prudent, overestimated the allowance to be made for shrinkage. And his blue serge herringbone coat and waistcoat, which he combined with his white flannels, was so unbending and indestructible it might have been woven from steel wool; it had seemed to absorb an inch from his height and add an inch to his stomach. For years whatever he wore looked pretentious on him, and yet underhandedly economical. Now in these terminal days of

* In 1949 Bob and Charlotte Lowell sold their 170 Marlborough Street house and moved to Beverly Farms, Massachusetts. Bob died August 30, 1950.

† French for "in one's Sunday best."

his life, Father dressed as if, lordly, tropical, Colonial, he had stepped out of Brooks Brothers into an illustration for Conrad, Kipling, or Maugham, once his favorite highbrow authors. And now he was vitally slim!

But it was otherwise in Father's fat days. I remember a maddening scene that occurred at 2129 Bancroft Place in Washington. I stood in Father's downstairs den. An unfinished mah-jongg game sprawled like the debris of Babel on a cheap card table. Father's dress sword with black crepe on its hilt for President Harding's death hung from a piano wire as large as a clothes-line. An eighteen-inch rectangular photograph of Father and his engineer-ing force aboard the Battleship "Pennsy," tilted over a fireplace without logs or andirons. Through a wide-open window and blowing organdy, drowsed the tepid, seedy, elephantine air of an April afternoon in Washington. Fa-ther and Commander K——, his classmate and immediate superior on the "Pennsy," knelt on strips of the Sunday paper. Both wore earphones and were busy fussing at the unshelled apparatus of Father's twelve-tube radio set designed to get stations in Australia and New Zealand. No one heard me when I asked for the third time to be taken to see the beavers at the Rock Creek Park Zoo. Father's sleeveless russet jersey gave him the unearned and quite disappointingly illusory appearance of a juicy land beaver. He squatted on the floor and fussed with the radio parts. And I, a twitchy, gan-gling child of seven, stood looking down on my father, and thinking how fat he was getting from overeating. I ran a sticky finger through my mop of unbrushed hair and gawked at his bald spot that seemed to be pinkly and visibly eroding. I saw myself as a haughty, gaunt, coughing Don Quixote, mounted on Rocinante, a bag of bones, and esquired by Father, the pedes-trian, plebeian, obese Sancho. I hoped Mother would come into the room and make this same invidious, venomous comparison. My rage had grown monstrous, causeless. As though I were trying to put the hex on Father, I kept mewing to myself, "Thick man, thin man!" In my mind, immovable as the vocabulary drill on our school blackboard, I saw the worst words I knew: *paunch* and *bald* . . . Then Mother *was* in the room and again nagging Father about my supposed asthma, and asking him again when he was going to request to be transferred from Washington to Boston. She looked wrath-fully at the crepe-hung sword, put an arm around my shoulders, and said, "I don't see how that stupid Dr. Brague or *Brag* can help Bobby, when he let President Harding die!"

Goodbye to all that ignominy! During his last days of retirement at Beverly Farms, Father hovered on the porch: a trim figure, an efficient hairless head, a Cheshire Cat smile over a cream-colored dinner jacket and an indigo cummerbund. He might have posed as General Eisenhower! Bronzed, cool-looking, a cool customer! Though perhaps a shade too ruddy, he would idle a minute under the six-pointed star lantern for his birthday present two months earlier in July. His eye would linger on the huge, unhewn boulder, which hulked, tamely and smoothly enough, on a slope in the center of his garden and must have reminded him of similar irregular effects in Chinese gardens on the Yangtze in 1908, when life had opened out utterly to him, a gentle, promising naval ensign, just two years out of Annapolis, and still possessing a boy's virginal, buccaneer imagination. And further down his garden slope he would have seen the gun-barrel blue rails of the commuters' railroad gleaming cleanly through the scarlet autumn leaves of the sumac sprouting like a jungle on the limits of his property. The nearness of the railroad would have been worse perhaps than looking down the barrels of a loaded gun for my parents in the shy early years of their marriage; but at this moment in their lives the railroad had been what had determined their settling at Beverly Farms. Its nearness meant that they were independent of their car. Father cared nothing for owning a house that overlooked some spur of the Atlantic drenched with breakers. If asked where he lived, he would answer with contempt for the poetic and pastoral, "Two minutes' walk from the Beverly Farms' Station and forty minutes by train from Boston." Often Father would stroll seigneurially down his garden path and pretend to be admiring his tiger lilies; but his mind would be solely on his small black Ford. Despite the strain on his heart, and like a conspirator, he would slide back the door to his garage. And there it lay: stripped of its superfluous nickel, sensationally sober, waxed, simonized within an inch of its life! It was like a garlanded, sacrificial steer with varnished hooves. It was like some old maid's spotless electric car decorated with twin vases of flowers. It was a car you would have been proud to ask to your dining room table! But the Ford was less expensive and more out of date than it appeared, and its gloss was fragile, like Father, or the dancing pumps he had bought while taking the waters at Bad Nauheim on the eve of World War II, when he could still boast that he had only three fillings in his teeth, twenty-twenty vision, and had never been sick for longer than two consecutive days.

All through this summer until the middle of August, Father and his Ford had been up and out on the road by nine-thirty in the morning. This was due to a little stratagem arranged by Professor X———, the husband of the sister of one of Mother's Reading Club cronies. During these latter years, ever since the termination of his last real job as MIT's liaison man for the Charlestown Naval Yard, it must be confessed that Father was almost unemployable. Employers were afraid of his heart condition, and quite astonished by a certain beaming inattentive languor that had been growing on him for years. But Professor X———, a retired archeologist, had put in a word with his naval connections at Newport, and these in turn had "contacted" the director of the Salem Marine Museum,* who had, in his turn, sent a note to Father. So each morning bright and early, and five days a week, Father and his black Ford set off for the museum, and as I saw them disappearing down the driveway, seeming to shake off the dust and dew of Beverly Farms, I thought of them as not merely man and thing, but as two boys playing hooky. Sheets of graph paper covered with figures and scaled drawings would flap negligently on their shelf by the Ford's back window. They had been safely, though hurriedly, weighted down with Father's valuable ivory slide rule, a graduation commemorative token from his mother. He worked with manic esprit de corps, in a tone of jovial awe spoke of the museum director as "the commandant," and with characteristic shyness kept putting off, though prodded by Mother, inquiring the amount of his salary. But it turned out that there was no salary at all. So one night Father said, "If they don't want to pay me, I won't work." After that the museum and its director dropped from conversation.

****

"Br-r-r-p!" said Prince Scharnhorst. My glass, glazed, ajar door crashed cheerfully, insolently against my desk. Ghostly, Strindbergian, the Prince stood stooping over my shoulder. "Br-r-r-p, br-r-r-p, br-r-r-p," he effervesced with his North German version of the Oxford accent. I hid the sheet of onionskin paper on which I had written the first and last lines of a sonnet entitled:

---

* Presumably Lowell here means the Salem Maritime National Historic Site, established in 1938.

TO MY FATHER

You sailed to China, Father, and knew your math . . .

. . . .

Friendly to all, and loving none, perhaps.*

The Prince was a chalky, unhappily elongated and freakishly Swedish-looking young German with platinum blond hair and the steely touch of a pianist. White as a mannequin cut out of paper, he held up a white whalebone model of a windjammer which he had just fitted together and which he wanted to lend me because my father, a naval man, had admired Count von Luckner, the Sea Devil.† Prince Scharnhorst wore black suede shoes, eccentrically broad at the middle, regular gunboats, but then suddenly narrowing to a point, like spades on a playing card. His flimsy plaid socks had faded to a monochrome without at all losing their original cheap, aristocratic loudness. His shirt, a pepper-and-salt check, was a thin cotton imitation of a lumberjack's flannel shirt. His suit was belted and made of apricot-orange corduroy. I used to point out to the Prince that his dress was courageously conservative—among the sporty Payne Whitney patients, he was the only man whose coat matched his trousers. His underdrawers were an important hearsay part of his getup. He boasted that these perplexingly buttonless fabrics had been copied from the regulation "issue" of a sanitarium at Colorado Springs or Antibes. He flamed in my doorway, a sunbeam—a man

* Here is the full text of the concealed sonnet. Lowell never published it. It is typed on a separate sheet and today filed in Robert Lowell Papers at the Houghton Library, Harvard University, with other draft poems in a folder labeled "Miscellaneous fragments and untitled poems":

> You sailed to China, Daddy, and knew your math
> Had all the answers. When you stood on tap,
> Reserved and beaming, just behind the scene,
> And did the dirty work as engineer
> Aboard the Pennsie. Daddy, your career
> Shot like a rocket from that Turkish bath
> Of pipes and coils and fell in Mother's lap.
> I prize the life you whittled to routine!
> As early as teatime you would spread your graphs
> To dodge our conversation, and to prove
> Systems to break the market, to collapse . . .
> Daddy, we cannot talk, and now you move,
> Shy Smiler, through my world of photographs,
> Friendly to all and loving none perhaps.

† Felix Graf von Luckner (1881–1966), a German nobleman and a naval officer, nicknamed *Der Seeteufel* ("The Sea Devil") for his exploits as a commander of the commercial raider SMS *Seeadler* during World War I.

so various in his moonshines and virtuosity that I half imagined he was an apparition, an actor.

"Br-r-p!" said Prince Scharnhorst. *Br-r-r-p* was his Russian roulette call, and was meant to signify the whir of a revolver cylinder spinning with five empty chambers and one loaded chamber. You put in a cartridge, spun the cylinder, "looked the barrel in the eye," and had five-sixths of a chance of not killing yourself. One night after his first discharge from Payne Whitney, the Prince had actually "gambled" on Russian roulette, and won five thousand dollars. He had returned to us. Miraculously still alive, bandaged like a victorious skier, with a nick off his left ear, a bullet burn along the left side of his head, stooping, smiling with ironic modesty, the Prince had returned to us. And now after seven weeks at the clinic, he was once again all but cured. In spare minutes, he had written a condescendingly lucid abridgement and revision of Goren's *Contract Bridge*. To the astonishment of the doctors, he had organized and presided over an interfloor duplicate bridge tournament. But today the Prince was doing hard time. While waiting for his baked apple at breakfast, he had remembered that there were only twenty-four hours in the day. Excited at being kept waiting, he began to brood on his stamp collection. The filing cabinet in his bedroom held twenty leather-bound volumes filled with stamps. They were turning mossy with neglect! His desk was a mare's nest of envelopes bursting with new unassorted stamps mailed to him from London, Oslo and an émigré uncle, an *oil* baron in Dallas. The Prince flung down his napkin, as though he were delivering a challenge to the nurses. He began to pester, storm, curse, scream. Leaving his breakfast untasted, he snuffled off to his bedroom. And there I had seen him sitting mute, efficient, steely-fingered. On a cold, empty stomach, as though fasting for the Communion at high mass, he pasted, sorted and resorted his stamps. And now he stood in my doorway. He had forgotten his stamps, and held a little model frigate, which he wished to lend me because my father had admired Count von Luckner. "Br-r-r-p!"

****

Three days after Father's death, the Beverly Farms house almost gave the impression of having once been lived in. Its rooms, open, eviscerated, empty and intimate, were rooms restored to "period": they only existed fifty years in the future, on exhibition. Perhaps this vacancy, this on-tiptoe air, came from my knowing that everything about me had waited three days for Father's return to us from the undertaker. But it was obvious that my parents had lived at Beverly Farms less than eighteen months: the house wasn't ready to own up to them; each piece of our old furniture seemed to say, "I was city-bred." Mother had bought the Beverly Farms house as a compensation for Father, whose ten-year dream of moving from Boston to Puget Sound had been destroyed by a second heart attack. Fearfully, she had looked out of her windows at Beverly Farms, as though she were looking from the windows of a train that was drawing into the station, one station beyond her destination. From the beginning, she had lived with an eye cocked toward Boston. She wanted to be in Boston, and she dreaded Boston's invasion and mockery of this new house, which was so transparently a sheepish toy house for Father. Organizing and tidying with prodigal animosity, she kept her rooms alerted—not to be judged by visitors but to judge them.

The third day after Father's death was an overcast day. His little ship's-cabin-sized bedroom, the blue bedroom, lay overlooking the sloping garden, the huge, smooth boulder, the gunmetal railroad tracks showing through scarlet sumac. White caps on a patch of black Atlantic appeared through the scenic, lopped tops of garden trees; chalk writing on a blackboard! The blueness of the bedroom had been achieved by Mother through an accumulation of inconspicuous touches: blue lines on the top of the bedspread, blue fringe on the curtains, blue velvet straps on the Chinese sandals, a blue kimono. Blue symbolized baths twice a day, a platonic virility, the sea; *Thalassa*! But the bedroom was ninety-nine one-hundredths white of course. Elbow grease, an explosive simplicity—the floor's old broad softwood boards seemed sandblasted into cleanliness! On a white enamel bedside table and beside a glass lamp with a lace lampshade lay Volume I of Lafcadio Hearn's *Glimpses of Unfamiliar Japan*. The cover, an olive green ornamented with silver bamboo stalks in leaf, was as wrinkled and punished and discolored as an old school book. On the flyleaf my grandmother Lowell had written "Rob, from Mother. September 1908." The book had originally been given her by someone named Alice on January 23, 1908. This, too, was noted down. On another page, she had written, "This book had hard usage on the Yangtze River, China, when R.T.S.L. was on the gunboat *Villalobos*. It was left

under an open porthole in a storm." This inscription* was unlike ones written by Mother's family, the Winslows: it was correctly spelled, and made no
attempt to amuse or improve.

Mother's bedroom was a better place. It was four times as large as Father's. Sensibly, world-acceptingly, it overlooked a driveway and faced
away from the ocean. Here were objects which proclaimed admirable pleasures: an adjacent, pavilion-like bathroom, a window seat, a boudoir table,
lending-library who-done-its with plastic covers, bedside lamps loaded
with red and yellow fruit and decent putti, an electric blanket; and perhaps
crowning all in its idyllic symbolism, a hot-water bottle, silver, engraved
like an old-fashioned hip flask with a family crest, and covered by a loosely
woven pink woolen slip which Mother had knitted herself. Mother's double
bed, her tall ornate bureau, her short plain bureau, her boudoir-table bench,
her telephone stand and stool, her rocker, her hearth broom and her breakfast tray with folding legs all matched, and were painted a mustard yellow
ornamented with wheels and ripplings of green and gold. Alas, her innocent
breakfasts in bed—*ubi sunt*!†

On the third day, one room, as though it were a person, seemed to experience Father's absence. This was the "den." All its soft, easeful, chilly
leather surfaces glistened and mourned: the brown-oak-and-iron escritoire
brought back from Palermo by Grandfather Winslow; the brown blotter,
rug, lampshades and curtains; the brown wood of the paper knife, chairs
and ship's-clock base. The brasses mourned: a second paper knife, the
helmsman's-wheel frame of the ship's clock, a hollow brass rod that was
a combination poker and bellows. (The financial page from a last week's
Boston Herald lay folded where Father had left it under his portable radio,
so placed to prevent the page from blowing away during one of Mother's
bracing, all-windows-open after-breakfast airings.) His ivory slide rule
protruded from a pigeonhole of the desk, where it rested in its leather case,
as handy as some more warlike householder's holstered revolver.

Also on the desk was a red and gold portfolio which held pitilessly complete and clear records of Father's interests since 1945. Here was the twenty-

* Here Lowell penciled in the following insertion in the manuscript: "signed K.B.L. 1911 was typical of
Gr. L." In Lowell's shorthand, "K.B.L." stands for Kate Bailey Lowell, and "Gr. L." for Grandmother
Lowell.

† Latin for "Where are [they]?" or "Where have they gone?"

page booklet of scaled diagrams executed in inks of five colors, and showing, a page to a room, each room at Beverly Farms. The position and measurements of each sofa, bed, table, chair, etc., were given. Father had spent a cheerful month devising and correcting this booklet; it had proved a godsend to the movers. Here was a similar booklet filled with hypothetical alternative plans for a rearrangement of the Salem Museum's display cases.

These furniture-position booklets were derivative art; Father had learned how to make them from his cousin A. Lawrence Lowell. When Lawrence Lowell was elected President of Harvard in 1908, he packed up the furniture in his Marlborough St. house and moved to the Yard.* He was a man who always landed on his feet, and who looked with modest foresight into the sands of time, and before moving he had accordingly drawn up a furniture-position plan of his old house. In 1936,[†] he had returned to Marlborough St.—an ex-president, a widower, an octogenarian, and an automobilist who had just been deprived of his license for reckless driving. But not a piece of the old furniture had been lost; the position plans were consulted and each piece unalterably reoccupied its old position . . . Here finally were Father's estimates and drawings for the installation of the new Sears Roebuck furnace, which by its low fuel consumption was to pay for itself in ten years. Missing only were the innumerable graphs on which Father had plotted out catastrophic systems for his private investments in those years before the War, when he had been an investment counsel and his own chief customer. On the table by Father's easy chair lay *Life* magazine, a sort of Bible, whose pro–Chiang Kai-shek editorial sermons and savagely red-bordered black-and-white cover photographs used to remind him with nostalgia of Chinese lacquers and dragons. Absence!

I was the only person Mother permitted to lift the lid of the casket. Father was there. He wore his best sport coat—pink, at ease, obedient! Not a twist or a grimace recalled those unprecedented last words spoken to Mother as he died, "I feel awful." And it was right that he should still have the slight over-ruddiness so characteristic of his last summer. He looked entirely alive, or as he used to say: *W & H*—Well and Happy. Impossible

* Abbott Lawrence Lowell's house was at 171 Marlborough Street in the Back Bay. Harvard Yard is a grassy plot of 22.5 acres, with dormitories, Harvard libraries, classroom buildings, the Memorial Church, deans' offices, and the President's House (known today as Loeb House).

† By all indications, Abbott Lawrence Lowell moved back to his Marlborough Street house in 1933, not 1936.

to believe that if I had pressed a hand to his brow to see if it were hectic, I would have touched the *cold thing*! There were flowers; not too many. To one side of the casket, someone had accidentally left Admiral K——'s framed photograph. This was the same K—— that I have described as squatting on a section of a Sunday paper in Washington, and helping Father to assemble his radio. In the Navy, officers are listed according to rank and age; Father and K—— had once been the only officers in their class, who were not outranked by younger men. And now in the photograph, Admiral K——, who had risen from glory to glory, stood on a part of his Mediterranean flagship that looked more like a laundry than a ship, only it was outdoors. K—— held his binoculars half-raised to his eyes, and seemed to squint through the sun's dazzling, difficult glare into what were either folds of an awning or thirty uniforms on hangers. The picture was inscribed: "To my old friend, classmate+shipmate '*Bob*' Lowell."

****

Occupational Therapy, or O.T., was held in a suite of rooms on the top floor of the Clinic. It was a sunny, improving world; and there, unable to "think" with my hands, I spent a daily hour of embarrassed anguish. There for weeks I saw my abandoned pinecone basket lying on the pile for waste materials. And as it sank under sawdust and shavings, it seemed to protest the pains Mr. Kemper, our instructor, had once taken to warp, to soak, to reweave, to rescue it. And there in an old cigar box I saw my materially expensive, massively hideous silver ring, which Mr. Kemper had mostly forged and then capped off with an intaglio of an Iroquois corn shock ripening under the arrowy rays of a crescent moon. And as I stood there, obsequious, scornful, fearful and fierce, Mr. Kemper would come to me in his mild, beach-colored smock. He was a shy, precise man, who, blushing as if at his own presumption, would tell gentle, instructive anecdotes so as to avoid crude, outright answers to my haphazard questions on techniques. He was used to the impatience of patients; but he seemed stunned when he discovered that my polite, hesitant, often erratically detailed questions seldom implied even an appearance of attending to his answers. I would interrupt in midsentence with new questions, or drive deafly, blindly, marringly into my work.

A white-haired, electrically neat and alert Miss Margate was the directress of O.T. She had an office of her own. In its window, there was a full view
of that great slice of life, hope and modern architecture—the U.N. Building.
On the walls hung Miss Margate's own watercolors of the stranded schoo-
ners and long bridge at Wiscasset, Maine. To avoid working with my hands,
I used to loiter in Miss Margate's office and ask her desultory, philosophical
questions in a patronizing mumble. I talked with exhilarating bluster of my
vocation, writing, and her *avocation*, painting. I pitied her talent smothered in
administration and suggested in a fine phrase that her "deftly faultless" watercolors were wise in avoiding both the "finesse and the folly of art." "We
will never see a Margate work in the Washington National Gallery," I used
to joke brutally, "but she'll never beg bread among the Washington Square
daubers!"

At Occupational Therapy, there was the room of the loom and the room
of the potters' wheels. I spent several mornings in each, inquiring. But when
the loom or the wheel was put in my hands, I excused myself by explaining
Charles Collingwood's theory that art could never be merely craft, "despite
all the attacks made on inspiration by our friends the anti-romantic critics."*
I pretended that my doctor had given me permission to read *Kim*.

But in the end, of course, I gravitated to young Mrs. Rodgers' painting
class, which was held in a long light room whose windows surveyed the East
River and its shipping. For a few mornings, I asked questions about method,
drew cones and tried to memorize the complementary colors; then wearying I began to shout out and make childish scenes against representation,
the laws of perspective and the Hollywoodization of America. I declaimed
paragraphs from a brochure on Cézanne written by Meyer Schapiro.† I
praised that "plodding dispositional ferocity" which had ruined Cézanne's
White Monk but later made possible the serene and triumphant *Madame
Cézanne Tête Baissée*.‡ Prince Scharnhorst was finishing a delicate and archi-

* Lowell here means not Charles but Robin George Collingwood, whose theory of art sets it apart from
craft in *The Principles of Art* (1938).

† Meyer Schapiro (1904–1996), Columbia University art historian, author of several publications on
Cézanne.

‡ In this sentence Lowell presumably refers to Cézanne's 1866 *Portrait d'un moine* (Portrait of a Monk) and
to one of his several paintings showing his wife, Hortense Fiquet, with bent head, perhaps *Madame Cézanne
aux cheveux dénoués* of 1885–1886, a painting Schapiro praises in a publication on Cézanne of the 1950s.
The exact quote that Lowell cites is nowhere to be found, though Schapiro does talk of "a rare vehemence,

tecturally correct nocturne of the U.N. Building. I enraged him by calling
his picture an "impromptu Whistler," and sneered pityingly at his "deploy-
ment of mass." I began my life-size copy of *Madame Cézanne dans la serre*;
obscenely tried to add the nude male bodies of *Les Baigneurs* as background,
and then, prompted by Mrs. Rodgers, consented to content myself with *Les
Grandes Baigneuses*. Mrs. Rodgers mixed my paints, measured my propor-
tions, steered my brush; halfway through I began to experiment with late
Van Gogh and Jackson Pollock palette-knife techniques. My picture was
finally almost a likeness, almost attractive, but in a moment of vandalistic
Freiheit,* I plastered a Dali mustache on Madame Cézanne and made my
picture hideous. Then I discovered Paul Klee.

Prince Scharnhorst had meanwhile abandoned painting in disgust, and
was casting about for more challenging media. He now sat putting the finishing touches on an exact replica of a new Swedish plywood sloop, which
he was modeling in deep relief to be mounted on a circular plaque of green
baize-covered wood, to be protected by a glass dome. I showed him a Klee
reproduction, *Die Hoehe*:† a girl, triangle body and pumpkin head, tight-
roped over a pink and purplish glare. The Prince said that this was work
that would disgrace a child or a criminal psychopath. So I began a Klee.
I used a formula that my grandmother Winslow, Gaga, had taught me as
a child. By making O's of different sizes and adding rectangles and a few
dots, I could draw a picture which began as a farmhouse, a yard, a path and
a pond; and then presto! was a man's face.

****

"But I don't want to go anywhere; I want to go to *Rock*!" That's how I
would stop conversation, when my mother and father talked about trips
to Paris, Puget Sound, Mattapoisett . . . anywhere! *Rock* was my name for
Grandfather Winslow's country place at Rock, Mass. On the letter paper

---

even ferocity" of execution of *Portrait d'un moine*. See Meyer Schapiro, *Paul Cézanne* (New York: Harry N. Abrams, 1952), 32, 58–59.

* German for "freedom."

† Probably Paul Klee's 1928 etching *Höhe!* (Heights!).

Rock had the name *Chardesa* for my grandfather's three children: Charlotte, Devereux and Sarah.

An avenue of poplars led from the stable to the pine grove. The leaves on these trees were always crisp, brilliant, dusty, athirst.

On an August afternoon in 1922, I sat squatting on the stone screen-porch. Before me on the red tiles, some crummy with ant droppings, some sweating with the secret dank, lay a pile of black earth and a pile of white earth. All about me were the works of my grandfather Winslow's hands: stogie-brown, twisted beams, mica-sparkling stones laid in a network of cement, and the screens, as transparent as the air from one angle, but from other and wrong angles, coarse-grained and black as soft coal drifting in the wind. And often in the basin hollowed out of a mill wheel, the fountain would clog. Or the antique gasoline pump would go on a strike. Or wind would bluster and topple over the basin's eighteenth-century statuette of a boy fishing with a broom straw. And sometimes the potted geraniums ailed and stank like humidors or the gasoline pump. The porch was ranch-style. Like everything my grandfather built, it was a well of comfort. Comfortable, yes; but stern, disproportioned, overbearing. What were those sunflowers? Those pumpkins floating in midair? They were the maids, Sadie and Nellie, bearing in frosted pitchers of ice tea, lemons, oranges and mint. Or it was the pitcher of *shandygaff*, which my grandfather made by blending yeasty, wheezing, exploding homemade beer with homemade root beer. *Chardesa* had been our family property and hobby for fifteen years. No one, except a silly gun-shy setter, had ever died there. Our lives there in 1922 were perfectly *ancien régime*. I sat on the tiles and mixed the black earth with the white.

I was all of three and a half. My new formal gray shorts had been worn for all of three minutes. Obsequious little drops of water pinpricked my face reflected in the basin. My perfection was that of those Olympian models in the plate glass windows of Rogers Peet's men's and boy's store below the Boston State House. The landscape in the store window was a false landscape. I felt like a stuffed toucan with a bibulous, multicolored beak.

Up in the air, on the glass porch, my great-aunt Sarah played the overture to *The Flying Dutchman*. She thundered on the keyboard of her dummy piano, a little soundless box bought to spare the nerves of her sister-in-law, my grandmother Winslow, who despaired of all music except the "Pastoral Symphony" from Handel's *Messiah*. But once in a vexed mood, my grandmother had said, "I don't see why Sally must thump all day on that thing she can't hear." Great-Aunt Sarah was the impractical one in our family. She looked down her structured nose, and sighed as she thought of all the statues of marble athletes collecting dust and wasting their manhood in Symphony Hall. Poor *Symphony*! It was like death during these empty off-season summer months. And there she had failed to appear for her great piano performance fifty years ago! That had been her classical moment, her fifth-century Athens. Great-Aunt Sarah lifted a hand dramatically to the mute keys of the dummy piano. "Barbarism lies behind me," she declaimed grandly, "mannerism is ahead." It was teatime in New England.

I scratched destructively at the blue anchors on my sailor blouse, which was like a balloon jib. What in the world could I be in want of? Nothing, except perhaps a wishes-are-white-horses horse; or a fluff of west wind to ruffle the waters, to stretch my canvas sail, to carry me kiting over the seven chimneys of *Chardesa*, the white farmhouse, and on over the bunched steel-blue barrels of the shotguns fortifying my uncle Devereux's duck blind, and on over the three ample, un-islanded miles of Assawompset the great lake. I was going far. Further than was useful. The wind fell.

I had always loved my uncle Devereux's hunting cabin at *Chardesa* on the island between the lakes Pocksha and Assawompset.* And now I entered. Uncle Devereux had already shut up shop for the winter almost. He was heaving a huge stillson wrench to fasten down the bars on the last window blind. I cowered in a corner behind a pyramid of Friend's Baked Beans cans. Sunlight from the open doorway struck the loud, period posters nailed everywhere on the cabin's raw, splintery wood. On the boards I saw Mr. Punch, watermelon-bellied, in Harvard crimson hockey tights, and tippling a bottle of Mr. Pimm's stirrup cup;† the remnants of a British battalion formed in hollow square on the terrible veldt, and dying to a man before the enfilading fire of the cowardly, nigger-hating unseen Boer; flocks of prewar opera stars with their goose necks, their beauty spots, their hair like rooster

---

* The cabin was on Wading Place Neck, a spit of land that cleaves the ponds and that at times is mostly submerged, creating an island at its tip. Right across Pocksha Pond from the mansion, the neck, too, was part of Arthur Winslow's property, which he purchased in 1908. In the *Life Studies* poem "My Last Afternoon with Uncle Devereux Winslow," Lowell disregards Pocksha and describes the island as "halving" Assawompset.

† "Hockey tights" is apparently a mistake for "jockey tights," one that is replicated in the corresponding line of "My Last Afternoon with Uncle Devereux Winslow." Pimm's Cup is a traditional British cocktail, based on Pimm's No. 1, which is a bottled liqueur.

tails and their glorious signatures; and finally, the patron of all good girls, *Entente Cordiale* himself, the porcine, proper, majestic Edward VII, who raised a model of a city, *gai Paris*, above Big Ben.* "What an eye for the girls," someone had scribbled tentatively in pencil.

I wasn't a child at all. Unseen and all-seeing, I was Agrippina at the palace of Nero.† I would beg my uncle Devereux to read me more stories about that Emperor who built a death barge for his mother, one that collapsed like a bombarded duck blind!‡

And now I sat in my sailor blouse, as clean as Bayard, our carriage horse. I rested my hands on the two piles of dirt, one black and one white. And Uncle Devereux stood behind me. His face was putty. His blue coat and white flannel trousers grew straighter and straighter, as though he were in a clothespress. His trousers were like solid cream from the top of the bottle. His coat was like a blue jay's tail feather. His face was animated, hieratic. His glasses were like Harold Lloyd's glasses.§ He was dying of the incurable Hodgkin's disease.¶ I mixed the sand of two colors to a single, victorious gray. Come winter, Uncle Devereux would blend to the one color.

****

For the first time in the two months since my acceptance by the Clinic, I enjoyed "sharps privileges." I pulled off the dingy, disfiguring adhesive tape marked "Lowell" from my newly returned nail clipper, and saw the whole morning flash blindingly from its chromium surface. My high window had nothing in it except a view of the white-brick New York Hospital, an iceberg against sky in the abstract. And three summers earlier almost to a day, I had sat among the goats on a hillside and watched five varieties of exotic

---

* *Entente Cordiale* was a set of agreements signed in 1904 between United Kingdom and France, establishing amicable relations between the two countries. King Edward VII's sexual life was bruited about as enacting the friendly relations across the English Channel: he was a frequent visitor to Parisian brothels.

† Julia Agrippina (15–59 CE), the mother of the Roman emperor Nero.

‡ According to Tacitus, Nero saw his mother, Agrippina, as the main obstacle to his marrying a noble woman named Poppaea Sabina. Therefore, he tried to assassinate her by having her embark on a self-sinking boat. This assassination attempt failed, however, for Agrippina managed to swim ashore.

§ Harold Lloyd (1893–1971), an American comedian who wore large black horn-rimmed glasses.

¶ John Devereux Winslow, Arthur Winslow's son and Charlotte's brother, died of Hodgkin's disease on November 16, 1922.

carrion hawk cruise on scimitar wings over the chalky, carious Christian tombs by the Golden Horn.* Muezzins, in their compulsory western dress, wailed from minarets, and already, almost in defiance of the "new order" and the memory of Kemal Atatürk,† arch-loather of *temporis acti*,‡ posters were being raised outside the iconoclastic mosques of Istanbul to celebrate the five hundredth anniversary of Mohammed II's conquest of Constantinople in 1453. History had been my only honor subject at boarding school, and 1453 was still more important to me than the dates of my parents' birthdays. I had sat and watched the "purifying" hawks. I had read in my copy of Gibbon about Mohammed II, who purified face and hands after speaking with infidels; about his "piece of brass ordnance" which drove "a stone bullet weighing over six hundred pounds";§ and about Constantine Palaeologus, the last Greek emperor, who died fighting and crying out, "Cannot a Christian be found to cut off my head?"¶ I had felt a sly sympathy with the triumph and "clean sweep" of the Crescent or Hammer and Sickle against my kind. And now three years later, I sat in a sanitarium and clipped my long owl's-talon fingernails with a giddy, drunken joy, I knew that I would be able now to scratch my head ad nauseam without danger of drawing blood.

Talk, talk, talk. But it was all empty, abstract mea culpa! My old R.C. *Instructions for the Confessional* had said, "Accuse yourself, and not others. Avoid tedious particularity."

As the regulations required, I sat in my armchair, and Dr. Masterson sat facing me in a hard straight-backed chair. Was I paying Dr. Masterson to talk to me or to listen? I couldn't give much mind to what I was saying because time seemed so precious to me. Dr. Masterson sat in his white smock,

---

* A narrow, horn-shaped inlet of the Bosphorus Strait constituting the harbor of Istanbul.

† Kemal Atatürk (1881–1938), the president of Turkey (1923–1938), who modernized the country and pushed for the adoption of European ways.

‡ The phrase "arch-loather of *temporis acti*" is the direct opposite of the well-known phrase from Horace, "*laudator temporis acti*," referring to someone constantly praising past times.

§ For Mohammed II's ablutions after his contacts with infidels, see Edward Gibbon, *History of the Decline and Fall of the Roman Empire*, vol. 5, edited by Thomas Bowdler (London: Longman, Rees, Orme, Brown, and Green, 1826), 401. Lowell quotes (somewhat inaccurately) Gibbon's description of the great cannon of Mohammed, which was to destroy the walls of Constantinople: "a piece of brass ordnance of stupendous, and almost incredible, magnitude; a measure of twelve palms is assigned to the bore; and the stone bullet weighed above six hundred pounds." See Gibbon, *History of the Decline and Fall*, vol. 5, 412.

¶ Constantine XI Palaeologus (1404–1453), the last Byzantine emperor, killed in the final defense of Constantinople against the Ottomans. Gibbon's version of the emperor's last words is slightly different: "Cannot there be found a Christian to cut off my head?" See Gibbon, *History of the Decline and Fall*, vol. 5, 433.

like the Snow Queen.* His tough, unbrushable hair, his horn-rimmed glasses and his hieratic, slightly wandering gaze made me remember my uncle Devereux. They were so much alike that I was put to it to find reliable distinguishing marks. My doctor was healthier, swarthier, alive.

And down below at the entrance to the hospital, a chauffeur placed twelve leather suitcases in the back of an initialed station wagon. A boy in a black Brooks Brothers suit was giving the doorman his final handshake.

And down at the end of the corridor, the day directress, Miss Morse, fussed with the balanced aquarium, a huge affair with snails, sanitary plants, little fish with seven tails, midget sunfish and midget silver tarpon. She complained that none of the nurses understood "balance" but were always casting breadcrumbs and dead flies on the waters, so that the fish and snails didn't know whether they were coming or going. I made my worn-out joke about the aquarium being a sanitarium within a sanitarium, "only I'm not on display."

And outside on the East River Drive,† traffic had come to sudden screeching stop. A car had stopped diagonally across the road. A door hung open, and a man had fallen out and now lay motionless, and with his shirt torn across the shoulders. In less than three minutes an ambulance came. The man hadn't moved. Then suddenly he jumped up and angrily escorted the stretcher-bearers off the highway, as though they were mentally deficient. And the seven-tailed fish, despite all our troubles, moved without artifice or disorder, and above them gulls moved across the Bronx and Brooklyn skyline without artifice or disorder.

And now the whole floor had returned from Occupational Therapy. They rushed about me excitedly, as though eager to be in time for the accident. But instead they congratulated me on my release from the sanitarium. I was going home that afternoon. "How did it feel?" And I answered that I was pleased, but that of course it hurt.

---

* The powerful, heartless title figure of Hans Christian Andersen's seven-part fairy tale called "Snedronningen" ("The Snow Queen").

† Today better known as the FDR Drive.

I suffer from periodic wild manic explosions

I SUFFER FROM periodic wild manic explosions that are followed by long hangovers of formless self-pity. What I ask of psychotherapy is that these extremes be cured, or at least moderated, and that in the future I will be in a position to take quick preventative measures and never again lose control.

I think both my depressed and manic periods are merely results of something else that is my real disease. I grew up as an only child, one that was always fighting off his parents and yet rejoiced at holding the center of the stage. I became stubborn, dreamy, silent, gauche, cold, furious, charming for brief moments, impenetrable. None of the normal exigencies and opportunities of either home or school education much drew me. I formed gangs, stole a little, won marbles, caught snakes, sailed by myself, trolled by myself, read bird books, read Napoleon books, read literature. I played games with a heavy energy and had a distaste for form. Here and there I imitated fragments and facets of people I felt were admired, or who excelled at some hobby that preoccupied me. But for the most part both my parents and everyone else seemed against me. If I could I ran off; if I couldn't I slept in a cowed silence—passionate paralysis, paralyzed passion.

Writing felt to me like a life preserver. At last I could dominate, despise, say nothing mattered except the great works of art. I think I really cared for these, but I enjoyed using them as a battering ram against everything and everybody that puzzled me or seemed indifferent or critical. I was certainly an albatross on land, and never really got over being churlish, inarticulate and critical when off my subject—most of life was off my subject, but much of the time I hardly knew it. When first married, I had some of the usual dreams: house, children, career, etc.; but mostly I thought of shutting myself to read and write works that would astonish. Society would be a little group of sympathizers and masters.

This wasn't enough. I discovered the Catholic Church, for me another mobile inner world, one that connected with the real world and was pleasantly critical of it. I tried to convert my wife. I read more books. After a while religion and poetry came together, and after a lapse of two years I started writing again and with more power and coherence. In my life religion was largely reading polemic and going to mass, but things had more order, or in a more orderly fashion I was even fiercer against the world. In the third year of my marriage I boiled over, became a conscientious objector, refused to report for the draft, and at odds with everyone except other objectors, especially Catholic objectors, went to jail.

Out of jail, I went back to writing, did some better work, had a hard time with living and my marriage, and thought we ought to be by ourselves. I thought of becoming a fisherman in Maine, but found I had no qualifications. I bought a house in Maine. My wife drank more and more and did all the practical work; I grew more and more depressed and silent. There were many fights. I ran off to a friend of my wife's who had been visiting us. I spent the winter in a shabby furnished room, seeing only this person and two or three literary acquaintances.

After that I received two poetry prizes and an appointment to the Chair of Poetry at Washington,* and for a year lived as a literary man—rather oddly having few acquaintances except other writers who would occasionally pass through Washington, and spending almost all my time either reading or pursuing another affair, this time with a much older woman. It had to

---

* In 1947–1948 Lowell held the position of consultant in poetry to the Library of Congress, which since 1985 has been called poet laureate.

be done secretly, and after five months ended very bitterly. I wanted to be free and by myself. I went to a writers' colony. There, after five months, it was suggested to me that the colony was controlled by a communist sympathizer. I put myself at the head of a little group,* became a practicing Catholic again, began to think I was Christ or the Holy Spirit, I didn't know which, had hallucinations and ended up in an asylum. Since then, I have married, spent two years in Europe, taught seven semester terms at different colleges (during two I had manic attacks and had to be put in a sanitarium and have shock treatments)."†

I find that I fall into two parts which roughly correspond to instinct and conscience. To use a figure, I might characterize both parts as writers. Neither one, as far as the simple daily calls of life go, is much of a success. Instinct likes to smoke cigarettes, drink cocktails, drink malted milks, lie on a bed; it thinks by means of images which are rather childish and secondhand. It is full of energy, likes to put off every task it can, including sustained conversation and thought. It likes novels, entertainments, music games, and perhaps most of all dreaming itself asleep at night. Conscience is a fine fellow, but it has never written anything, not even a thought-out critical essay, and its experience derives almost entirely from what instinct has felt. An angel's abstract mind and a brute's body, it talks against everything conceivable, for it cannot conceive of anything that might make its queer centaurish being work like a man.

Now coming back to the question of what I would like to get from my therapy. I must say that I find it difficult to be sensible, concrete and sustained on this subject. I am tempted to use empty clichés, rhetoric, irrelevances, unexplained images—then feeling none of these will do, I face a blank and want to avoid answering. My great need of the moment is to keep up a front, that is, I think I am quite up to going through with an orderly day, making sense and not complaining that I am helpless then asking help. I know that life went fairly well for long stretches in the past, and that I am at least able to come up to certain minimum requirements. I feel drawn to ask

---

* Lowell refers to a well-known imbroglio of his early career. In February 1949, suffering from an as-yet-undiagnosed mood disorder, he led a group of intellectuals attempting to remove the director of Yaddo, Elizabeth Ames, on the grounds of knowingly harboring Communist influences at the writers' colony. The Yaddo board ultimately dismissed Lowell's charges and reinstated Ames.

† These last two sentences do not appear in the hardcover edition of this book because we subsequently discovered them on a stray sheet, hidden away among unpublished poems in the Lowell Collection at Harvard.

impossible things of myself and then do nothing. I see very well that I need to find a middle path and that ecstasy and despair will always be problems. I think I can use therapy to get through these forks. I want to live the life I have—married, teaching, writing. I think therapy can help me not to give up or run away. I think I can learn to use my head and eyes together. I want to be able to see my faults, do something about them, and be a good husband, a writer who can grow, and a steady, capable teacher.

Seven years ago I had an attack of pathological enthusiasm

SEVEN YEARS AGO I had an attack of pathological enthusiasm. The night before I was locked up, I ran about the streets of Bloomington, Indiana, crying out against devils and homosexuals.* I believed I could stop cars and paralyze their forces by merely standing in the middle of the highway with my arms outspread. Each car carried a long rod above its taillight, and the rods were adorned with diabolic Indian or voodoo signs. Bloomington stood for Joyce's hero and Christian regeneration. Indiana stood for the evil, unexorcized, aboriginal Indians. I suspected I was a reincarnation of the Holy Ghost and had become homocidally† hallucinated. To have known the glory, violence and banality of such an experience is corrupting.

---

* In early April 1949, right after the Yaddo incident, Lowell visited Peter Taylor at Indiana University in Bloomington and had the psychotic episode described here. He was committed to Baldpate Hospital, a small psychiatric institution in Georgetown, Massachusetts; diagnosed with acute mania; and treated with electroshock therapy. After three months, he emerged feeling shaken, depressed, and remorseful. See Paul Mariani, *Lost Puritan: A Life of Robert Lowell* (New York: W. W. Norton, 1994), 183–86; and Kay Redfield Jamison, *Robert Lowell, Setting the River on Fire: A Study of Genius, Mania, and Character* (New York: Alfred A. Knopf, 2017), 102–5.

† Presumably a mistyping or misspelling of "homicidally." Nevertheless, given that he cried out against homosexuals, a trace of the word "homosexual" may still be present in the apparent mistake.

For two years I have been cooling off

FOR TWO YEARS I have been cooling off from three months of pathological enthusiasm. I go to sleep now easily, but sometimes I wake up with a jar. In my dreams I am like one of Michelangelo's rugged, ideal statues that can be tumbled downhill without injury. When I wake, it is as though I had been flayed, and had each nerve beaten with a rubber hose.

I am writing my autobiography literally to "pass the time."* I almost doubt if the time would pass at all otherwise. However, I also hope the result will supply me with my swaddling clothes, with a sort of immense bandage of gauze and ambergris for my hurt nerves. Therefore this book will stop in the summer of 1934.† A few months after the end of this book, I *found* myself.

As I try to write my own autobiography, other autobiographies naturally come to mind. The last autobiography I have looked into was a movie about a bull terrier from Brooklyn. The dog's name was, I think, *House on Fire*. The district he came from was so tough that smoking had to be per-

---

* The autobiography is "My Autobiography," reproduced in Part I of this volume.

† This sentence originally read "Therefore this book will stop with an account of a period of enthusiasm that happened more than twenty years ago in the summer of 1934." During a subsequent revision Lowell crossed out the sentence's midsection.

mitted in the last three pews at high mass. House on Fire's mother had been deserted by his father. House knows that his father is a great dog in the great world, either as a champion fighter or as a champion in exhibitions. House on Fire keeps saying with his Brooklyn accent, "I want to be a champ so that I can kill my father." In the end there is peace.

My own father was a gentle, faithful and dim man. I don't know why I was so agin him. I hope there will be peace.

Arthur Winslow at the beach, March 1915 (Courtesy of Sarah Payne Stuart)

Arthur Winslow, March 1916 (Courtesy of Sarah Payne Stuart)

TOP Arthur Winslow holding Bobby at Chardesa, 1918 (Courtesy of Sarah Payne Stuart)

ABOVE LEFT Bobby and Charlotte Lowell in front of an ornate water well at Chardesa, 1918; the well appears in "The House at Rock" in "My Autobiography" as well as in "The Neo-Classical Urn" in Lowell's *Collected Poems* (Courtesy of Sarah Payne Stuart)

ABOVE RIGHT Bobby in a playpen, presumably with his nurse, at Chardesa, 1918 (Courtesy of Sarah Payne Stuart)

ABOVE LEFT From left to right: Mary Winslow, Aunt Sarah Winslow (standing), Charlotte, Great-Aunt Sarah Stark Winslow, and Bobby in front of Chardesa, summer 1920 (Courtesy of Sarah Payne Stuart)

ABOVE RIGHT "Emily" (unidentified) and Young Aunt Sarah behind the "neoclassical urn," 1920 (Courtesy of Sarah Payne Stuart)

Charlotte at 2129 Bancroft Place, Washington, D.C., March 1925
(Courtesy of Sarah Payne Stuart)

ABOVE LEFT John Devereux Winslow on the "ranch-style" screened-in stone porch
with the cement basin, as in "Pictures of Rock," June 1922
(Courtesy of Sarah Payne Stuart)

ABOVE RIGHT Mary Winslow, "Mrs. B." (unidentified), and Arthur Winslow,
August 28, 1922 (Courtesy of Sarah Payne Stuart)

Charlotte, Bobby, and Mary Winslow at Chardesa, September 1922
(Courtesy of Sarah Payne Stuart)

Bobby at Chardesa, summer 1927 (Courtesy of Sarah Payne Stuart)

Mr. Burroughs and Bobby at Dunbarton, May 18, 1929. Mr. Burroughs was the caretaker at Dunbarton, mentioned in "Arthur Winslow III: Dunbarton" in "My Autobiography" and in "Dunbarton" in *Collected Poems* (Courtesy of Sarah Payne Stuart)

Bobby (first row, far left) at Rivers School, 1930 (Courtesy of Harry Ransom Center)

Aunt Sarah Winslow, Charlotte, Robert T. S. Lowell III, and Mary Winslow
at Chardesa, July 5, 1931 (Courtesy of Sarah Payne Stuart)

ABOVE Bobby jumping in front of James MacDonald's house on Perry Street in Rock Village, March 27, 1931. James MacDonald was the farmer at Rock and caretaker at Chardesa; he appears in "Arthur Winslow V" in "My Autobiography" and in "Dunbarton" and "Two Farmers" in *Collected Poems* (Courtesy of Sarah Payne Stuart)

RIGHT Bobby on the porch of the farmer's house on Perry Street in Rock, with Mrs. MacDonald, March 27, 1931 (Courtesy of Sarah Payne Stuart)

Chardesa, May 7, 1931 (Courtesy of Sarah Payne Stuart)

Bobby at Chardesa, August 1931

(Courtesy of Sarah Payne Stuart)

Robert Lowell in Boston, Massachusetts, January 1, 1964

(Photograph by Steve Schapiro; reproduced by permission of Getty Images)

Our dining room at 239 Marlborough St.

OUR DINING ROOM at 239 Marlborough St. is a casual, frayed, gently downhill reconstruction of my parents' dining room at 170 Marlborough St. Stationed in similar positions are all those pieces that my parents inherited: the English sideboard with a key in one side door, the patriotic American highboy, topped by a gold eagle, stray bits of colonial silver, stamped with the Pollock Boar.* The little, almost souvenir-like, eighteenth-century oval portrait of a scarcely identifiable Judge Bailey† still hangs next to our more historic, very black and dimming copy of a portrait of red-coated Edward Winslow, the Sheriff and Georgian silver-smith.‡ Great-Grandfather R. T. S. Lowell still represents our more intellectual heritage by holding the place of honor over the fireplace. My parents described him as the headmaster of St. Mark's School; I described him as James Russell Lowell's brother. All their lives my parents used a complete set of Tiffany silver, a wedding present. The largeness and usefulness of the set pleased them, the squarish modern design embarrassed. I feel the

* The crest of the Scottish clan Pollock features a boar passant shot with an arrow.

† Presumably Judge William Bailey (1763–1840), who held several public offices in the upstate New York counties Franklin and Clinton. He was a great-grandfather of Kate Bailey Myers Lowell, Lowell's paternal grandmother, who lived on Staten Island.

‡ Edward Winslow Jr. (1669–1753) was a great-great-great-grandfather of Arthur Winslow.

same pleasure and embarrassment. Mother's one personal innovation was to trade a massive Victorian dining room table for a thin mahogany table, airy yet conservative in design. This table still seems impiously new to me; its faded blue chair cushions still seem an uninvited invasion—blue sea and blue sky.

The house facing us in the back alley has its shades drawn to about noon. At night its fire escapes are crowded, sometimes with as many as fifteen girls in wrappers, who shout at drunken shouting boys who climb the alley garages and even my car. Mother would have done something about them. Even in these changed rooming-house times, we might have succeeded. We do nothing.

I might have been fifteen, or
I might have been thirty-five

I MIGHT HAVE been fifteen, or I might have been thirty-five, my father might have been alive or dead, the location might have been our good (not grand) half-a-lifetime's house in the Back Bay, or Mother's adequate Boston apartment, or Mother and Father's sprawly, slightly citified, unbalanced, battleship-gray commuters' house in Beverly Farms, where they had migrated towards the end for a change, and of course changed as little as possible. Thus, one didn't start with a place or even a room that could be labeled such and such and no other. You had to begin with Mother's furniture, and *that* didn't change at all—if it did, the new or different pieces always managed to retell the same story.

A young literary fan of our family psychiatrist used to do fieldwork of a kind by coming to tea with my parents. She was acid, deep and Hawaiian. Her scarlet tea dress was transparent here and there, and unbelievably opaque over her vitals. The skirt was in the style of the mid-twenties, and made a diving diagonal from the dead center of her knees. The girl summed up her visits by reporting that the furniture was Mother. But neither she nor anyone else was happy or produced much of a revelation in trying to expose just what Mother's characteristic possessions expressed. "Things, things, things," Mother used to scold, "things have taken me in!" They had, and they hadn't, for in a funny arbitrary way, everything Mother arranged connected with what it hid and was meant to expunge. The slow pushing Nile of Mother's life was behind each crackle of lacquer and each ounce of cushion. But it was as though some Japanese stage director with over-severe notions on uniformity and pattern had invented a single mask for both Clytemnestra and Orestes, and was saying in a riddling bottom-to-top singsong, "These personae look different, but their ghosts are one cut. Oh verily!" I feel that my reference to the Greeks and particularly to Orestes is bad manners and perhaps a blind alley. Paul Valéry has stated that the old poetry prior to Mallarmé is as arithmetic to algebra.* But over half a century ago Freud was cautioning Hofmannsthal and Strauss that classical myths (particularly Orestes and his mother) were as *simpliste* and useless to the modern dramatist as algebraic formulae.†

Now to get back to my subject, I am writing about one person and not two, and it would be stupidly overstepping myself to call this person Clytemnestra and empty out a whole picture book of far-fetched parallels, such as the only child who held the center of the stage till the age of five, one jut-chinned sister of the plastic Helen, the grave ignorant bride of the unknown great king and so on and so on down to, God help us, matricide. I am now waving my arms so wildly that I forget what I am proposing not to propose. Shall I say that all the phases of Clytemnestra, crown of the moon, from tender young slip to haft of the battle-axe were chips on the same old block? The old wooden mask?

I know a composer from South Boston. When he was five he knew Bee-thoven's quartets backwards. When he was twenty-seven he was trying to blot out all of Beethoven and Stravinsky note by note from beginning to end. For three hours he dogged after some friends who were taking in the copies of copies of Hellenistic statues in the museum at Naples. He timed himself with a chronometer and didn't open his mouth for two hundred

---

* Lowell slightly misremembers the analogy. Valéry praised Mallarmé for making a rare move from his poetic principles to "the extraordinary task of grasping in all its generality the nature of his art and [. . .] of distinguishing all its means and classifying all its potential." He compared this "search" to "the invention of algebra" from arithmetic. Paul Valéry, *Collected Works of Paul Valéry*, vol. 8: *Leonardo, Poe, Mallarme*, translated by Malcolm Cowley and James R. Lawler (Princeton, NJ: Princeton University Press, 1972), 297.

† Hugo von Hofmannsthal, a Viennese poet and playwright, collaborated with Richard Strauss, writing libretti for his operas. These operas are often said to have anticipated Freud's psychoanalytical models. Strauss's May 1905 opera, *Elektra*, with the libretto by Hofmannsthal, performed in Vienna, provoked Freud to call the Wednesday Society to a meeting on May 24, 1905. Reportedly, afterward the psychoanalyst began to distance himself from the "Electra complex."

minutes and two hundred and fifty statues with negligently obtruding right arms. Then he said, "Who were the Greeks?" I want to get back in touch, or rather with my twentieth-century mother. Her life, like anyone else's, was all tangles of one thread. There was no noose or sword or anything ominous at the end, only a slight fraying.

On Black Israelites

ISPENT April, May, June, July and August of 1954 at the Payne Whitney Clinic of the New York Hospital. I was recovering from an attack of pathological enthusiasm. One morning towards the end of my stay, I told my psychiatrist about an experience I had had during the War when I was serving a five months' sentence in jail as a conscientious objector.* I belonged to a gang that walked outside the prison gates each morning and worked on building a barn. The work was mild; the workers were slow and absent-minded. There were long pauses, and we would sit around barrels filled with burning coke and roast wheat seeds. All the prisoners were sentenced for a cause, all liked nothing better than talking the world to rights.

Among the many eccentrics one group took the prize. They were Negroes who called themselves Israelites. Their ritual compelled them to shave their heads and let their beards grow. But the prison regulations forced them to shave their beards. So with unnaturally smooth and shining faces and naked heads wrapped in Turkish towels, they shivered about the coke barrels and talked wisdom and nonsense. Their nonsense was that they were the chosen people. They had found a text in the Bible which said, "But I am black, though my brother is white."† This convinced them that the people

---

* The memories that follow also inform "In the Cage" and "The Mouth of the Hudson," in Robert Lowell, *Collected Poems*, edited by Frank Bidart and David Gewanter (New York: Farrar, Straus and Giroux, 2003), 55, 526, 328.

† There is no such line in standard editions of the Hebrew Bible. Lowell may be misremembering or revis-

of the Old Testament were Negroes. The Israelites believed that modern Jews were impostors.

Their wisdom was a deep ancestral knowledge of herbs and nature. They were always curing themselves with queer herbal remedies that they gathered from the fields. Once, as we sat by the coke, the most venerable and mild of the Israelites stretched out his hand. Below him lay the town of Danbury, which consisted of what might be called *filling-station architecture*; the country was the fine, small, rolling land of Connecticut. One expected to see the flash of a deer's white scut as it jumped a boulder wall by a patch of unmelted snow. My friend stretched out his arm and said, "Only man is miserable." I told my doctor that this summed up my morals and aesthetics [. . .]

---

ing verses from Job 30:30–31: "I am a brother to dragons, and a companion to owls. My skin is black upon me, and my bones are burned with heat."

Dreams

The place is a modification of Yaddo or a sanitarium. A succession of gray dreary corridors alternating with white bare rooms—bleak warmth of snow in city. Someone (Ed Maisel) writing book, sentence by sentence, on the New England composer Ives*—the biography is accomplished somehow not by writing but more like working out a series of mathematical problems. I'm not doing my biography. Talk with an attendant who has been there thirty years. He says he has met no one he couldn't love. I feel guilt. I am not allowed to leave unless I write and mingle. Am somehow talking to Mary McCarthy in a passage both in and outdoors.† She jokes and I encourage her about the Maisel book. She has written a sensible book on the same subject. I pretend I am doing my writing.

SUN. MARCH 6TH

A school, a sanitarium, a country house. Conversations and maneuvers in corridors with glass panes. Trial (am I the husband, the wife or a spectator?). A wife is on trial. She goes through motions like a warrior on a Japanese

---

* Edward Maisel (1917–2008), a writer on music, especially on Charles T. Griffes. Maisel is not known to have written a book on Charles Ives. He was a guest at Yaddo in the winter of 1948–1949 when Lowell and Elizabeth Hardwick were there.

† Mary McCarthy (1912–1989), American critic and novelist. Lowell became friends with her through Hardwick.

print or a football player, in underwear putting on shoulder guards. She goes through all the required motions but is too slow. She must be expelled. Discovery that the husband intends to enforce his rights. Even go to law. Slow elaborate procedure, gentleness, timidity that doesn't dare do enough, fear of coming out of my shell even though not coming out involves expulsion from the house.

MON. MARCH 7TH

A large country house—Columbia conference, boarding school etc.—I am going through the men's dormitory (Frelinghuysen's)* with a letter to Allen Tate from T. S. Eliot. The letter is a note on Tate's work; I manage to indicate that Eliot has let me know the contents. I have a reply of my own that Eliot expects from me (publishing details connected with my book). I dawdle about bringing them to E's room. Take pride in my witty phrasing.

2) Driving through Austria with Tate and someone else. Small clayish lakes, which Allen compares with North Carolina. I feel relieved that Tate is there, someone I feel sure of, someone with a sufficiently objective grasp of both places Austria and N.C. to make comparison; feel I couldn't; annoyed that anyone would dream of comparing anything American (even the South) with Austria, which everyone knows is better and is also less known to me. Want Tate to do the talking—relief, jealousy.

3) Scene between Aunt Alice† and Eliot. I hope they will marry; Aunt A's vigor and enthusiasm will do Eliot good; Eliot's mind, wit, sense of reality and precision will be good for Aunt A. Add Eliot to my family.

4) Going down almost endless iron staircase (Intimate Relations) with Tate-Rilke (looked like neither), a young blond man and one other. Feel rivalry as we descend; when we emerge in dormitory area I am loudly and more or less sincerely reassuring Rilke: "But you shouldn't worry about your work. You have a voice of your own, a real personal bray; and such quantity."

---

* Most likely Peter Hood Ballantine Frelinghuysen Jr. (1916–2011), a New Jersey congressman from 1953 to 1975. He attended St. Mark's School with Lowell, appearing in a photo of the football squad in the 1933 issue of *The Saint Mark's Lion*, along with his twin brother, Harry O. H. Frelinghuysen, and Lowell. Peter Frelinghuysen graduated from Yale Law School in 1941 and did graduate study in history at Columbia University in 1946 and 1947.

† Presumably, Alice Thorndike Winslow (1895–1964), the wife of John Devereux Winslow and Charlotte's sister-in-law.

TWO DREAMS—MAY 3RD

Confrontation with a young man, the long puzzle of finding out a common language, following some problem, circles of thought, consciousness that he was younger, even that the relationship was homosexual, but not physical, this part of the dream, sedentary, motionless, intellectual. Second part, group walking, feel I break the ice by saying, "if you don't do something, we'll (I'll?) have the young man rape you." Rough gay tones of men being fellows together.

Dream two—world has ended, or wasted, suffered a disaster. Two groups, one American (?), which I head, the other Russian, headed by Khrushchev, much bigger and physically stronger than in life, conscious of the round hardness of his arms, the special idiomatic way of talking that must be learned and caught—incomplete sentences. A barrenness, a stench. Struggle to survive, in second part of the dream, the corner has been turned, stench receding, also barrenness, very fond and intimate with K. Our American group is somehow more agile and ahead of his group, but I rely on K. as a weight to test myself against, as someone to talk to, somehow in the end as my guide. Parades, horses (?), action and recovery.

My dreams at night are so enjoyable to me that I am willing to accept the nothingness of sleep. My dreams in the morning are so enjoyable that I am willing to accept life. I suppose these two sentences are the worst I can say for myself.

Death, the Rich City

I WAS A couple of miles from San Juan in Puerto Rico, and walking along the beach.* A frank, straightforward warm beach, seductive to the wintering northerner, but sadly disfigured with sea-tar and phallic safeguards. I was thinking of the resurrection of the body, almost the sole surviving thread of my once total Catholic faith. Stumbling violently on something like a child's sagged, discolored balloon, I looked up and saw fourteen fourteen-story, erect housing skyscrapers. They were wonderfully alike, all of mild wasp-nest gray. "The wasps," I said, "just like home." Strangely, this identification brought no wholesome feeling of nostalgia and protection. "To hell with the Catholic Church," I said, "how can bodies survive without embalmers. From the Pharaohs to Lenin no dead Christian lives in his body. No body lives—" Suddenly, to my humiliation, I saw his now familiar Bentley racer skidding from side to side, now splashing water, now grinding the wasp-gray cement boundary wall of the beach—driving on me a hundred miles an hour. Behind the sandswept windshield leered the dusky, drunken face, El Butano, the country's highest-prized and bravest

* Lowell was in Puerto Rico with Elizabeth Hardwick and their daughter, Harriet, from March 20 through March 30, 1962. They wanted, as Lowell wrote in a letter to Ezra Pound, to "bake away our colds and the midwinter grayness and grind of the city"; see Robert Lowell, *The Letters of Robert Lowell*, edited by Saskia Hamilton (New York: Farrar, Straus and Giroux, 2005), 405. Immediately after they returned, on March 31, Lowell wrote to Edmund Wilson: "I'm just back from Puerto Rico, sunned and shaken—partly by the country, all the sun and water, all the creeping Puerto Rican life, which is all around us here on the West Side, but which is revealed there in greater purity perhaps, that creeping life that will survive all the crust of our culture—or will it?"; see *Letters*, 405.

enemy—boss and idol of Puerto Rico's ultra-socialist guerrillas, uproariously lifting both hands from the wheel, and holding in one the works of Marx and a cigarette lighter, and in the other his ten-gallon gray milk tin of butane, weapons with which he sent not only the soul but the body of the white gringos to literal extinction.

The car screeched to a halt, and severed the toes on my left foot. I screamed, bunched with agony, "What will he do with my body at the second coming, El Butano?" "El liberdad,"* laughed El Butano with honest, democratic bonhomie. "If I don't have a whole left foot left," I pled, "how will I walk when the Bridegroom comes?" "Nada," he roared, "you'll be nada. Why you think I buy this butane?"

---

* Botched Spanish for "liberty." It should be "*La libertad.*"

The Raspberry Sherbet Heart

IT WAS THE DAY when Rose Sharon from three skyscraper apartment houses down the street brought Frisky to call on Charles. Frisky was a silky, tired, white-colored buck rabbit. He weighed ten pounds and took two hands to lift because he lay like dough in Rose's arms and wouldn't stretch a claw to help her carry him. Frisky wasn't at all frisky, and all through the visit sat panting and stolid by the claw foot of the sofa where Charles's father was skimming through book reviews.

"That rabbit looks like a worn-out pillow," said Charles's father, who was wishing that he could shake his shoes off and go to sleep.

But Charles, who was much more on his toes then than his father and besides had been learning new words one after another all winter, said, "That's not right at all! Frisky is like a mop and a heartbeat."

Frisky and Rose went home, but Charles was so surprised by what he had just said that he kept on repeating *heartbeat*, sometimes to himself and sometimes out loud. "Heartbeat," he said, as he swiveled around creaking a hundred times in his tumble-bowl. "Heartbeat, heartbeat," he shouted, as he bounced a hundred times on his huge inner tube from a truck. It was night.

Charles's father said, "Another day."

Charles's mother said, "The day is over. Go to bed Charles."

Charles ran upstairs. He knew that a day is never over, and he lay in his dark bedroom squinting first through one eye and then through the other at his small orange wall light bulb that stuck up like a glowing arrowhead. Over and over, he said, "One heartbeat, two heartbeats, three heartbeats, four heartbeats, five heartbeats, six heartbeats, INFINITY*ZERO heartbeats."*

He whispered the first six numbers, but when he came to INFINITY*ZERO, his voice rose to a bellow and was so loud that he thought his giant blue Japanese paper tarpon that hung from the ceiling was swinging *tick-tock, tick-tock*, like a pendulum. The animals stacked helter-skelter in his tumble-bowl seemed to stir their fur as if breathing. He found he had squeezed his pillow so hard that chicken down was coming out and worming on his cheek.

Downstairs, his mother's voice said, "If I hear another word!"

His father said, "Look, it's long after eight o'clock."

His mother said, "Don't you know tomorrow is a school day?"

Then they both said, "If we have to come upstairs another time!"

They said these things over and over, and sometimes even made walking sounds on the stairs. Finally Charles was quiet. He didn't feel in any mood for sleep, so he clapped a hand to one ear and tried to listen while his mother and father talked. Their talk was less tightly plotted and amusing than a television program, but Charles could never entirely tell what might come next, and there was always the chance that they might begin to talk about Charles. Once, a year ago, he had heard his mother say, "Charles *is* unusual." Charles's father had said, "What's peculiar about him? We'd be peculiar if we were illiterate and only four feet high." Charles's mother had said, "I didn't say he was peculiar. No, he is a most unusual child." Next day when Charles asked Miss Baskin at the Ethical Culture School what peculiar and unusual meant, she said, "Peculiar is the unusual we laugh at."

Another night Charles had heard his mother say, "He is a dreamboat, he is divine, he hasn't sucked his thumb since last Thursday." Charles's father had said, "Poor little embryonic man, it must be like giving up smoking." Charles had thought, "Some people can't be told. It's much harder than that. A cigarette isn't tied to your body and part of you." Next morning when he had said to his father, "When are you going to grow up and stop smoking?" his father had answered, "Someday, someday, God willing, when all the

---

* Though often believed to equal zero, the expression infinity*zero (or infinity times zero) is rather an indeterminate form, a puzzle, because infinity is a concept rather than a number that can be multiplied.

doctors quit." His father had turned red, and then white, and said, "That's how you'll answer when you've achieved the years of wisdom."

Once or twice a month, there were tumultuous nights when the mother and father would light into each other and have what they afterwards called a real set-to. Their voices would mumble and grumble and rumble. The paper fish would swing, the animals would stir their fur, and the feathers would wriggle out of Charles's pillow and tickle his cheek. "I may be unusual," Charles would think, "but grownups are *really* unusual. They are as soft as lambs for weeks, then one night they'll say everything." They said everything rough Charles had ever thought about them, and oceans more that he couldn't understand, because they used long words and sentences that lasted five minutes. They seemed able to breathe while they spoke. All he could remember was his father saying, "You notice everything. I haven't been able to finish a sentence all winter." And his mother had said, "*You* never notice anything. You don't know we exist." One night he heard continual crashing sounds of grown-up music and shoes clicking on the floor. He had come down the stairs in his pajamas, pointed a finger at them and said two sentences he had been wanting to say for weeks, "Turn that phonograph down. I keep hearing it." Then they had suddenly gotten very long-faced and quiet. Once or twice a week when they were talking very quietly, Charles would run downstairs and kiss them both, and often they would kiss him and kiss him and tell him they loved him more than anything in the world. But grown-ups were unusual. Sometimes they would just go on thinking.

Charles too went on thinking. He thought, "They're funny. They always have money to buy anything they want to eat, they have reasons for everything they do." When Charles tried to think of reasons for everything he did, the reasons spun around in his head like water in the washer, and he grew dizzy. Then he thought, "I may not have reasons, but I can always argue with them." Then he thought of how his father always gave a little smile when he spoke of the "years of wisdom." "I guess," he said, "they are just me infinity times zero." Once when he had been arguing with them about why he wanted to wear his soft brown sweater instead of the rough blue one to school, they had said, "What's the matter with us? We're not too bad." And he had answered, "You are only too bad right now. Most of the time you are quite sweet really." That's what they had said about Miss

Gerassi when she brought him his third TWA Flight Commander's hat. His father had seemed to think it a wonderful joke that poor Miss Gerassi had never married, but his mother had said, "Men! I can't imagine what she sees in them." Charles had thought about marrying Rose Sharon. He imagined Rose with rose-red cheeks and all dressed up in gauze and lace and plastics and dragonfly wings like a fairy. He thought, "Maybe I'd rather marry Mummy. Daddy could stay around if he wanted to." He thought, "I want to marry Mummy now, but when I'm older I don't suppose I will." He imagined his mother dressed in her wedding gauze and lace and plastic and dragonfly wings. No matter how far off he saw her and himself in the years of wisdom, her face was always higher than he could reach.

Downstairs he could hear his mother and father talking. "Not about me, not about Miss Gerassi, not about each other!" He thought about what fun it would be to call his father "Mummy" and his mother "Daddy." "You can do anything with parents if you scramble and mix them up." What they were saying was hard for him to follow. He imagined them without faces. His father was a black-and-white bear doll with a dumbbell for a head and patent-leather ears. His mother was a red-and-gold Chinese doll wearing the tumble-bowl instead of her head.* Then he saw them as long thin lumps of limp dough covered with powdery flour. He stuck his beaver's head on one, and then on the other. "Ha ha, beaverboards," he cried, "masticate your food." Then he saw how lumpy and limp they were, and almost cried as he pushed a finger gently against their sides. "Heartbeat, heartbeat," he whispered.

He crept to the head of the stairs. His mother and father were watching the Kentucky Derby on their television set. His mother said, "This is the first time we've seen the Derby in three years."

His father said, "It's all over when it starts."

His mother said, "Now, now!"

Then after about a minute, his father said, "Spare-ribs has won. Now the race-track is fading like the smile on Happy Chandler's face."†

His mother said, "Delicious Spare-ribs, what a name for a winning

---

* A revision shows that Lowell considered the possibility of Charles's mother wearing the tumble-bowl instead of her hat, though he neither accepted nor rejected this change.

† Happy Chandler is a nickname of A. B. Chandler (1898–1991), a Democratic governor of Kentucky and U.S. senator as well as a commissioner of American baseball. He earned his nickname by his pasted-on smile.

horse! Happy Chandler calls his wife Mother. Look, there's Mother. Her shoes hurt her something awful."

Charles thought, "I want to call my father Mummy."

Then his mother's voice was edgy with emphasis. She was saying, "Gambling on the horses is the only gambling that makes sense. If we only knew horses, we'd be rich."

Charles's father said, "I was talking to Dr. Hamlin, the head stretcher. He said he'd had scores of patients who gambled on the horses. All of them lost their money. He said they were all reverting to childhood."

Charles's mother said, "Dr. Hamlin has never even seen the dust of the kind of person I'm talking about."

Charles said to himself, "The trouble with Daddy is that he doesn't talk English. *Reverting to childhood!* He means hurt child." Then he thought, "Their voices are going to get edgier and edgier. They always do when Father stops talking English."

The voices didn't get edgier. Charles's mother said, "Oh heavenly Spare-ribs running over the blue grass!"

Charles's father said, "Spare-ribs is a far cry from Man of War. I wonder if Man of War's statue is still nibbling the blue grass."

Charles said, "Daddy's off again. Why doesn't he talk English? How can a statue nibble grass?" But when Charles crawled down the stairs a little way and could see the television screen, he saw a great bronze statue of a horse.* "Daddy does make sense, but you can never tell when or how. He was teasing when he called that statue of a horse Man of War. I don't see the war."

Charles crept off back to bed. He thought about the way his father made wonders happen with words. He began to make wonders happen himself. He imagined a green Irish derby swinging in the window. When the orange light of the little wall bulb struck it, it changed to a big blade of blue grass, then it was a blue jay, then it was a blue ribbon that said, "First Prize." Under the ribbon, a lovely green frog was panting and looking like the rabbit Frisky. Charles thought about carrying the frog in both his arms to Rose

---

* Man o' War, a chestnut Thoroughbred, one of the greatest racehorses of all time. A year after he died in 1947 and was buried at Faraway Farm in Lexington, Kentucky, the horse was commemorated with a bronze statue erected over his grave. The statue was moved, along with the grave, to the Kentucky Horse Park in 1977.

Sharon. "I must be awfully gentle and not let the frog gum up her dress of gauze and lace and plastics and dragonfly wings. I won't let a frog spoil our wedding." But the frog was quietly sitting under the first-prize blue ribbon and blowing soap bubbles from a white clay pipe. Each time the frog blew a bubble, his throat would blow out into a greenish, cream-colored ball that was the same size as the bubble. Then the bubble would drift slowly like a balloon up the frog's shiny nose and escape, and at the same time the ball in the frog's throat would pop back flat, and the frog would say, "Chug-umm, chug-umm, chug-um!" A tremendous rainbow-colored bubble floated over Charles's head. When he looked into it, everything in the room had doubled in size. Charles's hand was as big as his father's when he lifted it to burst the bubble. But the bubble didn't burst. Touched, it beat once or twice like a heart and then became two bubbles. When he touched the two bubbles, they became four.

The four became eight, the eight became sixteen. And so they went on doubling until the bedroom was crammed in bubbles. They covered the floor, they stacked up to the ceiling, they covered the window, the dresser, the door, and soon there would be no more room for the bubbles, but they kept on doubling. Squashed together, each beat like a heart and shone like a rainbow. Soon there would be infinity*zero bubbles. Charles was asleep.

While he slept, he dreamed, and at first the dream made a good deal more sense than the roomful of bubbles he had been thinking up to himself. He saw a man, a stumpy little fellow who wore khaki shorts, a khaki shirt, a khaki necktie, and a khaki mouth veil like an Arabian woman. His legs were wrapped in khaki bandages and so were his hands. On his head was a shining aluminum kitchen pot. He had smaller aluminum pots on his feet. In his two hands he held a broom with a carving knife tied to the handle. He kept saying all in one breath, "I am Man of War, I am Man of War." Rose Sharon and Charles were sitting holding hands on a stone above a little brook. The man ran by them and began jumping on foot from rock to rock across the brook. Each time he jumped, he called to the children, "I bet I can jump higher and higher than you can."

Then he took his broom and carving knife and began to dive it like a bird into the water, and it would come up with old graying soggy newspapers stuck on the point of the carving knife. Each paper had a runny brown picture of a runny brown soldier, all dressed in khaki, with bandages on his arms and legs, pots on his head and feet, and a broom with a carving knife in his hands. It was like the bubbles that Charles had imagined, one thing always led to more of the same thing. Then suddenly the brown man fished up a beautiful green Irish derby. It began to sprout and soon it was like a big elm tree in full leaf, and as the brown man held it over his head, the leaves began to shake and rustle. The man too began to shake and rustle, but instead of turning into a tree, he fell forward on his arms. His arms turned into horses' legs, his legs turned into horses' legs. The kitchen pots became hooves and horseshoes. Then the man's head stretched into a gray log that was soon a very sad-looking log that changed into a long sad gray horse's head. The nostrils were horses' nostrils that shivered and quivered and sneezed, as the man, now entirely a horse, stretched up his long thin neck and began to nibble the green derby, as though it were an armful of hay. Then Rose and Charles helped each other onto the horse's back. They lightly beat its behind with the broom, and soon they were flying like the wind through a great field, whose grass wasn't true grass but thousands of blue ribbons. Half of them had *First Prize* written on them, the other half simply said *Blue Grass*.

Charles said to Rose, "He is a real live horse. He is really ours even though we live in New York City."

Rose said, "He is ours, he is ours!"

But at that very moment, the horse began to harden. When they smelled him, he didn't smell like a horse or hay, but like a silver coin. When they slapped his sides with their hands, their hands stung and they heard the hollow sounds of a bronze bell. The horse was a statue.

"Bing, bang, bong, bwawng," went the four little gilded Near Eastern bells that Charles's Mother always rang to call him to breakfast.* Before the last had sounded, Charles was asleep again and dreaming. This dream was so lifelike that Charles later decided it was a memory. He was back with Rose at the brook. His father was lounging on a stone, still wearing his

---

* In Lowell's typescript, the protagonist's name changes here from "Charles" to "David" for the duration of one dream sequence lasting one page. Numbered "5a," the page was inserted between pages 5 and 6 of Charles's story, and was evidently taken from a now-lost draft in which the boy had a different name. Assuming that there is no significance to the boy being called "David" five times, we have retained "Charles" throughout.

detestable loud, heart's-red necktie, and playing with a scarlet pirate's sash that hung to his ankles.

"Rose," said Charles's father, "you mustn't lose your heart to a horse. That one was always hollow and now he is gone. Listen, I'll tell you my favorite story."

Charles knew he would, he knew that now nothing on earth could stop his father from telling the detestable story.

"There was a woman," said Charles's father, "who all her life wanted to get to heaven. She couldn't wait, and unlike most people, she really had a reason for her wish. She was literally dying to meet the Virgin Mary. What do you think happened next? The woman died like everyone else. What do you think happened next? Believe it or not, the woman got to heaven. And what happened next? The woman actually met the Archangel Michael. I'm sorry to say she wasn't prepared to be impressed by Michael and only said to him, 'I am dying to meet the Virgin Mary.' And Michael was very hurt, and said, 'What do you mean you are dying, you are already dead.' You see he wanted to make it hard for the woman, and he really did make it hard. The woman had to fill out questionnaires, she took intelligence tests and aptitude tests and vocational tests. She estimated her quarterly income for the next decade. She met sleepy, pompous, important officials, and she met sharp, impertinent, promising, unimportant officials. Finally she was brought before the Virgin Mary. 'Oh, Virgin Mary,' said the woman, 'I have been dying all my life to meet you. You must be the happiest woman ever to have had such a rapturous son as Jesus.' The Virgin Mary looked at the woman sadly for a long time, then she answered, 'I don't know. We always had wanted a girl.'"

"Where does that leave me?" Charles thought as he woke up. "My Daddy wouldn't settle for a son, even if it were Jesus."

"Bing, bang, bong, bwawng!" went the gongs for a second time. Charles was very glad to be in the real world again, even though he had lost Rose Sharon and the hollow horse. Something funny though had happened to him. When he laid his hand on his heart just to be sure that he too hadn't turned into a bronze statue, he found he didn't have a heart. Way down below his ribs, something was sluggishly rising and dropping, but it wasn't his ordinary everyday heart of flesh and blood and muscle and friendly warmth. Instead, somewhere in the depths of his chest slowly bulging and still more slowly shrinking down like a leaking balloon were two loose fist-fuls of pinkish snow. Of course he couldn't see them but he knew they were like two containers of raspberry sherbet. He knew this just as he knew his mother and father were his mother and father though nothing he could see in them said Mother and Father.

"I know so much that I can't see," Charles said to himself.

Breakfast was extraordinary. Everyone seemed to be eating different courses, to be living through different hours of the day, and even to have been pieced together from different families and different apartments. Charles's father was going through the gestures of eating a solid, old-fashioned, spaced-out breakfast, gloomily mixing his bacon into his poached eggs and rubbing Charles's modeling dough from his heavy morning paper. His mother was darting about in robin's-egg-blue trousers, tossing last night's dishes along with any loose, unguarded breakfast dish she could find into the washer, and now and then taking little gulps from her one morning course, a whiff of coffee steam without cream or sugar. Charles faced and buried his fingers in a cereal bowl filled with the splattered bulk of his yesterday's modeling dough. He stared at his orange juice until everyone wondered why he didn't drink. This often happened, but today he seemed neither to see nor to eat. He was deciding that he would not tell his mother and father about his changed heart. If they couldn't even see it, what was the use in his saying, "It's nice, isn't it, to have a refreshing raspberry sherbet heart on this hot May morning"? Clenching his brows, he could clearly see the large grains of snow, a little discolored with pink and looking much like coarse grains of beach sand. He felt how delicious it would be to cool his hot sticky hands on this snowy stuff, and scrunch it into new shapes. He could work it into two red doughnuts, or chisel at it with his butter knife until he had carved a lovely five-pointed star. He thought, "My heart is a star. I must be Baby Jesus. The kings and shepherds will come to me. Santa Claus will come too. He was only Daddy this year, but I don't mind." Then he drank his orange juice and said to himself, "My heart is turning golden, its two fistfuls of snow will turn into one shining circle, I will be carrying the sun inside me." A million sunbeams or golden coins seemed to be flickering through his chest. Then he found he really didn't much fancy having the sun inside him. "What's the sun?" he said. "It's only a light bulb fastened up in the sky. It's small potatoes being the only boy with a sun inside him. I want my own heart that is me and only me and beats like my heart."

Then he wolfed down all the fresh strawberries on top of his bran flakes, and sure enough his heart began to grow red and heart-colored again. But it wasn't a real heart. It wasn't warm and flesh and blood, it really wasn't anything, for although it gave off a vague cold feeling, it really wasn't a cold you could touch, or say was here, there or anywhere. "It's like a cold thought," he said, and when he had said this, he began to be scared. "I'm not very scared," he said, "but it's hard to be funnyfeeling when I am already much too small." He climbed onto his father's knees and put a finger to where his heart was, where it should have been, where it used to be. He said, "Daddy, feel my heart. It's old and cold."

The father laid a hand on Charles's chest. It was hot. The father said, "You are hot, but not too hot because this is the warmest day in May."

Charles said, "I am as cold as Greenland in winter. My heart is lying in the refrigerator. Please take it out."

Neither Charles's mother nor his father had any idea what he was saying, but being grown-up they thought they had. They said, "Charles is a surrealist. He is improving on nature. Last night he said the stars are blossoming. He said the stars were blowing on brass horns and he couldn't hear what we were saying." That's what they thought, so they didn't bother to understand Charles and were already looking forward to telling their friends how their son was able to mingle all sorts of beautiful and unlikely things together in his mind.

Charles said, "Help me."

His father said, "I don't know any doctor who can take a heart out of a refrigerator. What you need is an ice surgeon." He didn't say this to tease Charles but only to make him laugh.

Charles laughed and screamed and kept repeating, "My heart is an icicle, my heart is a popsicle, my heart is a creamsicle." He knew it was hopeless to try and make the grown-ups understand anything really unusual. "I don't want to pull a long face," he thought. "It's always safer to laugh and be silly." "Hello, long-face," he said to his father. "Hello, ink-eraser-face." He pulled his father's face by the nose and chin as though it were made of rubber. Everybody laughed.

When they laughed, it was queer though. He wasn't with them. He was away somewhere trying to lay his hands on two fistfuls of pink snow that were miles deep in his chest and growing colder. "It's infinity*zero deep," he said. And it was really so, that was where his heart was, and he was with it, and it was silly all the while to be sitting in the dining room with his mother and father and to be hearing them laugh and not to be able to feel them laugh. He had to pretend he could feel them, but soon they too seemed to be moving away. His mother and father hadn't moved an inch, yet now they appeared to have whizzed backwards whole continents out of reach. Now it was as though they were looking at him from the grass-green swaying world of a fish tank, behind miles and miles of plate glass, flattening and whitening their flippers against its sides. "It is glorious, it is like being God," he thought, "this seeing them feel and not feeling them feel." And then again, it wasn't so glorious. "I am awake and I am watching myself sleep. I am lying here in front of myself. I am snoring at myself. I am snowing on myself. I am a lump of clay without any hands trying to model a lump of clay without any hands."

"It's time for school," the mother said.

Charles didn't hear a word, but something that didn't make a sound kept telling him inside his head, "It's time for school." "My heart is red snow," he said. "My mother is inside a fish tank." He put on his school cap and picked up his toy beaver that didn't look very much like a real beaver because its hair was gray grizzled at the ends like a porcupine, and its tail was pudgy and roundish and more like a blown-up rat's tail than the flat shovel-like tail a beaver uses to pat down mud and build its dams and igloo houses of mush and branches. "Whatever it is," Charles said, "it has two teeth. They're not baby teeth. They're teeth as big as my thumbs."

"Old beaverboard," he cried to the toy beaver once he was out of his apartment. "Nestle up close to me, chew through my ribs. Chew very gently so as not to hurt me. Old beaverboard, move your teeth like baby spider legs and pretend my ribs are only in my mind so you can take out my red-snow heart that is only in my mind and put back my real heart, so that my real heart will be back in my mind."

He was a very brave boy to think all this, and as he walked on across the park to school, he grew still braver and imagined the two handfuls of pink snow inside him were beginning to harden and solidify into two bright lumps of ice. Then he imagined something worse. The two lumps of ice were beginning to harden and solidify into two stones. "Nothing is harder than a stone," he said. "A stone is a stone forever." Then he thought, "Forever is a very long time."

He was thinking so hard, he hardly noticed anyone he passed. People were only thin black posts or bars or zebra stripes. They had no shape or beauty or anything about them to make Charles like them. "They are all just as much alike as a box of pins," he said. And this worried him, and he kept studying the people and trying to tell them apart, and finally, after a long time, he began to see that one was shorter than another and that one was a lighter black than another. At last they began to have legs, then arms, then faces, though the faces were all one face. He saw this one had a bran-colored suit and yellow leather patches on his sleeves. The next one had a torn pocket hanging down from his coat. Another had a glorious white beard like God, but walked heavily and slowly because he was old. Then he saw a very old lady snapping peanuts off her thumbnail to the squirrels. Finally a lady who was not so old but middle-aged and brown-haired passed, dragging a fat brown spaniel on a chain leash. The lady and the spaniel looked exactly the same to Charles, except that the spaniel wore transparent plastic ear-sheaths that hung to the ground. A boy pulling a kite shaped like a bird came by. He said to the lady, "Winter is over. Your pooch can take off his earmuffs." Then the lady said, "Those aren't earmuffs, they are ear-*sheaths*. My darling dog wears them to keep clean in New York City. Besides his ears are so long they drag on the ground like your kite." The boy with the kite didn't seem to hear her, and only said, "Winter is finished, take off your earmuffs." The man with the great white beard said, "This is a heat wave. The thermometer has already risen to eighty degrees."

Then Charles looked up over the skyscrapers and he saw a sign that said *eighty*. "That old man is eighty," Charles thought, and suddenly all about him everything stopped being gray and black and stiff and sticklike. Spreading before him were thousands of blades of grass. Each was a different length and stuck its point out in a different direction. There were dandelions and clover, and each was different. He looked up at the skyscrapers on the skyline, and though they looked just alike, each was different. And under the skyscrapers, there were trees—some had pale pink blossoms, some had dark pink blossoms, some had pink and white blossoms, and some had white blossoms with yellow centers. Each tree was a different height and had branches that pointed off in different angles. He saw a thorn hedge—the thorns were hay-colored and as alike as a box of pins, but each had a different leaf pointing off in a different way near it. Then he watched the people. They all wore different colors. Their neckties had different patterns. Some were happy, some were sad, some were both happy and sad. Some were worn, some were torn, and some were neither worn nor torn. Some spoke English and some spoke Spanish. Suddenly each had a face, each had his own face.

Then Charles began to skip over a little brook, and as he was standing in the middle on one foot, he heard a beautiful birdsong. Nothing could have been better. Charles circled around the tree where he had heard the bird. He looked on this side, he looked on that side, he squinted up into the highest branches, he pulled the lowest branches which almost swept the ground. He circled the tree five times, and he couldn't see a thing. Then a common robin hopped on a twig, dropped to a rock, sang its song, the song, and went darting its head out after a worm.

Charles remembered someone saying to him, "Don't waste your time listening to robins." He thought about the robin's red breast. "Its song is red too," he thought, then he looked down and saw to his surprise that he was holding his own heart. For better or worse, the two pink lumps of snow had melted. All morning Charles had been wearing and holding his father's heart-colored necktie.*

* In this sentence we have followed Lowell's penciled-in revisions, though the phrases he struck are significant; in the original sentence Charles was "pulling off" his "own" necktie.

PART III

A Life Among Writers

INTRODUCTION

ETWEEN 1959 AND his death in 1977, Lowell wrote a series of brief memoirs of other writers, plus a memoir of himself as a writer. These memoirs, twenty in all, are mostly about poets, though they include a philosopher (Hannah Arendt) and two writers celebrated more for their fiction than for their poetry (Ford Madox Ford and Robert Penn Warren). Still, Lowell seemed to regard all of them essentially as poets. The memoirs were a way of remembering and recording a group of admired and often beloved literary artists. They were also an effort to position himself as a valued member of that cohort. Finally, these memoirs were attempts to compose small works of art in prose—jewel-like compendia of personal observation, textual elucidation, and powerful feeling.

Lowell wrote all of these literary memoirs after he abruptly ceased work on his personal memoirs. Beginning in 1954, he spent about two and a half years working assiduously on "My Autobiography" and his memoirs of psychic crisis. Except for the two concluding items in Part II, he dropped those projects in early 1957. Months later he began to write the "Life Studies" sequence, which appeared in 1959 as the final section of *Life Studies*. Also in 1959, Lowell inaugurated a new phase by publishing his very first literary memoir, "Visiting the Tates." Others appeared at a fairly regular pace for the rest of his life: William Carlos Williams in 1961, Robert Frost in 1963, Ezra Pound and Randall Jarrell in 1965, Ford Madox Ford and Sylvia Plath in 1966, John Berryman in 1972, John Crowe Ransom in 1974, Hannah Arendt in 1976, and his memoir of his own career in 1977. Three other memoirs appeared posthumously: his short, seemingly reluctant memoir of Anne Sexton in 1978; a second memoir of Ford in 1981; and the T. S. Eliot memoir, in a rather inaccurate version, in 1987. Other memoirs—of Allen Tate, Pound, Jarrell, Warren, and Plath—have not been published until now.*

A distinctive feature of Lowell's literary memoirs is that they usually interweave commentary on texts and careers along with the more expectable recollections of meetings and conversations. For Lowell, the writer and the writing were a unity. In his poem "For John Berryman I," he asserted that he and Berryman "are words,"† and he apparently assumed that the same was true for other writers. Beyond recalling the writers and their work, these memoirs also evoke Lowell's experience of reading these writers. The memoirs disclose his grappling with his friends' written language, his effort to assess their artistry.

In these memoirs we see a very different Lowell from the person we glimpse in his memoirs of childhood and psychic crisis. In those earlier memoirs we encounter a wounded person, at odds with himself and circumstance, seeking to discover a viable self within the chaotic elements of his makeup, and hoping to find a way to live and to be of use. It's a flawed Lowell we meet there, hoping to make something valuable of his one "consuming chance."‡ In these literary memoirs, conversely, we discover a capable Lowell. He is a poet interacting with other notable writers of his time, who recognize him as a worthy professional. He observes, socializes with, and gossips about writers who are his elders (Tate, Caroline Gordon, Ransom, Ford, Eliot, Pound, Frost, and Williams), writers who are his own age or only slightly senior (Jarrell, Berryman, Warren, and Arendt), and younger writers who took a class from him (Sexton and Plath). He is open to the world and confident of his place in it.

In these memoirs Lowell has made something of himself. He has achieved the aspirations underlying the anguish of his childhood and early adulthood. These literary memoirs represent the fulfillment of his promise,

---

* A memoir of Philip Rahv, which Lowell started but soon abandoned, appears in the Appendix.

† Robert Lowell, *History* (New York: Farrar, Straus and Giroux, 1973), 203; reprinted in Robert Lowell, *Collected Poems*, edited by Frank Bidart and David Gewanter (New York: Farrar, Straus and Giroux, 2003), 600.

‡ "After Enjoying Six or Seven Essays on Me."

the vindication of his struggle. No less true or revealing than the memoirs of personal brokenness, these vocational memoirs expose the threads binding incapacity to accomplishment, fragility to strength. They provide an image of the power and humanity a marginal person can sometimes achieve.

We have presented these memoirs roughly in the order of Lowell's friendships, not in the order of composition or publication. This ordering system permits us to keep multiple memoirs of the same poet together. Lowell never published his literary memoirs with a date attached, seeming more interested in the stories he was telling—and in the larger story about creativity that they implied—than in his linear development as a memoirist. In the "Note on the Texts," we indicate the compositional and publication history of each memoir.

Yet the chronological order of Lowell's interactions with the other writers does roughly parallel the order of composition. At first, Lowell wrote about the mentors who helped him and admitted him to their social circles. (Ransom, though encountered early in Lowell's life, was written about later.) These memoirs are exuberant and funny. They suggest Lowell's exhilaration at being accepted by such literary giants—and also the pleasure many of his mentors took in helping him and in finding themselves reflected admiringly in his eyes.* Then came Lowell's memoirs of his friends in the profession, poets of about his own age who had died too young: Jarrell and Berryman. The glass darkens. The mood changes from youthful joy to mourning. Lowell called these memoirs "undertaker's pieces."† These eulogies were closely followed by memorials to other writers, both a little older and younger than he. All of the later pieces, except the one on Warren, were generated by a writer's death, and three or four of them concern suicides: Berryman, Sexton, Plath, and possibly (probably) Jarrell. Wordsworth's elegiac lines echo in the mood shift of Lowell's story arc: "We Poets in our

---

* Frost, ever suspicious of other poets, was an exception. In a conversation with Cleanth Brooks and Robert Penn Warren, Lowell recalled how as a Harvard freshman he went to see Frost after the Norton Lectures in 1936: "I had a huge blank verse epic on the First Crusade and took it to him all in my undecipherable pencil-writing, and he read a little of it, and said, 'It goes on rather a bit, doesn't it?'"; see *Robert Lowell: Interviews and Memoirs*, edited by Jeffrey Meyers (Ann Arbor: University of Michigan Press, 1988), 38. Lowell saw Frank Parker that night, and Parker says Lowell was quite shaken. He told him Frost didn't even bother to read the epic. Ian Hamilton, interview with Frank Parker, March 14, 1979, recording, C939/09, British Library, London.

† "On Ezra Pound I."

youth begin in gladness; / But thereof come in the end despondency and madness."*

While these memoirs make writers such as Tate, Eliot, Pound, Williams, Jarrell, Berryman, Arendt, and Plath highly present to us, they barely even mention Lowell's closest literary friend, Elizabeth Bishop. He names her only once, in "After Enjoying Six or Seven Essays on Me," where he identifies her as one of three major influences on his poetry, along with Tate and Williams. Lowell's friendship with Bishop may have been too deep and enduring to be metonymically reproduced in a brief memoir. His lasting memorial to her does not appear in the memoir genre at all but in their correspondence, which both of them carefully preserved, and which has been published as *Words in Air*.†

---

* William Wordsworth, "Resolution and Independence," lines 48–49.

† *Words in Air: The Complete Correspondence Between Elizabeth Bishop and Robert Lowell*, edited by Thomas Travisano with Saskia Hamilton (New York: Farrar, Straus and Giroux, 2008). Other missing pieces appear as mini-memoirs in his letters—for example, his accounts of Marianne Moore, Flannery O'Connor, and Delmore Schwartz; see *The Letters of Robert Lowell*, edited by Saskia Hamilton (New York: Farrar, Straus and Giroux, 2005), 323–24, 452–53, 472, respectively.

A NOTE ON THE TEXTS

O UR COPY-TEXT OF "Visiting the Tates," Lowell's memoir about
his student days in Tennessee, is the essay's first publication, in a
special 1959 issue of *Sewanee Review** celebrating Allen Tate's sixtieth birthday. No divergent manuscript drafts of the text have survived, there
being only some 1975 typescripts, today held at the Harry Ransom Center at
the University of Texas, Austin. These are secondary to the version printed
in 1959, as they are mere transcriptions retyped for a collection of prose
called *A Moment in American Poetry*, which Lowell and his publisher, Robert Giroux, had planned but never published. Another clean version of this
memoir printed in Lowell's lifetime appears in the seventieth-anniversary
Festschrift for Tate, *Allen Tate and His Work: Critical Evaluations.*[†] This
version differs from the 1959 original only in very minor corrections (for
example, the spelling of "moccasins" is fixed, a missing comma is provided,
and a superfluous one deleted). Working from the first publication, we made
these and similar improvements: besides fixing the spelling of "moccasins"
and correcting comma mistakes, we updated, as usual, the hyphenation and
word division of some of the compounds (for example, "mail box" was
replaced with "mailbox"). Most important, we disregarded the redactions

* Robert Lowell, "Visiting the Tates," *Sewanee Review* 67, no. 4 (1959): 557–59.

† Robert Lowell, "Visiting the Tates," in *Allen Tate and His Work: Critical Evaluations*, edited by Radcliffe
Squires (Minneapolis: University of Minnesota Press, 1972), 34–36.

made by Giroux in his 1987 republication of the memoir in Lowell's posthumous *Collected Prose*, preferring to retain Lowell's original wording. For instance, we restore the more colloquial sentence "A few days later, I returned with an olive Sears-Roebuck-Nashville umbrella tent," where Giroux had chosen to intervene; his revision made the sentence grammatically clearer but also more formal: "A few days later, I returned from Nashville with an olive Sears, Roebuck umbrella tent."

Lowell began his other Tate memoir, "On Allen Tate," as a preface for Tate's Festschrift at a time when Lowell was still its official editor. His editorship fell through, and the memoir was neither finished nor published. Only one unpublished draft exists, at the Harry Ransom Center. We regularized one slightly garbled sentence, replaced the phrase "social thing" with "social thinking" (surmising from the Eliot text Lowell cites that that was what he intended), and provided one phrase, bracketed, that we thought was missing.

The memoir of Ransom was first printed as "John Crowe Ransom 1888–1974" in the British journal *The New Review** and then soon afterward, titled "John Crowe Ransom: A Tribute," in the United States by James Laughlin in his anthology *New Directions*†—the latter, of course, using American spelling. These early versions (nearly identical except for the spelling) differ from the one Giroux included in his 1987 edition of Lowell's *Collected Prose* in about two hundred instances of varied significance. The large number of revisions complicate Giroux's claim in his "Notes and Sources" that the version in *The New Review* constituted his copy-text for the memoir. The character of the revisions in Giroux's version suggests that many or perhaps all of them were made by Lowell himself, who presumably at some point went about touching up the text for the purpose of reprinting it in the planned but never-published collection of prose pieces he wanted to call *A Moment in American Poetry*. This hypothesized revision, however, has been misplaced or lost, so it is presently impossible to be confident about the provenance of the changes. As was typical of Lowell's revisions in the 1970s, the changes are sometimes successful and sometimes not. Ironically, one is reminded of

---

* Robert Lowell, "John Crowe Ransom 1888–1974," *New Review* 1, no. 5 (August 1974): 3–5.

† Robert Lowell, "John Crowe Ransom: A Tribute," in *New Directions: An International Anthology of Prose and Poetry*, vol. 31, edited by James Laughlin (New York: New Directions, 1975), 1–8.

his comment on Ransom's own erratic revisions, "A little ground is gained for the more that is lost."* Taking all of these facts into consideration, we decided to return to the original text, as printed by Laughlin, which seems to have a freshness and directness often spoiled by the subsequent effort at succinctness and finish. In our footnotes we quote the most significant changes appearing in the later version.

In the case of "Memories of Ford Madox Ford," Lowell's contribution to a radio program taped in New York City on November 5, 1961, only one transcript of the talk exists, printed in *The Presence of Ford Madox Ford.*† We transcribed it from there verbatim. The more elaborate and richer "Foreword to Ford Madox Ford's *Buckshee*" was first prepublished, with the title "Ford Madox Ford," in *The New York Review of Books,*‡ though from the start it was intended as a foreword to *Buckshee*§ and appeared there the same year. Later reprinted verbatim by Frank MacShane in his collection *Ford Madox Ford: The Critical Heritage,*¶ the foreword is on the whole better edited than the version printed in *The New York Review of Books*, and that is why we use it as the copy-text.

The tribute "Robert Frost: 1875–1963" is mistitled; the poet was born in 1874, not in 1875. However, the memoir has been known by this flawed title for more than fifty years, and we thought it best to preserve it. Four drafts of the essay have survived and are part of the Robert Lowell Papers at the Houghton Library, Harvard University. Of the four, only one is significantly different from the version published in *The New York Review of Books,*** which is the latest and best developed and which we chose as our copy-text. We quote the most significant alternative passages in the notes.

Our initial Pound item, "A Tribute to Ezra Pound (Two Versions)," comprises two texts written in the same days—one so far unpublished, ex-

---

* "John Crowe Ransom: A Tribute."

† [I met him in Boston in 1937], in Robert Lowell, *The Presence of Ford Madox Ford*, edited by Sondra J. Stang (Philadelphia: University of Pennsylvania Press, 1981), 204–205.

‡ Robert Lowell, "On Two Poets: 1. Ford Madox Ford," *The New York Review of Books*, May 12, 1966, 3.

§ Robert Lowell, Foreword to *Buckshee*, by Ford Madox Ford (Cambridge, MA: Pym-Randall Press, 1966), xi–xv.

¶ Robert Lowell, Foreword to *Buckshee*, in *Ford Madox Ford: The Critical Heritage*, edited by Frank MacShane (London: Routledge and Kegan Paul, 1972), 264–67.

** Robert Lowell, "Robert Frost: 1875–1963," *The New York Review of Books*, February 1, 1963, 47.

isting only in manuscript at the Houghton Library, and the other previously published in *Agenda*.* We print the newly discovered tribute as we found it, while the *Agenda* piece is also transcribed with almost no changes—we corrected only one spelling error and deleted one superfluous comma.

"On Ezra Pound I" and "On Ezra Pound II" derive from Lowell's two apparently independent attempts to write a eulogy for Pound after his death in November 1972. "On Ezra Pound I" is a typescript at the Harry Ransom Center, consisting of two sheets that accidentally got separated, and that today are misfiled in two different folders and have not been identified so far as belonging together. As for "On Ezra Pound II," the text exists in several related typescript drafts at the Houghton Library. (The Harry Ransom Center has only a carbon copy of the Houghton Library's best-developed version of the item, which includes Lowell's final corrections.) Neither of these two memoirs of Pound has been published so far. Eventually, in his effort to honor Pound, Lowell limited himself to only two anecdotes from the drafts before and while reading selections from *Cathay* and *Pisan Cantos* at a memorial event on January 4, 1973. This was called "A Quiet Requiem for E. P.," organized by the Academy of American Poets and the New York Public Library, and held at the Donnell Library Center in Manhattan. A recording of the memorial evening demonstrates that he didn't read from either of the two memoirs that night. Neither does a pamphlet advertising the memorial evening, entitled "The Academy of American Poets Presents 'A Quiet Requiem for E. P.'" and published by the New York Public Library, feature or quote from either of Lowell's memoirs; instead, it includes an excerpt from one of Lowell's letters.

Lowell's 1965 eulogy "On T. S. Eliot" was to be his contribution to the winter 1966 memorial issue of *Sewanee Review* on Eliot, guest-edited by Allen Tate.† Because this memoir, for unknown reasons, did not actually appear in that issue, we had to rely on the only existing typescript at the Houghton Library, which we have faithfully transcribed. We disregarded Giroux's version in the *Collected Prose* (1987), one to which the editor seems

---

* Robert Lowell, "A Tribute," *Agenda* 4, no. 2 (October–November 1965): 22.

† Lowell's letter to Elizabeth Bishop of June 15, 1965, in *Words in Air: The Complete Correspondence Between Elizabeth Bishop and Robert Lowell*, edited by Thomas Travisano with Saskia Hamilton (New York: Farrar, Straus and Giroux, 2008), 575.

to have given his own title, "Two Controversial Questions." The reader will find our text to be rather different from that version. For instance, Giroux tacked onto the beginning a paragraph we think comes from Lowell's other prose project, "New England and Further," which he started in the same weeks in 1965; Giroux also omitted three sentences from the middle. Our method of handling Lowell's manuscript corrections was the same one we employed throughout this volume: We reviewed all the corrections individually, and automatically entered them if Lowell indicated his intention to do so by striking the original word or phrase. Whenever his intentions seemed uncertain or unclear, we considered the variants and chose the one that seemed to us most authoritative. As we did in the previous transcriptions, we fixed punctuation and spelling, and modernized hyphenation.

Several typescript drafts of "William Carlos Williams" have survived and are housed at the Houghton Library. Different as they are, they evince steady development toward the final version published in *The Hudson Review*.* The printed version has many minor editorial idiosyncrasies, some of which we've fixed in very much the same way as Giroux fixed them for his edition. Just as often, however, we decided to fall back on Lowell's slightly rough editing, especially where the irregularities seemed to be less errors than Lowell's shorthand, casual notations ("beats" rather than "Beats," definite articles omitted in titles, etc.), showing him attempting a slightly more informal, vernacular style. Whenever Lowell slightly misquotes Williams we generally preserved Lowell's rewrites except for the most obvious typos; at times we fell back on the way Lowell quotes Williams in his manuscripts, having discovered that they are more faithful to the original than as later revised by an overzealous copy editor.

Lowell's brief "Introduction for Randall Jarrell," circa 1963, exists only in one typescript draft at the Houghton Library with handwritten revisions. It has remained unpublished until now. We reproduce it with only a few minor spelling corrections. We follow that piece with Lowell's longer and more eloquent memorial for Jarrell, "Randall Jarrell, 1914–1965." Lowell first read the latter memoir, in a much shorter version, at a dinner meeting of the National Institute of Arts and Letters, probably in November 1965.

---

* Robert Lowell, "William Carlos Williams," *Hudson Review* 14, no. 4 (Winter 1961–62): 530–36.

This version was printed in *Proceedings of the American Academy of Arts and Letters and the National Institute of Arts and Letters*.* Soon after it was given, the talk was made available to the general reader in *The New York Review of Books*,† but not before the poet added eleven more paragraphs—two at the beginning and nine in the middle. He then picked five paragraphs from this text to read at the Randall Jarrell Memorial Service on February 28, 1966, at Yale. *The New York Review of Books* version was then reprinted, though without a title, in *The Alumni News* of the University of North Carolina at Greensboro in the spring of 1966, and as "An Appreciation" in Jarrell's last volume, *The Lost World*, published by Collier Books that year. Virtually the same text, though with a dozen or so needed corrections and titled simply "Randall Jarrell," was eventually printed in the Farrar, Straus and Giroux memorial volume, *Randall Jarrell, 1914–1965*,‡ which collected memorial tributes to Jarrell by many of his friends. This final, most polished version—in a volume Lowell coedited with Peter Taylor and Robert Penn Warren—served as our copy-text. We made only a few spelling corrections of our own. We retained the birth and death dates in the memoir's title, which had been eliminated in the memorial volume.

The history and the intended use of "For Robert Penn Warren" are unknown. Only one typescript draft has survived and today is held at the Harry Ransom Center. Lowell later quarried its material for the poem "Louisiana State University in 1940," included in *Day by Day*. The text of "For Robert Penn Warren" required only some minor typographical corrections.

"For John Berryman" appeared in *The New York Review of Books* in 1972.§ No other version with authorial provenance exists to complicate our editorial choices. The text misquotes slightly in reproducing Berryman's two poems, which we identify in footnotes.

The commemorative tribute to Hannah Arendt was initially written—as was the tribute to Jarrell more than ten years earlier—for a dinner meeting of the National Institute of Arts and Letters. Lowell delivered the talk, by all

---

* Robert Lowell, "Randall Jarrell, 1914–1965," *Proceedings of the American Academy of Arts and Letters and the National Institute of Arts and Letters* 15 (1965): 82–85.

† Robert Lowell, "Randall Jarrell, 1914–1965," *The New York Review of Books*, November 25, 1965, 3–4.

‡ Robert Lowell, "Randall Jarrell," in *Randall Jarrell, 1914–1965* (New York: Farrar, Straus and Giroux, 1967), 101–12.

§ Robert Lowell, "For John Berryman," *The New York Review of Books*, April 6, 1972, 3–4.

indications, on April 7, 1976, and later that year it was printed in the society's *Proceedings of the American Academy of Arts and Letters and the National Institute of Arts and Letters*.* (One manuscript draft has survived, today at the Harry Ransom Center, but it doesn't differ significantly from the version printed in *Proceedings*.) Just weeks after the dinner, however, the tribute was also published in *The New York Review of Books*† in a version in which Lowell made some significant changes. It is this version that served as our copy-text, though one passage in the original version, which we judged significant even though Lowell revised it for *The New York Review of Books*, is also quoted in a footnote.

Printed in *Anne Sexton: The Artist and Her Critics*, a volume edited by J. D. McClatchy, "Anne Sexton"‡ posed no problems, as it was carefully redacted by its first editor. We reproduce McClatchy's version here as originally published, including the extended excerpt from Sexton's poem "Some Foreign Letters."

"Sylvia Plath" is transcribed from a Houghton Library manuscript and has never been published until now. It was Lowell's first attempt to draft a memoir of Plath for use as a foreword to Plath's *Ariel*. Lowell abandoned this attempt and started over, eventually writing the "Foreword" that is also included in this volume. Because "Sylvia Plath" was never revised or finished, it includes some repetitions, and because it was part of the same writing process that produced the published "Foreword," it also has one significant overlap with that memoir. In editing "Sylvia Plath," we had to cope with some redundancy issues. In the first instance, we left an ellipsis in square brackets where Lowell wrote a sentence followed by a quotation from "Death & Co." that he then transferred to a spot later in the essay without crossing out the prior iteration. In another, a paragraph closely parallels a memorable paragraph in "Foreword"—the one about Russian roulette. We kept it but footnoted the resemblance and the significant differences. In still another, Lowell quotes the same Plath poem, "Berck-Plage," twice; we dropped the second quote, on the assumption that he forgot to cross it

---

* Robert Lowell, "Hannah Arendt, 1906–1975," *Proceedings of the American Academy of Arts and Letters and the National Institute of Arts and Letters* 26 (1976): 87–92.

† Robert Lowell, "On Hannah Arendt," *The New York Review of Books*, May 13, 1976, 6.

‡ Robert Lowell, "Anne Sexton," in *Anne Sexton: The Artist and Her Critics*, edited by J. D. McClatchy (Bloomington: Indiana University Press, 1978), 71–73.

out. Finally, a passage about Plath's voice is repeated with slight differences. We dropped its gist when it first appears (again leaving an ellipsis in square brackets) and kept it where it is more developed. In short, we only trimmed the text where it was obviously repetitious, adding no words of our own.

"Foreword to Sylvia Plath's *Ariel*" is Lowell's final version of the memoir of Plath, first printed in *The New York Review of Books*,* in tandem with a memoir on Ford, before it appeared as a foreword to the 1966 edition of *Ariel*.† There are no significant differences between the magazine article and the book foreword. That said, the *Ariel* version is better punctuated and is free from several oddly hyphenated compounds and spelling errors overlooked by the magazine editors. Therefore, it's the foreword to Plath's volume rather than the text's earlier publication in *The New York Review of Books* that served as our copy-text. As elsewhere, we've left Lowell's misremembered quotations intact but noted significant deviations by way of footnote.

"After Enjoying Six or Seven Essays on Me" was first published in the spring 1977 issue of *Salmagundi*.‡ Absent from the 1987 *Collected Prose*, it was reprinted in Steven Gould Axelrod's *Critical Response to Robert Lowell* (1999) and then in Frank Bidart and David Gewanter's 2003 edition of Lowell's *Collected Poems*. The *Salmagundi* version served as our copy-text, it being far better developed than an early manuscript draft housed in the Houghton Library collection among materials donated by Bidart. Following Bidart and Gewanter, we corrected one or two spelling errors; we also fixed or regularized the punctuation of several sentences and the styling of some poem titles.

Poems that Lowell quotes are often different from the versions printed in standard editions. He could be quoting from editions different from the standard ones; he could be quoting from manuscripts he got directly from those poets, many of whom were his friends; or he could be deliberately

---

* Robert Lowell, "On Two Poets: 2. Sylvia Plath (1932–1963)," *The New York Review of Books*, May 12, 1966, 4.

† Robert Lowell, Foreword to *Ariel*, by Sylvia Plath (New York: Harper and Row, 1966), vii–ix.

‡ Robert Lowell, "After Enjoying Six or Seven Essays on Me," *Salmagundi* 37 (Spring 1977): 112–15.

misquoting them. Most likely, however, he is quoting from memory as he said the poems to himself. Lowell's way of misremembering a poem could be precisely something that should be salvaged. Added or changed words, such as "there" in a line from Frost's "The Investment" or pluralized "gunnels" in "The Flower Boat," are important because those are the words he probably spoke to himself; they are *his* Frost. Therefore, we silently corrected only the divergences that seemed insignificant, careless typos; in all other cases, we added a footnote commenting on the divergence.

We provided titles for some of the pieces that, in manuscript, have remained untitled. This was the case with "On Allen Tate," "Memories of Ford Madox Ford" (which was actually the title of the radio program including Lowell's talk), "On T. S. Eliot," and "On Ezra Pound I." (Lowell called the second, longer essay on Pound "On Ezra Pound," and we added the Roman numeral II.) Certain titles, originally abridged—such as "A Tribute" (to Ezra Pound) or "Foreword" (to *Buckshee* or *Ariel*)—had to be written out in full for clarity. Although Lowell never affixed dates to any of his prose pieces, we decided to provide them here, in parentheses, again for the sake of clarity. The date refers to the first publication or—where no publication occurred until now—the date of composition. In this section, and throughout the book we have carefully preserved Lowell's extra line spaces, which he liked to use to organize texts.

Visiting the Tates

A PRIL 1937—I WAS wearing the last summer's mothballish, already soiled white linens, and moccasins, knotted so that they never had to be tied or untied. What I missed along the road from Nashville to Clarksville was the eastern seaboard's thin fields chopped by stone walls and useless wilderness of scrub.* Instead, plains of treeless farmland, and an unnatural, unseasonable heat. Gushers of it seemed to spout over the bumpy, sectioned concrete highway, and bombard the horizon. Midway, a set of orientally shapely and conical hills. It was like watching a Western and waiting for a wayside steer's skull and the bleaching ribs of a covered wagon.

My head was full of Miltonic, vaguely piratical ambitions. My only anchor was a suitcase, heavy with bad poetry. I was brought to earth by my bumper mashing the Tates' frail agrarian mailbox post.† Getting out to dis-

---

* On a leave of absence from Harvard, a twenty-year-old Lowell had just arrived in Nashville, where he was to attend, at Vanderbilt University, the classes of John Crowe Ransom. Soon afterward, he drove out to Benfolly, the old columned house of Allen Tate and Caroline Gordon on an eighty-five-acre hillside property overlooking the Cumberland River, just south of Clarksville, Tennessee. Lowell originally intended to reconnect with Ford Madox Ford, whom he'd met in Boston a few weeks earlier through Merrill Moore, a family friend and psychiatrist who was the true architect of the transfer. Ford suggested that they see each other again at the Tates' house, though he was later dismayed to find his perfunctory invitation treated so seriously.

† Caroline Gordon's letters to her friend Sally Wood Kohn provide a valuable alternative perspective on Lowell's visit at Benfolly. For instance, here is how she describes the moment of his arrival: "The other day we had what I believe is the strangest visitation we ever had. Allen and I were standing in the circle admiring the lemon lilies when a car drove up to the gate and a young man got out. He stopped down there by the

guise the damage, I turned my back on their peeling, pillared house. I had crashed the civilization of the South.

The Tates were stately yet bohemian, leisurely yet dedicated.* A schoolboy's loaded twenty-two rifle hung under the Confederate flag over the fireplace. A reproduced sketch of Leonardo's *Virgin of the Rocks* balanced an engraving of Stonewall Jackson. Below us, the deadwood-bordered Cumberland River was the color of wet concrete, and Mr. Norman, the token tenant,† looked like slabs of his unpainted shack padded in workclothes. After an easy hour or two of regional anecdotes, Greenwich Village reminiscences, polemics on personalities, I began to discover what I had never known. I, too, was part of a legend. I was Northern, disembodied, a Platonist, a Puritan, an abolitionist. Tate handed me a hand-printed, defiantly gingersnap-thin edition of his *The Mediterranean and Other Poems*. He quoted a stanza from Holmes's "Chambered Nautilus"—"rather beyond the flight of your renowned Uncle." I realized that the old deadweight of poor J. R. Lowell was now an asset. Here, like the battered Confederacy, he still lived and was history.

All the English classics, and some of the Greeks and Latins, were at Tate's elbow. He maneuvered through them, coolly blasting, rehabilitating, now and then reciting key lines in an austere, vibrant voice. Turning to the moderns, he slaughtered whole Chicago droves of slipshod Untermeyer Anthology experimentalists. He felt that all the culture and tradition of the East, the South and Europe stood behind Eliot, Emily Dickinson, Yeats and Rimbaud. I found myself despising the rootless appetites of middle-class meliorism.

---

post box and answered the calls of Nature then ascended the slope. We stood there eyeing him sternly and were on the point of shouting 'defense d'uriner' when he came up to Allen, regarded him fixedly and muttered something about Ford. Something made us treat him more gently and ask him into the house. He is a young man named Lowell from Massachusetts who heard Ford lecture in Boston and as he wasn't getting on well at Harvard decided to come south to learn how to write. We kept him overnight and sent him on to Nashville to learn further about writing. I think Ford really rescued him from a bad situation. His family decided he was crazy because he wants to be a poet and had him in a psychopathic sanitarium. He does have a queer eye on him but is very well behaved and affable, but imagine a Lowell (yes, the poor boy's mother is a Cabot)—imagine one coming all the way from Boston to sit at Southern feet." See Sally Wood Kohn, ed., *The Southern Mandarins: Letters of Caroline Gordon to Sally Wood, 1924–1937* (Baton Rouge: Louisiana State University Press, 1984), 209.

* When Lowell arrived, Ford hadn't appeared yet, so Lowell "got to know the Tates quite well before his [Ford's] appearance." Robert Lowell, "An Interview with Frederick Seidel" (1961), in *Collected Prose*, edited by Robert Giroux (New York: Farrar, Straus and Giroux, 1987), 257.

† Tenant farmer.

Tate said two things this afternoon that at once struck me as all but contradictory and yet self-evident. He said that he always believed each poem he finished would be his last. His second pronouncement was that a good poem had nothing to do with exalted feelings of being moved by the spirit. It was simply a piece of craftsmanship, an intelligible or *cognitive* object. As examples of cognitive objects, Tate brought forward Mr. Norman, the hand-printed edition of *The Mediterranean*, and finally a tar-black cabinet with huge earlobe-like handles. It was his own workmanship. I had supposed that crafts were repeatable skills and belonged to the pedestrian boredom of manual training classes. However, something warped, fissured, strained and terrific about this cabinet suggested that it would be Tate's last.

I came to the Tates a second time. Ford Madox Ford, the object of my original visit, was now installed with his wife and secretary.* Already, their trustful city habits had exhausted the only cistern. On the lawn, almost igniting with the heat, was a tangle of barked twigs in a washtub. This was Ford's Provençal dew pond.† The household groaned with the fatigued valor of Southern hospitality.‡ Ida, the colored day-help, had grown squint-eyed, balky and aboriginal from the confusion of labors, the clash of cultures. Instantly, and with keen, idealistic, adolescent heedlessness, I offered myself as a guest. The Tates' way of refusing was to say that there was no room for me unless I pitched a tent on the lawn. A few days later, I returned with an olive Sears-Roebuck-Nashville umbrella tent. I stayed three months. Every other day, I turned out grimly unromantic poems—organized, hard and classical as a cabinet. They were very flimsy. Indoors, life was Olympian and somehow crackling. Outside, Uncle Andrew, the calf, sagged against my tent sides. I sweated enough to fill the cistern, and breathlessly, I ached for the conviction that each finished poem would be my last.

Like a torn cat, I was taken in when I needed help, and in a sense I have

---

* Ford's life partner during his last decade—though never his wife—was the Polish Jewish American painter Janice Biala (1903–2000). Ford's secretary was Wally Tworkov, the wife of Biala's brother.

† Presumably believing that morning dew would suffice as the source of water, Ford tried to make a dew pond of the kind he saw at home in France. He sank into the ground a washtub, which he then filled with twigs. As Tony Roberts writes, "It proved a dismal failure"; "With the Topnotch Tates at Benfolly, 1937," *PN Review* 42, no. 3 (January 2016): 33–37.

‡ As Lowell described in a letter to Richard Eberhart, "The Fords are spending two months with the Tates and there is a certain amount [of] buried conflict. Water is supplied by a cistern, toilets must hardly ever be flushed, French as opposed to Tennessee cooking." See Robert Lowell, *The Letters of Robert Lowell*, edited by Saskia Hamilton (New York: Farrar, Straus and Giroux, 2005), 17.

never left. Tate still seems as jaunty and magisterial as he did twenty years ago. His poems, all of them, even the slightest, are terribly personal. Out of splutter and shambling comes a killing eloquence. Perhaps this is the resonance of desperation, or rather the formal resonance of desperation. I say "formal" because no one has so given us the impression that poetry must be burly, must be courteous, must be tinkered with and recast until one's eyes pop out of one's head. How often something smashes through the tortured joy of composition to strike the impossible bull's-eye! The pre-Armageddon twenties and thirties with all their peculiar fears and enthusiasms throb in Tate's poetry; imitated ad infinitum, it has never been reproduced by another hand.

(1959)

On Allen Tate

MY ESSAY PRECEDES, though it doesn't preface, other essays on Allen Tate here selected and gathered in this volume.* A seventieth-anniversary volume. The pressures to be polite and empty are almost irresistible. But not from Allen Tate who on such occasions has a talent for being most gracious and generous without giving up an impertinence and even rudeness, without which friendly criticism would be unreadable, inconsequential.

When I met Allen Tate in 1937, I think I must have had a bias toward his temper and ideas. I had a temper, but no distinct ideas. I still have too little interest in sustained argument, sustained polemic, to much want to write a critical essay. In this instance, I shall try to be erratic and conversational. I will have succeeded if I can describe what has knocked off on me. Talking with Tate was always exciting; later I have always thought of him with a mixture of awe and amusement. He has been my beloved friend.

---

* In the late 1960s Lowell reluctantly agreed to edit a Festschrift for Allen Tate to be published on the occasion of his seventieth birthday. Tate sent him all the criticism about himself and his work that he had collected over the years. Lowell kept putting off the project, eventually offering the excuse that it was the writing of this prefatory essay—published here for the first time—that was his main "stumbling block." In the end, his maid mistakenly threw out all the materials in his absence, and he never completed the project. In a letter of apology to Tate, he wrote that he felt like John Stuart Mill when his maid had burned the only copy of Carlyle's *The French Revolution*; see Robert Lowell, *The Letters of Robert Lowell*, edited by Saskia Hamilton (New York: Farrar, Straus and Giroux, 2005), 530. Though Tate's birthday anniversary was missed, many of the essays and tributes (though not Lowell's) were re-collected by his biographer Radcliffe Squires and published in *Allen Tate and His Work: Critical Evaluations* (Minneapolis: University of Minnesota Press, 1972).

T. S. Eliot, in writing a short note for Tate's sixtieth birthday,* notices his poetry, prose fiction, literary criticism and social thinking, and suggests that considerable as was the accomplishment in each of these forms, the whole is greater than the sum of its parts. This is a compliment that might possibly give the recipient more honor than pleasure. By slightly changing this statement, I can make it more pleasurable. The accomplishment is in the critical essays and the poetry, the bulk lying in the essays, the hardest steel in the best poems.

Before looking at the poems and fiction, I want to look at four or five points all found in the essays and which have given me trouble and instruction, almost always both.

First the form. I like the way Tate confesses that he has no plan or system and hardly knows how or what sentences will follow the last. In this he follows Eliot and, still earlier, Arnold. He is close to both in his interest in society, in his mingling of literary judgment, morality and religion. In this last and of course in his specific literary likes, Tate is closer to Eliot. Both perhaps use religion to hedge off the graceless, verbally graceless, expert in modern science and part science. The age-old terminology of Aristotle and the scholastics might seem so open to everyman that it can withstand an abstruseness no less withering than that of science.

Tate sometimes seems a Tennessee version of Eliot, so close are their prejudices, so close are their discoveries. Tate is much the more overt and direct and chivalrous. I mean this as a tribute and a limitation. Tate is much the more physical, open and simple-minded. He is much closer to the body with its colors, habits, sudden angers and courtesies. Often I feel Tate is hammering some belief or obsession to death. Then he suddenly switches with some flashing, inconsistent figure of speech, makes some gay, destructive concession, admits confusion, complexities beyond his argument—or nails down an opponent he has merely been nagging. The New Englander, fulfilling Tate's prejudice about us, may find him naive, only to be amazed by some instant, off-hand and accurate [turn of] mind. What a good mind, I say, thinking less of the long reasoning than of the humor, the quick terms, the relaxed hit.

(Composed circa 1968)

---

* T. S. Eliot, "A Note," in a featured section entitled "Homage to Allen Tate: Essays, Notes, and Verses in Honor of His Sixtieth Birthday," *Sewanee Review* 67, no. 4 (Autumn 1959): 576.

John Crowe Ransom:
A Tribute

H E WAS BORN in 1888, my father's birthdate, and was the intellectual father I would have chosen.* Twenty-five years ago, I wrote
a short *festschrift* piece on Ransom's conversation.† I thought his
poetry was conversation as much as his criticism. Since then his accomplishment hasn't changed except for half a dozen fine elegiac essays, and
eight poems curiously and dubiously revised. I have nothing new to offer but my wonder. My lasting, almost daily, picture of Ransom is slightly
oversymbolic, and such as he couldn't have been. I was nineteen or twenty
then, loud-humored, dirty and frayed—I needed to be encouraged to comb
my hair, tie my shoes and say goodbye when leaving a house. I knew more
about Dryden and Milton than most students, but had never read a word by
a philosopher or Greek. I could not decode John's (none of us wished‡ to
call him this until after graduation) metaphysical terms, *ontology*, *catharsis*,

* In his letter of recommendation for Lowell to Cleanth Brooks and Robert Penn Warren, Ransom wrote:
"Lowell is more than a student, he's more like a son to me." Ian Hamilton, *Robert Lowell: A Biography* (New
York: Random House, 1982), 72.

† Robert Lowell, "John Ransom's Conversation," *Sewanee Review* 56, no. 3 (Summer 1948): 374–77.

‡ When revising for his never-published 1975 prose volume, *A Moment in American Poetry*, Lowell replaced
the verb "wished" with "dared."

with their homely Greek derivations and abstract, accurate English signifi-
cations so unlike language.

Ransom detested laurels and Byronic bravery, but his poetic calling
showed in the fine fiber of his phrases, and in a convivial shyness. His recre-
ations were games, all the brisk and precise ones, golf, croquet, crossword
puzzles, bridge, charades, the Game. For someone so gracious, he was surprisingly put out by violations. An enemy charade team once divided
Churchill into *church* and *hill* instead of *church* and *ill*. This brought out his
sustained aesthetic scoldings; so did the illegal moving of his croquet ball.
He could live without cheating and within the rules of a game. His rather
repelling and unwayward rows of flowers seemed laid out by tape measure
and flower advertisements.* "I would fill rows of separate plots with flowers
to my liking; and very congenial would be the well-clipped horizontal turfs
between adjacent plots to walk upon. But I would replace the end-flowers
of the two central plots with ten plants of Burpee's *Climax Marigold*, which
bear blazing orange flowers; and the end-flowers of the upper and lower
plots with Wayside Gardens' *Aster Frikartii*, whose blossoms are bright lavender . . . Think how the farmer and the visitors would be intrigued by
the displacements of the sloping front border, which do not subtract a foot
from its lawful length." His parlors in three successive houses were the same
room, bleak, comfortably barren, just-moved-into-looking; no games or
students sipping a beer on the rug could injure it or alter. Most of Ransom's
original paintings were loaned him by Kenyon's art instructor. They were
coarse-textured and large, an affront to the instructor's rival, the Impres-
sionist wife of the coeditor of the *Kenyon Review*. Ransom would say, "Mr.
Mercer, like William Turner, is better at the sea than farmland."

Ransom's mouth was large and always in slow perceptive motion,[†]
tight-drawn to deflect ignorant rudeness, giving an encouraging grimace,
or relaxed, though busy, in reason. It was a mouth more expressive than the
small, beautiful mouths of the girls in his poems. He liked to be a poet, but
not to be tagged as one; he preferred the manner of a country philosopher[‡]

---

* For more on Ransom's passion for order and regularity in his Gambier, Ohio, garden, see Thomas Daniel
Young, *Gentleman in a Dustcoat: A Biography of John Crowe Ransom* (Baton Rouge: Louisiana State University Press, 1976), 328.

† In the manuscript for *A Moment in American Poetry*, Lowell added, "quivering with tedium."

‡ Lowell later replaced this phrase in the *Moment* manuscript with "provincial minister."

or classics professor—a man from his father's generation. He roughened his musical voice as with gravel, just as he revised to roughen meter. Once we watched my classmate, Mr. Nerber,* lope in his apricot corduroy suit across the Kenyon campus. "Nerber is our only Kenyon man whose trousers match his coat." Poor Nerber, nothing else in his whole life matched. Ransom could paraphrase a faculty meeting and make it interesting. He could make a sad comic masterpiece of a happening under his nose. My classics professor was a close friend of his and mine, and was a child prodigy, who entered Harvard at thirteen, wrote the best Greek verse by an American in England, and later married another classics child prodigy—egregious people but fated for divorce and tragedy. They were plain and Socratic, yet their divorce was marked with violence and absurdity: a sheet wetted to cause pneumonia, a carving knife left threateningly on a stair post, a daughter held *incommunicado* by the Ransoms from both parents, insomnia, evidence, floods of persuasive, contradictory and retold debate. On the much adjourned day of trial, the presiding judge, the master of sarcasm, was kicked and incapacitated by a mule. Ransom told this story for a season as if possessed, and in an honest rococo style that left listening moralists pale and embarrassed. It was his version of the Southern tall story—one of the strangest and most fascinating, though true. Ransom's natural conversation was abstract and soft-spoken, as if leading a slow actress.[†]

There were moments in Ransom's ironic courtesies that reduced even Allen Tate to white-faced finger twitching, so far had the conversation dropped from brave sublimity. In a letter just written me, Tate rightly boasts of being Ransom's oldest living student. But the relationship could never have been this, they were so near genius, close in age, and different in character. Ransom affected fear, lest Tate, though matchless, prove too strong. He [Tate] roamed in the danger areas, France, Rimbaud, Hart Crane, *The Waste Land*, was too eloquent, obscure, and menacing. Ransom liked to stand behind and later off from the Agrarian rush, an antislavery Southern commander with liberal connections in the East. I suppose I don't need to explain the decentralist provincial hopes of the Tennessee agrarians and neo-traditionalists,

---

* John Nerber (1915–1969), an editor, writer, and poet; a graduate of Kenyon College; and the managing editor of the Kenyon College students' literary magazine, *Hika*, when Lowell was contributing to it.

† Lowell revised that final remark to read "as if he were leading a slow actor."

a utopia as impractical and permanent as socialism, though for now fallen away from the sunlight.

Ransom spent his last thirty-five years, over a third of his whole life, at an adopted college in Ohio. His affections warmed slightly to the bohemian; his politics grew less slashing and heroic. His Southern first love leveled or dimmed into an unoptimistic, though airy, Northern reasonableness. The powerful Midwestern farms never became his soil, or harvest; not even a spot to sightsee. Who knows what was the choice? Did leaving Tennessee strengthen his health by derailing his inspiration? Health is the nurse of our functioning, according to the Stagirite, to use his ironic word.*

Randall Jarrell said the gods who took away the poet's audience gave him students. No student was more brilliant than Jarrell, but Ransom had dozens, Allen Tate, Robert Penn Warren, Andrew Lytle, Peter Taylor, John Thompson, Robie Macauley, James Wright. We carried his academic brand, but were diverse, unsortable, ungroupable. Ransom's neatness fathered the haphazard. He was known throughout the English departments of America; in Southern universities, he is a cult, everyone has studied under him or under someone who has; any student can repeat scraps of Ransom dialogue, epigram and dogma, or laugh at his legendary defeat of some notable or boor. His classes were usually for a dozen or more students; they were homemade, methodical yet humdrum. For five years, he coolly taught *The Faerie Queene*; though he found Spenser's allegory without intellectual pith, it amused him like a crossword puzzle or a problem for his flowers.†
More brilliance and flare often came in his casual gossip. Sometimes classes would crackle with fire. Most often in Aesthetics. "I must give Hegel's Triad an accurate terminology. When a teacher says that, he means his own." He had a fairly rich though sketchy and out-of-vogue acquaintance with the old classical-romantic music. Once in Aesthetics, we were taken to hear a record of Beethoven's *Seventh Symphony*.‡ It upset Ransom's spleen with the nineteenth century; he had discovered Shelleys everywhere in that unmetaphysical darkness. "Beethoven is a romantic . . . he is too good."

---

* Here Lowell presumably means Aristotle's remarks in *De Anima* on the nature of health as harmony between the contraries of the body.

† Lowell later revised it to read "a blueprint for his garden."

‡ Lowell's later revision: "Thirteenth or Fifteenth Quartet."

Ransom's Prose. He thought philosophy more intellectually stimulating than literary criticism; criticism more masculine than scholarship; scholarship more solid than criticism; poetry more intuitive than philosophy, though a florid and slipshod thinker. Technique was skeletal without intuition; intuition was soft. "The minds of man and woman grow apart; and how shall we express their differentiation? In this way, I think: man at his best is an intellectualized woman." Or, "The philosopher is apt to see a lot of wood and no trees, his theory is very general and his acquaintance with particulars is not persistent or intimate, especially his acquaintance with technical effects." In the world of the sentiments and art's particularity, child, woman, art and creature are perfect, though they mostly fail before the verification— bodies without heads. All Ransom's thoughts are dialectical, games of pieces in opposition. None can be expelled, or maneuvered without bumping. I hope I haven't suggested that everything is equal to everything in his aesthetics, that college course jars against college course without umpire or outcome. He could suffer breakage and bloodshed, he was a tough and untiring constructor.

Ransom received a low but passing grade for writing his final classics exam at Oxford in the Latin of Tacitus. No other Latin style seemed close and intelligent enough. He studied romantics with fear and pity, and never confused extravagance with sublimity. He himself, though, was a romantic, and had the underdog courage of someone always smaller, quicker, and brighter. He was happier than us, though easily injured. My friend Jarrell was romantic in another style than Tate or Ransom. He was educated in the preoccupations of the Thirties, Marx, Auden, Empson, Kafka, plane-design, anthropology since Frazer, the ideologies and news of the day. He knew everything, except Ransom's provincial world of Greek, Latin, Aristotle, and England. His idiom was boyish, his clothes Southern collegiate. Our college President, Dr. Chalmers, was a thoughtless disciple of the great American humanists, Paul Elmer More and Irving Babbitt. Unlike Ransom, he believed in his anti-romanticism and forever called out barbarously for measure, order, the inner check. For him, Socrates was a brand-new humanist professor at Harvard. He watched Randall going down a ski crest in his unconventional, unlovely clothes, crying, "I am like an angel." Ransom suggested that Randall had shocked Dr. Chalmers's belief. The Aristotelian schoolmen had known no such enthusiastic and inordinate angel. "That boy needs a more generous vocabulary." He knew that Randall had already *swallowed the dictionary*.

When Ransom wasn't playing games, golfing or taking us on hikers' discussions, or gardening in structured solitude, he was in his den. It was a compact, unwomanly room, the twin of last year's moved-out-of den— fresh and secure, though seasoned with pipe smoke, Greek, Latin, English, an infirm volume or two in French or German bought at college, a firm density of philosophy, criticism, a volume or two of Jane Austen, four by Faulkner, a fair spread of modern poetry, weakened by signed copies from friends. He talked metaphysics if he could, and poetry if he could, and gossip if he could. The strands were indistinguishable; one of his obsessive critical terms was *nostalgia*. Unlike the poet, he could write of women, and the fresh things of the sexes.

When he changed his poetry for criticism, everyone asked why he stopped writing. They discussed this behind his back, or studied him silently with a pained, consolatory eye. Perhaps the reverse question had only been put to him by himself. Why make pretty rhyming instead of an honest essay? Critics condescend to poets yet often must abase their own medium before poetry. Even so Ransom; but he was lucky to find criticism in his unoccupied hour, a more flexible and controlled sentence, and stricter sequence. No need to tinsel out syllogism and sorites with meter; no passion to puff like balloons. Through criticism, Ransom discovered his *Review*, entered in correspondence with the first New Critics. He assembled critics annually each summer at Gambier, Ohio, to teach his School of Criticism. *O bel eta del oro*,* when criticism had an air of winning! When Ransom's classical pessimism renounced its half-warning, "They won't be content until the old work is done over." Somehow in the next generation, the great analytical and philosophic project turned to wood, the formidable inertia of the pedagogue and follow-up man.

Ransom's poems, if anything, think more clearly than his prose. Yet the essays have the same language, and the same intent. His charming, biting criticism of Edna Millay is like one of his poems on Southern ladies. It has wit and flirtation yet skillfully avoids poetry. In his prose, Aristotle, Santayana and Sir Arthur Quiller-Couch breathe, though introduced as intel-

---

* That is, *O bella età dell'oro* (O beautiful golden age).

lectual presences not portraits. His unruffled rhetoric and arguments against blur and enthusiasm once seemed to me perverse. They are medicine now.

Ransom wanted to go back to his poetry. Someone found an envelope he had scribbled with bizarre and hitherto unused off rhymes. No other words. After the War, he published his first *Selected Poems*, with minor though magical revisions.* Long after, he spent years rewriting and trying to perfect his old, almost perfect poems in a disastrously new style.† I leave this insolent sentence as I wrote it. Not all of Ransom's changes are disastrous, some improve, almost all show surprising ways in which passages can be turned into variations. We are given a thousand opportunities to misrevise. A little ground is gained for the more that is lost. One new quatrain in "Prelude to an Evening" has the richness of lines from *Macbeth*. Ransom's prose *defenses* of his new poetic versions are autobiographical and critical; they sometimes change the life story. "During the *Fugitive* days of my fourth decade I was at great pains to suppress my feelings in what I wrote. I was both sensitive and sentimental . . . My friends seemed to think I managed it." "The third stanza, where chill replaces fever, is almost unutterably painful; but I was most intent upon it, and managed to the best of my ability. Lines two and three are the saddest; perhaps in all my poems."‡ I hope these saddest lines were those of the first version, not those he ruined by revision.

His *Selected Poems* is no longer than single volumes by other poets; all his work is no longer than two such volumes. He made one or two debatable inclusions, and three or four omissions; these were missed and later restored. What he wrote could have come from knowing Hardy, E. A. Robinson, early Graves, Shakespeare, Milton, Mother Goose, ballads, Plato, and Aristotle. His poems stick apart, and refuse to melt into their neighbors. They seem few until one tries to discover as many in some favorite, more voluminous author. Ransom's essays, even the most dazzling and strong, are like didactic poems (some of Auden's perhaps), a little monotonous and ill-jointed. The charm of his true poems seems to be first in their colors,

---

* Robert Lowell, *Selected Poems* (New York: Alfred A. Knopf, 1945).

† Here Lowell has in mind Ransom's *Selected Poems* of 1963 and 1969 (both volumes published in New York by Knopf).

‡ Slightly misquoted, these are Ransom's comments on, respectively, "Of Margaret" and "Here Lies a Lady" in his third edition of *Selected Poems* (1969), 146, 142. Ransom actually wrote, "My friends seemed to think that I managed it" and "Lines two and three are the saddest in the poem; perhaps in all my poems."

people, beautiful, observant imagery, grace of rhyme and speed—his undefinable voice. They are short.

Ransom is able to like women, and the young, find them delightful, irritating, mortal, though not quite human. His women cannot be spoiled by abstraction, or impressed into drudgery. They are supporting figures; man stands in the middle, one unchangeable man wherever he is—troubled, gaunt, conscienced, philosophizing to no good, Quixote, Prufrock, too serious to see his own shadow or children . . . heavily unlike Ransom in life. Men and women court, quarrel, and whirl into disequilibrium, not tragic but pained. Nowhere a thoughtless happiness, a worldly innocence, places to "hear the maiden pageant ever sing / Of that far away time of gentleness." Man goes creased and sometimes finds his puzzling joy.

In his art, too, Ransom discovered pain, or a harmony of disequilibrium. Why do we not come back, he asks, to a photograph for aesthetic pleasure, no matter how colorful and dramatic it is, not even if it is a picture of someone dead? We cannot feel, here, as in paintings, the artist's mother work of hand and mind. I asked the master photographer, Walker Evans, how Vermeer's *View of Delft* (perhaps the first *trompe l'oeil* of landscape verisimilitude) differed from a photograph. He paused, staring, as if his eye could not give an answer. His solution was Ransom's—art is the intelligent pain or care behind each speck of brick and spot of paint.

Ransom made no case for a poetry of onomatopoeia, superior eeriness, passionate intensity. He liked his language to be elegant and unpainted, not far removed, except in its close texture, from written or spoken prose. He wished poetry to show its seams, and show the uncouthness caused by rhyming, compression, managing syntax. Out of pain, the art that can hide art. The poetic in the old sense was all to Ransom. He told me his poems came from brief, unevoked daydreams, a wisp of imagery, or a new fable. Many dreams, few poems. When the daydreams stopped or became inappropriate, so did the muse.

I think of Ransom on a hill, as a student must see his loved master. Kenyon had a sentimental hill celebrated in student songs.* I have left out my friend's personal life, his charming, healthy household, where with Jarrell I spent my second and key college year. I leave out too his wife, Robb

---

* Presumably it is Gambier Hill, the site of the college campus.

Reavill, whose humor and particularity held him back from the ether* of the metaphysics.

In his seventies, he confessed that he could not control his feeling when finishing two poems. "But I must add that they are fictions."†

(1974)

---

* Lowell replaced "ether" with "small air" in his unpublished manuscript *A Moment in American Poetry*.

† Again, a line from his comment on "Of Margaret." The other poem that moved him was "Here Lies a Lady." For the comment, see Ransom's *Selected Poems* (1969), 146.

Memories of
Ford Madox Ford*

I MET HIM in Boston in 1937, two years before he died, and it was a crucial moment in my life. I was having a good deal of trouble, personal trouble with my parents, and it was arranged that I meet Ford at a cocktail party. And I remember him coming in, and I had the fantastic impression that he was very much like the Republican elephant—not that he resembled that elephant, but he was a large man and . . . perhaps that's the key word to him, big in bulk, big in the qualities underneath that bulk . . . I once asked him the young writer's question, "What does a writer need more than anything else?" and he said, "Memory." And whether that's true or not, it is certainly true of his kind of writing, which was full of a great abundance of things he'd retained.

And after you speak of the largeness of Ford, my second impression would be that he had two qualities almost equally pronounced that are almost contradictory, but were not, and that is the generosity and contempt. No person warmed and was more sensitive to young writers, and he was like a bear more than an elephant. He could hit you with his elbow and knock

* Lowell presented this reminiscence at the WBAI studio in New York City on November 5, 1961. Taped by Richard Elman, the talk was part of the station's program "Memories of Ford Madox Ford." Unpublished in Lowell's lifetime, the memoir appeared in *The Presence of Ford Madox Ford*, edited by Sondra J. Stang (Philadelphia: University of Pennsylvania Press, 1981).

you down in sort of a blunt way . . . and I think those qualities went together. In my case I will give an illustration. After I met him he told some people that I was—I was nineteen at the time—that I was the most intelligent person he had met in Boston. Now I think that was more his low opinion of Boston than his high opinion of me.

I might say too that Ford is the first Englishman I think I ever met intimately, and he had certain generic qualities of an Englishman—their humor, their rhythm, and so forth, is different from ours—disconcerting and marvelous. And his opinion of Boston . . . I think that was the part of America he perhaps liked least: he saw through Boston. Its English pretensions and its Puritanism were very distasteful, and no man was less puritanical than Ford. Big and easygoing, and I might even say that he knew he was big, and he acted the role, and he could fill the role he chose, . . . ate great amounts.

I remember Colorado when he was lecturing at Boulder at the college. He said he was going to give a dinner with venison, which was illegal at that time, and the dinner was arranged, and I think it's still the best I ever had. The wines were balanced, and every course came as it should, and the venison came, and we ended with syllabub, and you felt in Paradise at the end. You never realized that the venison was mutton that Ford had cooked.

He was writing *The March of Literature* at that time, and I went to Olivet College with him, and his way of writing was to dictate, and I must say that was agony for me. I didn't know shorthand and took down what he said in illegible print, and he mumbled and had a Yorkshire voice, and it was quite difficult to get what his sentences were, and he slurred his words, and I often had to guess, and he would make remarks that I had no sense of prose rhythm when I couldn't hear him. Then in the afternoon—I could hardly type—I would painfully type out what I took down in longhand, which had many gaps, and with my terrible sense of prose rhythm had to improvise phrases here and there which I think still remain in *The March of Literature*—little blemishes that have been undetected.

The Ford I knew was very much like the Ford you find in *The Nightingale*,* one of the later books of autobiography: that is, he dictated his books, and the books went very much as his conversation did. He used that

---

* Ford Madox Ford, *It Was the Nightingale* (Philadelphia: J. B. Lippincott, 1933).

method, and it's quite subtle that good conversationalists don't necessarily write well and good writers are not necessarily good conversationalists. He'd got something that *joined* the two, so that being a writer changed his conversation. I've often thought that if you could listen to Ford talk for an hour, say, as he does in *The Nightingale*, . . . you would say this was the most astonishing speaker you'd ever heard, and he gave that impression. He was not quite as consecutive and sustained in presence as on paper, but he was very much that way. Something happened when he had a plot and characters that changed the style, though even there I think he dictated those books—certainly the Tietjens*—and they too have something of that quality of someone speaking.

I met my first wife through him.† I think she was present when we remet in New York. What I remember is something that didn't happen there. He was so near the end of his life, which I never would have guessed. It must have been six or seven months before he died, so that after I heard about his death, somehow that last meeting stood out in some peculiar way which I have no image of.

(Composed 1961)

---

* Lowell's synecdoche for Ford's *Parade's End* (1924–1928), a tetralogy whose protagonist is Christopher Tietjens.

† Jean Stafford (1915–1979); Lowell was married to her between 1940 and 1948.

Foreword to
Ford Madox Ford's *Buckshee*

I FIRST MET Ford in 1937, a year or so after the publication of *Buckshee*,* and two years before his death. Reading these poems is like stepping back in time to Ford in his right setting, France, to a moment when both he and Europe between the wars were, imperceptibly, miraculously, a little younger, hopeful, and almost at a pause in the onrush. When I knew Ford in America, he was out of cash, out of fashion, and half out of inspiration, a half-German, half-English exile in love with the French, and able to sell his books only in the United States. Propped by his young wife, he was plodding from writers' conference to writers' conference, finally ending up as writer in residence at Olivet College in Michigan.† He seemed to travel with the leisure and full dress of the last hectic Edwardian giants—Hudson, James, and Hardy. He cried out, as if wounded, against the eminence, pomp, and private lives of Tennyson, Carlyle, and Ruskin, the false gods, so he

---

* Ford's late poetic sequence "Buckshee" first appeared in a British anthology in 1931 and then in *Poetry* magazine in 1932. Lowell wrote this memoir as a foreword to a new edition of the sequence published in Cambridge, Massachusetts, by Pym-Randall Press in 1966.

† Janice Biala, an American painter, was not Ford's wife, though that is how he usually referred to her. Ford was still married to Elsie Martindale, whom he never divorced. They all—Ford, Biala, Lowell, Allen Tate, and Tate's wife, Caroline Gordon—drove from Tennessee to Olivet College for a writer's conference that began on July 18, 1937. From there Ford and Biala took a train to Boulder, Colorado—as did Lowell soon afterward—to another writers' conference, where Ford gave a lecture on August 3.

thought, of his fathers. He was trailed by a legend of personal heroism and slump, times of great writing, times of space-filling, past triumph and past humiliation, Grub Street drudgery, and aristocratic indolence. He was the friend of all good writers, and seemed to carry a concealed pistol to protect them and himself against the shoving non-creative powers of editors, publishers, businessmen, politicians, college presidents, literary agents—his cronies, his vultures.

Always writers and writing! He was then at work on his last book, *The March of Literature*, and rereading the classics in their original tongues. At each college stop he picked up armloads of Loeb classics, and reams of unpublished manuscript. Writers walked through his mind and his life— young ones to be discovered, instructed, and entertained, contemporaries to be assembled, telegraphed, and celebrated, the dead friend to be resurrected in anecdote, the long, long dead to be freshly assaulted or defended. Ford was large, unwieldy, wheezy, unwell, and looked somehow like a British version of the Republican elephant. His conversation, at least as finished and fluent as his written reminiscences, came out in ordered, subtly circuitous paragraphs. His marvelous, altering stories about the famous and colorful were often truer than fact. His voice, always *sotto voce*, and sometimes a muffled Yorkshire gasp, made him a man for small gatherings. Once* I watched an audience of three thousand walk out on him, as he exquisitely, ludicrously, and inaudibly imitated the elaborate periphrastic style of Henry James. They could neither hear nor sympathize.

Largeness is the key word for Ford. He liked to say that genius is memory. His own was like an elephant's. No one admired more of his elders, or discovered more of his juniors, and so went on admiring and discovering till the end. He seemed to like nothing that was mediocre, and miss nothing that was good. His humility was edged with a mumbling insolence. His fanatical life-and-death dedication to the arts was messy, British, and amused. As if his heart were physically too large for his body, his stamina, imperfection, and generosity were extreme.

* At the writers' conference at the University of Colorado, Boulder, in August 1937.

Ford's glory and mastery are in two or three of his novels. He also never stopped writing and speaking prose. He had a religious fascination in the possibilities of sentence structure and fictional techniques. About poetry, he was ambivalent. He had a flair for quoting beautiful unknown or forgotten lines, yet called poetry something like "the less civilized medium," one whose crudity and barbarism were decked out with stiff measures and coarse sonorities. Like Boris Pasternak, he preferred Shakespeare's prose to his blank verse, and thought no poetry could equal the novels of Flaubert.

He himself wrote poetry with his left hand—casually and even contemptuously. He gives sound and intense advice to a beginning poet: "Forget about *Piers Plowman*, forget about Shakespeare, Keats, Yeats, Morris, the English Bible, and remember only that you live in our terrific, untidy, indifferent empirical age, where not a single problem is solved and not a single Accepted Idea from the poet has any more magic . . ." Yet he himself as a poet was incurably of the nineteenth century he detested, and to the end had an incurable love for some of its most irritating and overpoetic conventions. His guides were always "Christabel," the Browning of "My Last Duchess," the Rossettis, Morris, and their successors, the decadents. He is Pre-Raphaelite to the heart. Their pretty eloquence, their passionate simplicities, their quaint neo-Gothic, their vocabulary of love and romance, their keyed-up Christianity, their troubadour heresies, and their terribly over-effective rhythms are always peeping through Ford's railway stations and straggling free verse. For Ford and his ablest contemporaries, Hardy, Hopkins, Housman, Yeats, de la Mare, Kipling, and Pound, the influence and even the inspiration of the Pre-Raphaelites was unavoidable. Each, in his way, imitated, innovated, modified, and revolted. Ford's early imitations have a true Pre-Raphaelite brio, but he is too relaxed and perhaps too interested in life to have their finest delicacy, conviction, and intensity. His revolt is brave and resourceful, but the soul of the old dead style remains to hamper him. Even in prose, except for *The Good Soldier* and *Parade's End*, he had difficulty in striking the main artery; in poetry, he almost never struck it. His good phrases and rhythms grow limp or hopped up with impatient diffidence, and seldom reach their destination. The doggerel bounce and hackneyed prettiness of lines like

The poor saint on his fountain
On top of his column
Gazes up sad and solemn*

(to choose a bad example) keep breaking in on passages that are picturesque
and lovely. His shorter poems are brisk, his longer diffuse.

Pound's famous command that *poetry be at least as well-written as prose* must
have been inspired by Ford, though I doubt if Ford believed this a possibility or really had much fondness for a poetry that wasn't simple, poetic, and
pastoral. I heard someone ask him about Pound's influence on Yeats's later
style. "Oh," Ford said, "I used to tell Ezra that he mustn't write illiterate
poetic jargon. Then he'd go to Yeats and say the same thing." This was
tossed off with such flippant finality that I was sure it was nonsense. Years
later, however, Pound told me the same story. He said too that Ford actually
lived the heroic artistic life that Yeats talked about. There must be more to
the story. Ford had no gift like Yeats for combining a conversational prose
idiom with the grand style. I think he must often have felt the mortification
of seeing the shining abundance of his novels dwindle away in his poetry to
something tame, absent-minded, and cautious. He must have found it hard
to get rid of his jingling, hard to charge his lines, hard to find true subjects,
and harder still to stick to them when found. Even such an original and personal poem as "On Heaven" is forever being beguiled from the road. Yet
a magnificence and an Albigensian brightness hover over these rambling
steps: Ford and Pound were companions on the great road from twelfth-
century Toulouse to twentieth-century London.

　　Buckshee is Ford, the poet, at his best. It too is uneven and rambling—
uneven, rambling, intimate, and wonderful. Gardening in Provence, or
hearing a night bell strike two in Paris, Ford ruminates with weary devotion
on his long labors, and celebrates his new young marriage—O minutes out
of time, when time was short, and the air stiff with Nazi steel and propaganda! In his last years, Ford's political emotions were to the left, but his

---

* From Ford's poem "In the Little Old Market-Place," reprinted in *Selected Poems*, edited by Max Saunders
(Manchester, UK: Carcanet Press, 2003), 69.

memory, pace, and tastes were conservative. He didn't like a place without history, a patina of dust, "Richelieu's Villa Latina with its unvarying *statu quo ante*." Above all he hated a world ruled by a "maniacal monotone of execration." I remember how he expressed his despair of the America he was part of, and humorously advised me to give up eating corn lest I inherit the narrow fierceness of the Red Indian. In "Coda," the last and supreme poem in this sequence, he is back in Paris, his great threatened love and symbol for civilization. In his dark apartment, he watches the lights of a taxi illuminate two objects, the "pale square" of his wife's painting, *Spring in Luxemburg*, and the galleys of his manuscript, momentarily lit up like Michelangelo's scroll of the Fates. Then he says to his wife, the painter:

I know you don't like Michelangelo
But the universe is very large having room
Within it for infinities of gods.*

Buckshee coughs and blunders a bit in getting off, but in "Champêtre," "Temps de Sécheresse," and "Coda," Ford finds the unpredictable waver of his true inspiration. In these reveries, he has at last managed to work his speaking voice, and something more than his speaking voice, into poems— the inner voice of the tireless old man, the old master still in harness, confiding, tolerant, Bohemian, newly married, and in France.

(1966)

* Lowell's quotation departs from Ford's actual lines as reprinted in the very book Lowell was introducing. In Ford's poem, there's a period after "Michelangelo," the words "Universe" and "Gods" are capitalized, and the sentence continues without a period after "Gods."

Robert Frost: 1875–1963*

A FTER FROST'S WIFE died in the thirties, he stepped up the pace of his public readings. He must have gotten consolation from being Robert Frost, from being the image of himself that he had perfected with such genius.† I have heard him say mockingly that hell was a half-filled auditorium. This was a hell he never had to suffer. Year after year after year, he was as great a drawing card as Dylan Thomas was in his brief prime. Yet there was a strain; never in his life was he able to eat before a reading. A mutual friend of ours once said with pity, "It's sad to see Frost storming about the country when he might have been an honest schoolteacher."

Frost had an insatiable yearning for crowds, circles of listeners, single

---

* Frost was born in 1874, not in 1875.

† One manuscript version of this essay (in the Lowell Collection at the Houghton Library, Harvard University) adds the following passage here: "It's easy to say that this figure is too good for life, and too easily cheapened by the public. I would rather praise his abundance and overflow. Still we mustn't simplify Frost by imagining he was much like the Great American Bard of his notoriety—that blurred and blown-up effigy shedding hayseed and floating like a national advertisement over our parades.

"His true story, necessarily still bowdlerized, would resemble Gorky's shrewd, fascinating reminiscences of Tolstoy. Like Tolstoy, though smaller, Frost was compact and life-size, he had the same small ruses, surprises and cunning agility. He knew how to speak his own words. He could talk forever. Often it was a lacework of teasing and frail, fresh testings. Here too, for brief flashes, one saw some stone statue, primitive yet sophisticated, a slab thrown up the great center of things."

After completing the Frost memoir, Lowell wrote to Elizabeth Bishop: "Walking by his house in Cambridge last Thanksgiving, I thought with some shame about how wrong I was to be bothered by his notoriety and showing off. Under the great display the life was really very bounded and simple"; see Robert Lowell, *The Letters of Robert Lowell*, edited by Saskia Hamilton (New York: Farrar, Straus and Giroux, 2005), 417.

listeners—and even for solitude. Can we believe him when he says he "took the road less travelled by"? He ran, I think, in no tracks except the ones he made for himself. The thinker and poet that most influenced him was Emerson. Both had something of the same highly urbane yet homemade finish and something of the same knack for verbal discovery. Both went about talking. Both leaned on and defied the colleges. A few of their poems are almost interchangeable. "In May, when sea-winds pierced our solitudes, / I found the fresh Rhodora in the woods."* Part of Frost was wary of Emerson. "Great is the art / Great shall be the manners of the bard." He knew better than anyone that his neighbors would find this manner boring and insufferable. He tried to make himself a man of many ruses, subtle surprises, and weathered agility. He was almost a farmer. Yet under the camouflage there was always the Brahma crouching, a Whitman, a great-mannered bard. If God had stood in his sunlight, he would have elbowed God away with a thrust or a joke.

He wasn't quite a farmer even in his early, isolated years. He didn't quite make a living; he got up at noon. He said the cows got used to his hours more easily than his neighbors. There was nothing very heroic or out of the ordinary here, yet these fifteen years or so of farming were as valuable to him as Melville's whaling or Faulkner's Mississippi. Without exactly knowing it, and probably not intending it, Frost found he was different from other men of letters. He used to tell a story about a Florida train trip he took with Wallace Stevens. The two poets were nervous with each other. Stevens, however, was more in the vacationer's mood. He made witty remarks, and finally said, "The trouble with your poetry, Frost, is that it has subjects." I don't want to spoil the weird, whimsical rightness of Stevens's taunt.† Frost had an unfashionable hold on subjects.‡ What were they?

---

* The lines are from Emerson's "Rhodora." The quotation in the next sentence is slightly misquoted from Emerson's "Merlin." The second verse should read, "Great be the manners, of the bard."

† Lowell means he doesn't want to quote Frost's alleged retort, which Frost prided himself on but which may be fictionalized. Frost claimed that he responded, "The trouble with you, Wallace, is that you write about—bric-a-brac." Lowell throughout this memoir seems to be quoting from memory, and his wording of Stevens's gibe varies slightly from the version recorded in the biography of Frost by Lawrance Roger Thompson and R. H. Winnick, *Robert Frost: The Later Years, 1938–1963* (New York: Holt, Rinehart and Winston, 1966), 61.

‡ Here again the early draft of the Frost essay (at the Houghton Library) diverges remarkably from the final version: "Frost is strong enough to withstand our seeing him momentarily as an outmoded, white-haired, Father Time–like creature covered with the splintered debris of the old ages."

I suppose what I liked about Frost's poems when I read them thirty years ago was their description of the New England country, a world I knew mostly from summer and weekend dips into it. It was a boy's world, fresher, grainier, tougher, and freer than the city where I had to live. "Back out of all this now too much for us," "Over back there where they speak of life as staying," "the dory filled to the gunnels with flowers," "the tar-banded ancient cherry trees," one man saying, "Weren't you relieved to find he wasn't dead?" and the other answering, "No! and yet I don't know—it's hard to say. / I went about to kill him fair enough."* I used to wonder if I knew anything about the country that wasn't in Frost. I always had the pleasure of either having my own knowledge confirmed or of learning something new that completed it. I hardly cared which.

The arts do not progress but move along by surges and sags. Frost, born in 1875, was our last poet who could honestly ignore the new techniques that were to shatter the crust. He understood the use of tools, often wonderful tools, that five or ten years later would be forever obsolete. He was a continuer and completer and not a copyist. When he began to write, the American cultural scene was unimaginably different from anything we now know. There were no celebrated masters to meet, no one to imitate. Poetry was the great English Romantics and Victorians and their famous, official American offshoots. Through their practice, criticism, and translations, the known past had been reborn in their image.

Frost had a hundred years' tradition he could accept without question, yet he had to teach himself everything. Excellence had left the old poetry. Like the New England countryside, it had run through its soil and had been dead a long time. Frost rebuilt both the soil and the poetry: by edging deeper and deeper into the country and its people, he found he was possessed by the old style. He became the best strictly metered poet in our history, and our best local observer, at least in meter. The high wind of inspiration blew through his long, packed, isolated rustication. By the time he was forty and had finished his second book, *North of Boston*, he had arrived. Step by step, he had tested his observation of places and people until his best poems had

---

* Lowell slightly misremembers several of these quotations, but gets the gist right. They derive from, respectively, "Directive," "The Investment," "The Flower Boat," "The Black Cottage," and "The Code."

the human and seen richness of great novels. No one had helped him to learn, and now no one could because no one wrote better.

Randall Jarrell has a fine phrase about Frost's "matter-of-fact magnificence." He writes that the poems' subjects are isolation, extinction, and the learning of human limitation. These three themes combine, I think, in a single main theme, that of a man moving through the formless, the lawless and the free, of moving into snow, air, ocean, waste, despair, death, and madness. When the limits are reached, and sometimes almost passed, the man returns.

This is what I remember about Frost. There was music in his voice, in the way he made his quotations ring, in the spin on his language, in the strange, intuitive waywardness of his toleration. He was less of the specialized literary man than other poets and more curious personally.

Last November I walked by his house on Brewster Street in Cambridge. Its narrow gray wood was a town cousin of the farmhouses he wrote about, and stood on some middle ground between luxury and poverty. It was a traveler from the last century that had inconspicuously drifted over the customs border of time. Here one night he was talking about the suicide of a young friend, and said that sometimes when he was excited and full of himself, he came back by thinking how little good his health could do those who were close to him.*

The lights were out that night; they are out for good now, but I can easily imagine the barish rooms, the miscellaneous gold-lettered old classics, the Georgian poets, the Catullus by his bedside, the iron stove where he sometimes did his cooking, and the stool drawn up to his visitor's chair so that he could ramble and listen.

(1963)

* Lowell also recalls this conversation with Frost in his *History* sonnet "Robert Frost," in Robert Lowell, *Collected Poems*, edited by Frank Bidart and David Gewanter (New York: Farrar, Straus and Giroux, 2003), 539.

A Tribute to Ezra Pound
(Two Versions)*

E ZRA POUND'S WORK wears very well and there's a lot of it. The *Cantos* is certainly *the* absorbing immense poem of the century in English. It's a heroic effort written at a time when it seemed almost as though all alive long works would be prose fiction. Many risks, many disasters, and big ones along the journey! The translation that might have been pedantry and inaccuracy and turned out to be wonder. The impossible politics that turned out to be at least a serious interest in politics. The coldness, the aloof, inhuman intensity, the egotism, that turned out to be humor, a Hardylike compassion for people and a reverence for the beautiful and heroic. I want to hail my old friend and praise his great, jagged and far-shining works.

(Composed 1965)

Ezra Pound's writings belong to the moment of experimental explosion—Stravinsky, Schoenberg, Picasso, Rilke, Joyce, Eliot, Proust. His work, like theirs, is alive with a radiant daring we now seem to have lost. As a man,

---

* The second paragraph alone was published as Robert Lowell, "A Tribute," *Agenda* 4, no. 2 (October–November 1965): 22.

he had the surpassing generosity of his sure, discovering eye. How often he encouraged other artists at the risk of breaking and dispersing himself! His translations have a glory of music, freshness of idiom and something exuberant, indefinable and personal that make others seem joyless and soiled. His *Cantos* are heroic, a poem as long as a long novel, written in a time when it seemed as if only prose fiction could bring off anything extended, important and readable. And yet the *Cantos* are not metered fiction, nor do they go against the grain of what is possible in poetry. I want to hail my old friend on his eightieth birthday, and reverence his courage and humor—a great, jagged, far-shining splendor!

(1965)

On Ezra Pound I

T HIS IS THE fifth undertaker's piece on the great poets I have written for *The New York Review of Books*.* I feel the gloomy perversity; I hope there will be no more. I hope . . .)

I met Pound in 1947 when I was Consultant in Poetry at the Library of Congress—1947–48, the years of Harry Truman's seeming exit before Thomas Dewey.

I had an introduction to Pound from Eliot, though this made little difference, for Pound was open to all and jocular about his friends and old enthusiasms. I used to go to St. Elizabeth's once a month, twice a month—in all many many times, a habit. The visits were hardly fun. On about the third or second, Pound suddenly said, "I know I'm the damnedest bore in America." And Dorothy Pound said, "I find nothing more boring than economics." But there they were, day after day, [visits] of dim afternoons in the ward for the criminally insane—hours only livened by crummy tinfoil cookies and Ezra's monologues. Yet the refreshment for me was unlike anything else in Washing-

---

* Indeed, had it been published (which it was not), his essay on Pound would have been his fifth eulogy for *The New York Review of Books*, after his Frost (February 1, 1963), Jarrell (November 25, 1965), Plath (May 12, 1966), and Berryman (April 6, 1972). Lowell seems to have lost confidence in this memoir of Pound and never completed it. Eventually, it was his reminiscence of Arendt (May 13, 1976) that became his fifth "undertaker's piece" for *The New York Review of Books*.

ton, and unique. Of course Ezra was a presence, numinous almost, and his reminiscences of the great were lovely and shrewd, on Yeats, James, Eliot, Ford—most of them in the *Pisan Cantos* or elsewhere, but many not.

Once it seemed necessary to ask Ezra if he had ever met Mussolini. "Once, I went to see Muss in 1936 (?),* and he was expecting a quiet half hour on Cavalcanti." (How could Mussolini have been expecting anything of the kind? It reminds me of Pound sending his last copy later in the year of his Confucian translation to Senator Taft . . . In this anecdote, I am surely garbling, but unintentionally and being true to a twenty-five-year-old memory.) "Instead I gave him an economics program that would have blown the lid off of Europe. Mussolini looked at it bewildered, and said something like 'It makes a point.'" Pound felt from this that Mussolini had the next quickest mind of anyone he had met, except the French painter Picabia. Pound suggested that he move to Rome where they could have weekly economics conferences. I can imagine the panic of Mussolini, who rapidly said, "No, go back to Rapallo and I'll send for you." The summons of course never came. Pound returned to Rapallo. No word. But when all was fall and Mussolini's Republic was ever retreating further north, as the Germans retreated—when all was lost, someone passing Rapallo told Pound the Boss would like to see him. Pound walked sixty miles through the American lines who didn't know then what to do with him—a grayish red sixty-year-old man still carrying "the economics program that would blow the lid off Europe" to Mussolini and the Italian Republican Army that had faded out of reach northward before the American and British advance.† Pound convalesced for a few days or a week in the deserted village, then walked back home. We know about his brutal captivity, the cage, the insane asylum.

(Composed 1972 or 1973)

---

* Lowell is clearly uncertain if he remembers the date correctly. In fact, Pound had an audience with Mussolini on January 30, 1933. For a more fact-based account of the meeting, see A. David Moody, *Ezra Pound: Poet*, vol. 1, *The Epic Years 1921–1939* (Oxford: Oxford University Press, 2014), 136–37.

† This passage conflates—as do the accounts of several early biographers—Pound's two separate journeys. First, on September 10–23, 1943, Pound by turns walked and took trains to get from Rome to Gais to see his daughter, Mary de Rachewiltz. Then, between November 23 and December 18, he traveled again, this time not on foot, from Rapallo to Salò and Milan to join the propaganda operation of the Italian Social Republic, a German puppet state led by Mussolini. Though he hoped to see Mussolini again, he didn't manage to obtain an audience. For details, see Moody, *Ezra Pound: Poet*, vol. 3, *The Tragic Years 1939–1972* (Oxford: Oxford University Press, 2015), 65–76; 548. There could not have been any American lines as yet between Rome or his home and his two destinations in late 1943. American troops had barely landed in Salerno and Sicily by then, much farther south, and had not yet started advancing north.

On Ezra Pound II[*]

FIRST I MUST step over the pit of Pound's politics in support of Mussolini, and his anti-Semitism in support of Fascism. Current political polemic is a byline in the *Cantos*, and turns up almost always as a hair, a shadow, a footnote, a pointing of past history, or a biased symbolic universal. In his Rome Radio Broadcasts during the War, controversy is naturally everything. Controversy also swarms through his prose of the Thirties. I haven't pursued the instances. The broadcasts swing between Social Credit lectures and Jew-cursing. The Social Credit is cranky, neither engrossing nor evil.[†] The writing on the Jews is evil and dull, often not much above Father Coughlin's newspaper, a now lost name in his forgotten yellow sheet.

---

[*] Lowell gave this speech on the evening of January 4, 1973, at a memorial service organized by the Academy of American Poets at the Donnell Library Center of the New York Public Library. The program also included reminiscences by Leon Edel, Robert Fitzgerald, James Laughlin, and Robert M. MacGregor. See the pamphlet *The Academy of American Poets Presents "A Quiet Requiem for E. P."* (New York: New York Public Library, 1973). Among the audience members were Pound's daughter, Mary de Rachewiltz; his son, Omar Pound; and Pound's lifelong companion, Olga Rudge. For one account of the event, see Thomas Lask, "'Quiet Requiem for E.P.' Recalls Turbulent Life of Embattled Poet," *The New York Times*, January 6, 1973, 31.

[†] During the memorial Lowell and Laughlin engaged in a friendly exchange—what Lowell would later call in a letter "our dispute and joking"—over Pound's economic theories. In response to Lowell's remark that he "did not understand" them, Laughlin retorted that maybe he "did, but would not let on." Lowell responded that Pound's theories seemed to him "like Christianity: One had to take them on faith." For an account of the discussion, see Lask, "'Quiet Requiem for E.P.'" See also Lowell to James Laughlin, October 23, 1974, in Robert Lowell, *The Letters of Robert Lowell*, edited by Saskia Hamilton (New York: Farrar, Straus and Giroux, 2005), 636.

Thirty or forty years ago, in the years of Stalin, Franco, Roosevelt, etc., one thought there was a left, right and middle. We were the middle, and we were right. And the Communists were right. And the Nazis were to the right of the left. And Liberalism and Conservatism? They do not mean upholding one's well-off contemporaries, or even inventing graceful or brutal theories to maintain these people. *Right* in those days had a dozen different and tenable meanings—all of them wrong. The true liberal or conservative should have followed none of the alleys and blind names. Who could choose? Such thoughts must have walked through Pound's frantic mind at that time; one this moment, another the next moment, all of them in jangling disarray to the inward glance.

It's not my duty as fellow poet, critic and his friend to defend or clear Pound's record. I can't see him as a bad man, except in the ways we all are. I do see him as a generous man to other artists, and this in a way none of us will touch. The Broadcast smears seem, if not acts of madness, at least acts of dementia and obsession. Was the poetry hurt? No one can say very surely and plausibly. Engagement, participation—certainly Pound *plunged*: in the American Army Camp at Pisa, in his imprisonments, in writing the *Pisan Cantos*, his most poignant work. To be occupied with something is better than nothing. Is it true that no bad ideas can hurt, if held with character? That no good ideas can help the shallow? That good and bad alike are fuel for an inspired mind? I wish to let the questions dangle.

If Shakespeare, in a seizure of paranoia, had murdered his wife, think of the new interpretations of *Othello*! Could we claim then that the sacred text was still unaltered? Wouldn't *Othello* have been dragged into court as evidence by a prosecuting attorney in the trial for murder? We will never see the *Cantos* as if they had been written by Carl Sandburg—or as they are. In a hundred years . . .

In a few sentences, no new interpretation is fortunately in order. I will hold myself down to personal impressions, some revised and others not, from thirty years of reading. When I first came on *Personae*, I was taken with the voice, a vibrance of nostalgia and slang—America to Europe, to the glisten of the master spirits. *Personae* has many lovely poems. They are still beautiful, but I cannot quite catch the old enchantment. Most are over-poetic now, too much of the Pre-Raphaelites. If they had come out in the day of Rossetti, Swinburne and the early Yeats, they would have made all

the Nineteenth Century anthologies—stars among those stars. This cannot
be. What has lasted best from that far past, and almost my favorite work of
Pound's, is *Cathay*. What better short poem in English than "The River-
Merchant's Wife"? That catches the feelings of a girl, of a young wife? Or
the poem on the frontier soldiers digging fern-roots?* In Saint Elizabeth's
Hospital, I tried to tell the Pounds that this was as good as the King James
"By the waters of Babylon." They answered, "We had hoped it was better."
Cathay has the sensuous firmness of the best poems in the King James Bible,
along with FitzGerald's *Rubaiyat*, the only English masterpiece that is an
Oriental classic. Pound's *Propertius*, much less of a translation and more of
an original, is also harder to get at and to follow. It too may have a larger and
less approachable excellence. *Cathay*'s magic endures, but when it was first
read, Chinese poetry was still new and exotic. This helped; but Latin, even
the *Elegies* of Propertius, is an old road. Pound's tone is one of ironic disil-
lusionment with the Roman Empire (the British? ours?), one that resembles
the different and old-world voices of Hardy and Chekhov. This is not the
stiff and mighty line of Propertius. In Pound, love affairs are nostalgic and
urbane; in Propertius, suicidal.

I am not sure why *Mauberley* seems so much better to me than Pound's
short early poems, which so much resemble it. The opening sections roll off
with a thunder. The metrical difficulties of the quatrains (anyone can write a
quatrain; the trick here is in the conversation and the live, but unlight-verse
rhymes) seem to guarantee the honesty of the portrait of World War I Europe, such an unlikely mass for quatrains, and impossible in anyone else's.
The length; it's hard to realize how short both *Mauberley* and *The Waste
Land* are. They seem to last as long as *Gatsby* and *The Sun Also Rises*.

Pound's greatness must hang on the *Cantos*. Seen on a table or bookcase,
the fat black silver-lettered twenty-year-old volume looks as thick as a best-
seller. No other poem by an American looks like that—except for unread
library curiosities, toils of scansion, languors of vers libre, and except for
Melville's *Clarel*, a work of genius by our greatest genius; not unread, but
unreadable, perhaps because of its monotonous line and rhyme. Pound is
read, I think, because of the loveliness of his ear, his variety of styles and
often-human material, the pleasing irregularity of his meter, moving from

---

* Ezra Pound, "Song of the Bowmen of Shu," in *Cathay* (London: Elkin Mathews, 1915), 5–6.

song, to painting, to talk, the relative brevity and completeness of his separate cantos. It seems worrying to fuss too much with the poem's structural
looseness. About half the lines twitch with life; few epics or long narrative
poems go farther than that. Parts that many critics have thought uninspired
seem so to me. I have never checked the Jefferson and Adams correspondence with Pound's use of it, but I suspect he has merely cut and anthol-
ogized. The later Chinese Cantos run too rapidly to interest me much in
their history and potentates. Randall Jarrell said, "To Pound, not only do
all Chinamen look alike, they think and talk alike." *Rock-Drill* and *Thrones*
are staccato and stuttering, china vases broken against a wall, or smashed,
laconic jottings from a workbook. Yet even as I list and dismiss, I am struck
by how fresh and unexpected this material once was, how much more in key
now. *Rock-Drill* and *Thrones* are inspired titles. Each misdirection Pound has
taken has fruitfully been followed by disciples and treasured with less skill.
The great solid parts the first thirty, the *Pisan*, scattered single cantos, many
pages and phrases. I name some of the best: the elegy on his friends killed
in the First World War, the lines following in French argot; the two pages
on the beginning of the Russian Revolution, taken from the lively prose of
Lincoln Steffens, and by a few alterations changed from wood to something
growing;* the canto beginning with "And Kung walked into the dynastic
temple," taken from Confucius, and if I can judge from prose translations,
including Pound's own, a heightening and improvement on its source;† and
so many others: Canto I, the Odyssey, the Usura Cantos, much of the Pisan
Cantos, especially the opening lines on Mussolini's lynching, the long passage beginning, "Oh to be in England now that Winston's out," the famous,
"What thou lovest best."‡

When I last saw Ezra Pound in Rapallo, emaciated, neat in blacks and
whites, silver beard, he looked like the cover of one of his books, or like an
El Greco, some old mural, aristocratic and flaking.§ He held up his blotched,
thinned-away hands, and said, as if he were joking at them, "The worms

* Canto XVI.

† Canto XIII, which in fact begins, "Kung walked / by the dynastic temple."

‡ At the conclusion of the 1973 memorial at the New York Public Library, Lowell read Canto CXV.

§ Lowell visited Pound for the last time in Rapallo in March 1965 on his way back from Egypt and the
University of Cairo, where he had lectured on poetry. See also Lowell's letter of August 31, 1966, to James
Laughlin in *Letters*, 473.

are getting to me."* Later, I must have said something about Hamilton or Pennsylvania College, where he had studied.† He said, "Yes, I started with a swelled head and end with swelled feet." He was thinking of Oedipus.‡ I said, "You are one of the few living men who has walked through Purgatory." Watching me like a cat, and catching my affectation and affection, he answered, "Didn't Frost say you'd say anything once for the hell of it?"

(Composed 1972 and early 1973)

* In his sonnet "Ezra Pound," in Robert Lowell, *Collected Poems*, edited by Frank Bidart and David Gewanter (New York: Farrar, Straus and Giroux, 2003), 537, Lowell recalls this last meeting somewhat differently. This sentence is condensed to "Worms," followed by a new sentence by Pound, then his "swelled head" sentence repeated almost verbatim, and then another new one.

† Pound first studied at the University of Pennsylvania (1901–1903), then at Hamilton College in Clinton, New York (1903–1905), and then returned to Philadelphia for further graduate work.

‡ Prophesied to murder his father and marry his mother, Oedipus, when still a child, was left to die on a mountainside with his feet pinned together. Hence his name, Oedipus, which in Greek means "swollen foot."

On T. S. Eliot

CRITICS HAVE SAID about all they can on Eliot.* There will be little more to the point, I think, until new and unforeseeably different masterpieces have been written and the world has changed. I have nothing fresh to say, and yet I will name a few things that strike me as singular and marvelous.

He hit British rather than American writing, as an American masked as a Frenchman, Laforgue. Laforgue grew dimmer, but to the end it's hard to say whether Eliot is American, British, or French. To the end, something impertinent, chilling, disturbing—even in the magister, the living classic, the Arnold of Criticism, the Christian preacher. Under the authority, something unreliable; fuming and smoky hell fires under the dandyism.

All the poems have one hero, the Laforguean Prufrock. Not only one hero, but one journey from frivolity and hell to somewhere in Purgatory. One man walking. One figure drawn with heavy black lines, slightly narrow,

---

* The opening of "On T. S. Eliot" originates from a powerful paragraph that Lowell later greatly revised as he worked on the piece. The initial version of the opening paragraph reads as follows: "I wept when T. S. Eliot died, and yet I keep putting off writing about him. We are fed up with Eliot elucidation, summations and tributes. They are all 'armed visions' and the most expert of their kind. He now almost seems like the fatal first example of the writer of works to be written about. He didn't deserve this; he was alive. Now nothing fresh seems to come, and perhaps nothing will until the world goes on a bit and new, very different masterpieces have been written." Lowell revisited this root paragraph twelve years later, in 1977, to prompt himself to write another Eliot text for a collection of sketches on New England's literary history titled "New England and Further." Robert Giroux did not include the paragraph in the version of "New England and Further" he published in Lowell's posthumous *Collected Prose*.

slightly caricatured, but always in motion, never quite saying the same things, or using the same technical means. The pieces can't be shifted. There is a destination, whether it was the destination intended or not, whether there was improvement or not. Certainly no drying up, no dying, no Waste Land, except perhaps in the plays.

Eliot is seldom, if ever, as highly charged as the later Yeats. But his best poems are much longer. His best works are very long short poems, or very short long poems.

His influence is everywhere inescapable, and nowhere really usable. The air, an American dressed up as a Frenchman preaching to the English; that air of a slightly square *poète maudit* missionary suited no one else, though there are traces in Stevens and the Pound of "Mauberley." His mixture of meter and irregularity really suited no one. Better the grand quatrains of Hart Crane, or the free verse of Williams, or the Robert Bridges–like boundaries and ingenuity of Auden. His style of writing religious poetry was far too heavy a cross for the religious, and anathema to the faithless. Yet not a poem can be written now without thoughts of Eliot. They are thoughts of dread. In comparison with him, we are likely to be dull, wasteful, academic, or at best little.

In what remains, I want to take up two controversial questions, *The Waste Land* and Eliot's religion, and then end with a brief personal impression.

What concerns me here is not the meaning of *The Waste Land*, the legitimacy of its technical method, or even primarily its importance in English poetry. I want rather to puzzle at the unanswerable question of whether it is a picture of the age. Perhaps I should claim no more than that it is an inspired cri de cœur, and even allow with Randall Jarrell that it is a personal and idiosyncratic, though heartfelt, cry. Isn't it meaningless to ask if the picture is true, just as it would be meaningless to ask if Shakespeare thought life was really as hideous as he showed it to be in *Lear* and *Macbeth*? Such subjects once chosen require horror. No more to say. But more must be said. Shakespeare's tragedies are his deepest thrust. Like *The Waste Land* and perhaps almost all literary tragedy, they are about sterility, cruelty and sex gone haywire. Of course, *The Waste Land* seems in its emblematic, allegorical New England way to be asserting more than just *a* truth. It's a symbolic key. I could easily say that *The Waste Land* was written after the First World War and that the reality that has followed has surpassed any nightmare. Yet

I feel the perversity of trying to prove anything, particularly that life is any worse than it is. Eliot with all his shortcomings has stabbed very deeply and cruelly. The wound, along with many another, is now part of our history. It cannot be refuted like a debater's thesis. Each new writer can only remember and forget, and make his own worse or gentler and inevitably different try.

I want to use a comparison to get at Eliot's religion. Probably the greatest American writer in my lifetime has been William Faulkner. When Faulkner is set beside his equals, I am thinking of Mann and Pasternak, he often strikes us as provincial, incoherent and blind in some universal sense. Mann and Pasternak were at the center, they could use the great riches of history, their nations and the age. I don't suppose Faulkner is quite the equal of the very greatest writers. Yet now we know that his bypath, Mississippi, was no bypath. He struck obliquely and landed in the thick.

Eliot's Christianity also may seem off the track, a detour and a bypath. Christianity for ages has had a spindly, undistinguished record. Ever more so, increasingly weak and irrelevant in fact, thought and imagination. Eliot's faith seems almost willfully crooked, dry, narrow and hard in comparison with what I would like to describe as the toleration, hope and intuition of Matthew Arnold's tragic liberalism. That silver age is irrecoverably gone maybe. If Christianity seems like a bypath to most of us, Eliot's kind of Christianity seems almost worse, a bypath off a bypath. We remember his slippery wisecrack, "The letter giveth life, the spirit giveth death."

Eliot in his poems seems surprisingly detached from the letter and orthodoxy. His letter is the agnostic's accuracy of the written word. Christ and the Virgin are present, but only as rather icy Congregationalist anatomies. Death and rebirth are at the heart of things in a rather universalist and symbolic guise that perhaps ignores any creed. Eliot has hit on one of the very few things that are still alive in religion. I don't see how man will ever quite be able to get rid of purification, contemplation and rebirth. Our orthodox sciences—sociology, social reform and psychiatry—and our orthodox prophets, Freud and Marx, still leave this loophole; alas, they must.

As a man, Eliot was a hero and lovable. He did the usual good works of little and great attentions, standing up for his values, reading manuscripts, giving piercing and modest guidance, giving endless hours. He had a way of his own of knowing his limits. People have named the time he lived in after him and called him the leader. A strange leader, one who gave thousands of speechless hours to listening to brilliant monologuists. He took a crooked pleasure in his martyrdom, and he was perhaps too intolerant of egotistical exuberance, which is after all one of the glories of life. Yet how dangerous. In America almost all our gods coarsen into giants or shrivel into hollow men. Eliot did neither. His fierceness was restrained, his dullness was never more than the possum's feigned death.

I have never met anyone more brilliant, or anyone who tried so hard to use his brilliance modestly and honestly. One could go on for a long time recalling his gentle, unobtrusive acts of kindness. I would like rather to recall two harsh companionable moments of honesty.

Sometimes Eliot's list of wearying great men seemed all-inclusive. One, by no means the most trying, was Robert Frost. For long years, Frost enjoyed taking lecture-hall swipes at Eliot, the "great British poet from St. Louis," etc. Later Frost eased up and toward the end of both their lives rather set his heart on having Eliot to dinner in Cambridge, Mass. Eliot whittled the dinner down to tea or cocktails. After it was over I asked him how it went. I can see and hear him very well now: a sidelong smirk, then the slow, deep, weary, "oh, you know." Then Eliot's eyes glistened with delight and joy: "you have to watch yourself with the old man, he is very *wicked*."

Eliot never condescended to young people he liked, or made them feel like hayseeds or just numbers. When I was about twenty-five, I met him for the second time. Behind us, Harvard's Memorial Hall with its wasteful, irreplaceable Victorian architecture and scrolls of the Civil War dead. Before us, the rush-hour traffic. As we were stuck on the sidewalk, looking for an opening, Eliot out of the blue sky said, "Don't you loathe being compared with your relatives?" Pause, as I put the question to myself, groping for what I really felt, for what I should decently feel and what I should indecently feel. Eliot: "I do." Pause again, then the changed lifting voice of delight. "I was reading Poe's reviews the other day. He took up two of my family, and wiped the floor with them." Pause. "I was delighted."

(Composed 1965)

William Carlos Williams

D R. WILLIAMS AND HIS WORK are part of me, yet I come on them as a critical intruder. I fear I shall spoil what I have to say, just as I somehow got off on the wrong note about Williams with Ford Madox Ford twenty-five years ago. Ford was wearing a stained robin's-egg-blue pajama top, reading Theocritus in Greek, and guying me about my "butterfly existence," so removed from the labors of a professional writer. I was saying something awkward, green and intense in praise of Williams, and Ford, while agreeing, managed to make me feel that I was far too provincial, genteel and puritanical to understand what I was saying. And why not? Wasn't I, as Ford assumed, the grandson or something of James Russell Lowell and the cousin of Lawrence Lowell, a young man doomed to trifle with poetry and end up as President of Harvard or ambassador to England?

I have stepped over these pitfalls. I have conquered my hereditary disadvantages. Except for writing, nothing I've touched has shone. When I think about writing on Dr. Williams, I feel a chaos of thoughts and images, images cracking open to admit a thought, thoughts dragging their roots for the soil of an image. When I woke up this morning, something unusual for this summer was going on!—pinpricks of rain were falling in a reliable, comforting simmer. Our town was blanketed in the rain of rot and the rain of renewal. New life was muscling in, everything growing moved on its one-way trip to the ground. I could feel this, yet believe our universal misfortune was bearable and even welcome. An image held my mind during these moments and kept returning—an old-fashioned New England cottage freshly painted white. I saw a shaggy, triangular shade on the house, trees, a hedge, or their shadows, the blotch of decay. The house might have been the house I was now living in, but it wasn't; it came from the time when I was a child, still unable to read and living in the small town of Barnstable on Cape Cod.* Inside the house was a bird book with an old stiff and steely engraving of a sharp-shinned hawk. The hawk's legs had a reddish brown buffalo fuzz on them; behind was the blue sky, bare and abstracted from the world. In the present, pinpricks of rain were falling on everything I could see, and even on the white house in my mind, but the hawk's picture, being indoors I suppose, was more or less spared. Since I saw the picture of the hawk, the pinpricks of rain have gone on, half the people I once knew are dead, half the people I now know were then unborn, and I have learned to read.

An image of a white house with a blotch on it—this is perhaps the start of a Williams poem. If I held this image closely and honestly enough, the stabbing detail might come and with it the universal that belonged to this detail and nowhere else. Much wrapping would have to be cut away, and many elegiac cadences with their worn eloquence and loftiness. This is how I would like to write about Dr. Williams. I would collect impressions, stare them into rightness, and let my mind-work and judgments come as they might naturally.

When I was a freshman at Harvard, nothing hit me so hard as the Norton Lectures given by Robert Frost. Frost's revolutionary power, however, was not in his followers, or in the student literary magazine, the *Advocate*, whose editor had just written a piece on speech rhythms in the "Hired Man," a much less up-to-date thing to do then than now. Our only strong and avant-garde man was James Laughlin. He was much taller and older than we were. He knew Henry Miller, and exotic young American poetesses in Paris, spent summers at Rapallo with Ezra Pound, and was getting out the first number of his experimental annual, *New Directions*. He knew the great, and he himself wrote deliberately flat descriptive and anecdotal poems. We were sarcastic about them, but they made us feel secretly that we didn't know

---

* Lowell is referring to the summers he spent in the 1920s in Rock and Mattapoisett, Massachusetts, often making extended visits with the Bowles household in Barnstable. See "Forty-Four West Cedar Street and Barnstable" in "My Autobiography."

what was up in poetry. They used no punctuation or capitals, and their only rule was that each line should be eleven or fifteen typewriter spaces long. The author explained that this metric was "as rational as any other" and was based on the practice of W. C. Williams, a poet and pediatrician living in Rutherford, New Jersey. About this time, Laughlin published a review somewhere, perhaps even in the *Harvard Advocate*, of Williams' last small volume. In it, he pushed the metric of typewriter spaces, and quoted from a poem, "The Catholic Bells," to show Williams' "mature style at fifty!" This was a memorable phrase, and one that made maturity seem possible, but a long way off. I more or less memorized "The Catholic Bells," and spent months trying to console myself by detecting immaturities in whatever Williams had written before he was fifty.

THE CATHOLIC BELLS

Tho' I'm no Catholic
I listen hard when the bells
in the yellow-brick tower
of their new church

ring down the leaves
ring in the frost upon them
and the death of the flowers
ring out the grackle

toward the south, the sky
darkened by them, ring in
the new baby of Mr. and Mrs.
Krantz which cannot

for the fat of its cheeks
open well its eyes . . .

What I liked about "The Catholic Bells" were the irrelevant associations I hung on the words "frost" and "Catholic," and still more its misleading similarity to the "Ring out wild bells" section of *In Memoriam*. Other things upset and fascinated me and made me feel I was in a world I would never quite understand. Were the spelling "Tho," strange in a realistic writer, and the iambic rhythm of the first seven words part of some inevitable sound pattern? I had dipped into Edith Sitwell's criticism and was full of inevitable sound patterns. I was sure that somewhere hidden was a key that would make this poem as regular as the regular meters of Tennyson. There had to be something outside the poem I could hang onto because what was inside dizzied me!—the shocking scramble of the august and the crass in making the Catholic church "new" and "yellow-brick," the cherubic ugliness of the baby, belonging rather horribly to "Mr. and Mrs. / Krantz," and seen by the experienced, mature pediatrician as unable to see "for the fat of its cheeks"—this last a cunning shift into anapests. I was surprised that Williams used commas, and that my three or four methods of adjusting his lines to uniform typewriter spaces failed. I supposed he had gone on to some bolder and still more mature system.

To explain the full punishment I felt on first reading Williams, I should say a little about what I was studying at the time. A year or so before, I had read some introductory books on the enjoyment of poetry, and was knocked over by the examples in the free verse sections. When I arrived at college, independent, fearful of advice and with all the world before me, I began to rummage through the Cambridge bookshops. I found books that must have been looking for a buyer since the student days of Trumbull Stickney: soiled metrical treatises written by obscure English professors in the eighteen-nineties. They were full of glorious things: rising rhythm, falling rhythm, feet with Greek names, stanzas from Longfellow's *Psalm of Life*, John Drinkwater and Swinburne. Nothing seemed simpler than meter. I began experiments with an exotic foot, short, long, two shorts, then fell back on iambics. My material now took twice as many words, and I rolled out Spenserian stanzas on Job and Jonah surrounded by recently seen Nantucket scenery. Everything I did was grand, ungrammatical and had a timeless, hackneyed quality. All this was ended by reading Williams. It was as though some homemade ship, part Spanish galleon, part paddle wheels, kitchen pots and elastic bands and worked by hand, had anchored to a filling station.

In the "Catholic Bells," the joining of religion and non-religion, of piety and a hard, nervous secular knowingness are typical of Williams. Further along in this poem, there is a piece of mere description that has always stuck in my mind.

(the

grapes still hanging to
the vines along the nearby
Concordia Halle like broken
teeth in the head of an

old man)

Take out the *Concordia Halle* and the grape vines crackle in the wind with a sour, impoverished dryness; take out the vines and the *Concordia Halle* has lost its world.* Williams has pages and pages of description that are as good as this. It is his equivalent of, say, the Miltonic sentence, the dazzling staple and excellence which he can always produce. Williams has said that he uses the forms he does for quick changes of tone, atmosphere and speed. This makes him dangerous and difficult to imitate, because most poets have little change of tone, atmosphere and speed in them.

I have emphasized Williams' simplicity and nakedness and have no doubt been misleading. His idiom comes from many sources, from speech and reading, both of various kinds; the blend, which is his own invention, is generous and even exotic. Few poets can come near to his wide clarity and dashing rightness with words, his dignity and almost Alexandrian modulations of voice. His short lines often speed up and simplify hugely drawn out and ornate sentence structures. I once typed out his direct but densely observed poem, "The Semblables," in a single prose paragraph. Not a word or its placing had been changed, but the poem had changed into a piece of smothering, magnificent rhetoric, much more like Faulkner than the original Williams.

The difficulties I found in Williams twenty-five years ago are still difficulties for me. Williams enters me, but I cannot enter him. Of course, one

---

* The old German Meeting Hall (today demolished) in East Rutherford. See William Carlos Williams, *Collected Poems of William Carlos Williams*, vol. 1: *1909–1939*, edited by A. Walton Litz and Christopher MacGowan (New York: New Directions, 1991), 541.

cannot catch any good writer's voice or breathe his air. But there's something more. It's as if no poet except Williams had really seen America or heard its language. Or rather, he sees and hears what we all see and hear and what is most obvious, but no one else has found this a help or an inspiration. This may come naturally to Dr. Williams from his character, surroundings and occupation. I can see him rushing from his practice to his typewriter, happy that so much of the world has rubbed off on him, maddened by its hurry. Perhaps he had no choice. Anyway, what others have spent lifetimes building up personal styles to gather has been snatched up on the run by Dr. Williams.* When I say that I cannot enter him, I am almost saying that I cannot enter America. This troubles me. I am not satisfied to let it be. Like others I have picked up things here and there from Williams, but this only makes me marvel all the more at his unique and searing journey. It is a Dantesque journey, for he loves America excessively, as if it were *the* truth and *the* subject; his exasperation is also excessive, as if there were no other hell. His flowers rustle by the superhighways and pick up all our voices.

A seemingly unending war has been going on for as long as I can remember between Williams and his disciples and the principals and disciples of another school of modern poetry. The "beats" are on one side, the university poets are on the other. Lately the gunfire has been hot. With such unlikely Williams recruits as Karl Shapiro blasting away, it has become unpleasant to stand in the middle in a position of impartiality.

The war is an old one for me. In the late Thirties, I was at Kenyon College to study under John Crowe Ransom. The times hummed with catastrophe and ideological violence, both political and aesthetical. The English departments were clogged with worthy, but outworn and backward-looking scholars, whose tastes in the moderns were most often superficial, random and vulgar. Students who wanted to write got little practical help from their professors. They studied the classics as monsters that were slowly losing their fur and feathers and leaking a little sawdust. What one did one's self was all chance and shallowness, and no profession seemed wispier and less

---

* We have omitted as probable mistakes the words "in" after "lifetimes" and "what" after "gather," and a question mark at the end.

needed than that of the poet. My own group, that of Tate and Ransom, was all for the high discipline, for putting on the full armor of the past, for making poetry something that would take a man's full weight and that would bear his complete intelligence, passion and subtlety. Almost anything, the Greek and Roman classics, Elizabethan dramatic poetry, 17th-century metaphysical verse, old and modern critics, aestheticians and philosophers, could be suppled up and again made necessary. The struggle perhaps centered on making the old metrical forms usable again to express the depths of one's experience.

For us, Williams was of course part of the revolution that had renewed poetry, but he was a byline. Opinions varied on his work. It was something fresh, secondary and minor, or it was the best that free verse could do. He was the one writer with the substance, daring and staying power to make the short free verse poem something considerable. One was shaken when the radical conservative critic, Yvor Winters, spoke of Williams' "By the road to the contagious hospital" as a finer, more lasting piece of craftsmanship than "Gerontion."

Well, nothing will do for everyone. It's hard for me to see how I and the younger poets I was close to could at that time have learned much from Williams. It was all we could do to keep alive and follow our own heavy program. That time is gone, and now young poets are perhaps more conscious of the burden and the hardening of this old formalism. Too many poems have been written to rule. They show off their authors' efforts and mind, but little more. Often the culture seems to have passed them by. And once more, Dr. Williams is a model and a liberator. What will come, I don't know. Williams, unlike, say, Marianne Moore, seems to be one of those poets who can be imitated anonymously. His style is almost a common style and even what he claims for it—*the American style*. Somehow, written without his speed and genius, the results are usually dull, a poem at best well-made but without breath.

Williams is part of the great breath of our literature. *Paterson* is our *Leaves of Grass*. The times have changed. A drastic experimental art is now expected and demanded. The scene is dense with the dirt and power of industrial society. Williams looks on it with exasperation, terror and a kind of love. His short poems are singularly perfect thrusts, maybe the best that will ever be written of their kind, because neither the man nor the pressure will be found again. When I think of his last longish autobiographical poems, I remember his last reading I heard. It was at Wellesley. I think about three thousand students attended. It couldn't have been more crowded in the wide-galleried hall and I had to sit in the aisle. The poet appeared, one whole side partly paralyzed, his voice just audible, and here and there a word misread. No one stirred. In the silence he read his great poem "Of Asphodel, That Greeny Flower," a triumph of simple confession—somehow he delivered to us what was impossible, something that was both poetry and beyond poetry.*

I think of going with Dr. Williams and his son to visit his mother, very old, almost a hundred, and unknowing, her black eyes boring through. And Williams saying to her, "Which would you rather see, us, or three beautiful blonds?" As we left, he said, "The old bitch will live on but I may die tomorrow!" You could not feel shocked. Few men had felt and respected anyone more than Williams had his old mother. And in seeing him out strolling on a Sunday after a heart attack: the town seemed to know him and love him and take him in its stride, as we will do with his great pouring of books, his part in the air we breathe and will breathe.

(1962)

---

* Williams's poem is titled simply "Asphodel, That Greeny Flower."

Introduction for
Randall Jarrell*

THIS IS ROBERT LOWELL introducing Randall Jarrell. My first introduction to Jarrell was in 1937 on the campus of Vanderbilt University in Tennessee. I showed him two or three scratchy little poems written in what I thought was a severe and classical style. I can still hear Jarrell's spontaneous sniff of disgust. "You call *that* form!" he said. This was cruel, but it was honest and accurate. I was just honest enough at the time to recognize Jarrell's honesty and authority. I knew I had heard a voice that I would have to trust on the long, unpredictable road of apprenticeship.

Jarrell is by far the finest critic of poetry in my generation. After my reminiscence, it will perhaps seem strange if I say that what inspires his criticism is the devastating enthusiasm of his intuitions. He not only always enlightens, he is also able to turn on his tracks and reverse and deepen an

* This is likely a draft of a speech Lowell was scheduled to give introducing Jarrell's reading at the 92nd Street Young Men's and Young Women's Hebrew Association Poetry Center in New York City—today commonly known as the 92nd Street Y—on April 28, 1963. Lowell never actually introduced his friend, perhaps as a result of being booed off the stage there a few months earlier, for reading from *Imitations*, reputedly his mere "translations" of the work of others instead of his own new poems. Jarrell to Robert Lowell, September 1962, in *Randall Jarrell's Letters: An Autobiographical and Literary Selection*, edited by Mary Jarrell (Boston: Houghton Mifflin, 1985), 457. Lowell was replaced by the critic Eric Bentley but went to the event anyway and found Bentley's introduction nothing short of foolish. For his critical account of the event, see Lowell to Elizabeth Bishop, May 8, 1963, in *Words in Air: The Complete Correspondence Between Elizabeth Bishop and Robert Lowell*, edited by Thomas Travisano with Saskia Hamilton (New York: Farrar, Straus and Giroux, 2008), 454.

earlier impression. His large essays on Frost, Stevens and Graves are all reversals and continuations of fiery first thoughts. A stream of witty insights makes his reverence overwhelming.

Tonight, however, I want to talk about the poet and not the critic. Jarrell's most thrusting, delicate and loaded intuitions are in his poetry. It has many subjects, but behind most of them is some child, some helpless person, some simpleton, some spinster, wife or widow, or some sophisticated person caught in a moment of pious openness. They dream through entranced scenes of images, memories and petty plots, almost the peasant kingdoms of the Brothers Grimm. Always at one's elbow, however, is the real modern world with its brilliant and terrible technology and methods. The great thinkers, Goethe, Marx, Freud and many others are watching—gracious in their European wisdom and razor-sharp, just as the poet has understood them.

One particular group of Jarrell's writings has always struck me in its wholeness. This is his war poems, a group that forms about half of his largest collection.* As I reread them yesterday, that whole age from the mid-thirties to the mid-forties, the preparation for war years and finally the war, came back. I saw not only the period's paraphernalia and decor, but its mind, so tense yet angular and oblique in its commitment. It's mysterious that one should look back on that grim season, perhaps our darkest, with a sort of summer's nostalgia. It was no summer, yet in a way it was a kind of passing autumn of the mind. There pushed to the limits of things, the spirit was forced to lash out with a more desperate and pathetic sincerity than is now possible. Greater gropings and a greater confusion were then controllable. Men yawned toward oblivion. Their plot was huge and obvious and could stand any amount of searching. Jarrell's war poems are more telling than any others for two reasons. Long before the war, he had become expert in all the machines and ideologies that would be engaged. To this fascination and knowledge, he brought his almost mythical feeling for the sorrows of the helpless. The soldiers and pilots he wrote about were his old companions and ex-aviation students. They were man suffering, and for Jarrell man suffering was truth. The picture wasn't touched up, all its flaws and twists were seen, and yet in the end the sympathy was unlimited.

* Randall Jarrell, *Selected Poems* (New York: Alfred A. Knopf, 1955).

Since then Jarrell has written many magical and serene peace poems, some of them refinements and extensions of his earlier portraits. He has made the best translations from Rilke and Goethe that I have read, translations that for me have the weight and clear edge of their originals. Tonight he is going to read long new poems in terza rima, the very hard meter of Dante's *Commedia*.* I feel Randall Jarrell has surpassed himself.

(Composed in 1962–1963)

* Probably the three-part poem "The Lost World."

Randall Jarrell, 1914–1965

W
HEN I FIRST met Randall, he was twenty-three or four, and
upsettingly brilliant, precocious, knowing, naïve, and vexing.
He seemed to make no distinction between what he would
say in our hearing and what he would say behind our backs. If anything,
absence made him more discreet. Woe to the acquaintance who liked the
wrong writer, the wrong poem by the right writer, or the wrong lines in the
right poem! And how those who loved him enjoyed admiring, complaining,
and gossiping about the last outrageous thing he had done or, more often,
said. It brought us together—whispering about Randall. In 1937, we both
roomed at the house of John Crowe Ransom in Gambier, Ohio. Ransom
and Jarrell had each separately spent the preceding summer studying Shakespeare's *Sonnets*, and had emerged with unorthodox and widely differing
theories. Roughly, Ransom thought that Shakespeare was continually going off the rails into illogical incoherence.* Jarrell believed that no one, not
even William Empson, had done justice to the rich, significant ambiguity of
Shakespeare's intelligence and images. I can see and hear Ransom and Jarrell
now, seated on one sofa, as though on one love seat, the sacred texts open on
their laps, one fifty, the other just out of college, and each expounding to the
other's deaf ears his own inspired and irreconcilable interpretation.

---

* At the time Ransom was working on his essay "Shakespeare at Sonnets," making precisely that claim. It
was first published in *Southern Review* 3 (1937–1938): 531–53, later reprinted in John Crowe Ransom, *The
World's Body* (New York: Charles Scribner's Sons, 1938), 270–303.

Gordon Chalmers, the President of Kenyon College and a disciple of the somber anti-Romantic Humanists, once went skiing with Randall, and was shocked to hear him exclaiming, "I feel just like an angel." Randall *did* somehow give off an angelic impression, despite his love for tennis, singular mufflers knitted by a girlfriend, and disturbing improvements of his own on the latest dance steps. His mind, unearthly in its quickness, was a little boyish, disembodied, and brittle. His body was a little ghostly in its immunity to soil, entanglements, and rebellion. As one sat with him in oblivious absorption at the campus bar, sucking a fifteen-cent chocolate milk shake and talking eternal things, one felt, beside him, too corrupt and companionable. He had the harsh luminosity of Shelley—like Shelley, every inch a poet, and like Shelley, imperiled perhaps by an arid, abstracting precocity. Not really! Somewhere inside him, a breezy, untouchable spirit had even then made its youthful and sightless promise to accept—to accept and never to accept the bulk, confusion, and defeat of mortal flesh . . . all that blithe and blood-torn dolor!

Randall Jarrell had his own peculiar and important excellence as a poet, and outdistanced all others in the things he could do well. His gifts, both by nature and by a lifetime of hard dedication and growth, were wit, pathos, and brilliance of intelligence. These qualities, dazzling in themselves, were often so well employed that he became, I think, the most heartbreaking English poet of his generation.

Most good poets are also good critics on occasion, but Jarrell was much more than this. He was a critic of genius, a poet-critic of genius at a time when, as he wrote, most criticism was "astonishingly graceless, joyless, humorless, long-winded, niggling, blinkered, methodical, self-important, cliché-ridden, prestige-obsessed, and almost autonomous."

He had a deadly hand for killing what he despised. He described a murky verbal poet as "writing poems that might have been written *by* a typewriter *on* a typewriter."* The flashing reviews he wrote in his twenties are full of such witticisms and barbs, and hundreds more were tossed off in casual conversa-

---

* Jarrell's comment, on a volume by Oscar Williams, was slightly different. He said that the book "gave the impression of having been written on a typewriter by a typewriter." See Randall Jarrell, *Kipling, Auden & Co.: Essays and Reviews, 1935–1964* (Manchester, UK: Carcanet Press, 1981), 137.

tion, and never preserved, or even repeated. Speaking of a famous scholar, he said, "What can be more tedious than a man whose every sentence is a balanced epigram without wit, profundity, or taste?" He himself, though often fierce, was incapable of vulgarity, self-seeking, or meanness. He could be very tender and gracious, but often he seemed tone-deaf to the amenities and dishonesties that make human relations tolerable. Both his likes and dislikes were a terror to everyone, that is to everyone who either saw himself as important or wished to see himself as important. Although he was almost without vices, heads of colleges and English departments found his frankness more unsettling and unpredictable than the drunken explosions of some divine *enfant terrible*, such as Dylan Thomas. Usually his wit was austerely pure, but sometimes he could jolt the more cynical. Once we were looking at a furnished apartment that one of our friends had just rented. It was overbearingly eccentric. Life-size clay lamps like flowerpots remodeled into Matisse nudes by a spastic child. Paintings made from a palette of mud by a blind painter. About the paintings Randall said, "Ectoplasm sprinkled with zinc." About the apartment, "All that's missing are Mrs. X's illegitimate children in bottles of formaldehyde." His first reviews were described as "symbolic murders," but even then his most destructive judgments had a patient, intuitive, unworldly certainty.

Yet eulogy was the glory of Randall's criticism. Eulogies that not only impressed readers with his own enthusiasms, but which also, time and again, changed and improved opinions and values. He left many reputations permanently altered and exalted. I think particularly of his famous Frost and Whitman essays, and one on the last poems of Wallace Stevens, which was a dramatic reversal of his own earlier evaluation. His mind kept moving and groping more deeply. His prejudices were never the established and fashionable prejudices of the world around him. One could never say of one of his new admirations, "Oh, I knew *you* would like that." His progress was not the usual youthful critic's progress from callow severity to lax benevolence. With wrinkled brow and cool fresh eye, he was forever musing, discovering, and chipping away at his own misconceptions. Getting out on a limb was a daily occurrence for him, and when he found words for what he had intuited, his judgments were bold and unlikely. Randall was so often right, that sometimes we said he was always right. He could enjoy discarded writers whom it was a scandal to like, praise young, unknown writers as if he were praising and describing Shakespeare's tragedies, and read Shakespeare's tragedies with the uncertainty and wonder of their first discoverers.

He once said, "If I were a rich man, I would pay money for the privilege of being able to teach." Probably there was no better teacher of literature in the country, and yet he was curiously unworldly about it, and welcomed teaching for almost twenty years in the shade or heat of his little-known Southern college for girls in Greensboro, North Carolina. There his own community gave him a compact, tangible, personal reverence that was incomparably more substantial and poignant than the empty, numerical long-distance blaze of national publicity. He grieved over the coarseness, unkindness, and corruption of our society, and said that "the poet has a peculiar relation to this public. It is unaware of his existence." He said bitterly and lightheartedly that "the gods who had taken away the poet's audience had given him students." Yet he gloried in being a teacher, never apologized for it, and related it to his most serious criticism. Writing of three long poems by Robert Frost, poems too long to include in his essay, he breaks off and says, "I have used rather an odd tone about [these poems] because I feel so much frustration at not being able to quote and go over them, as I have so often done with friends and classes." Few critics could so gracefully descend from the grand manner or be so offhand about their dignity. His essays are never encrusted with the hardness of a professor. They have the raciness and artistic gaiety of his own hypnotic voice.

Randall was the only man I have ever met who could make other writers feel that their work was more important to him than his own. I don't mean that he was in the habit of saying to people he admired, "This is much better than anything I could do." Such confessions, though charming, cost little effort. What he did was to make others feel that their realizing themselves was as close to him as his own self-realization, and that he cared as much about making the nature and goodness of someone else's work understood as he cared about making his own understood. I have never known anyone who so connected what his friends wrote with their lives, or their lives with what they wrote. This could be trying: whenever we turned out something Randall felt was unworthy or a falling off, there was a coolness in all one's relations with him. You felt that even your choice in neckties wounded him. Yet he always veered and returned, for he knew as well as anyone that the spark from heaven is beyond man's call and control. Good will he demanded, but in the end was lenient to honest sterility and failure.

Jarrell was the most readable and generous of critics of contemporary poetry. His novel, *Pictures from an Institution*, whatever its fictional oddities, is a unique and serious joke book. How often I've met people who keep it by their beds or somewhere handy, and read random pages aloud to lighten their hearts. His book *A Sad Heart at the Supermarket* had a condescending press. When one listened to these social essays, they were like *dies irae* sermons, strange ones that cauterized the soul, and yet made us weep with laughter. A banal world found them banal. But what Jarrell's inner life really was in all its wonder, variety, and subtlety is best told in his poetry. To the end, he was writing with deepening force, clarity, and frankness. For some twenty-five years he wrote excellent poems. Here I only want to emphasize two of his peaks: what he wrote about the war, and what he completed in the last years of his life.

In the first months of the war, Jarrell became a pilot. He was rather old for a beginner, and soon "washed out," and spent the remaining war years as an aviation instructor. Even earlier, he had an expert's knowledge. I remember sitting with him in 1938 on the hill of Kenyon College and listening to him analyze in cool technical detail the various rather minute ways in which the latest British planes were superior to their German equivalents. He then jokingly sketched out how a bombing raid might be made against the college. Nine-tenths of his war poems are air force poems, and are about planes and their personnel, the flyers, crews, and mechanics who attended them. No other imaginative writer had his precise knowledge of aviation, or knew so well how to draw inspiration from this knowledge.

> In the turret's great glass dome, the apparition, death,
> Framed in the glass of the gunsight, a fighter's blinking wing,
> Flares softly, a vacant fire. If the flak's inked blurs—
> Distributed, statistical—the bombs' lost patterning
> Are death, they are death under glass, a chance
> For someone yesterday, someone tomorrow; and the fire

That streams from the fighter which is there, not there,
Does not warm you, has not burned them, though they die.*

More important still, the soldiers he wrote about were men much like his own pilot-students. He knew them well, and not only that, peculiarly sympathized with them. For Jarrell, the war careers of these young men had the freshness, wonder, and magical brevity of childhood. In his poetry, they are murderers, and yet innocents. They destroyed cities and men that had only the nominal reality of names studied in elementary geography classes.

In bombers named for girls, we burned
The cities we had learned about in school—
Till our lives wore out†

Or

In this year of our warfare, indispensable
In general, and in particular dispensable

Finally, the pilot goes home for good, forever mutilated and wounded, "the slow flesh failing, the terrible flesh / Sloughed off at last . . . / Stumbling to the toilet on one clever leg / Of leather, wire, and willow." There, knowledge has at last come to him:

And it is different, different—you have understood
Your world at last: you have tasted your own blood.‡

Jarrell's portraits of his pilots have been downgraded sometimes as unheroic, naïve, and even sentimental. Well, he was writing beyond the war, and turning the full visionary powers of his mind on the war to probe into and expose the horror, pathos, and charm he found in life. Always behind the

---

* Excerpted from "Siegfried," in Randall Jarrell, *The Complete Poems* (New York: Farrar, Straus and Giroux, 1969), 149.

† From "Losses," in *Complete Poems*, 145.

‡ From "Siegfried," in *Complete Poems*, 149.

sharpened edge of his lines, there is the merciful vision, *his* vision, partial like all others, but an illumination of life, too sad and radiant for us to stay with long—or forget.

In his last and best book, *The Lost World*, he used subjects and methods he had been developing and improving for almost twenty years. Most of the poems are dramatic monologues. Their speakers, though mostly women, are intentionally, and unlike Browning's, very close to the author. Their themes, repeated with endless variations, are solitude, the solitude of the unmarried, the solitude of the married, the love, strife, dependency, and indifference of man and woman—how mortals age, and brood over their lost and raw childhood, only recapturable in memory and imagination. Above all, childhood! This subject, for many a careless and tarnished cliché, was for him what it was for his two favorite poets, Rilke and Wordsworth, a governing and transcendent vision. For shallower creatures, recollections of childhood and youth are drenched in a mist of plaintive pathos, or even bathos, but for Jarrell this was the divine glimpse, lifelong to be lived with, painfully and tenderly relived, transformed, matured—man with and against woman, child with and against adult.

One of his aging women says:

When I was young and miserable and pretty
And poor, I'd wish
What all girls wish: to have a husband

But later, thinking of the withering present, she says:

How young I seem; I *am* exceptional;
I think of all I have.
But really no one is exceptional,
No one has anything, I'm anybody,
I stand beside my grave
Confused with my life, that is commonplace and solitary.*

* From "Next Day," in *Complete Poems*, 279–80.

In so reflecting, she is a particular woman—one sad, particular woman reaching into Jarrell's universal Everyman, poor or triumphant. Speaking in his own person and of his own childhood, he says,

> . . . As I run by the chicken coops
> With lettuce for my rabbit, real remorse
> Hurts me, here, now: the little girl is crying
> Because I didn't write. Because—
>   of course,
> I *was* a child, I missed them so. But justifying
> Hurts too . . . *

Then in a poem called "Woman," the speaker, a man, addresses the woman next to him in bed:

> Let me sleep beside you, each night, like a spoon;
> When, starting from my dreams, I groan to you,
> May your I love you send me back to sleep.
> At morning bring me, grayer for its mirroring,
> The heavens' sun perfected in your eyes.†

It all comes back to me now—the just under thirty years of our friendship, mostly meetings in transit, mostly in Greensboro, North Carolina, the South he loved and stayed with, though no agrarian, but a radical liberal. Poor modern-minded exile from the forests of Grimm, I see him unbearded, slightly South American–looking, then later bearded, with a beard we at first wished to reach out our hands to and pluck off, but which later became him, like Walter Bagehot's, or some Symbolist's in France's *fin-de-siècle* Third Republic. Then unbearded again. I see the bright, petty, pretty sacred objects he accumulated for his joy and solace: Vermeer's red-hatted girl, the Piero and Donatello reproductions, the photographs of his bruised, merciful heroes: Chekhov, Rilke, Marcel Proust. I see the white sporting Mercedes-Benz, the ever better cut and more deliberately jaunty clothes, the

---

* From "The Lost World: III. A Street off Sunset," in *Complete Poems*, 291.

† From "Woman," in *Complete Poems* 329.

television with its long afternoons of professional football, those matches he thought miraculously more graceful than college football . . . Randall had an uncanny clairvoyance for helping friends in subtle precarious moments—almost always as only he could help, with something written: critical sentences in a letter, or an unanticipated published book review. Twice or thrice, I think, he must have thrown me a lifeline. In his own life, he had much public acclaim and more private. The public, at least, fell cruelly short of what he deserved. Now that he is gone, I see clearly that the spark from heaven really struck and irradiated the lines and being of my dear old friend—his noble, difficult, and beautiful soul.

(1965)

For Robert Penn Warren*

AGOOD TEACHER'S student is always a student. I am stalled by my first memories of Red Warren, and his casual, three-months-delayed return to the University of Louisiana† in 1940, when I was putting off my master's thesis.‡ The bright scholar, the young master— nothing was daunting about Warren, except the hard, discordant duties he undertook, a novel on Huey Long,§ a course given on the pre-Renaissance humanists, Petrarch, Erasmus, More, Wyatt, all presented with huge erudition. His interest in character couldn't be confined to the close textual analysis of the New Critics. One afternoon, he spoke for three hours in praise of Machiavelli, citing fifty authors in Italian and English, and then picked his way through the contradictions to a judgment of his own. He

---

* This essay gave impetus to Lowell's poem "Louisiana State University in 1940," subtitled "For Robert Penn Warren," which was published in Robert Lowell, *Day by Day* (New York: Farrar, Straus and Giroux, 1977), reprinted in *Collected Poems*, edited by Frank Bidart and David Gewanter (New York: Farrar, Straus and Giroux, 2003), 735. On September 4, 1976, Lowell wrote to Jean Stafford: "I got a letter last month from Vanderbilt to write for Red's 70th festschrift. After struggling with a laborious prose compliment, I dropped it for a poem, more of the tone, the humidity, less critique"; in Robert Lowell, *The Letters of Robert Lowell*, edited by Saskia Hamilton (New York: Farrar, Straus and Giroux, 2005), 657.

† Lowell means Louisiana State University in Baton Rouge, where he entered the graduate program in the summer of 1940. He had graduated from Kenyon in June and received, with the help of Ransom's contacts, a junior fellowship for a year at LSU.

‡ Lowell was to take a master's degree under Warren's tutelage in the spring of 1941 (note Lowell's error in dating). But then, unexpectedly, Warren took an unpaid leave and decamped to the University of Iowa for the second term, from January until May 1941. See Joseph Blotner, *Robert Penn Warren: A Biography* (New York: Random House, 1997), 187.

§ *All the King's Men*, published in 1946.

examined at length the discoveries of Petrarch, the first introspective nature and mountain poet, yet disliked his even music. He disliked the tepid polish and tolerance of Erasmus. The course was climaxed and crowned by two three-hour lectures on Wyatt. Now, as we had expected, Warren was at last let loose, and spoke with poetic eagerness, yet not as an ignorant enthusiast or amateur. He quoted from everything written on or by Wyatt, even his translations of the psalms, to prove the artistry of his harsh, irregular line, rhythm and metaphor, a dramatic embodiment that went beyond Petrarch's sweet music. These lectures were talks, delivered from notes, never published, and perhaps never given to another class.

Warren's writer's workshop was of another species, and apparently slackly taught. He read aloud stories by his students and classics from his own anthology. His voice was confused by his Todd County Kentucky accent, frequently half-audible, and sometimes interrupted by a dry, desperate smoker's cough. The seminar room was green and waterlogged with Louisiana. One catnapped through the hour, then awoke to the questions, to an interrogation. No one had to answer, but now the room changed to the heat of a hunt. Poems, though accepted for credit, were never discussed. Perhaps because poetry, except for Browning's monologues, conceals no meaning. In time, it dawned on me that each short story had an intention, a key even, though this was dangerous, allegorical simplification.

That was one revelation, the other was when I brought Warren five poems to be considered for the *Southern Review*, perhaps *the* little magazine to reach. Certainly it was grander and more impersonally universal than Ransom's unpredictable *Kenyon Review*, a generous accepter of student work, though usually in small quantities and just once. Warren liked one poem, and surprisingly returned all five, saying, "Your best is too good to be printed alone. We will wait for a Lowell group." I should have felt encouraged, but my poems were not easily disposable. They now lay about, swollen to immobility by the Southern heat—longish, aggressively labored, the largest written in Miltonic blank verse imitating the rhetoric of Burke's denunciation of Hastings . . . each line fifty times improved. I stopped writing for two years, forever I thought then, stopped mercifully by life's intruding jolt.

I remember plain things he said at the time. They were somehow accepting and optimistic because of their lack of side, almost a rule with him, except in a rare, often shocking conversational narrative. On America: "You can't beat a country where every boy of eighteen can repair a car."* On exercise: "It's hell to do it, and hell not to." He exercised violently and with more pleasure than he thought courteous to press on sedentary friends. On a Vanderbilt professor forbidden to close his office door while meeting girl students: "The awful thing is the old bastard never succeeded." On Dreiser's *American Tragedy*: "It's heresy, but I like it better than James." On Marvel's "Coy Mistress": "I'd give up all Tennyson and Wordsworth to have written it." He liked to say some author was better than others acclaimed by intelligent fashion. Who were these others? [...]

(Composed circa August 1976)

* In the poem "Louisiana State University in 1940," the boy is "twelve," the vehicle he repairs is "a motorcycle," and the "country" seems to be the Soviet Union.

For John Berryman

I SIT LOOKING OUT a window at 3:30 this February afternoon. I see a pasture, green out of season and sunlit; in an hour more or less, it will be black. John Berryman walks brightly out of my memory. We met at Princeton through Caroline Gordon, in 1944, the wane of the war. The moment was troubled; my wife, Jean Stafford, and I were introduced to the Berrymans for youth and diversion. I remember expected, probably false, images, the hospital-white tablecloth, the clear martinis, the green antiquing of an Ivy League college faculty club. What college? Not Princeton, but the less spruce Cambridge, England, John carried with him in his speech rhythms and dress. He had a casual intensity, the almost intimate mumble of a don. For life, he was to be a student, scholar, and teacher. I think he was almost *the* student-friend I've had, the one who was the student in essence. An indignant spirit was born in him; his life was a cruel fight to set it free. Is the word for him courage or generosity or loyalty? He had these. And he was always a performer, a prima donna; at first to those he scorned, later to everyone, except perhaps students, his family, and Saul Bellow.

From the first, John was humorous, learned, thrustingly vehement in liking . . . more adolescent than boyish. He and I preferred critics who were writers to critics who were not writers. We hated literary discussions animated by jealousy and pushed by caution. John's own criticism, mostly spoken, had a poetry. Hyperenthusiasms made him a hot friend, and could also make him wearing to friends—one of his dearest, Delmore Schwartz, used to say no one had John's loyalty, but you liked him to live in another city. John had fire then, but not the fire of Byron or Yevtushenko. He clung so keenly to Hopkins, Yeats, and Auden that their shadows paled him.

Later, the Berrymans (the first Berrymans, the first Lowells) stayed with us in Damariscotta Mills, Maine.* Too many guests had accepted. We were inept and uncouth at getting the most out of the country; we didn't own or drive a car. This gloomed and needled the guests. John was ease and light. We gossiped on the rocks of the millpond, baked things in shells on the sand, and drank, as was the appetite of our age, much less than now. John could quote with vibrance to all lengths, even prose, even late Shakespeare, to show me what could be done with disrupted and mended syntax. This was the start of his real style. At first he wrote with great brio bristles of clauses, all breaks and with little to break off from. Someone said this style was like Emily Dickinson's mad dash punctuation without the words. I copied, and arrived at a manner that made even the verses I wrote for my cousins' *bouts rimés* (with "floor," "door," "whore," and "more" for the fixed rhymes) leaden and unintelligible. Nets so grandly knotted could only catch logs— our first harsh, inarticulate cry of truth.

My pilgrimage to Princeton with Randall Jarrell to have dinner with the Berrymans was not happy. Compared with other poets John was a prodigy; compared with Randall, a slow starter. Perpetrators of such mis-encounters usually confess their bewilderment that two talents with so much in common failed to jell. So much in common—both were slightly heretical disciples of Bernard Haggin, the music and record critic. But John jarred the evening by playing his own favorite recordings on an immense machine constructed and formerly used by Haggin. This didn't animate things; they tried ballet. One liked Covent Garden, the other Danilova, Markova, and the latest New York Balanchine. Berryman unfolded leather photograph books of enlarged British ballerinas he had almost dated. Jarrell made cool,

* Lowell's marriage to Jean Stafford lasted from 1940 to 1948; Berryman's to Eileen Simpson from 1942 to 1953. The summer stay in Damariscotta Mills occurred in late July and early August 1946.

odd evaluations drawn from his forty, recent, consecutive nights of New York ballet. He hinted that the English dancers he had never seen were on a level with the Danes. I suffered more than the fighters, and lost authority by trying not to take sides.

Both poet-critics had just written definitive essay-reviews of my first book, *Lord Weary's Castle*. To a myopic eye, they seemed to harmonize. So much the worse. Truth is in minute particulars; here, in the minutiae, nothing meshed. Earlier in the night, Berryman made the tactical mistake of complimenting Jarrell on his essay. This was accepted with a hurt, glib croak, "Oh thanks." The flattery was not returned, not a muscle smiled. I realized that if the essays were to be written again . . . On the horrible New Jersey midnight local to Pennsylvania Station, Randall analyzed John's high, intense voice with surprise and coldness. "Why hasn't anyone told him?" Randall had the same high, keyed-up voice he criticized. Soon he developed chills and fevers, ever more violent, and I took my suit coat and covered him. He might have been a child. John, the host, the insulted one, recovered sooner. His admiration for Randall remained unsoured, but the dinner was never repeated.

Our trip a year later to Ezra Pound at St. Elizabeth's Hospital near Washington was softer, so soft I remember nothing except a surely misplaced image of John sitting on the floor hugging his knees, and asking with shining cheeks for Pound to sing an aria from his opera *Villon*. He saw nothing nutty about Pound, or maybe it was the opposite. Anyway his instincts were true—serene, ungrudging, buoyant. Few people, even modern poets, felt carefree and happy with Pound then . . . When we came back to my room, I made the mistake of thinking that John was less interested in his new poems than in mine . . . Another opera. Much later, in the ragged days of John's first divorce, we went to the Met Opera Club, and had to borrow Robert Giroux's dinner jacket and tails. I lost the toss and wore the tails. I see John dancing in the street shouting, "I don't know you, Elizabeth wouldn't know you, only your mother would."

Pound, Jarrell, and Berryman had the same marvelous and maddening characteristic: they were self-centered and unselfish. This gave that breathless, commanding rush to their amusements and controversies—to Jarrell's cool and glowing critical appreciations, to Berryman's quotations and gossip. His taste for what he despised was infallible; but he could outrageously hero-worship living and dead, most of all writers his own age. Few have died without his defiant, heroic dirge. I think he sees them rise from their graves like soldiers to answer him.

Jarrell's death was the sadder. If it hadn't happened, it wouldn't have happened. He would be with me now, in full power, as far as one may at fifty. This might-have-been (it's a frequent thought) stings my eyes. John, with pain and joy like his friend Dylan Thomas, almost won what he gambled for. He was more eccentric than Thomas, less the natural poet of natural force, yet had less need to be first actor. He grew older, drier, more toughly twisted into the varieties of experience.

I must say something of death and the *extremist poets*, as we are named in often prefunerary tributes. Except for Weldon Kees and Sylvia Plath, they lived as long as Shakespeare, outlived Wyatt, Baudelaire, and Hopkins, and long outlived the forever Romantics, those who really died young. John himself lived to the age of Beethoven, whom he celebrates in the most ambitious and perhaps finest of his late poems, a monument to his long love, unhampered expression, and subtle criticism. John died with fewer infirmities than Beethoven. The consolation somehow doesn't wash. I feel the jagged gash with which my contemporaries died, with which we were to die. Were they killed, as standard radicals say, by our corrupted society? Was their success an aspect of their destruction? Were we uncomfortable epigoni of Frost, Pound, Eliot, Marianne Moore, etc.? This bitter possibility came to us at the moment of our *arrival*. Death comes sooner or later, these made it sooner.

I somehow smile, though a bit crookedly, when I think of John's whole life, and even of the icy leap from the bridge to the hard ground. He was springy to the end, and on his feet. The cost of his career is shown by an anecdote he tells in one of the earlier *Dream Songs*—as a boy the sliding seat in his shell slipped as he was rowing a race, and he had to push back and forth bleeding his bottom on the runners, till the race was finished.* The bravery is ignominious and screams. John kept rowing; maybe at the dock no one noticed the blood on his shorts—his injury wasn't maiming. Going to one

---

* #70, in John Berryman, *The Dream Songs* (New York: Farrar, Straus and Giroux, 2014), 77.

of his later Minnesota classes, he stumbled down the corridor, unhelped, though steadying himself step by step on the wall, then taught his allotted hour, and walked to the ambulance he had ordered, certain he would die of a stroke while teaching.* He was sick a few weeks, then returned to his old courses—as good as before.

The brighter side is in his hilarious, mocking stories, times with wives, children, and friends, and surely in some of the sprinted affairs he fabled. As he became more inspired and famous and drunk, more and more John Berryman, he became less good company and more a happening—slashing eloquence in undertones, amber tumblers of Bourbon, a stony pyramid talking down a rugful of admirers. His almost inhuman generosity sweetened this, but as the heart grew larger, the hide grew thicker. Is his work worth it to us? Of course; though the life of the ant is more to the ant than the health of his anthill. He never stopped fighting and moving all his life; at first, expert and derivative, later the full output, more juice, more pages, more strange words on the page, more simplicity, more obscurity. I am afraid I mistook it for forcing, when he came into his own. No voice now or persona sticks in my ear as his. It is poignant, abrasive, anguished, humorous. A voice on the page, identifiable as my friend's on the telephone, though lost now to mimicry. We should hear him read aloud. It is we who are labored and private, when he is smiling.

I met John last a year or so ago at Christmas in New York. He had been phoning poems and invitations to people at three in the morning, and I felt a weariness about seeing him. Since he had let me sleep uncalled, I guessed he felt numbness to me. We met one noon during the taxi strike at the Chelsea Hotel, dusty with donated, avant-garde constructs, and dismal with personal recollections, Bohemia, and the death of Thomas. There was no cheerful restaurant within walking distance, and the seven best bad ones were closed. We settled for the huge, varnished unwelcome of an empty cafeteria-bar. John addressed me with an awareness of his dignity, as if he were Ezra Pound at St. Elizabeth's, emphatic without pertinence, then brownly inaudible.

---

* Berryman was a professor at the University of Minnesota from 1955 until his death in 1972.

His remarks seemed guarded, then softened into sounds that only he could understand or hear. At first John was ascetically hung over, at the end we were high without assurance, and speechless. I said, "When will I see you again?" meaning, in the next few days before I flew to England. John said, "Cal, I was thinking through lunch that I'll never see you again." I wondered how in the murk of our conversation I had hurt him, but he explained that his doctor had told him one more drunken binge would kill him. Choice? It is blighting to know that this fear was the beginning of eleven months of abstinence . . . half a year of prolific rebirth, then suicide.

I have written on most of Berryman's earlier books.* *77 Dream Songs* are harder than most hard modern poetry, the succeeding poems in *His Toy* are as direct as a prose journal, as readable as poetry can be. This is a fulfillment, yet the *77 Songs* may speak clearest, almost John's whole truth. I misjudged them, and was rattled by their mannerisms. His last two books, *Love & Fame* and *Delusions, Etc.*, move. They may be slighter than the chronicle of dream songs, but they fill out the frame, alter their speech with age, and prepare for his death—they almost bury John's love child and ventriloquist's doll, Henry. *Love & Fame* is profane and often in bad taste, the license of John's old college dates recollected at fifty. The subjects may have been too inspiring and less a breaking of new ground than he knew; some wear his gayest cloth. *Love & Fame* ends with an intense long prayer sequence. *Delusions* is mostly sacred and begins with a prayer sequence.

Was riot or prayer delusion? Both were tried friends. The prayers are a Roman Catholic unbeliever's, seesawing from sin to piety, from blasphemous affirmation to devoted anguish. Their trouble is not the dark Hopkins discovered in himself and invented. This is a traditionally Catholic situation, the *Sagesse*, the wisdom of the sinner, Verlaine in jail. Berryman became one

---

* Indeed, in his earlier essay "The Poetry of John Berryman," which was ostensibly a review of Berryman's *77 Dream Songs* (in *The New York Review of Books*, May 28, 1964, 3–4), Lowell devoted some space to a discussion of his friend's previous work—that is, *Poems* (1942), *The Dispossessed* (1948), and "Homage to Mistress Bradstreet" (1956).

of the few religious poets, yet it isn't my favorite side, and I will end with two personal quotations. The first is humorous, a shadow portrait:

> . . . My marvelous black new brim-rolled felt is both stuffy and raffish.
> I hit my summit with it, in firelight.
> Maybe I only got a Yuletide tie
> (increasing sixty) & some writing paper
>
> but ha(haha) I've bought myself a hat!
> Plus strokes from position zero!*

The second is soberly prophetic and goes back twenty-six years to when John was visiting Richard Blackmur a few days before or after he visited me:

UNDERSTANDING†

> He was reading late, at Richard's down in Maine,
> aged 32? Richard and Helen long in bed,
> my good wife long in bed.
> All I had to do was strip & get in my bed,
> putting the marker in the book, and sleep,
> & wake to a hot breakfast.
>
> Off the coast was an island, P'tit Manaan,
> the bluff from Richard's lawn was almost sheer.
> A chill at four o'clock.
> It only takes a few minutes to make a man.
> A concentration upon now and here.
> Suddenly, unlike Bach,

---

* From "Lauds," in John Berryman, *Delusions, Etc.* (New York: Farrar, Straus and Giroux, 1972), 3. The excerpt diverges slightly from the original.

† The final version of the poem, printed in *Delusions, Etc.*, is titled "Henry's Understanding" (53). Lowell's version differs from it in a number of details, two of which are quite prominent—the title and the sixteenth line, which in *Delusions, Etc.* reads: "& cross the damp cold lawn & down the bluff."

& horribly, unlike Bach, it occurred to me
that one night instead of warm pajamas,
I'd take off all my clothes
& cross the damp cold lawn & totter down the bluff
into the terrible water & walk forever
under it out toward the island.

(1972)

On Hannah Arendt*

HANNAH ARENDT WAS an oasis in the fevered, dialectical dust of New York—to me, and I imagine to everyone who loved her. We met in the late Fifties or early Sixties in Mary McCarthy's apartment. She seemed hardly to take her coat off, as she brushed on with purpose to a class or functional shopping. In her hurry, she had time to say to me something like "This is an occasion," or more probably, "This is a meeting." I put the least intention into her words, but later dared telephone her to make a call. The calls were part of my life as long as I lived in New York—once a month, sometimes twice.

I was overawed. Years earlier Randall Jarrell had written me in Holland that if I wanted to discover something big and new, I would read Hannah Arendt's *Origins of Totalitarianism*. Randall seldom praised in vain, but my Dutch intellectual friends, as usual embarrassingly more into whatever was being written in America, were ahead of me, and were discussing *Origins* with minds sharpened by the Dutch Resistance, a hatred of Germany, and a fluency with German philosophers. I felt landless and alone, and read Han-

---

* Arendt (1906–1975) was a prominent political theorist, philosopher, and cultural analyst. Months after her death, Lowell read this memoir at the American Academy of Arts and Letters, subsequently publishing it in *The New York Review of Books*. He explained to Elizabeth Bishop his difficulty in composing it: "How different prose is; sometimes the two mediums just refuse to say the same things. I found this lately doing an obituary on Hannah Arendt. Without verse, without philosophy, I found it hard, I was naked without my line-ends"; in Robert Lowell, *The Letters of Robert Lowell*, edited by Saskia Hamilton (New York: Farrar, Straus and Giroux, 2005), 648.

nah as though I were going home, or reading *Moby Dick*, perhaps for the second time, no longer seeking adventure, but the voyage of wisdom, the tragedy of America.

Writing when Stalin was still enthroned and the shade of Hitler still unburied, Hannah believed with somber shrewdness, like Edmund Burke, that totalitarian power totally corrupts. Compared with Melville, however, she might seem an optimist about America. *Origins*, like many of her books, is apparently a defense of America, one that overstates and troubles us by assuming that we must be what we declared ourselves to be in our Revolutionary and post-Revolutionary beginnings. Her dream, it is both German and Jewish, now perhaps seems sadly beyond our chances and intentions. Yet the idea is still true, still taunting us to act. What is memorable, and almost uniquely rare and courageous in a thinker, is that Hannah's theory is always applied to action, and often to immediate principles of state. Her imperatives for political freedom still enchant and reproach us, though America has obviously, in black moments one thinks almost totally, slipped from those jaunty years of Harry Truman and the old crusade for international democracy. We couldn't know how fragile we were, or how much totalitarianism could ameliorate, bend, adulterate itself, and succeed.

Hannah's high apartment house high on the lower Hudson always gave me a feeling of apprehension, the thrill, hesitation, and helplessness of entering a foreign country, a north German harbor, the tenements of Kafka.* Its drabness and respectability that hid her true character also emphasized her unfashionable independence. On my first visit, I blundered about a vacant greenish immensity unable to find the name of any owner. Then I ran through the small print cards, uniform as names in a telephone book, that filled a green brass plaque camouflaged to lose itself in the dark green hall. No Arendt; then I found what I was seeking: *Blucher 12a*. It was inevitable for Hannah to use her husband's name for domestic identification. The elevator was brusque and unhurried; through my ineptitude, it made false premature stops. A vehemently not-Hannah German woman appeared and gave me advice that sent me to the top of the building. Did another lady dart

---

* Arendt lived in Manhattan at 370 Riverside Drive, 12A.

out shouting wrong directions? So it seemed, but memories magnify. Later when my arrivals were errorless though gradual, it seemed an undeserved rescue to find Hannah in her doorway and ready to kiss me.

Once inside, the raw Hudson, too big for New York, was chillingly present, but only in a window at an angle and raised several feet above the floor. We almost had to stand to see it, and it was soon lost in the urgency of conversation. I sometimes had an architectural temptation to cut away the unalterable window.

How many fine views have given me comfort by their nearness, yet were only taken in by chance over a typescript or the head of a friend. How unconsciously Hannah held the straying mind. Though a philosopher in every heartbeat of her nervous system, she belonged, like all true thinkers, to culture and literature. Coming to America in early middle age, she had the pluck not only to learn English but to write it with a power of phrase and syntax that often made her a master, the strongest theoretical writer of her age. Phrasing, syntax, and vehemence—her finest sentences are a wrenching then a marriage of English and German, of English instantness and German philosophical discipline. She translated many of her books into German, but I imagine if she had written in German and let someone else translate her into English her freshness, nerve, and actuality would have suffered a glaze, a stealing of her life.

Because I once failed to speak out, yet was stirred almost to hysteria by the smearing reception of Hannah's book *Eichmann in Jerusalem*, I want to take it up now, yet evade what is beyond my non-Jewish limitation.* I read her book innocently in *The New Yorker* before the anger of faction could accumulate and burst.† I was astonished to discover a new kind of biography, a blueprint of a man flayed down to his abstract moral performance, no color, no anecdote, nothing kept that would support a drawing or even

---

* As will become even clearer further into the memoir, Lowell felt he should have spoken out in defense of Arendt during a public symposium on the book, held in October 1963 in New York City under the auspices of *Dissent* magazine and chaired by the editor in chief, Irving Howe. It was attended by, among others, Lionel Abel, Daniel Bell, Alfred Kazin, Marie Syrkin, and Lowell. Howe recalled that, after a barrage of attacks on Arendt from the floor, "The chairman, myself, therefore asked twice for speakers who might support her. None rose to speak, though several of her supporters were present. [. . .] Only after the chairman announced that discussion from the floor was over, did Alfred Kazin jump up to speak." See Howe's description of the event in "Arguments: More on Eichmann," *Partisan Review* 31, no. 2 (1964): 253–83, 260. For Lowell's rich account of the evening, see his letter to Elizabeth Bishop of October 27, 1963 in *Letters*, 438.

† The book was first published as a series of articles in *The New Yorker* between February 16 and March 16, 1963.

a snapshot—yet a living kicking anatomy, Eichmann's X-ray in motion. It was a terrifying expressionist invention applied with a force no imitator could rival, and to a subject too sordid for reappraisal. The book's lesson seemed to be that given the right bad circumstances, Eichmann is still in the world. I have never understood why Hannah's phrase "the banality of evil" excited such universal polemic. She wasn't writing of Attila or Caesar, but Eichmann. The Eichmann who managed the railroading of thousands, perhaps millions, to their death camps was an appallingly uninteresting man both in his criminal efficiency and in his irrelevant pedantry and evasions while on trial for his life. Since Hannah has written, who has dreamed of painting Eichmann as colorful? Hannah's rage against Eichmann's mediocrity was itself enraging.

It was far more so when she turned with the same heat against the rhetoric and window dressing of the Eichmann trial in Israel; and far more still when she said that certain Jews, themselves martyrs, cooperated in the destruction of other Jews.* Who can expound the sober facts? Must not justice allow that Hannah Arendt, where she was wrong, wrote with the honest foolhardiness of a prophet? Perhaps her warnings to us to resist future liquidation are too heroic to live with, for nearly all of us are cowards if sufficiently squeezed by the hand of the powerful.†

No society is more acute and over-acute at self-criticism than that of the New York Jews. No society I have known is higher in intelligence, wit, inexhaustible willingness to reason, bicker, tolerate, and differ. When Hannah's *Eichmann* was published, a meeting was summoned by Irving Howe and Lionel Abel, normally urbane and liberal minds.‡ The meeting was like a trial, the stoning of an outcast member of the family. Any sneering overemphasis on Hannah, who had been invited but was away teaching in Chicago,§ was greeted with derisive clapping or savage sighs of amazement.

---

* In the commemorative speech Lowell delivered at the dinner of the National Institute of Arts and Letters, he worded Arendt's argument in *Eichmann* much more harshly: "she accused the privileged Jews, themselves martyrs, of conniving in the destruction of the less privileged." In the revision published in *The New York Review of Books* little over a month later (and reproduced here), he adopted a significantly less specific rhetoric.

† The clause "where she was wrong" as well as the adverb "nearly" qualifying his sweeping "all of us are cowards" were also his later revisions for *The New York Review of Books*.

‡ Here Lowell again refers to the symposium of October 1963 organized by Howe.

§ This clause was another new addition in *The New York Review of Books* version, seemingly another attempt to be fair to the opposing side.

Her appointed defenders drifted off into unintelligibly ingenious theses and avoided her name. When her tolerance was eloquently and unfavorably compared with Trotsky's, Alfred Kazin walked self-consciously to the stage and stammered, "After all Hannah didn't kill any Jews." He walked off the stage laughed at as irrelevant and absurd. His was the one voice for the defense. I admire his bravery, and wish I had dared speak. Half my New York literary and magazine acquaintance was sitting near, yet their intensity was terrifying, as if they were about to pick up chairs.*

Hannah did other portraits, genial, penetrating, good-humored ones, and had an unlikely genius for the form, as if the universal could win in a contest for hunting down particulars. How Disraeli and Clemenceau shine in her *Origins of Totalitarianism*. A subtle, relentless search for truth animates her essays on Rosa Luxemburg, Brecht, and Auden.

My meetings with Hannah were most often alone and at four in the afternoon. They had the concentrated intimacy of a tutorial. Large nuts were spread out on the table, the ashtrays filled, the conversation rambled through history, politics, and philosophy, but soon refreshed itself on gossip, mostly about people one liked, the dead and still living. Hannah made crushingly laconic sentences, but narrow slander, even of one's enemies, bored her. She thought and breathed within boundaries, ones held with such firm belief that she could function safely with almost torrential carelessness. She used to talk with merry ease, revising my definitions and her own, as if haphazard words could be as accurately attuned as writing. Yet all was warm, casual, and throwaway. It seems immoral to remember her epigrams I used to repeat, her acuteness and good temper seemed to inspire me to make sense beyond my custom.

I felt so much at home, I used to bring her poems. Rhythms with mean-

---

* In his first effort to make up for his silence at the meeting, Lowell made his own contribution to the *Partisan Review* symposium "Argument: More on Eichmann": "Both Hannah Arendt and Lionel Abel have written with such intelligence and force that any comment by me is likely to seem weak and impertinent. I particularly wish to avoid saying anything about the Jewish committees, or Abel's unanswerable, 'What would you have done?' and 'What could you have done?' I do think he distorts the painfully patient examination Miss Arendt gives this question. Her portrait of Eichmann, far from being lenient, is a masterpiece in rendering the almost unreadably repellent. I never felt she was condescending, or hard, or driven by a perverse theory, or by any motive except a heroic desire for the truth"; see "Arguments: More on Eichmann," 260.

ing would delight her, but she was quick to find obscurities and uncouth, pretentious generalizations. Mostly the poems were a device to diversify our talk about history, politics, and persons. I tried not to overstay, but sometimes I left in the dark and was late for supper—so cooling and kind was her affection, a parenthesis in the unjust blur of ordinary life.

(1976)

Anne Sexton[*]

I MET ANNE SEXTON in 1957,[†] and at a moment to be impressed, because I was writing my first autobiographical poems and was carried away by Snodgrass's marvelous *Heart's Needle* sequence. Anne was lean-faced, white-armed, thirty, and a poet for only a few months. She had met Snodgrass that summer and become a "confessional" poet overnight. How many laborious, often useless, steps of apprenticeship she had bypassed. Unlike Snodgrass and Sylvia Plath, she was an amateur. I am not sure I know what I mean by this. In my writing class, which she attended for a year or so, her comments and questions were more to the point than the more studious. In the beginning, her lines were overpoetic; she gave promise of becoming a fifties Edna Millay. Yet on her own, she developed a more sensitive, realistic idiom. Her gift was to grip, to give words to the drama of her personality. She did what few did, cut a figure. What went wrong? For a book or two, she grew more powerful. Then writing was too easy or too hard for her. She became meager and exaggerated. Many of her most

---

* Lowell wrote this memoir at the request of the poet and critic J. D. McClatchy for inclusion in his collection of reminiscences and reviews, *Anne Sexton: The Artist and Her Critics*, edited by J. D. McClatchy (Bloomington: Indiana University Press, 1978). As McClatchy explains in the preface, "I had asked those who wrote (many others refused to write at all, the subject being still too painful for them) to address themselves primarily to the artist they had worked with rather than to the friend they remembered" (viii). McClatchy and Lowell corresponded intermittently in the last years of Lowell's life.

† In fact, Lowell did not meet Sexton until September 1958.

embarrassing poems would have been fascinating if someone had put them in quotes, as the presentation of some character, not the author.

At a time when poetry readings were expected to be boring, no one ever fell asleep at Anne's. I see her as having the large, transparent, breakable, and increasingly ragged wings of a dragonfly—her poor, shy, driven life, the blind terror behind her bravado, her deadly increasing pace . . . her bravery while she lasted. For relief, I quote one of her finest and quieter poems.*

I knew you forever and you were always old,
soft white lady of my heart. Surely you would scold
me for sitting up late, reading your letters,
as if these foreign postmarks were meant for me.
You posted them first in London, wearing furs
and a new dress in the winter of eighteen-ninety.
I read how London is dull on Lord Mayor's Day,
where you guided past groups of robbers, the sad holes
of Whitechapel, clutching your pocketbook, on the way
to Jack the Ripper dissecting his famous bones.
This Wednesday in Berlin, you say, you will
go to a bazaar at Bismarck's house. And I
see you as a young girl in a good world still,
writing three generations before mine. I try
to reach into your page and breathe it back . . .
but life is a trick, life is a kitten in a sack.†

. . . .

This is Italy. You learn its mother tongue.
I read how you walked on the Palatine among
the ruins of the palaces of the Caesars;
alone in the Roman autumn, alone since July.
When you were mine they wrapped you out of here
with your best hat over your face. I cried
because I was seventeen. I am older now.

* The quoted lines are excerpted from Sexton's "Some Foreign Letters," which appeared in her first book, *To Bedlam and Part Way Back* (Boston: Houghton Mifflin, 1960), reprinted in *The Complete Poems* (Boston: Houghton Mifflin, 1999), 9.

† Here Lowell omits two stanzas.

I read how your student ticket admitted you
into the private chapel of the Vatican and how
you cheered with the others, as we used to do
on the Fourth of July. One Wednesday in November
you watched a balloon, painted like a silver ball,
float up over the Forum, up over the lost emperors,
to shiver its little modern cage in an occasional
breeze. You worked your New England conscience out
beside artisans, chestnut vendors and the devout.

Tonight I will learn to love you twice;
learn your first days, your mid-Victorian face.
Tonight I will speak up and interrupt
your letters, warning you that wars are coming,
that the Count will die, that you will accept
your America back to live like a prim thing
on the farm in Maine. I tell you, you will come
here, to the suburbs of Boston, to see the blue-nose
world go drunk each night, to see the handsome
children jitterbug, to feel your left ear close
one Friday at Symphony. And I tell you,
you will tip your boot feet out of that hall,
rocking from its sour sound, out onto
the crowded street, letting your spectacles fall
and your hair net tangle as you stop passers-by
to mumble your guilty love while your ears die.

(Composed 1978)

Sylvia Plath[*]

S YLVIA PLATH'S LAST and best poems seem to have an excellence
that might almost be proved and measured out in inches, like the
breaking of some athletic record. One feels that years before any
of these poems were written, she had set herself a plausible but impossible
mark, that she went through her long, prescribed hours of training, and
then suddenly and recklessly sure of her force and daring let herself go in a
blaze of inventiveness. She must hardly have had the time to see she had left
the terrible mark behind her, when her life ended.

Miss Plath's poems are so unlike other poems that they seem without
models, and yet many of their characteristics are orthodox and almost unavoidable for a writer of her moment. Her humility and willingness to accept
what was admired seem at times to give her an air of maddening docility and
to obscure her unfashionable patience and boldness.

In the work of her apprenticeship, Miss Plath was unusually conscientious
and steady in hammering what might have come to her first as simple images
and impressions into hard meter, rhymes and stanzas. Logic and syntax were
fiercely kept and twisted, and armed with an alliterative rhetoric that seemed
like a makeshift and protection against the greater discipline and abandon
of finding a true voice. In the later poems all this is pulverized, one feels the

* This piece is apparently an early draft of the foreword to Plath's *Ariel*. Overlapping in only a few passages,
it is more impersonal toward Plath than the later memoir-essay, though equally introspective. Still, it does
reflect an implicit sense of Plath's personal presence and calls her at one point "Sylvia."

wild energy of a horse throwing off its trappings, a grace of archery shooting without pause from a hundred unexpected postures and angles. [. . .]

Sylvia Plath's first book of poems, *The Colossus*, was somber, expert in meter, had a feeling for harsh sounds, and avoided clichés. Only a lover of *all* competent poetry could say much more of it, and no one I talked to really makes much more of a claim; it had the desolate brilliance of some fine machine produced by the poetry workshops of the American universities. How stupid we were! Yet each time I reread these early poems, I feel dull.

"The restlessness of his mind has forbidden him to marshal his thoughts carefully and logically; the pain, if it ever found any better expression than a beating of the breast and a tearing of the hair could be satisfied only with phrases of the most condensed and perverse imagery." This is Robert Graves writing on Keats's "La Belle Dame,"* and he writes truly, though in the idiom of our own age rather than Keats's. Yet how unperverse and uncondensed "I saw their starved lips in the gloam / with horrid warning gaped wide" and the rest of Keats's magical and terrible little ballad become after reading Sylvia Plath.

> He tells me how sweet
> The babies look in their hospital
> Icebox, a simple
>
> Frill at the neck,
> Then the fluting of their Ionian
> Death-gowns,
> Then two little feet.†

Some essential quality in these poems makes me evasive, benumbed. Something in these poems makes one despair of writing one's self.

---

* Perhaps misremembering, Lowell somewhat misquotes Graves's comment on Keats in *The Meaning of Dreams* (London: Palmer, 1924), 145. Nevertheless, he accurately reproduces Graves's key words, the last eight.

† Slightly misquoted from "Death & Co.," in *Ariel* (London: Faber and Faber, 1965), reprinted in Sylvia Plath, *The Collected Poems*, edited by Ted Hughes (New York: Harper, 1992), 254. This quotation, with one added line, also appears in Lowell's foreword to *Ariel*.

Sometimes after reading these poems, I have wanted to give up writing. The terrible audacity, rightness and ease of their inspiration make most other poems sound like birthday odes to George the First.

For several weeks, I have been reading and brooding over *Ariel*, and wondering with some anguish why so much of it made me feel empty, evasive, and worst of all, wordless.* It is like listening to some conversationalist who makes all other conversation fraudulent. The voice of the serpent whispers, "Come, if only you had my courage, you too could have my rightness, audacity and ease of inspiration." And what is this courage? It's the finality of playing Russian roulette with a full cylinder, or a game of "chicken" with locked wheels that will allow neither car to swerve. And one knows the game is not worth it, and even if played would turn out to be more phony than prudence. These poems are not the celebration of some desperate and debauched existence, that of the "damned" poet, glad to settle for the continuous intensity that burns out his body. They offer no such career. They say simply that life, even when endured with discipline, is hell.

If poor Sylvia Plath could return now three years from her abrupt, defiant death, she would find herself established. Usually poets, even the very good ones, pay the penalty of their dense, brief medium, and are thought of not as presences, but as workmen. If they cheat and fill their poems with lucid, shocking, immediate oral effects, these effects quickly pass from the mind into nothingness, transparent and frail as dandelion fluff.

The poems in *Ariel* are surrealist, confessional free verse. Nothing very new in these techniques singly, or even in combination. Yet with Sylvia, each was given a diamond edge of distinction, one instantly felt her sureness, her careless, assured daring. Behind the free verse is a break-loose, deft certainty of touch, the joy of feeling that a laborious and measured metric is being thrown to the winds, recklessly shattered, and then resurrected in little fragments of scansion and sound effects, law lost and reborn as life.

---

* A highly revised version of this paragraph appears in Lowell's foreword to *Ariel*. There he softens the chilling adjective "wordless" to merely "inarticulate," and he refers to Plath's "courage" only once instead of twice. In a subsequent 1975 revision, and in Lowell's posthumous *Collected Prose*, "courage" disappears entirely, and he settles for "rightness, audacity and ease of inspiration." See Robert Lowell, *Collected Prose*, edited by Robert Giroux (New York: Farrar, Straus and Giroux, 1987), 124.

Bastard
Masturbating a glitter,
He wants to be loved.

I do not stir.
The frost makes a flower,
The dew makes a star,
The dead bell,
The dead bell.

Somebody's done for.*

This is lawless, but has the scanned, sophisticated, calculated intricacy of touch of de la Mare.

Miss Plath has her recognizable ways of working, but her surrealist jumps seem without method or formula. Many poems, such as "Gulliver," "The Bee Meeting" and "Daddy," are beautifully imagined and organic, no phrase that doesn't cohere. Others, like "Medusa," seem like an unarranged flow of language. Perhaps the unorganized poems will someday seem as clear and satisfactory as the organized. Phrase by phrase they almost always seem authentic, fresh and earned. Language never dies in her hands. Yet I must admit the sprawling poems seem less satisfactory to me, to be thrown out waiting for a further and last triumphant swoop of imagination. I rejoice when I find in "Berck-Plage," a long ambitious, steadily startling, but incoherent composition, such a solid nugget as the following lines on death.

On a striped mattress in one room

An old man is vanishing.
There's no help from his weeping wife.

Where are the eye-stones, yellow and valuable,
And the tongue, sapphire of ash.

_____

* From "Death & Co.," in *Ariel*, reprinted in *The Collected Poems*, 254–55.

A wedding-cake face in a paper frill.
How superior he is now.

It is like possessing a saint.
The nurses in their wing-caps are no longer so beautiful.

They are browning like touched gardenias . . .
This is what it is to be complete . . . *

As so often in Sylvia Plath, each image, even the most unnatural and grotesque, could be shown in a film.

What makes her a supreme poet is her personal voice. [. . .] "Fever 103°" is sinewed together by this voice:

. . . dull, fat Cerberus
Who wheezes at the gate. Incapable
Of licking clean

The aguey tendon, the sin, the sin.†

And in a much greater poem, "Lady Lazarus," one of Miss Plath's masterpieces, this ever certain voice thrusts into and captures the deepest and most terrible personal experience.

I have done it again
One year in every ten
I manage it—
A sort of walking miracle, my skin
Bright as a Nazi lampshade,
My right foot

---

* Slightly misquoted from *Ariel*, reprinted in *The Collected Poems*, 198.

† *Ariel*, reprinted in *The Collected Poems*, 231.

A paperweight,
My face a featureless, fine
Jew linen.

Peel off the napkin
O my enemy.*

What makes Sylvia Plath a supreme poet is her personal voice: it is a sour, witty, very fanciful voice, jumping precisely and unexpectedly like a spry bird from object to object, tone to tone. It is often grindingly cruel. Into it enters all the postwar world's writing philosophies, homicidal science, liquidation camps, and driving man-killing iron. There are times when we can hardly face or bear the poet's fierce, amused, aristocratic rasp. Among her most perfect and powerful poems are: "Lady Lazarus," "Death & Co.," "Daddy," "The Bee Meeting," "The Arrival of the Bee Box," "Getting There," "Lesbos" and the poem about bees and Napoleon.† They are among the melancholy triumphs of twentieth-century imagination.

(Composed 1966)

* *Ariel*, reprinted in *The Collected Poems*, 242.

† "The Swarm," in *Ariel*, reprinted in *The Collected Poems*, 215.

Foreword to Sylvia Plath's
Ariel

I N THESE POEMS, written in the last months of her life and often rushed out at the rate of two or three a day, Sylvia Plath becomes herself, becomes something imaginary, newly, wildly and subtly created—hardly a person at all, or a woman, certainly not another "poetess," but one of those super-real, hypnotic, great classical heroines. This character is feminine, rather than female, though almost everything we customarily think of as feminine is turned on its head. The voice is now coolly amused, witty, now sour, now fanciful, girlish, charming, now sinking to the strident rasp of the vampire—a Dido, Phaedra, or Medea, who can laugh at herself as "cow-heavy and floral in my Victorian nightgown." Though lines get repeated, and sometimes the plot is lost, language never dies in her mouth.

Everything in these poems is personal, confessional, felt, but the manner of feeling is controlled hallucination, the autobiography of a fever. She burns to be on the move, a walk, a ride, a journey, the flight of the queen bee. She is driven forward by the pounding pistons of her heart. The title *Ariel* summons up Shakespeare's lovely, though slightly chilling and androgynous spirit, but the truth is that this *Ariel* is the author's horse. Dangerous, more powerful than man, machinelike from hard training, she herself is a little like a racehorse, galloping relentlessly with risked, outstretched neck, death hurdle after death hurdle topped. She cries out for that rapid life of starting pistols, snapping tapes, and new world records broken. What is most heroic in her, though, is not her force, but the desperate practicality of her control, her hand of metal with its modest, womanish touch. Almost pure motion, she can endure "God, the great stasis in his vacuous night,"[*] hospitals, fever, paralysis, the iron lung, being stripped like a girl in the booth of a circus sideshow, dressed like a mannequin, tied down like Gulliver by the Lilliputians . . . apartments, babies, prim English landscapes, beehives, yew trees, gardens, the moon, hooks, the black boot, wounds, flowers with mouths like wounds, Belsen's lampshades made of human skin, Hitler's homicidal iron tanks clanking over Russia. Suicide, father-hatred, self-loathing—nothing is too much for the macabre gaiety of her control. Yet it is too much; her art's immortality is life's disintegration. The surprise, the shimmering, unwrapped birthday present, the transcendence "into the red eye, the cauldron of morning," and the lover, who are always waiting for her, are Death, her own abrupt and defiant death.

> He tells me how badly I photograph.
> He tells me how sweet
> The babies look in their hospital
> Icebox, a simple
>
> Frill at the neck,
> Then the flutings of their Ionian
> Death-gowns,
> Then two little feet.[†]

There is a peculiar, haunting challenge to these poems. Probably many, after reading *Ariel*, will recoil from their first overawed shock, and painfully wonder why so much of it leaves them feeling empty, evasive and inarticulate. In her lines, I often hear the serpent whisper, "Come, if only you had the courage, you too could have my rightness, audacity and ease of inspi-

[*] Misquoted from "Years," which includes the lines "O God, I am not like you / In your vacuous black" and "And you, great Stasis"; see *Ariel* (London: Faber and Faber, 1965), 72; reprinted in Sylvia Plath, *The Collected Poems*, edited by Ted Hughes (New York: Harper, 1992), 255.

[†] From "Death & Co.," in *Ariel*, 28, reprinted in *The Collected Poems*, 254.

ration."* But most of us will turn back. These poems are playing Russian roulette with six cartridges in the cylinder, a game of "chicken," the wheels of both cars locked and unable to swerve. Oh, for that heaven of the humble copyist, those millennia of Egyptian artists repeating their lofty set patterns! And yet Sylvia Plath's poems are not the celebration of some savage and debauched existence, that of the "damned" poet, glad to burn out his body for a few years of continuous intensity. This poetry and life are not a career; they tell that life, even when disciplined, is simply not worth it.

It is poignant, looking back, to realize that the secret of Sylvia Plath's last irresistible blaze lies lost somewhere in the checks and courtesies of her early laborious shyness. She was never a student of mine, but for a couple of months seven years ago, she used to drop in on my poetry seminar at Boston University. I see her dim against the bright sky of a high window, viewless unless one cared to look down on the city outskirts' defeated yellow brick and square concrete pillbox filling stations. She was willowy, long-waisted, sharp-elbowed, nervous, giggly, gracious—a brilliant tense presence embarrassed by restraint. Her humility and willingness to accept what was admired seemed at times to give her an air of maddening docility that hid her unfashionable patience and boldness. She showed us poems that later, more or less unchanged, went into her first book, *The Colossus*. They were somber, formidably expert in stanza structure, and had a flair for alliteration and Massachusetts's low-tide dolor.

> A mongrel working his legs to a gallop
> Hustles the gull flock to flap off the sand-spit.†

Other lines showed her wit and directness.

> The pears fatten like little Buddhas.‡

---

* In the posthumous Robert Lowell, *Collected Prose* (New York: Farrar, Straus and Giroux, 1987), as well as in a 1975 typescript Lowell prepared for *A Moment in American Poetry*, this sentence is truncated so as to eliminate the word "courage."

† Quoted, slightly incorrectly, from Sylvia Plath, "Suicide Off Egg Rock," in *The Colossus* (London: William Heinemann, 1960), 35; reprinted in *The Collected Poems*, 115.

‡ Quoted, again slightly incorrectly, from Sylvia Plath, "The Manor Garden," in *The Colossus*, 3; reprinted in *The Collected Poems*, 125.

Somehow none of it sank very deep into my awareness. I sensed her abashment and distinction, and never guessed her later appalling and triumphant fulfillment.*

(1966)

---

* Lowell's letter of October 27, 1963, to Bishop is filled with similarly poignant remarks on Plath's *Ariel* poems: she "almost makes one feel at first reading that almost all other poetry is about nothing. Still, it's searingly extreme, a triumph by a hair, that one almost wished had never come about"; see *Words in Air: The Complete Correspondence Between Elizabeth Bishop and Robert Lowell*, edited by Thomas Travisano with Saskia Hamilton (New York: Farrar, Straus and Giroux, 2008), 513.

After Enjoying Six or Seven Essays on Me[*]

I AM NOT an authoritative critic of my own poems, except in the most pressing and urgent way. I have spent hundreds and hundreds of hours shaping, extending and changing hopeless or defective work. I lie on a bed staring, crossing out, writing in, crossing out what was written in, again and again, through days and weeks. Heavenly hours of absorption and idleness . . . intuition, intelligence, pursuing my ear that knows not what it says. In time, the fragmentary and scattered limbs become, by a wild extended figure of speech, something living . . . a person.

I know roughly what I think are my better poems, and more roughly and imperfectly why I think they are; and roughly too, which are my worst and where they fail. I have an idea how my best fall short. To have to state all this systematically, and perhaps with controversial argument, would be a prison sentence to me. It would be an exposure. But which is one's good

---

[*] Lowell's memoir of his poetic career was written for a section of *Salmagundi* 37 (Spring 1977) honoring him on his sixtieth birthday. It appeared months before his death. The section included a preface by Robert Boyers, and essays by Helen Vendler, Robert Fitzgerald, John Peck, Philip Booth, Frank Bidart, Robert Hass, G. S. Fraser, Mary Kinzie, Robert Pinsky, and Vanessa Ryder—eleven essays in all. One wonders if Lowell was speaking figuratively in calling them "six or seven," or whether he meant that he only enjoyed that number.

poem? Is it a translation? Can one write something that will sing on for
years like the sirens, and not know it?

Reading other critics on me, as I have the pleasure of doing here, gives me
the surprise of seeing my poems through eyes that are not mine. Younger,
older . . . refreshingly different and perhaps keener eyes . . . mercifully
through the eyes of another, for a poem changes with each inspection.
Variability is its public existence. Yet variety has limits; no one could call
Macbeth or my "Quaker Graveyard" hilarious minuets. That would take an
insensately amusing theorist.

Politics? We live in the sunset of Capitalism. We have thundered nobly
against its bad record all our years, yet we cling to its vestiges, not just out
of greed and nostalgia, but for our intelligible survival. Is this what makes
our art so contradictory, muddled and troubled? We are being proven in a
sort of secular purgatory; there is no earthly paradise on the horizon. War,
nuclear bombs, civil gangsterism, race, woman—the last has always been
the writer's most unavoidable, though not only, subject, one we are too seriously engaged in to be fair, or . . . salvationists.

It seems our insoluble lives sometimes come clearer in writing. This
happens rarely because most often skill and passion are lacking, and when
these are not lacking it happens rarely because the goddess Fortuna grudg-
ingly consents. It is easier to write good poems than inspired lines.

Influences: I assume this is a live subject. When I began to publish, I
wrote literally under the rooftree of Allen Tate. When I imitated him, I
believed I was imitating the muse of poetry. When I erred, I failed, or accidentally forced myself to be original. Later, I was drawn to William Carlos
Williams and Elizabeth Bishop. I can't say how much I hope I learned. Yet
I differed so in temperament and technical training (particularly with Williams) that nothing I wrote could easily be confused with their poems. How
many poets I wish I could have copied, the Shakespeare of *The Winter's
Tale*, the Wordsworth of "The Ruined Cottage," the Blake of "Truly my
Satan . . . ," the Pound of the best *Pisan Cantos*. Baudelaire? Hardy? Maybe
I have. The large poet of the nineteenth century who attracts and repels us
is Robert Browning. Who couldn't he use, Napoleon III, St. John, Cardinal Manning, Caliban? He set them in a thousand meters. Nor was his

ear deficient—take the opening of "Andrea del Sarto," hundreds of lines of "Christmas Eve," all of "The Householder," most of "Mr. Sludge the Medium." And yet Browning's idiosyncratic robustness scratches us, and often his metrical acrobatics are too good. One wishes one could more often see him plain, or as he might have been rewritten by some master novelist, Samuel Butler or George Eliot, though not in her Italian phase. Yet perhaps Browning's poems will outlast much major fiction. Meanwhile he shames poets with the varied human beings he could scan, the generosity of his ventriloquism.

Looking over my *Selected Poems*, about thirty years of writing, my impression is that the thread that strings it together is my autobiography, it is a small-scale *Prelude*, written in many different styles and with digressions, yet a continuing story—still wayfaring. A story of what? Not the "growth of a poet's mind."* Not a lesson and example to be handed to the student. Yet the mind must eventually age and grow, or the story would be a still life, the pilgrimage of a zombie. My journey is always stumbling on the unforeseen and even unforeseeable. From year to year, things remembered from the past change almost more than the present.

Those mutilating years are often lenient to art . . . If only one's selected poems could keep their figure like Madame Bovary!

I haven't said what I wished to write in poems, the discordant things I've tried. It isn't possible, is it? When I was working on *Life Studies*, I found I had no language or meter that would allow me to approximate what I saw or remembered. Yet in prose I had already found what I wanted, the conventional style of autobiography and reminiscence. So I wrote my autobiographical poetry in a style I thought I had discovered in Flaubert, one that used images and ironic or amusing particulars. I did all kinds of tricks with meter and the avoidance of meter. When I didn't have to bang words into rhyme and count, I was more nakedly dependent on rhythm. After this in the *Union Dead*, I used the same style but with less amusement, and with more composition and stanza structure. Each poem was meant to stand by itself. This stronger structure would probably have ruined *Life Studies*, which would

---

* The subtitle and stated theme of Wordsworth's *The Prelude*.

have lost its novelistic flow. Later on in *For the Union Dead*, free verse subjects seemed to melt away, and I found myself back in strict meter, yet tried to avoid the symbols and heroics of my first books. After that I wrote a long sequence in Marvell's eight-line four-foot couplet stanza.* God knows why, except that it seemed fit to handle national events. Indeed the stanza was a Godsent task that held me almost breathing couplets all one summer and deep into the next autumn. Shine compensated for the overcompression. For six years I wrote unrhymed blank verse sonnets.† They had the eloquence at best of iambic pentameter, and often the structure and climaxes of sonnets, with one fraction of the fourteen lines balanced against the remaining fraction. Obscurity and confusion came when I tried to cram too much in the short space. Quite often I wasn't obscure or discontinuous. I had a chance such as I had never had before, or probably will again, to snatch up and verse the marvelous varieties of the moment. I think perfection (I mean outward coherence not inspiration) was never so difficult. Since then, I have been writing for the last three years in unrhymed free verse. At first I was so unused to this meter, it seemed like tree-climbing. It came back—gone now the sonnet's cramping and military beat. What I write almost always comes out of the pressure of some inner concern, temptation or obsessive puzzle. Surprisingly, quite important things may get said. But sometimes what is closest to the heart has no words but stereotypes. Stereotypes are usually true, but never art. Inspired lines from nowhere roam through my ears . . . to make or injure a poem. All my poems are written for catharsis; none can heal melancholia or arthritis.

I pray that my progress has been more than recoiling with satiation and disgust from one style to another, a series of rebuffs. I hope there has been increase of beauty, wisdom, tragedy, and all the blessings of this consuming chance.

(1977)

---

* The "Near the Ocean" sequence in *Near the Ocean*.

† In Robert Lowell, *Notebook 1967–68*, *Notebook*, *History*, *For Lizzie and Harriet*, and *The Dolphin*.

Selected Fragments from the Manuscripts

A NOTE ON THE TEXTS

THE APPENDIX COLLECTS fourteen memoir fragments from the Robert Lowell Papers at the Houghton Library, Harvard University, and one from the Harry Ransom Center at the University of Texas, Austin. These fragments are the most brilliant offshoots of the three prose memoir projects collected in Parts I, II, and III of this volume.

We've made the following editorial choices in the texts collected here:

- In each case but the last, the titles are derived from the opening sentences.
- In "For over an hour Mother and Father" we drop the final seven sentences, which duplicate material already in the main text of "Washington, D.C."; similarly, in "I sat looking out" we end the text where it begins to cover material from "The Balanced Aquarium."
- In "Mother was talking to Miss Frieda" we provide quotation marks to help identify quoted speech.
- "The stripped logs" comes from a manuscript with its first six pages missing. We elide words that finish the last sentence from page 6, indicating the omission with three dots in square brackets. "The stripped logs" handles the same material as "Pictures of Rock" and "The Balanced Aquarium," but makes the material vivid in a new way. We include this version, despite some redundancy, because of the light it casts on Lowell's creative decisions.

- In "But I don't want to go anywhere" we preserve a crossed-out but unreplaced phrase required for the last sentence in the opening paragraph to make sense.
- In "My grandmother Winslow" we omit the first sentence, in which Lowell explains the origins of the name "Chardesa." The sentence or a close variant appears in several other memoirs and drafts (for example, "Arthur Winslow IV," "The Balanced Aquarium," "But I don't want to go anywhere," and "The farm at Rock"), and it makes a particularly odd opening for this piece. In his drafts Lowell would sometimes use a sentence from an already written memoir as a prompt for new writing.
- In "The farm at Rock," we keep the piece's central sentence about Arthur Winslow being known "as a sort of Titanic," even though Lowell struck it.
- We group "Mother's neatness was compulsive" with the drafts for "My Autobiography," even though it may just as well pertain to "The Balanced Aquarium" and other texts in Part II. It includes an extended passage that Lowell says is quoted from a diary by Charlotte Winslow he found in 1954. Since he claims the excerpts are "exactly as she wrote" them and their "spelling is a miracle of inaccuracy due to [her] ignorance, but also due to impatience," we left this passage unedited. The text may include Lowell's own unintended or fabricated errors or typos, beside those he says he found in Charlotte's writing.
- "Philip Rahv" derives from a two-page typescript housed at the Harry Ransom Center. It is a very rough first draft of an opening for a memoir that never materialized. In seven places we had to re-sort to words that Lowell struck, because he failed to offer feasible alternatives for them. Most notably, we keep the phrase describing Rahv as seeming to be a few years "more than any youngish person he was with" and another depicting Randall Jarrell as straining to look "unrattled by Tate's harsh rebuff."

My Autobiography

What I know about the first three years

WHAT I KNOW about the first three years of my life comes from what I have been told and from what I remember—what I have been told and later imagined, what I see, or at least once, saw clearly, but have later corrected with what I have been told.* Such knowledge is a disorderly mixture. There are scenes so over-allegorized and made significant that they appear trifling—like a child sticking his tongue out and growing black in the face as he imitates one of the seven deadly sins. The meaning is even now deep beyond my plumbing, but the expression is starved and trite past grasping by any except the feebleminded. Then there are still other pictures that are all picture, a play of white sunlight on white sand; these stay in the mind with a brute, unlocked dumb insistence, and by their staying an inexpressible significance of expression. Both kinds of knowledge concern me; I come with signposts in one hand lettered Boston, Beacon Hill, the Atlantic Ocean, etc.; in the other I hold a handful of dust picked up somewhere along the road, true stuff, but unsorted, unlabeled.

* Alternative opening paragraph of "Philadelphia."

For over an hour Mother and Father

FOR OVER AN hour Mother and Father had been squabbling about Father's cheap Army Navy Store socks, garters, underwear and shirts.* Father liked to remember how he had once been a Plebe, though barely fifteen years old at Annapolis. By practicing a hundred miserable petty economies, he had been able to send monthly checks to his mother and grandmother. This was an image of himself that he liked to water and keep green. A sample of each article was spread on the sofa. Father's socks looked like inked cheese cloth; his garters were loud and their metal parts were made to resemble harps; his underwear were of a strange buttonless design that the Navy seems to have borrowed from an oriental insane asylum; the shirts, though plain white, were only too obviously shoddy material and over-decisive in their cut. Even the blue eagle tattooed on Father's right forearm gave offense. It had been done in China for a dollar. What Father liked about China was that one American dollar had the buying power of ten. This morning, for the first time since her marriage, Mother looked squarely at Father's tattoo. "Why, Bob," she said to Father, "it's a rubber stamp!"

Father stuck up for his purchases. They meant asceticism, self-sacrifice

---

* This fragment is an offshoot of material in "Washington, D.C."

and modesty. He felt certain at such times at least that he was one of the fittest and was surviving. He was a boy of fifteen, Robbie. His mother and grandmother's praises rang in his ears. But for Mother they meant only a tasteless perverse meanness. It wasn't as though these little savings mattered, for my father, as she never wearied of saying, could count pennies, but couldn't add dollars. And it was true that big sums somehow made Father tired.

Mother was talking to Miss Frieda

MOTHER WAS TALKING to Miss Frieda and Miss Frances Mims, two mousy almost transparent spinsters who made her feel almost Rabelaisian. They had stopped off for Mother on their way to Church. "But I can't believe that you are actually related to poor dear feather-witted Eunice Loring." Miss Loring was Bobby's Sunday school-teacher in Washington. She really thought that the Bible was a boys' classic, and spent a whole year telling him about Gideon cupping water in his hands, King David picking five smooth stones, Kings David's son hanging by his yellow hair, and even about King David dancing naked before the arc of the Covenant.

But Mr. Waterman, the Trinity Church* Sunday School teacher, had no such charms. He was interested only in theology and church history. And his only connection with the Bible was his deep slow Adam's apple. The first day he met with us, he said, "I am taking you off bread and milk. I am giving you meat and wine. I shall talk to you as men." Mr. Waterman's talks were drafts of papers he was writing for a course at the Harvard Divinity School. One was called "The Beauty of Bishops," another "The Bishop of Rome secedes from the main line."

---

* Trinity Church Boston is an Episcopal church at 206 Clarendon Street.

The stripped logs

[. . .] THE STRIPPED LOGS were again as pale as Grandfather's legs without stockings.* The knots looked like his varicose veins. I had no idea what I was searching for. Destruction perhaps; but at last I saw columns of yellow flies each as big as my thumb. Slowly, they moved; as slowly as drops of sweat growing silver-dollar-sized under a magnifying glass. Yellow torsos, black shoulders—they were coal miners with lamps stuck on their caps. Then needle, needle, needle. I felt my whole body was being riveted or stitched together like a baseball. The yellow hornets had stung me thirty-two times. Then I was out. I came to. I was far down the lawn, lying on my belly and plastered with mud and Vaseline. People kept saying, "Thirty-two hornet bites." I knew that for once I had really lived.

Then I was lying on a fluffy, lettuce-green Turkish towel that had been set in the center of the diamond on a huge Navajo rug. I was the hub of a wheel on a wheel of red tiles, octagonal red tiles that sweated, red tiles that were crumby with the droppings of ants. A Matisse picture, a mosque, a mammoth bathroom. All about me were the works of my grandfather's hands—stogie-brown beams, unhewn stone-and-cement walls, screens as clear as air from one angle, and blacker than railroad engines from another. The porch was ranch style. Like everything my grandfather built, it was stern, overgrown, unfashionable—and a well of comfort. What were these

* This text reworks material from "Pictures of Rock" and "The Balanced Aquarium."

orange trees, these sunflowers? They were pitchers of ice tea afloat with oases of homegrown mint. Nowhere in the world could drinkables gurgle so, or taste colder. My grandfather had stronger medicine. Into his old Stuttgart student stein that was shaped like a potbellied Cossack, he poured a pint of yeasty stinking homemade beer; on top of that chugged and exploded a pint of homemade root beer. All the while and quite unperturbed by either the drinking or my wounds, a fountain feebly tinkled. Clearly it was on its last legs from the midsummer drouth. The fountain basin was a saucer of unfinished cement, the size of a mill wheel. On the rim a china statuette with dim Boucher boudoir colors was fishing with a bent pin, tied to a thread, tied to a straw. It wore a conical hat and looked from the distance like a coolie—nearer it was Huck Finn. But about the neck my grandfather had hung a little card on a green ribbon. The card said in my grandfather's slanting green-ink letters, "I am a callow youth. My name is Verdant Greene." This was for me. Great-Aunt Sarah stretched out on her straw chaise longue. Beautiful, frail, blue-eyed Aunt Sarah, more blessed than bee or ice tea. An exotic bug in one of Harvard's exotic glass flowers. She was saying, "There's always the world, and the world and the world. Always another on top of the one you've got. They [are] all given to Bobby Lowell by his fond Grandfather Arthur Winslow. He gives them away to us," she said, "for free and for keeps." Great-Aunt Sarah resembled gigantic delicate pink and gray ribbons arranged on a coat hanger. She pointed to the statuette. "Poor Huck is deaf as a post," she said. "And just slobbering for game." She rolled up her copy of *Illustration* and indicated the basin's feeble sprinkle. "How frail, miserly and pale, the fountain's failing dole!" she said. My grandfather began poking at the main pipe of the fountain with a little stick that no one else was allowed to handle. Water spouted to the beams. A starry sprinkle in the basin. My grandfather looked as though he had produced a six-foot white bunny. Great-Aunt Sarah made a dumb show of clapping her hands. "Arthur," she said, "you have fetched the sacred water of the Ganges to the fountains of Versailles."

A day at *Chardesa* many years later. I am about ten years old. I have been joking with Great-Aunt Sarah and the guests a little too enthusiastically. I have been advised to "rest it off." Sunlight and afternoon whiten every inch of my bedroom. I haven't bothered to turn down my transparent gauze bedcover ornamented with solid white bunches of grapes. On the wall behind my head is the print of a blinding yellow row of daffodils blown by the wind. Underneath Wordsworth's lines were quoted, "My heart . . . dances with the daffodils." The afternoon, however, had blanched them white. Locusts whirred in the elms outside. On, on and on went the afternoon wind through the leaves. It was water coming to a boil; you couldn't stop it. *Away, away, away*, said the leaves. *Hey, hey, hey*, said the leaves, *let us pass out of life today, let us pass out.* I could see my grandmother, Great-Aunt Sarah, and Aunt Dora all growing daily whiter and whiter—air!

On the wall at the side of my bed, and not at all high up, hung a picture of a brown fish. It wasn't an honest fish, though, with its outline and scales all drawn equally distinctly. I wasn't like what I saw in my catalogue or *Field and Stream*, something you could give the weight and species of. Instead it was some sort of Chinese fraud, finely etched here, a fog there. "The head's all fog, and no fish," I thought. Following the head into the picture's background, I remembered the gross granulated gouge in the plaster—this was what the picture had been hung to conceal. Suddenly another afternoon came back to me. I was on the same bed, but in daylong darkness. I was a baby of three. With a big key hidden up my sleeve I tried to punish the wall. As I worked with the key, I again lived through the previous day, the one for which I was being punished.

Here's how it went. At eight-thirty in the morning, I was sitting in the music sitting room. Great-Aunt Sarah was giving a virtuoso performance on her dummy piano. We could hear the Pierce and the little Ford maneuvering out of the stable. My grandfather, grandmother and Young Aunt Sarah were off for the Brockton Fair, and they were taking all the more responsible servants with them. Great-Aunt Sarah and I listened. "I can't wait, I can't wait, I can't wait," we seemed to be saying in unison. My grandfather's sister, Sarah Stark Winslow, and his wife, Mary Livingston Winslow, were the two politest women I have ever met. They never quarreled or showed suppressed ill will. Yet they didn't entirely get on. My grandmother was an elegant, worldly and witty petite. Her interests were childish. She liked to manage a house and play sedentary games. She was pliant, orderly and always in a stir. Great-Aunt Sarah was deep, dreamy and always afloat on someone else's shoulders. The only music my grandmother could endure was Strauss waltzes. This was because she liked everything about dancing— dancing herself, remembering dances, and watching her daughters dance.

Strauss made her think of Vienna, Vienna made her think of Raleigh, North Carolina where she had grown up. But Great-Aunt Sarah loved the real thing. As a girl she had been a prize pupil of the Abbé Liszt. Always somehow when the day had come for her to give the public recital that would have launched her on her career, she had been prostrated with nerves and fatigue. Strangely enough, she was very charming, gay and brave about her failure. She never snapped or sniffled. But for months she lived in the dim throbbing realms of Debussy, Liszt and Wagner. The reason Great-Aunt Sarah played the dummy piano was that she was afraid of disturbing my grandmother. Therefore it seemed a bit thick for my grandmother to keep saying in her mischievous commonsense voice, "I don't see why Sally drums all day on that thing no one can even hear." That's why Great-Aunt Sarah was counting each turn of the Pierce's motor and saying to herself, "I can't wait."

Really Aunt Sarah was a perfect brick, never a severe word, but under her smile there was a turn at the corners of her mouth that said, "Boy, in unlimited quantities you might make me tired." She stopped playing. "Bobby," she said, "let's play the game of Sole and Souls. I am going to be myself today. You are going to be yourself. Your grandfather doesn't believe this is possible, but nothing is easier. We are going to be *by* ourselves—separately! Come back at five and tell me about it."

Aunt Sarah retired to her bedroom. In the doorway, she turned back to me, and pointed inward to the fragrant darkness. "It's all mine until five and teatime," she said. I stood on the stair landing. I could hear her. She pulled down the heavy green window shades. She pulled down the white summer dust shades. She undressed. She dressed. She wrapped her hairpins in tissue paper. She unwrapped her hairpins. She played her dummy piano. Then I was off. Stalking, climbing, stumbling, I tried to run away from myself. I was Captain Hook, the crook laying a powder-chain. Soon I was getting all the keys out of the doors. Soon I had twenty-seven. They looked identical, but each only fitted its own door. I shook them up in Young Aunt Sarah's conical garden hat. Then I shook them up in my grandfather's silver cocktail shaker. Then I took all the cartridges out of my grandfather's bedside revolver. At five I banged on Aunt Sarah's door. "Ice-tea man," I shouted, "ice-tea man."

Aunt Sarah believed that my grandfather was ruining me with excessive

correction. "Shake your shaker," she said, "you are going to play continue."
Then she began to tell a fantastic version of Little Black Sambo. Sambo was
Sir Walter Raleigh. She held up a scarlet jacket she was knitting. She said,
"this is Sir Walter's cloak. No, these aren't tigers that are running around
him. They are ladies in cloth-of-gold dresses. They wear stomachers, ropes
of pearls and red wigs. They are seven. They are all called Good Queen
Bess, and they are running around Sir Walter because they want to marry
him. They join hands. They hold the trains of each others' dresses in their
mouths. They bob and go in circles like wooden horses on a merry-go-
round. Faster, faster, faster. They lap up each others' dresses like pea soup.
They spin like the yellow spokes of carriage wheels. Look, look; they are by
now so hot and bored that they have all turned into a beautiful yellow puddle of butter. As they deliquesce they sing, *Butter won't melt in our mouths.*"
At this point, suddenly a cartridge exploded and burst through my cocktail
shaker, a mirror was shattered. Keys, water and cartridges gushed over Aunt
Sarah's long haired white rugs. When my grandfather returned, I was sent
to bed for three days. On the second, I had gouged the hole, later covered
over with the Chinese fish. And now seven years later, everything was passing. Away, away, away, sang the leaves. Out of life, out of life, out of life,
answered the locusts.

And between the day of the keys, and this later day of rest and recollection, my uncle Devereux actually has passed out of life. I can remember
his last appearance. It was afternoon, late, late in August. We were drifting
through the screen porch—the geraniums smelled like trolleys. Above us,
as though she were raised on a platform, my great-aunt Sarah was playing
her dummy piano on the glass porch. Her nose was structured, with a beauty
that even in age went beyond belief. She wore a simple gold cress.* Her tremendous Wagnerian themes were soundless. She didn't fit into the setting.
The very curtains that waved about in the hot wind seemed to snuffle, "You
didn't give your recital." She didn't fit. Yet her kindness and tact had kept
her in the ring and performing though not for money. Taste, nuance and
simplicity cherished her. Unchanged and in midair, she had survived, just
as she was at eighteen. No child pointed a finger at her, she wasn't a black
sheep, a skeleton. She liked to think of herself as a chaste Madame de Pom-

* Perhaps a cross, crest, or dress.

padour who had suffered the sorrows of Werther. But in fact she had done nothing worse than fail to marry a Long Island millionaire, and habitually spend too much time packing. The sun blasting through the orange slatted shades made the glass porch where she sat seem like a blazing cow barn, or like Valhalla. My grandmother said half audibly and with unparalleled crossness, "Why does Sally play on that sewing machine all day when no one can even hear her?" I knew something was wrong.

We stood or sat about the back lawn. I was all of three and a half years old. I had been wearing my creased pearl gray flannel shorts for all of three minutes. They felt and looked like the slate under the green baize on my grandfather's pool table. My blue serge coat and jockey's cap had been chosen for me as a joke, and were replicas of those worn by Shem, my grandfather's stuffed ape. My left hand rested on a small pile of black earth; my right rested on a small pile of white sand. I was acting up. I was trying to be perfect and Olympian. I was the model boy in the plate glass window of Rogers Peet's Men's Store below the State House on Tremont St. in Boston.

My grandfather was making a little speech. We were assembled, he said, to celebrate the completion of the *Chardesa* root house, a project long cherished and now brought to completion. He wished to thank his collaborators, John Devereux Winslow, and Harold Pittman, our farmer. "Our wives and fair ones," he said, "can now have fresh Chardesa apples and tomatoes even in the depths of an inclement Massachusetts winter." I don't think my grandfather himself knew if he were joking or in earnest. He brought out two bottles of a champagne that he had brewed himself. It tasted and looked like grasshopper juice, as some said. It didn't pop. No one looked happy.

I wanted unbearably to scratch the red eagle on my sailor blouse, but I kept my stance and neatness. I knew I was dressed to kill, and was setting my cap for Marion Gannon, my nurse. She was just two years out of Ireland. Her eye was as blue as an indoor swimming pool. Her hair had the unearthly pale red of Young Aunt Sarah's French dolls. She was so blankly beautiful that even my grandfather, a rock of sobriety, and a walking decalogue, seemed to wince and wipe his eye whenever she passed. This afternoon I was nettled with Marion because she was monopolizing Mr. Pittman, and actually talking about me to my face, just as my mother did. I might have been deaf and dumb and a pillar of salt. She said, "He's not bad, just simplelike. You can lead him by the nose like a pig, if you flatter the pants off him."

Great-Aunt Sarah was wearing slippers that were as simple as a man's black pumps, only they had old silver buckles and rosettes of lace. One of them was swinging over my piles of sand and dirt. Her laugh gave me the shivers. "Animal, vegetable or mineral?" she said. My mouth opened. It stayed open. I couldn't answer. Then my grandfather explained that sand is "stone ground down by the unpropitious air, by inopportune glaciers . . ." "Listen to the geologist," Aunt Sarah broke in. "All earth still comes out of the woods."

Great-Aunt Sarah is talking to my uncle Devereux. His face is thin, hieratic, animating. His coat and vest are deep blue. His trousers and complexion were cream from the top of the bottle. His glasses kept slipping half an inch down his nose, and were like glasses worn to be comic by someone in a play. Aunt Sarah put a hand on my shoulder. "Barbarism lies ahead," she said. She raised a finger playfully to her heart. "Pit-a-pat. Mannerism lies behind."

My uncle had worked his way up in the cotton mill. Now I knew that he was going to die. He was going from top to bottom. He wasn't coming again in the morning to brighten Mother up and give a tool chest and collapsible ruler. He wasn't going to drag afternoon long on the frozen Charles. He was dying of Hodgkin's disease. I scratched angrily at the red anchor on my white sailor blouse that was like a new jib ballooning. What in the world could I be in want of? Nothing. But fluffs of the west wind came ruffling over the waters, stretched my canvas, and carried me kiting over the seven chimneys of *Chardesa.* I was going far, further than was useful. Already I was passing over the blue steel shotgun barrels, bundles of baby crowbars that fortified my uncle's duck blind, I was passing Assawompset, the great lake. And I was descending for a second visit, to the cabin between the waters. I cowered in shadow under a table in a corner where the nearest windows were boarded because my uncle was shutting up shop for the winter. Light from the ajar door struck loud placards nailed everywhere on the raw splintery wood. Girls, girls, girls. They had goose necks, hair like rooster tails, moles and signatures like the cat's pajamas. Some advertised stockings, but they were pre-War and dressed to extinction. Here was a fat Mr. Punch or Pickwick; he was selling Pimm's stirrup cup. And here was a whole English square going down on the veld before the baboon-brewed Boers. Above them all stood a life-size portrait of Edward VII. Porcine and proper, he was holding up a model of the houses of Parliament, and seemed to be pledging the Eiffel Tower. I could see he had an eye for the girls. My uncle and his friends kept passing me, as though they were walking round and round on the deck of a steamer. In imagination, I still crouched in my corner under a table. The young men kept speaking cheerfully of my grandfather as the old man. "He's not the old man," I would say to myself, "he's just a child." I kept trying to tell them a story I had had from my mother about the Emperor Nero, who had built a golden barge especially for his queen mother—one that had collapsed like a bombarded duck blind. I was no child. Unseen and all-seeing, I was Agrippina in the palace of Nero.

Blue coat, pale cream, stage glasses—my uncle's shadow fell on my piles. Making a terrible effort I mixed the sand and the earth. They mixed to perfect in-between gray. I knew that, come autumn, my uncle would blend to the one color.

But I don't want to go anywhere

BUT I DON'T want to go anywhere; I want to go to Rock."* This was how I used to answer my mother and father, when they planned their highly colored summer trips to Paris, Puget Sound and Bar Harbor. Sometimes my grandfather, Arthur Winslow, would back me up. "Bob," he would say to Father, "that's a hell of a hypothesis." So, summer after summer we went to Mattapoisett, a semi-fashionable Massachusetts seaside town on Buzzards Bay, and some fourteen miles from my grandfather's farm at Rock. Here we found neither society nor solitude. Whenever anyone of us asked, the answer would always be "anywhere but Matt." But we always came back. In my teens I was often fed up, and wished somehow to be true to what I knew and yet tell everyone to drop dead. So I'd say, "I don't want to go anywhere; I want to go to Rock." One of the charms of Rock was that it was more or less nowhere. [. . .]†

This afternoon, Mother was angrier. "Bobby, Bobby!" she said, "why must you stop every rational discussion of places and travel dead by lugging in

---

* This fragment is an alternative version of material in "Rock."

† Here one leaf seems missing from the manuscript. That said, with the possible exception of a five-word sentence, the two surviving pages seem almost contiguous.

Rock?" My father had sighed and answered, "Yes, the same old record. If only the little fellow would use new words." Mother still, however, looked on my obsession with Rock with a certain pride and conspiratorial sympathy. "Bobby does express himself with a rather bloodcurdling monotony and single-mindedness. But he loves Papá better than anyone in the world." That's how she would explain me to the Reading Club, or excuse me to my father.

But what was Rock? Rock was my Carcassonne. And here is a detail that seems make-believe. For many years my favorite poem and one of the few I could tolerate was *Carcassonne*. One night at Rock I was sitting on a carved Swiss music-box bear and reading Bartlett's *Familiar Quotations*. Pinecones popped, copper flashed, stained wood beams threw crooked Teutonic fairy-story shadows. That's how I discovered Nadaud's poem in an English translation.*

> *They* see parading on the wall
> Two bishops and a general;
> But *I* have never been to Carcassonne.

Right away, I knew that I had always been one up on the author of this poem. I had never really been *out* of Carcassonne. When I was away from Rock, Rock was with me to distraction. When I visited the Rock of my distraction was with me. Only in dreams was I out of my dream. Rock was my opium and my breath of fresh air.

But what *was* Rock? Rock was our name for *Chardesa*. *Chardesa* stood for Charlotte, Devereux, and Sarah, my grandfather Winslow's three children, and was the title he gave to his two-hundred-acre farm in Rock, Massachusetts. Rock fitted my grandfather like one of his old London suits. The farmed part of the estate, some twenty acres, was laboriously and awkwardly "in the harness" as one might say. Nothing was neglected; nothing was done without fuss and waywardness. Another five acres was occupied by a spectacular stand of spaced off pine trees. The rest of the estate was just trees cut by big looping paths that my grandfather was always clearing. Nowhere was there any dirt; everywhere there was wilderness.

---

* Gustave Nadaud (1820–1893), a French songwriter, author of the poem "Carcassonne" (1887).

Rock was a fairly, but not very, efficient farm. Rock was a fairly, but not very, attractive park. Rock was a fairly, but not very, wild and fruitful place to hunt and fish. Rock had a pretty bad climate, but not an atrocious one. Rock was short of running water for the baths and toilets. Rock's lake had bloodsuckers, dangerous mussel shells, and was too hot for swimming in mid-July and August. But mostly, and this was its key characteristic, Rock was away from anywhere and anyone. This had surely been my grandfather's secret desire. In the beginning *Chardesa* had been bought ostensibly so that we could be near James Leland, one of Grandfather's business friends.* "Why go to Bar Harbor?" my grandfather had asked my timid grandmother. "People, people, people! You have them all winter in Boston. Mattapoisett is only a fourteen-mile ride from Rock." Once when Mother was telling this story, she recalled an odd and unlucky figure of speech that my grandfather used on this occasion. "James and Mary Leland† are worth any number of fashionable North Shore blue jays." But shortly after my grandparents settled at Rock, Mr. Leland's wife died. A year later he married his housekeeper. My grandfather paid the Lelands two icy visits, but he forbade my grandmother to be at home for their return calls. Soon it turned out that the land we had bought from Leland had a disputed boundary. My grandfather said one day at breakfast, "The ABCs of rectitude require that I sacrifice the charms of amenity." He walked out of the house and called Mr. Leland a thief. The two gentlemen stopped speaking. Strange things began to happen to Leland. He grew a pointed beard like a European monarch. He put up an eight-foot galvanized and perhaps electrified fence wherever his property bordered on *Chardesa*. He bought bloodhounds, and became a recluse. Both Leland and my grandfather stayed on in their houses at Rock for thirty years. I sometimes fear that my grandfather enjoyed driving Leland like a wolf to his burrow, and that later he just couldn't tear himself away from watching and gloating. Leland scarcely spoke to anyone; to accomplish this, Winslow was willing to spend all his summers in a region where he had no friends to speak to. Why, why, why, though, did my grandfather stay on at Rock. Because he wanted to teach his children the country, be-

---

* Indeed, the property immediately to the south of Winslow's was owned by William Sherman Leland, the vice president of the Elliott Five Cents Savings Bank of Boston, and then in 1906 a director of the People's National Bank of Boston.

† Leland was a bachelor all his life, and no records have been found for "James and Mary Leland."

cause he loved solitude, because he wanted to put iron in my grandmother's blood, because he fancied he was holding an outpost like Isaac Winslow the Sheriff and his other seventeenth-century Puritan ancestors, because he couldn't face the wrench of pulling up stakes. Because, because, because . . . My grandfather liked being away, he liked children, he liked giving children the feeling of being away. Besides, there was always Boston in the winter.

My grandmother Winslow

M Y GRANDMOTHER WINSLOW was a bright, sociable little lady from Raleigh, North Carolina.* She enjoyed playing bridge at least two afternoons a week, and reading French novels and French history. By 1930 she had spent some twenty-five summers at *Chardesa*, and loathed each more than the one before it.† My grandmother, or Gaga as I used to call her, always spoke with a tone of cheerfully amused apathy about *Chardesa* and her yearly banishments. Her delight was the garden. And here you could discover something you might otherwise miss in my grandmother's character, so timid and superficial on the surface—she was at bottom vigilant, tolerant and stubborn. My grandparents had long daily arguments; Gaga somehow almost always won by giving up, and then explaining several days later exactly why she was unconvinced. Like America, she lost every battle and won every war—only she was too civilized and sensible to talk or even think about winning.

But to return to *Chardesa*—my grandfather was a Puritan; he saw himself as a changeable Jehovah, one day he was hell on wheels, the next he was raining manna, trips, money and dinners. *Chardesa* was his idea of what this earth should be—Purgatory, and one he could take in his stride. Indeed

---

* This unfinished draft is a variant of "Arthur Winslow III: Dunbarton."

† Indeed, by 1930 it may have been precisely twenty-five years, for Arthur Winslow bought the first lot, with the big house, in February 1905.

there was nothing comely or spectacular about either *Chardesa*'s scenery or its architecture. Its two hundred acres were nine-tenths scrub woods, an endless quarry for making paths, my grandfather's delight. His house was an overgrown farmhouse. Rock was only fourteen miles from New Bedford and the Atlantic Ocean, but its climate, one Southern feature that my grandmother had no desire to import, was like North Carolina's. A Purgatory? Yes, but one Grandfather could take in his stride. Things were often glaringly rough-hewn and even tasteless; yes, but they were grandly comfortable. Gaga was always trying to give up a little luxury for *looks*, as she phrased it. Sweets, settees, beds, poolrooms; surely the good things of the world were everywhere, and yet *Chardesa* often seemed a network of minor and even major discomforts. Such were the hard paths of loneliness that my grandfather built in his search for solitude. *Chardesa* had no neighbors, but it did have Mr. Samuel Hill.* Grandpa had chosen Rock instead of a hundred cooler, more amusing places, solely in order to be near Mr. Samuel Hill. Then two years later the two gentlemen weren't speaking. Mr. Hill had done something unmentionably dishonest in his Boston real estate negotiations. Unmentionably dishonest, no not exactly, somehow it was constantly in the air—only no one could ever quite make clear exactly what Mr. Samuel Hill had done.

---

* Samuel Hill seems to be a different name for a neighbor previously remembered in "But I don't want to go anywhere" as James Leland. Whereas Leland was the actual name of Winslow's neighbor, Hill seems entirely Lowell's invention.

I remember very well
the moment

I REMEMBER VERY WELL the moment when Mother learned that she was to keep house for my grandfather during the summer of 1930. It was a dull winter afternoon. My grandfather was having tea in, of all places, the small Louis Quinze room in his house on Chestnut St. in Boston. He stood up to greet us, but instead of shaking hands, he swung his arms in a circle around the room. "No place for man, boy or post-Victorian woman to sit down in," he said, and gave the fragile little sofas and chairs a pitying smile. "Charlotte," he said, "your mother's fatigued by this simulacrum. She is sailing to France with Sarah for the original." "If they'll wait till June," Mother said, "I'll run Rock for the summer." "Ah," my grandfather said with courtly irony, "Charlotte shall reign at Chardesa."

I can remember when
everybody and his dog

I CAN REMEMBER when everybody and his dog began to tease me with the jingle about Boston being the city of beans, Cabots and cod, where the Lowells spoke only to God.* I was at St. Mark's Boarding School in Southborough, and away from home for the first time. My classmates mostly came from Tuxedo Park and Westport. They found the school's tone penurious and chafing; they felt out of sorts with the New England climate. One afternoon, Billy Butler chased me under the stone hood of the chateau-sized fireplace in the junior common room. We had been reading in Roman history about the Burgundian braves who greased their long yellow hair with rancid butter. Billy's hair was like that, or like a girl's. His nose was arched like Garbo's or an Assyrian's. He was sensitive, powerful, backward and cruel. Billy so terrified me that afternoon, that today, almost thirty years later, I have no need to close my eyes to see him. In front of my nose, he was shaking an expensive compass stolen from mechanical drawing class. The legs opened and shut like the claw of a lobster. "Lowell R.," Billy shouted, "If God talks to the Lowells in Boston, God talks Yiddish, by God!"†

---

* This text is related to material in "Entering St. Mark's."

† In this paragraph Lowell alludes to a well-known toast usually attributed to John Collins Bossidy (1860–1928), which he offered at a 1910 Holy Cross College Alumni Dinner at Harvard: "And this is good old Boston, / The home of the bean and the cod, / Where the Lowells talk to the Cabots / And the Cabots talk

I asked my father about this Yiddish business. Father was a naval offi-cer by profession and faith. Despite his name and connections, he felt like an outsider in Boston. "I don't know about the Lowells," he said, "but of course God talks Yiddish." Father then slipped off into his typical whimsy. "God," he said, "has promised the Zionists that he will brush up on his Hebrew. He finds it hard work talking the King's English and Beacon Hill British to Bishop Lawrence."* Suddenly, Father dropped his eyes, as though he had been blinded by sunlight. He studied the blue naval eagle tattooed on his forearm. He said, "You Bostonians want everyone, even God and Calvin Coolidge, to be cold fish and close as clams." I was no more than twelve years old and a blithe second-former, but something in my father's voice made me feel meant and insulted. [. . .]

---

only to God." Lowell also seems to be reworking—or so does the boy who stalked him—a later parody of the same toast, which ended with the line "And the Cabots speak Yiddish, by God!" The parody became popular in 1923 after a Jewish immigrant, Harry H. Kabotchnik from Philadelphia, was permitted by the U.S. courts to change his name to Cabot, against the petitions of the Boston Cabots.

* William Lawrence (1850–1941), the bishop of the Episcopal Diocese of Massachusetts.

The farm at Rock

T
HE FARM AT Rock, Massachusetts[,] was called *Chardesa* after my grandparents' three children, Charlotte, Devereux and Sarah.* Some fifteen years ago, the main building was torn down for its glass, metal and timber, and people in the neighborhood will still tell you that these raw materials brought the new owner double his purchase price for the entire farm and its two hundred acres.† They will also tell you that real estate speculations once trebled the fortune of my grandfather, Arthur Winslow—trebled his fortune only to fail him utterly during the crash and reduce him almost to bankruptcy. For a short time Mr. Winslow and his tribulations were known locally as a sort of Titanic, and exemplar of the pride of life. Towards the end of his life, when he was impoverished, disgusted and dying, he spoke of the sale of *Chardesa* as his last bad bargain. "All topsy-turvy," he used to say about his life and principles. Be that as may be, he made heroic maneuvers with trusts and insurance policies, and really pretty well took care of his wife, daughters and dependents. What more could one ask—he was a vigorous generous man; he had lived.

* This material is related to "Arthur Winslow VI."

† The house was purchased from the Winslow estate in 1940 by Edward Dunn and torn down in early 1943.

Mother's neatness was compulsive

OTHER'S NEATNESS WAS compulsive, competitive, romantic and *chic*. In a diary begun thirty years later, and almost immediately firmly discontinued, she once wrote, "I have loved beauty and . . ."

The other day I came across an autobiographical [piece] written by my mother in 1937 at the request of her psychologist.

A few months after Mother's death in 1954,* I went through her papers and discovered a notebook, written in 1937, when she had just begun to have interviews with a psychiatrist, Freudian like mine. The spelling is a miracle of inaccuracy due to ignorance, but also due to impatience. The notes soon become mere quotations from psychiatry books that Mother was reading. However, the first five or six pages are personal: they are an autobiographical sketch disguised as a third-person description of Miss B.

Mother's account shows courage and self-knowledge, and refuses to evade. Here are excerpts exactly as she wrote:

"Miss B's father was a conscientious discipinarian, so busy in uprooting what was bad that he distroyed and damaged much that was good. Her

---

* This sentence appears on the same manuscript page as the preceding sentence. It seems as though Lowell wanted to change the point in time when he allegedly discovered his mother's notebook.

mother was suppressed and unhappy, rather superficeal, but was completely dominated by her husband, who insisted on running everything, with constant criticism and direction." Her father's discipline was "eratic but severe." As a child Miss B was "selfconscious, intreverted, aggressive and rather deceitful." "Being a rather lonely and malajusted child, retreated into a world of dreams and unreality, And spent an increasing amount of time in this way (Began at about 10, years, encreased till about 26, ans lasted until over 40)." She was "absolutely powerful and perfect in this way and resisted exeration of any kind."

"Miss B. married, because she thought it was time to. She was not at all in love with the man, nor did she really admire him, but he seemed the best that was offered, She rather enjoyed his admiration, and thought she might improve him, and would be free herself, and away from the constant family frictions and quarrels, which she thought degrading."

"But she also thought she was doing a very wrong thing in marrying this man whom she did not love, and often felt that she would be punished for it, as she was always punished for doing what was wrong."

"After this marriage . . . having to live in constant companionship with this comparative stranger, whom she found neither agreeable, interesting, nor admirable, was a terrible nervous strain. She became increasingly critical and unappreciative. She wished to do nothing and see no one. She was utterly hysterical, and would have liked to die, but the idea of (Playing the game,) kept her from doing it. So to the world, her family, and her friends, she appeared happy and serine. She was determined not to whine and be a Coward; but what a lot of care she made for herself!"

Her husband "could not understand at all, was always kind, though irresponsible; and thought her half crazy."

Grandfather died in 1937

GRANDFATHER DIED in 1937.* Ages before that, he had entered into the Kingdom. This happened when he first connected the profits of his Liberty Bell Mine in Telluride, Colorado, with the possibility of cutting a figure in Boston. In the imagination, alas, and for our children, all our big wishes come true. What Mother inherited was the metallic bareness of glory. At twelve, a stout girl sleeping on an army cot and reading lives of Napoleon, she was already fated to become a Mrs. Lowell of Boston.

Thus, all through life, she was to have the joyful energy of a colt or a boy. How she adored walking out into our violently changing climate, breasting the stiff river winds of the Esplanade, and dreaming about her hot bath! Yet her brow always trembled with worry. She had such true, contradictory and unspeakable reflections. When the question of moving to another city came up in conversation, she could never own up and say, "I believe in my father's City," or "I crave what I am used to," or "What I've stood, I'll stand," or "I'm stuck here like a pigeon on a spike."

Poor Mother! She had buckets of courage. But even in her final years, when her education was jumping ahead like a yearling poodle, her heart was so much stronger than her brain! She knew that not only propriety, but life's very blood and marrow required that she believe her own half-

* Arthur Winslow died March 28, 1938.

understood verbal evasions. Thought and struggling were somehow impossible for her without evasion; evasion was impossible without struggle. She salted and resalted her leisure until her lips winced with the tartness. Her conscience and her lassitude were always simultaneously bawling for their pints of blood. In her diary, Mother once wrote, "I have loved luxury and Jung." Yes; but she had to have them together and strangling one another. To her, mere luxury was criminal; mere Jung was cant. Whenever the question of moving to another city would come up in conversation, Mother would answer with a comfortable smile and a delicate fluttering frown, "Boston is more practical."

Crisis and Aftermath

On a flashing morning in July

O N A F L A S H I N G M O R N I N G in July of 1954, I sat in my bedroom on the third floor of the Payne Whitney Clinic.* I heard the elevator clang as it soared to Occupational Therapy with the last of my fellow patients. The luxury of their absence inebriated me, blinded me; for a few seconds I felt the yeasty manic lift of my sickness. Two unfinished and penciled drafts of a letter lay on the blotting paper before me. The letter, a trial balloon, was addressed first to one person, then to a second, then to a third. "Although I of course cannot kick against having committed myself, I . . ." I had so mastered the right tone of voice that whenever I snoozed a little my argument seemed to creak forward for whole paragraphs filled with passion, logic and eloquence . . . and I had nothing, nothing to say. My mother. My father.

The deep drop of the side of the hospital right below my window was in shadow, a splinter of cold stone and unsunned air, a sliver of rigor mortis standing out against the gross, swarming swelter of summer in New York City.

---

* An alternative beginning of "The Balanced Aquarium."

I began writing about
myself in 1954

I BEGAN WRITING about myself in 1954, when I was recovering from a violent manic seizure in the Payne Whitney Clinic.* The mornings there were long because after breakfast and bed making and an informal lounging and television news period we were all expected to walk for some forty minutes in the courtyard. It was a formal, flowerless place, covered with bright gray, octagonal paving stones and looking like some unaccountably secluded and clean French place.

Two and two, we walked round and round and without any props or screens or diverting games, we tried to make conversation. It was thought uncooperative and morbid if we walked with another man. The women were terrible to me. Some were concave and depressed, some worried endlessly about their doctors' feelings and remarks, some flattered, some flirted, some made fierce, well-expressed sarcastic thrusts—they all talked. Distant, thorny, horny, absent-minded, ineptly polite, vacantly rude, I walked with the ladies. They were hurt, and I was hurt. The men were almost as bad. I had my cronies, but I had soon exhausted their novelty, which mattered little to me. What hurt me was that I in a matter of minutes used up any strength I had to be new or fresh or even there. Then there were the student nurses,

* This is an alternative version of the courtyard scene near the beginning of "The Balanced Aquarium."

crisp-fronted, pageboy-bobbed, pale-blue-denim-bloused, reading new *Herald Tribune*s and idling watchfully at strategic angles of the courtyard; they were ready to gently engage me and bring me back if ever I dawdled into single file or sat down by myself on a bench.

The unflowering shrubbery was healthily a full green, the leaves were all there and in spite of the dusty dreariness of midsummer New York all about us, all seemed cool, spontaneous and adequate. That's how all the other patients seemed. And a great iron gate, some twenty feet high, protected us from the city and living, as we often told each other, meaning nothing. The gate was just a gate, though not quite because, like everything else at the clinic, it was a little bit prettier and more ornate than use demanded. It was really locked, and a patient would have to have been an athlete or a thief to have gotten by it. Beyond it we could see the blinding blue sparkle of the East River. Often an orange tugboat was moored a few feet away from us. It had a swollen fleece-and-rawhide buffer on its prow. As if begging admission to our asylum, the boat kept rising with chafing sounds against the concrete embankment.

I sat looking out

I SAT LOOKING out of my bedroom window at the Clinic, and once more began to type at a poem, my substitute for the regulation Occupational Therapy requirement.* I wrote:

I was already halfway through my life,
When I woke up from Mother on the back
Of the Hill in Boston, to a skyline of Life
Insurance buildings,† still in blueprint.

Then the labor, cynicism, and maturity of writing in meter became horrible. I began to write rapidly in prose and in the style of a child.

...name, Bobby Lowell. I was all of three and a half. My new formal grey shorts had been worn for all of three minutes. Autumn played cops and robbers over my ankles. [...]

* This sketch is related to the material in "The Balanced Aquarium."

† Presumably, 501 Boylston Street, originally a multiunit building built between 1939 and 1942, the headquarters of New England Mutual Life Insurance.

A Life Among Writers

Philip Rahv

T HE WINTER OF 1942,[*] the Pennsylvania Railway Station, New York—out of the black brown smelly barrenness, two figures, both substantial, one gold and white,[†] one cropped black hair, wan brown face, in a fudge brown suit. Rahv wasn't fat, just sizable; this was reassuring, like his age, no age, yet always five or ten years more than any youngish person he was with. There have been others, the ancients, to whom Rahv seemed five or ten years younger, someone to be spoken to casually, but with etiquette.[‡] Except for Marianne Moore, he seldom sought them. It seems impossible, but the Rahvs and my wife and I became instant friends. I don't remember any conversation on the train; we were too shy,

* Lowell's January 18, 1974, letter to Elizabeth Hardwick explains why he left the piece unfinished. It had become his habit to write eulogies on their dead friends, especially for *The New York Review of Books*, but this time—after Philip Rahv's death on December 22, 1973—she relieved him of the task and published hers in the magazine's January 24, 1974, issue. Seeing her piece, he abandoned his draft and wrote to her with praise: "Delighted with your Philip. It seems to say everything for and against imaginable in your short space—and more than what is possible in a funeral speech. Yet I don't imagine anyone is hurt. I started a piece on him for *Commentary* and had actually written a little less than two pages . . . when I read you. I felt a great relief of not having to go on, you made it unnecessary; mine was a rambly reminiscence beginning during the War with going with the first Rahvs to hear Randall lecture at Princeton with Allen very himself presiding." See Robert Lowell, *The Letters of Robert Lowell*, edited by Saskia Hamilton (New York: Farrar, Straus and Giroux, 2005), 619. Lowell misremembers the season in the memoir's opening. The recollection takes place not in winter but on April 30, 1942, that being the date of Jarrell's Mesures Lecture at Princeton.

† Nathalie Swan, Rahv's first wife, an architect whom he married in 1941.

‡ The crossed-out alternative was "consideration."

the Rahvs were laconic. The train was going to Princeton; we were making the burdensome trip together to hear the first public lecture by Randall Jarrell, still in the Air Force. The Rahvs were the first non-Catholic intellectuals we had met in five months; we were to be the only readers of *Partisan Review* at the lecture who were New Yorkers.

The lecture, Jarrell's first, half bristled with Kenneth Burke, Arnold Toynbee, and Marx.* It was lumpily abstract, hard to follow and fifteen minutes too long. It was fireworks, so much so that Randall would often pause and look smilingly at his audience. He assumed our sympathy against wittily disguised opponents. Sometimes he would chuckle. As he stepped from the platform, intoxicated—he didn't drink—Allen Tate came up, took his arm, and said, "Randall, the thesis in your paper is remarkable, but take it from an old hand, your delivery is appalling."

The party after this at the Tates flitters—except for Rahv. My wife, Jean Stafford, was escorted by a bodyguard, the publisher (also Jarrell's) of her still-unwritten first novel.† But there were other novelists there who had published many novels and were unescorted. There was a confrontation between the Tates and Richard Blackmur. "Dick, I hear some stupid students think my husband is more interesting as a novelist."‡ Then Blackmur, prim Charlie Chaplin mustache, beautiful metallic New England voice, a slight, steady irrelevant smile, answered, separating Tate's poetry, criticism and novel. He was so merry, unruffled and absorbed in his points that one forgot if he had ever been lofty. Jarrell strained so greatly to show himself cool, unrattled by Tate's harsh rebuff, that [he] kept by a wall and talked to no one except his wife, us, [and] a rather dubious academic, an Ameri-

---

* At first thought lost, the manuscript of Jarrell's Princeton lecture, entitled "Levels and Opposites: Structure in Poetry," was rediscovered by Thomas Travisano and published in *The Georgia Review* 50, no. 4 (1996): 697–713.

† The publisher is Robert Giroux, who was a young editor at Harcourt Brace at the time, and the two books in question were Stafford's *Boston Adventure* (1944) and Jarrell's *Blood for a Stranger* (1942). Giroux actually brought Stafford's contract to Princeton for her to sign at the very party occasioned by Jarrell's lecture. Caroline Gordon, Tate's wife, turned the signing into a mock lavish ceremony with candles. See Ann Hulbert, *The Interior Castle: The Art and Life of Jean Stafford* (New York: Alfred A. Knopf, 1992), 140–41.

‡ If the Tates were arguing with Blackmur about "my husband . . . as a novelist," the speaker would be Caroline Gordon and the husband Allen Tate, whose novel *The Fathers* (1938) received more attention than any of Gordon's novels—for example, *Green Centuries* (1941). It sounds more like a confrontation "between the Tates," with Blackmur as an onlooker trying to defuse the situation.

can instructor in French at Rutgers. One fled and came back to this circle of constraint. Somehow one was reassured by Rahv, his almost silent substance, his hoarse, husky, Slavic whisper cutting through the hysteria of the Anglo-Saxon.

(Composed January 1974)

GENEALOGICAL CHART I:
THE WINSLOWS, THE STARKS,
AND THE DEVEREUXS

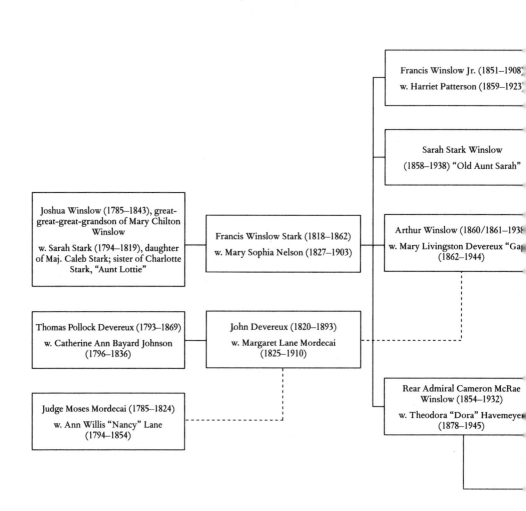

Francis Winslow Jr. (1851–1908)

w. Harriet Patterson (1859–1923)

Sarah Stark Winslow
(1858–1938) "Old Aunt Sarah"

Joshua Winslow (1785–1843), great-great-great-great-grandson of Mary Chilton Winslow

w. Sarah Stark (1794–1819), daughter of Maj. Caleb Stark; sister of Charlotte Stark, "Aunt Lottie"

Francis Winslow Stark (1818–1862)

w. Mary Sophia Nelson (1827–1903)

Arthur Winslow (1860/1861–1938)

w. Mary Livingston Devereux "Gaga" (1862–1944)

Thomas Pollock Devereux (1793–1869)

w. Catherine Ann Bayard Johnson (1796–1836)

John Devereux (1820–1893)

w. Margaret Lane Mordecai (1825–1910)

Judge Moses Mordecai (1785–1824)

w. Ann Willis "Nancy" Lane (1794–1854)

Rear Admiral Cameron McRae Winslow (1854–1932)

w. Theodora "Dora" Havemeyer (1878–1945)

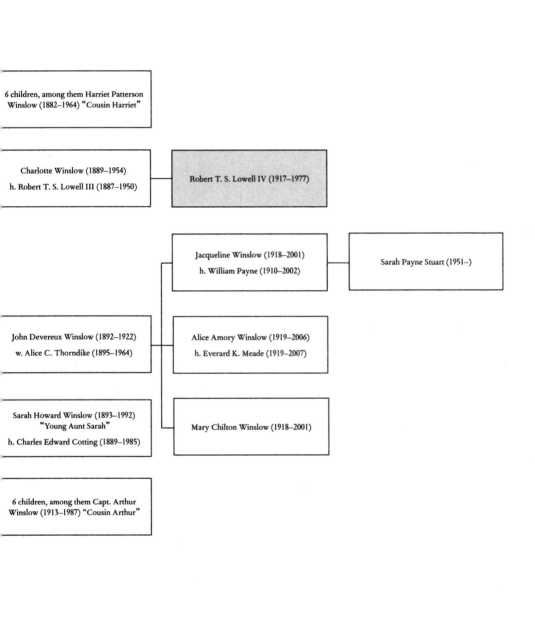

6 children, among them Harriet Patterson Winslow (1882–1964) "Cousin Harriet"

Charlotte Winslow (1889–1954)
h. Robert T. S. Lowell III (1887–1950)

Robert T. S. Lowell IV (1917–1977)

Jacqueline Winslow (1918–2001)
h. William Payne (1910–2002)

Sarah Payne Stuart (1951–)

John Devereux Winslow (1892–1922)
w. Alice C. Thorndike (1895–1964)

Alice Amory Winslow (1919–2006)
h. Everard K. Meade (1919–2007)

Sarah Howard Winslow (1893–1992)
"Young Aunt Sarah"
h. Charles Edward Cotting (1889–1985)

Mary Chilton Winslow (1918–2001)

6 children, among them Capt. Arthur Winslow (1913–1987) "Cousin Arthur"

GENEALOGICAL CHART II:

THE LOWELLS AND THE MYERSES

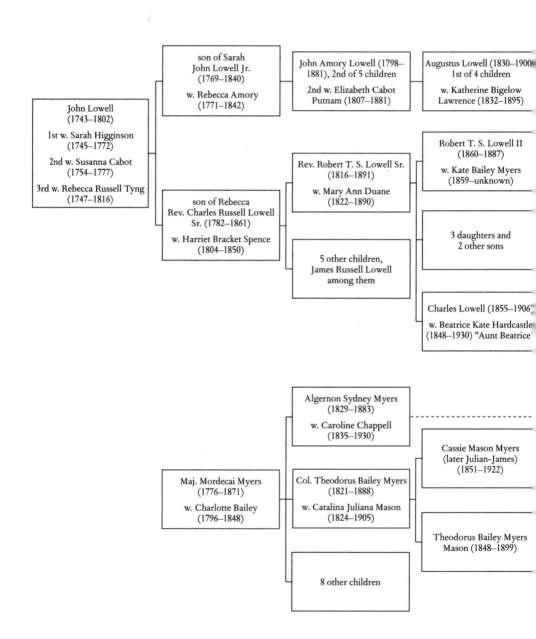

John Lowell (1743–1802)
1st w. Sarah Higginson (1745–1772)
2nd w. Susanna Cabot (1754–1777)
3rd w. Rebecca Russell Tyng (1747–1816)

son of Sarah
John Lowell Jr. (1769–1840)
w. Rebecca Amory (1771–1842)

John Amory Lowell (1798–1881), 2nd of 5 children
2nd w. Elizabeth Cabot Putnam (1807–1881)

Augustus Lowell (1830–1900) 1st of 4 children
w. Katherine Bigelow Lawrence (1832–1895)

son of Rebecca
Rev. Charles Russell Lowell Sr. (1782–1861)
w. Harriet Bracket Spence (1804–1850)

Rev. Robert T. S. Lowell Sr. (1816–1891)
w. Mary Ann Duane (1822–1890)

5 other children, James Russell Lowell among them

Robert T. S. Lowell II (1860–1887)
w. Kate Bailey Myers (1859–unknown)

3 daughters and 2 other sons

Charles Lowell (1855–1906)
w. Beatrice Kate Hardcastle (1848–1930) "Aunt Beatrice"

Maj. Mordecai Myers (1776–1871)
w. Charlotte Bailey (1796–1848)

Algernon Sydney Myers (1829–1883)
w. Caroline Chappell (1835–1930)

Col. Theodorus Bailey Myers (1821–1888)
w. Catalina Juliana Mason (1824–1905)

8 other children

Cassie Mason Myers (later Julian-James) (1851–1922)

Theodorus Bailey Myers Mason (1848–1899)

7 children, among them Percival Lowell, the astronomer; Amy Lowell, the poet; and Abbott Lawrence, Harvard president

Robert T. S. Lowell III
(Jul 15, 1887–1950)

w. Charlotte Winslow

Robert T. S. Lowell IV
(1917–1977)

1st w. Jean Stafford
(1915–1979)

2nd w. Elizabeth
Hardwick (1916–2007)

3rd w. Caroline Blackwood
(1931–1996)

daughter of Elizabeth
Harriet Winslow Lowell
(1957–)

son of Caroline
Robert Sheridan Lowell
(1971–)

Alfred Putnam Lowell
(1890–1954)

w. Catherine Hayward Bowles
(1890–1969)
daughter of Adm. Francis
T. Bowles and Adelaide H.
Savage ("Dada")

Frances Bowles Lowell
(later Hunsaker)(1916–2011)

h. James Peter Hunsaker Sr.
(1915–1959)

Beatrice Hardcastle Lowell
(later Magruder),
"Biddie"(1918–2013)

h. Lloyd Burns Magruder Jr.
(1917–1999)

Christina Lowell
(later Brazelton),
"Chrissie"(1921–2015)

h. T. Berry Brazelton
(1918–2018)

TIME LINE

1915   In the winter, Robert Traill Spence Lowell III (Bob) and Charlotte Winslow meet at the engagement party of Catherine Hay Bowles and Alfred Putnam Lowell, in the house of Alfred and his mother, Beatrice Hardcastle Lowell.

1916   Bob Lowell and Charlotte Winslow marry on April 26 in Trinity Church in Boston. On their honeymoon, they travel to the Grand Canyon. Soon afterward, Bob is transferred to Jamestown Naval Station, near Newport, Rhode Island, and Charlotte accompanies him. In the fall, Bob is transferred to Guantánamo Bay in Cuba. In the meantime, Charlotte, who is pregnant, moves to Staten Island to stay with her mother-in-law, Kate Bailey Lowell, and her husband's grandmother Caroline Myers, née Chappell.

1917   Robert Traill Spence Lowell IV (RL) is born on March 1 at his grandfather Arthur Winslow's town house at 18 Chestnut Street in Beacon Hill. The Lowells move to a house at 50 Brimmer Street.

1918   RL at 50 Brimmer Street.

1919   In January, Bob is transferred to the naval yard in Philadelphia. Arthur and Mary Winslow, presumably with Charlotte Lowell and RL, spend the summer at Annisquam, Massachusetts. In September, Charlotte and RL take a train to follow Bob to Philadelphia. The reunited family moves into "a pleasant house near Rittenhouse Square."

1920   Either at Christmas 1919 or in March 1920, Grandfather Arthur Winslow makes a surprise visit to the Lowells in Philadelphia. The Lowells, or at least Charlotte and RL, spend the summer at Arthur Winslow's farm at Rock Village, in Middleborough, Plymouth County, Massachusetts.

1921   The Lowells stay in Philadelphia until the summer, when Bob is reassigned to the Charlestown Navy Yard. Back in Boston, they move into 44 West Cedar Street, with RL spending the summer between Rock and Barnstable on Cape Cod. The Lowells' first house, 50 Brimmer Street, is sold.

1922   RL is enrolled in kindergarten at the Brimmer School at 67–69 Brimmer Street at the corner of Chestnut Street, in Beacon Hill (today Park Street Elementary School). John Devereux Winslow, RL's uncle and Charlotte's brother, dies of Hodgkin's disease on November 16.

1923   Brimmer School kindergarten. In July, or just before, Bob is transferred to Washington, D.C. The family's new address is 2129 Bancroft Place. Lowell attends the Potomac School at 2144 California Street. In August President Warren G. Harding dies. Bob, as a U.S. Navy commander, participates in the funeral.

1924   Still in Washington, D.C., Charlotte and RL spend the summer in Massachusetts, probably at a Sarah Barnard Estate cottage in Cannonville, Mattapoisett, presumably at 6 Shipyard Lane.

1925   Washington, D.C., until at least May. In the summer or fall, the Lowells move back to Boston. Bob obtains the position of second-in-command at Charlestown Navy Shipyard. RL is reenrolled at the Brimmer School. In about August, the family buys and moves into the house at 91 Revere Street.

1926   RL at Brimmer School.

1927   RL at Brimmer School. Bob resigns from the navy to begin his career at the American branch of Lever Brothers Soap. With high financial expectations, the Lowells buy a house at 170 Marlborough Street in the spring, probably in March. They also sell their old Hudson and buy a new Buick. In June, RL graduates from Brimmer; in September, he is enrolled in the Rivers School at 290 Dean Road in Brookline, one of the "open-air"—that is, unheated—schools.

1928   RL at Rivers School.

1929   RL at Rivers School.

1930   RL at Rivers School. Spends the summer with his family between Rock and Mattapoisett. Arthur Winslow, Gaga, and Great-Aunt Sarah probably go on a tour to Europe, leaving Charlotte in charge of her father's summer house "Chardesa." In September RL enters St. Mark's School.

1931   RL at St. Mark's School. Plays football and ice hockey.

1932   RL at St. Mark's School. In January, RL's great-uncle Cameron Winslow dies.

1933   RL at St. Mark's School. Poet Richard Eberhart joins faculty. RL develops close friendships with Frank Parker and Blair Clark.

1934   In the summer, RL becomes a counselor at Brantwood Camp, run by St. Mark's for poor boys from the Boston area, in Peterborough, New Hampshire. Inspired by the camp's notions of self-discipline and self-development, he "finds" himself. The epiphany consists of his resolution to become a (prose) writer. In the fall RL becomes the associate editor of *Vindex*, the literary magazine of St. Mark's. He is also a fullback on the varsity football team.

1935   Between March and June, five of RL's articles are published in *Vindex*. He enters Harvard in the fall, moving into Lowell House, room A-41.

1936   In March, RL visits Robert Frost, who stays at Harvard to give the Norton Lectures. Financial adversity forces Arthur Winslow to sell 18 Chestnut Street and to move to an apartment at 10 Otis Place, near the Charles River Esplanade. He also sells most of his other Beacon Hill real estate. In May, RL meets Anne Tuckerman Dick. They become engaged. In December, RL knocks his father down in a quarrel about the engagement.

1937   RL abandons Harvard and his engagement in the spring. He travels south to Tennessee. Attends lectures by John Crowe Ransom at Vanderbilt. In the summer, he sets up a tent on the lawn of Allen Tate and Caroline Gordon at Benfolly in Clarksville, Tennessee. In July and August, he serves as a secretary to Ford Madox Ford. In September, RL enrolls at Kenyon College in Gambier, Ohio, to study under Ransom, who has transferred there. RL moves into a second-floor bedroom at Ransom's house, where he rooms with fellow student Randall Jarrell. He also becomes friends with Peter Taylor. In December, RL visits his grandfather Arthur Winslow at his apartment on Otis Place.

1938   RL at Kenyon College. On March 28, Grandfather Winslow dies of prostate cancer at the Phillips House, a luxury section of the Massachusetts General Hospital. Starting in April, RL becomes a regular contributor to *Hika*, a student magazine at Kenyon College. In July, Great-Aunt Sarah dies. In December he has a car crash in which Jean Stafford breaks her nose.

1939   RL at Kenyon College. In the spring and summer, Stafford undergoes facial surgeries. She sues the Lowells for compensation. In June, Ford Madox Ford dies. In the fall RL proposes to Stafford.

1940   On April 2, RL marries Jean Stafford. He graduates summa cum laude from Kenyon. Rock farm is sold. RL receives a fellowship at Louisiana State University in Baton Rouge, for graduate study under Robert Penn Warren.

1941   In March, RL is baptized and received into the Catholic Church. In September, he takes a job with the publishing house Sheed & Ward. He and Stafford move to 63 West 11th Street in New York City.

1942   In the summer, RL and Stafford travel to Tennessee to stay with the Tates in Monteagle, Tennessee. There RL prepares to write a biography of Jonathan Edwards, but in the fall starts working on his first volume of poems instead.

1943   The house in Rock is torn down in April. In September, RL writes an open letter to President Roosevelt explaining his reasons for refusing the draft. In October, RL is sentenced to a year and a day in prison. Sent first to West Street Jail in New York, then, after ten days, to the Federal Correctional Center in Danbury, Connecticut.

1944   In March, RL is released on parole. When free, he moves, with Stafford, to an apartment in Black Rock, Connecticut. In July, RL's *Land of Unlikeness* is published. In September, RL and Stafford move to "the Barn" in Westport, Connecticut. RL meets John Berryman at Princeton. Grandmother Mary Livingston Devereux "Gaga" Winslow dies on November 24.

1945   In September, RL and Stafford move into a house in Damariscotta Mills, Maine, which Stafford buys with money earned from her novel *Boston Adventure*.

1946   Between January and March, the Lowells stay with Delmore Schwartz in Cambridge, Massachusetts. In September, after a difficult summer in Damariscotta Mills, RL and Stafford separate. Both move to New York City. RL begins a relationship with Gertrude Buckman. In December, *Lord Weary's Castle* is published.

1947   *Lord Weary's Castle* wins the Pulitzer Prize for Poetry. Beginning in October, RL serves for a year as the poetry consultant to the Library of Congress. He visits Ezra Pound at St. Elizabeth's Hospital. Meets T. S. Eliot and William Carlos Williams.

1948   RL and Jean Stafford divorce. He spends the summer at Yaddo, and then serves on the Bollingen Prize committee.

1949   In June, Charlotte and Bob Lowell sell the house at 170 Marlborough Street to move to Beverly Farms, a posh neighborhood in Beverly, Massachusetts, an hour and twenty minutes by train from Boston's North Station. In July, RL marries Elizabeth Hardwick. Suffers acute manic episode at Yaddo.

1950   Bob dies on August 30 at Beverly Hospital. In September, RL and Hardwick embark for Europe. They arrive in Florence, where they rent a house. They visit George Santayana in Rome.

1951   From Florence, RL and Hardwick make trips to southern France, Pisa, and Siena, and also travel to Turkey, Austria, France, and Spain. Eventually RL and Hardwick settle in Amsterdam for the winter, at his insistence. In the fall, *The Mills of the Kavanaughs* is published.

1952   In the summer, RL teaches at the Salzburg Seminar in American Civilization. Descending again into mania, he is confined in the American Army Hospital in Salzburg, then in the U.S. Army Hospital in Munich. In September, RL and Hardwick travel to Venice and Torcello before settling in Rome.

1953   In January, RL and Hardwick return to the United States. He obtains a teaching position at the University of Iowa Writers' Workshop.

1954   Starting February, RL assumes a teaching position at the University of Cincinnati. On February 13, RL's mother, Charlotte, dies in Rapallo, Italy. Lowell delays arriving until after she has died. He has his mother's body transported home and interred in the Stark Cemetery in Dunbarton, New Hampshire. On April 8, RL is committed to the Jewish Hospital in Cincinnati; in May he is moved to the Payne Whitney Psychiatric Clinic in New York. Payne Whitney discharges him on September 17. He and Hardwick move to 33 Commonwealth Avenue, a block from the Boston Public Garden. RL writes autobiographical prose.

1955   In February, Hardwick's novel *The Simple Truth* appears. In April, RL signs a contract with Farrar, Straus and Cudahy for an autobiography in prose. In the fall, he and Hardwick move to 239 Marlborough Street in the Back Bay. RL begins teaching at Boston University.

1956   In July, RL gives a talk titled "Art and Evil" at Bard. In the fall, *Partisan Review* publishes "91 Revere Street."

1957   On January 4, Hardwick gives birth to Harriet Winslow Lowell. RL ceases work on his prose autobiography. In March, RL goes on a West Coast reading tour. RL and Hardwick spend the summer in Castine, Maine. He may have met Anne Sexton for the first time. Begins writing "Skunk Hour" in August. In December, again manic, he is confined to Boston State Hospital and Massachusetts Mental Health Center in Boston.

1958   RL is moved to McLean Hospital just outside Boston, where he stays inter-
        mittently until May. In the fall, he teaches a poetry workshop (English 306)
        at Boston University, with Sexton as one of his students.

1959   In the spring, he continues to teach the creative writing course. Sylvia
        Plath joins class as an auditor. In May *Life Studies* is published.

1960   Sometime this year, RL becomes acquainted with Hannah Arendt through
        Mary McCarthy. Around the turn of the year, the Lowells move to New
        York City.

1961   In January, RL, Hardwick, and Harriet move into an apartment at 15 West
        Sixty-Seventh Street, off Central Park in Manhattan. In March, RL is di-
        agnosed with mania, admitted to Columbia-Presbyterian Hospital in New
        York. In July, the Lowells sell 239 Marlborough. In November, *Imitations*
        is published.

1962   From June through September, RL travels in South America as a guest of
        the Congress for Cultural Freedom. Between September and November,
        he suffers another bout of mania; is hospitalized at the Institute of Living
        in Hartford, Connecticut.

1963   In January, Robert Frost dies. In February, Sylvia Plath commits suicide.
        Also in February, *The New York Review of Books* is launched, cofounded by
        Hardwick. In March, William Carlos Williams dies. RL begins teaching at
        Harvard. He has a mild manic attack in December and is admitted again to
        the Institute of Living.

1964   *For the Union Dead* is published. *The Old Glory* is rehearsed and staged.

1965   In January, T. S. Eliot dies; RL has another manic attack and is hospital-
        ized, until February, at the Institute of Living. In March, RL visits Ezra
        Pound in Rapallo. In June, RL writes an open letter to President Johnson,
        citing Johnson's escalation policy in Vietnam as the reason for his decision
        not to accept an invitation to the White House Festival of the Arts. In Oc-
        tober, Randall Jarrell dies under the wheels of a car. In December, RL is
        hospitalized for mania at McLean Hospital.

1966   Hospitalized at McLean until February. RL spends the summer in Castine,
        and in the fall, begins teaching another seminar at Harvard. Composing
        Near the Ocean and a version of *Prometheus Bound*. In December, he is
        again hospitalized at McLean.

1967   RL stays at the hospital until March. In April, he helps produce his adap-
        tation of *Prometheus Bound* by Yale Drama School. In about May, RL is

prescribed lithium carbonate for his bipolar mood disorder. *Near the Ocean* is published. In October, RL participates in the antiwar March on the Pentagon. In December, he and Hardwick participate in a Congress for Cultural Freedom conference in Venezuela.

1968   In the spring, RL participates in Senator Eugene McCarthy's campaign for the presidency. In August, he attends the Democratic National Convention in Chicago. In November, he engages in a debate with Diana Trilling concerning antiwar protest.

1969   In the spring, RL travels to Israel and Spain. In June *Notebook 1967–68* is published. After the summer spent in Castine, he resumes teaching at Harvard.

1970   RL moves to England, initially as a Fellow at All Souls College at Oxford. He meets Caroline Blackwood, and in May, he moves into her apartment at 80 Redcliffe Square. In the summer, he is hospitalized for mania at Greenways Nursing Home in London. In the fall, he moves into a rented apartment at 33 Pont Street in London. He teaches at the University of Essex. He spends Christmas with Hardwick and Harriet, working on *The Dolphin*.

1971   In January, RL returns to London and resumes teaching at the University of Essex. In February, he learns that Blackwood is pregnant with their child. In June, they move to Milgate Park in Maidstone, Kent, and RL commutes from Maidstone to Colchester. In September, the couple's son, Robert Sheridan Lowell, is born.

1972   In January, John Berryman commits suicide. RL writes a memoir of Berryman for *The New York Review of Books*. He continues to teach at the University of Essex. In Santo Domingo, Dominican Republic, in October, he divorces Hardwick and marries Blackwood. In November, Ezra Pound dies.

1973   On January 4, RL attends Pound's memorial service. *History*, *For Lizzie and Harriet*, and *The Dolphin* are published.

1974   In April, RL is awarded the Pulitzer Prize for *The Dolphin*. In July, John Crowe Ransom dies. In October, Anne Sexton commits suicide.

1975   In February, RL leaves Milgate for Boston to teach at Harvard. During spring and early summer, he prepares, with the help of Frank Bidart and Robert Giroux, a two-hundred-page manuscript collecting much of his critical prose, *A Moment in American Poetry*, which is never published. In November, back in Kent, he has a manic attack and is confined at Priory Hospital in London, then Greenways Nursing Home. In December, Hannah Arendt dies.

1976   RL is hospitalized for mania until mid-February, in its last stage at St. An-
        drew's Hospital in Northampton. In May, *The New York Review of Books*
        prints RL's eulogy for Arendt. In September, he is readmitted to Greenways.

1977   *Day by Day* is published. RL is reunited with Hardwick and summers with
        her in Castine. He dies from heart failure in a taxicab ride from the airport,
        having just returned to New York from a visit with Caroline Blackwood,
        their son, and her three daughters at Castletown House in rural Ireland.
        The funeral service is held at the Episcopal Church of the Advent in Bos-
        ton; RL is buried in the Stark Cemetery beside his parents' graves.

ACKNOWLEDGMENTS

The editors want to thank the Robert Lowell Estate, and especially Harriet Lowell and Frank Bidart for their great help and kindness.

We are immensely grateful to Jonathan Galassi, who read all the materials in this book and helped us make our own words more focused and accurate. We thank Katie Liptak and Victoria Fox at Farrar, Straus and Giroux for their help as well. Also we are indebted to the FSG copy editors, production editors, and proofreaders—Karla Eoff, Christine Paik, Nancy E. Elgin, Janet Renard, and Laura Starrett.

Many thanks to Sarah Payne Stuart for permission to publish selections from her invaluable photograph collection. She generously let us search through her photographs and was brave in helping us secure the scans in the midst of the COVID-19 pandemic. Her own memoir of Lowell, *My First Cousin Once Removed: Money, Madness, and the Family of Robert Lowell* (New York: HarperCollins, 1998), served as a model of insight and generosity.

We are grateful to the historian Jeremiah B. C. Axelrod for his guidance with the reproduction and contextualization of the photos.

Steven Axelrod is grateful to Richard Lehan and the late J. C. Levenson for guiding him through his first efforts to write about Lowell; to Lowell himself for friendly replies to his inquiries; and to the late Rodney Dennis, the late Patrick Miehe, and Donald Gallup for introducing him to the Lowell manuscripts at Harvard and Yale. The many-years support of Stephen

Tapscott of MIT helped Greg Kosc become conversant with the Lowell archives.

We are happy to acknowledge the helpful advice from other Robert Lowell scholars, particularly Thomas Austenfeld, Eve Cobain, Philip Coleman, Jeffrey Gray, Kay Redfield Jamison, Frank Kearful, Saskia Hamilton, Kathleen Spivack, Craig Svonkin, and Thomas Travisano. Also helpful were two Robert Penn Warren experts, William Bedford Clark and the late James (Bo) Grimshaw; John Crowe Ransom expert, the late Ashby Bland Crowder of Hendrix College; and the rhetorician Rise B. Axelrod.

Special thanks also goes to Michael J. Maddigan, a local historian in Middleborough, Massachusetts; an author of several historical books about the region; and a founder of Recollecting Nemasket, a small publishing press. Maddigan shared with us his expert knowledge and his own research on Rock Village, Middleborough County, and the entire Cape Cod area.

Steven Axelrod thanks his outstanding research assistant Raymond Hong Jig Rim. He is also grateful to David Lloyd for inviting him to speak about Lowell's memoirs at the first annual Faculty Lecture, and to the undergraduate and graduate students who studied Lowell's life writing along with him. Greg Kosc wants to thank his graduate students in his 2016–2017 course Learning by Research.

The archival research was supported with a research grant of the National Science Center Poland (2012/07/B/HS2/01590). In the final stages of our work on the manuscript, Greg Kosc received a Frederic D. Weinstein Memorial Fellowship from the Harry Ransom Center at the University of Texas, Austin. The University of California, Riverside, also provided Steven Gould Axelrod with research assistance.

Special thanks should go to the several libraries we worked with. We are grateful to Susan Halpert, Joseph Zajac, Rachel Howarth, Peter X. Accardo, Heather Cole, Leslie Morris, and James Capobianco of the Houghton Library, Harvard University, where Lowell's main archive is housed.

We also thank Rick Watson, Kate Hayes, Bridget Gayle Ground, and Elizabeth L. Garver of the Harry Ransom Center, University of Texas, Austin, where the archive of Lowell's British years is located.

In addition, thanks are due to Laura Russo at the Howard Gotlieb Archival Research Center, Boston University; to Jessica Pigsa at the Brooke Russell Astor Reading Room for Rare Books and Manuscripts, New York

Public Library; to Michael Frost and Steven Ross at the Department of Manuscripts and Archives, Sterling Memorial Library, Yale University, for a recording of the poet's speech at the Randall Jarrell Memorial Service in 1963; and to Christina Davis, the curator, and the staff members at the Woodberry Poetry Room, Houghton Library, Harvard University, for a recording of Lowell's remarks during a 1973 memorial event for Ezra Pound, "A Quiet Requiem for E. P."

Steve wants to thank his wife and partner, Rise B. Axelrod, without whom nothing he does would be possible, and his son, Jeremiah Axelrod; his daughter-in-law, Lil Delcampo; and his granddaughters, Amalia and Sophie Axelrod-Delcampo. Greg is most grateful to his wife, Beata Dabrowa-Kosc, for being the first reader of all drafts, and to his sons, Szymon and Maciek, for their support and patience.